National Systems of Education

National Systems of Education

Dr Ismail Thamarasseri

KALPAZ

First Published, 2018

Published by

Kalpaz Publications
C-30, Satyawati Nagar,
Delhi – 110052
Ph.: 011-47034999, 9811692060
www.kalpazpublications.com
E-mail: kalpaz@hotmail.com

Printed at: G. Print Process, Delhi

Cataloging in Publication Data—DK
Courtesy: D.K. Agencies (P) Ltd. <docinfo@dkagencies.com>

Thamarasseri, Ismail, author.
National systems of education / Dr Ismail Thamarasseri.
pages cm
Includes bibliographical references.
ISBN 9789353240110

1. Education, Elementary—India. 2. Education, Secondary—India. 3. Education and state—India. 4. School management and organization—India. I. Title.

LCC LA1151.T43 2018 | DDC 370.954 23

Contents

Preface

Education, one of the thrust areas, is a critical input in development in general and in human resource development in particular and is a catalyst for empowerment, poverty reduction and growth per se. Education can act as a powerful tool for reducing poverty and unemployment, improving health and nutritional standards, and achieving a sustained human development-led growth. Within the purview of overall education, school education is recognized as a basic human right, vital both to the development of individuals and societies.

A national system of education is often defined from the perspective of formal education system. This includes institutionalized formal education from early childhood education, elementary education, secondary education, and higher education. The informal and non-formal education subsets are often assumed to be part of the formal education and if not ignored altogether, they are given little attention. However, it is important the national educational system should be wholly inclusive of all the subsets of the educational system, that is, formal, informal and non-formal education.

The Constitution of India represents the values on which the national system of education imagines of National System of Education means, up to a particular level every student irrespective of location, caste, gender or belief have contact to education of a similar class. For obtaining the quality the authority will make the first move to fund the plans. Useful dealing should be taken in the track of the *Common School System* advised in the 1968 Policy. The National System of Education foresees an ordinary structure of education.

This book critically examines the establishment and development of the national system of education in India. This is followed by an overview of the impact of wider contextual developments, including political, socio-economic, cultural and religious factors. The curricula developed and implemented in educational institutions throughout the period are used as the framework around which the wider educational developments at school level are structured. By focusing on what was taught, why it was taught and how it was taught, this book provides an insight into the evolving educational experiences of children in national schools in India during the contemporary period. This book also analyses the educational and skill development programmes of some other selected countries. Behind every national system of education, there are factors or features that determine or influence and hence shape each one of the system. However, the national character of a given system of education is never determined by one factor, but rather a combination and interweaving of several factors. Consequently national factors of a country are closely related with national system of education. As such, this book analyses the factors which make the education of a country national.

In preparation of this book the author had to refer to the works of other authors and information sources. The author extremely indebted to various writers, editors, educationists and scholars whose views and opinions are integrated in this book. The author shall ever remain obliged to his teachers, parents, friends, colleagues, family members and students for their kind directions, guidance and assistance. The author take this opportunity to express his sincere thanks to Prof. N.A. Nadeem, Prof. Nighat Basu, and all staff members of Central University of Kashmir for their valuable support. To them all, the author offer his grateful thanks to ***M/s. Gyan Books Pvt. Ltd. Delhi*** who came forward willingly undertakes the publishing of this book.

July, 2018 **Dr. Ismail Thamarasseri**

Srinagar, J&K

UNIT - 1

Elementary Education in India

Introduction

Free and compulsory education to all children up to the age of fourteen years is a constitutional commitment in India. The Government of India initiated a number of programmes to achieve the goal of Universalisation of Elementary Education (UEE). India is well aware of the importance of ensuring universal basic education. In 1950, the Constitution had resolved in Article 45 under the Directive Principles of state Policy that the '…State shall endeavour to provide, within a period of ten years from the commencement of this Constitution, for free and compulsory education for all children until they complete the age of fourteen'. Since then, many documents including every Five Year Plan, the National Policies on Education have attempted to refine India's efforts at Universal Elementary Education (UEE). There have been important Constitutional amendments as well that were intended to give a boost to elementary education. The 42nd Amendment to the Constitution in 1976 brought education, which was largely a state responsibility, into the Concurrent List and made universalizing elementary education the responsibility of both the central and state governments. In 2002, Government of India took another significant step by making elementary education a fundamental right through the 86th Constitutional Amendment. In 2009, India went further and passed the Right of Children to Free and Compulsory Education Act (2009).

Many positive developments have been recorded, especially after the 1990s. Demand for basic education continues to grow with increasing recognition of the importance of educating children among parents and guardians. Infrastructural facilities have improved over the past two decades, gross enrolment is almost universal, dropout rates have declined even for girls at the primary level, and many more teachers have been appointed. More school incentives (such as free textbooks and the serving of cooked meals) have led to better outreach and coverage. In most parts of the India, children studying in Grade I to V have a minimum education facility available to them within a radius of one km and, for Grade VI to VIII, within three kilometres of their residence. However, these statistics are dampened by the fact that more than 49 per cent of the children drop out from the school before they reach Grade VIII. The importance of universal primary education has now been widely recognized by everyone involved. Policies and pledges are easy to make but implementation can be difficult and goals hard to achieve, especially in a vast and populous country such as India. International agencies, the government of India, and the numerous NGOs will have to work together with will, wisdom and tremendous energy to make their desire for universal primary education a reality in India.

Objectives of Elementary Education

The importance of aims and objectives of education is recognised by all the educational, professional, political, non-political and religious associations, organisations and groups at various levels in their memoranda, letters and brochures. It is said that education without clear cut aims is like a rudderless ship. The following comparisons emphasise this point fully well. Every pilot has a route-chart and set timing of landing at predetermined destination. There is constitution or set of Principles and traditions through which a country is governed Similarly, there should be properly defined and declared principles, aims and objectives of education or the basis of which policies and programmes of education nave to be formulated to achieve the set goals wit out wasting scarce energies and resources in chasing the wild goose. It is generally felt that our educational system has not followed the desired aims as a result that it does not produce ideal citizens in the country. It has followed, rather an arrow aim of preparing individuals for livelihood, as mentioned in one of the documents received from an organisation. The main reason of failure of educational system is that it basically stands or, pre-independence system. The main Objective of its products was how to take degree and to earn money and to be careerist without consideration of ethical values and national spirit. On the other hand, it has also been pointed out that it is unreasonable to criticise educational system alone because it is based on the other subsystems accepted by us. On the one hand we are developing and cultivating the British given economy, judicial system and system of administration and parliament, and on the other we are decrying and Criticising the education system which merely fulfils the needs of the British systems that we are propagating. As pointed out in a memorandum of an association, "the main defect of the old education policy. is that it had completely ignored the Indian culture and the interest of the masses of India and have left them economically too backward and socially too fragmented to articulate their miseries...."

- The first objective is **Literacy**. The child should learn the first language i.e., Mother tongue.

- The second objective is attainment of **Numeracy**. The child should develop ability in the four fundamental numerical operations. i.e. Addition, Subtraction, Division, and Multiplication, and be able to apply in practical life.
- The third objective is **technocracy**. The child should learn the method of inquiry in Science & Technology and also begin to appreciate them.
- Child should develop a respect for national symbols. H/he should know about the composite / plural culture of India.
- Child should acquire healthy attitude towards dignity of labour.
- The child should develop habits of cleanliness, healthful living and an understanding of proper sanitation and hygiene.
- The child should acquire a taste for good and beautiful.
- The child should learn to co-operate others and appreciate the usefulness of working together for the common good.
- Develop desirable qualities of character, personality such as initiative, leadership, kindness and honesty.
- Develop an understanding of constitution on India, democratic process, structures and institutions in our country.
- Prepare the child for wider participation in society and the nation.

Primary education should provide the learner with opportunities to:

- acquire literacy, numeracy, creativity and communication skills
- enjoy learning and develop desire to continue learning
- develop ability for critical thinking and logical judgment
- appreciate and respect the dignity of work
- develop desirable social standards, moral and religious values
- develop into a self-disciplined, physically fit and healthy person
- develop aesthetic values and appreciate own and other people's cultures
- develop awareness and appreciation of the environment
- develop awareness of and appreciation for other nations and international community
- instil respect and love for own country and the need for harmonious co-existence
- develop individual talents
- promote social responsibility and make proper use of leisure time
- develop awareness and appreciation of the role of technology in national development

The **goals and objectives of Education for All in India** are as follows (MHRD, Annual Report: 1997-98):

Access

- Universal enrolment of all children, including girls and persons belonging to Scheduled Castes and Scheduled Tribes;
- Provision of primary school for all children within one kilometre of walking distance and of facility of non-formal education; and
- Improvement of ratio of primary to upper primary school to at least 1:2.

Retention

- Reduction of dropout rates between Classes I to V and I to VIII to 20 and 40 percent respectively; and
- Improvement of school facilities by revamped Operation Blackboard, to be extended to upper primary level also.

Achievement

- Achievement of minimum levels of learning by approximately all children at the primary level, and introduction of this concept at the middle stage on a large scale.

Monitoring

- Local level committee, with due representation to women and teachers, to assist in the working of primary education to oversee its functioning; and
- Improvement of the monitoring system for universalisation of elementary education.
- The Government of India has initiated a number of schemes to achieve the goals of EFA amongst which the scheme of Operation Blackboard (OB) is the most prominent one. The main objectives of OB Scheme (1987) are as follows (MHRD, Annual Report: 1993-94):
- A building comprising at least two reasonably large all-weather rooms with a deep varandah and separate toilet facilities for boys and girls;
- At least two teachers in every school, as far as possible one of them a women; and Essential teaching-learning material including blackboards, maps, charts, toys and equipment for work experience.

The scheme is recently revised so as to:

- Provide flexibility to schools in providing teaching-learning materials relevant to their curriculum and local needs:

- To relate the scheme with micro planning wherever undertaken, so that supply of inputs is matched by demand side interventions to promote participation;
- Intensify training in the use of teaching-learning equipment's; and
- Extend the scheme to upper primary schools.

In addition, a number of externally funded projects and programmes are also currently under implementation amongst which the World Bank assisted District Primary Education Programme is the most prominent one. The programme that was launched in 1994 in 42 districts of seven states is currently under implementation in about 150 districts spread over fifteen states. The main objectives of DPEP programme are as follows:

- Emphasizing the local area planning with district plans being formulated in their own right instead of being derived from a state plan project document;
- Infusing greater rigor and professional inputs in planning and appraisal;
- More focussed targeting in educationally ward districts and districts where total literacy campaign have been successful;
- More focussed coverage would initially focus on primary stage (Classes I-V and its NFE equivalent) with stress on girls and for socially disadvantaged groups; and
- Emphasizing capacity building and networking of district, states and national level institutes in the fields of education management and social services to provide the resource support for the programme.

Operation Black Board (OBB)

The Scheme of Operation Blackboard is designed to provide minimum essential infrastructure in the primary schools. Launched in 1987, in pursuance of the National Policy on Education, 1986, it had three objectives-(a) to provide at least two teachers in all primary schools: (b) to ensure that every school has essential teaching learning material' and (c) to provide each school at least a two roomed all weather building. As of 31st August. 1995, 522,902 primary schools have been sanctioned teaching learning material. 150,000 posts of teachers have been sanctioned, out of which 125,000 posts have been filled up. Approximately. half the posts have been filled by women. 150,000 school rooms have been constructed. An amount of ₹ 1.280 million has been spent on the scheme till now. It is proposed to cover all the remaining primary schools under the scheme of Operation Blackboard during the remaining period of the Eighth Five Year Plan. This would mean that all the primary schools located in SC/ST habitations will be covered under Operation Blackboard. The scheme is being expanded to provide 3 teachers and 3 rooms to primary schools and also to cover the upper primary stage. The State Governments have been instructed to accord priority to areas of concentration of Scheduled Castes and Scheduled Tribes while implementing the expended scheme of Operation Blackboard.

Background: One of the important objectives of educational development is universalisation of primary education. Free and compulsory education to all the children up to the age of 14years is included in the guiding principles of the Indian Constitution and is also a part of Minimum Needs Programme and 20-Point Programme. Free and compulsory education to all the children up to the age of 14 years by 1995 was the objective in the educational policy declared by Central Government in 1986. In the different measures to achieve this target the scheme viz. "Operation Blackboard" is included.

Implementing programme

This scheme is implemented by the Director of Education, Maharashtra State at State level and by Education Officer (Primary), Zilla Parishad at district level in the rural areas. In the urban areas the funds are provided by Regional Deputy Director of Education to Municipal Councils and Municipal Corporations and they implement the scheme. The scheme was started in 1988-89 and in the first round 3,294 posts of primary teachers were created and 8,100 schools were provided with the material. For this purpose, expenditure of ₹ 23.23 crore and ₹ 4.90 crore was made respectively. The second and the third round of the scheme were started in 1992-93 and 12,231 posts of teachers were created. For this purpose, ₹ 18.57 crore were spent. Besides this, 27,469primary schools were provided with teaching material and expenditure of ₹ 15.90crore was made. By the end of March, 1993, construction of 9,071 classrooms has been completed and an expenditure of ₹ 14.73 crore was made on this.

External evaluation of the scheme has indicated that lack of training of teachers in using the teaching material, specification of a large number of uniform facilities to be provided without modification according to local needs and lack of provision for breakage of equipment have been some of the draws of implementation of the scheme. In order to operationalise the Revised Policy Formulations, the modified OBB will contain the following three sub schemes:

- Continuation of ongoing OBB to cover all the remaining primary schools especially those in SC/ST areas;
- Expanding the scope of OBB to provide three teachers and three rooms to primary schools wherever enrolment warrants them; and
- Expanding OBB to upper primary schools to provide (a) at least one room for each class/section (b) a Headmaster-cum-office room, (c) separate toilet facilities for girls and boys, (d) essential teaching

learning equipment including a library, (e) at least one teacher for each class/section and (f) a contingency grant for replenishment of items, consumable and minor repairs, etc.

The following measures will be taken to improve the quality of implementation of OBB:

- Teachers will be trained in using the OBB teaching materials under a specially designed teacher training programme.
- State Governments will make provision for breakage and replacement of equipment.
- Enough flexibility will be provided for purchase of teaching learning materials relevant to the curriculum and the local needs.
- At least 50 percent of the teachers appointed will be women. This will have a positive impact on girls' enrolment and retention.
- Wherever Micro-planning projects are taken up OBB will form an integral part of Micro planning.
- As far as possible low cost and locally available designs relevant to the local conditions will be adopted for school buildings. *Nirmithi Kendras* (Building Centres) and local technical institutes will be associated in this endeavour.

As in the past, Central Government will provide funds for equipment and teachers' salary for the plan period. The State governments will mobilize resources under Jawhar Rozgar Yojana (JRY) and other schemes for construction of school buildings, including Headmaster-cum-office room and toilet facilities. The State Governments will also provide contingency and replacement funds for equipment. Ongoing OBB will cover all schools by 1993-94. Other two sub-schemes will be started in the second half of the 8th Plan. About 30 percent of the eligible schools will be provided three rooms and three teachers under the expanded OB by the end of 8th Plan and the remaining schools will be covered by the year A.D. 2000. Under the expanded OBB a limited number of upper primary schools will be covered during the 8th Plan. Depending on the availability of funds, all upper primary schools will be covered by the year A.D. 2000.

In pursuance of the NPE, 1986, the Department of Education launched a number of measures for the educational development of Scheduled Castes and Scheduled Tribes in addition to continuing the existing programmes, The programmes cover all stages of education.

Universalisation of Elementary Education (UEE)

Article 45 of the Constitution enjoins upon the state the responsibility to provide free and compulsory education to all children up to the age of 14 years. In pursuance -of the Constitutional directive, a number of measures have been taken up by the Department of Education for Universalisation of Elementary Education (UEE). Special measures are included in these programmes for Scheduled Castes and Scheduled Tribes. Provision of access is the primary concern in UEE. In order to enhance the access to primary education by the SC and ST children. the norms for opening of primary schools, which are generally one Km. walking distance from habitations of 300 population, has been relaxed in the case of SC and ST habitations in whose case the norm is to have a primary school within one Km. walking distance from habitations of 200 population. All state governments have abolished tuition fees in government schools at least up to upper primary level. In most of the States, education is also free in the schools run by local bodies and in private aided institutions.

Most of the States provide assistance to students belonging to economically backward, SC and ST communities for meeting other costs of education, such as textbooks, uniforms, school bags, transport, etc.: their number, however. is quite small. According to the Fifth All India Education Survey Report for the year 1986. free uniforms were provided to 146,36,266 children at the primary and upper primary stage, which constitute only about 12 percent of the enrolled elementary stage students. At all stages of school education. 160.73,242 students got free uniform. Among them, 33.04 percent belong to SC and 11.50 percent to ST Girls constitute 49.98 percent. Out of the beneficiaries 77.44 percent are in rural areas.

Non-Formal Education: Non-Formal Education (NFE) is seen as a vital aspect of India's current strategy on education as it can reach out to working children, girls and those children who cannot attend full time schools due to several socio- economic factors. Implemented through state governments and voluntary organisations, the NFE programme draws on a high level of community participation and is characterised by flexibility relevance and a decentralised administrative structure. The benefits of the scheme are accruing to the children of all communities including those of SC and ST So far, 260.000 NFE centres; have been set up catering to 6.5 million children. About 100.000 centres are exclusively for girls. Over 450 NGOs are implementing NFE.

Lok Jumbish: The goal of Lok Jumbish is to achieve education for all by 2000 A.D. in Rajasthan. The programme is aimed at enhancing access and participation in basic education system and focus specially on children from disadvantaged section of society. The project develops special strategies to reach out to SC/ST children through micro-planning at the village level. The project is also distributing free school uniforms and textbooks and provide for construction of low cost hostels and Ashramshalas for the children of SCs and STs families.

District Primary Education Programme (DPEP)

The District Primary Education Programme (DPEP) is conceived as a beach head for overhauling the primary education system in India. Building upon accumulated national experience as well as drawing from the best features of several state level initiatives. the programme is being implemented in the mission mode. The DPEP moves away from the earlier schematic, piecemeal approach and takes a holistic view of elementary education, emphasises decentralised management and community mobilisation and undertakes district and population-specific planning. It is a scheme sponsored by the Central Government and the Central share of funding has been raised from multilateral and bilateral sources. DPEP goes beyond conventional packages such as opening of new schools and appointing teachers and addresses issues of content, process, quality and equity in education. The programme takes an integrated view of pedagogic issues in primary education development and seeks to build and strengthen institutional capacity in the states as well as local levels. so as to address the challenges of UEE.

The DPEP has been prepared in pursuance of the strategy of district specific projects envisaged in the Programme of Action (POA) 1992. The specific objectives of DPEP are:

- to reduce differences in enrolment, dropout and learning achievements among gender and social groups to less than five percent.
- to reduce overall primary drop-out rates for all students to less than 10 percent.
- to raise average achievement levels by at least 25 percent over measured baseline levels and ensuring achievement of basic literacy and numeracy competencies and a minimum of 40 percent achievement levels in other competencies, by all primary school children; and
- to provide, according to national norms, access for all children, to primary education classes (I-V), i.e.. primary schooling wherever possible, or its equivalent non-formal education.

The criteria for selection of districts have been that those districts where female literacy rate is lower than the national average according to the 1991 census and where Total Literacy Campaigns have successfully generated a demand for education.

The target is to cover 110 districts in a phased manner during the Eighth Five Year Plan period. So far. 42 districts in the seven states of Madhya Pradesh, Maharashtra, Tamil Nadu, Kerala, Haryana, Karnataka and Assam have been covered under the programme. These are: Dhubri, Darrang, Morigaon and Karbi in Assam; Sirsa, Hissar, Jind and Kaithan in Haryana; Kolar, Madhya, Belgaum and Raichut in Karnataka; Kasargod, Waynad and Malppuram in

Kerala; Aurangabad, Osmanabad, Nanded, Parbhani and Latur in Maharashtra; Dharmapuri, Thiruvannamalai Sambuvarayar and South Arcot in Tamil Nadu; and Sidhi. Raigarh, Sarguja, Guna, Panna, Tikamgarh, Shahdol, Dhar, Chhatarpur, Schore, Raisen, Raigarh, Rewa, Bilaspur, Satna, Rajnandgaon, Mandsaur, Ratlam and Betul in Madhya Pradesh.

Out of these districts 9 districts in Madhya Pradesh and Chattisgarh namely; Sidhi, Sarguja, Bilaspur, Dhar, Shahdol, Ratlam, Raigarh, Rajnandgaon and Betul are predominantly tribal districts with tribal sub-plan areas.

The DPEP specifically provides for developing strategies for tribal districts for improving primary education of Scheduled Tribes along with implementation plans and budgets, allocating projects resources for tribal students at least in proportion to the share of the tribal population in relevant DPEP districts.

Studies were conducted in 15 districts of seven states with a view to assess the present status and identify special needs of tribals so that tribal specific programmes can be developed. Specific interventions for education of tribals are as below:

- New Schools in tribal habitation
- Strong linkages with other central and state programmes like Integrated Childhood Development Services (ICDS) and Creches which would help siblings being taken care of so that girl child can attend to school
- Supplementary instructional material in tribal languages
- Tribal sensitisation of teachers and educational administration
- Appointment of tribal teachers
- Thrust to training of teachers in tribal languages
- Ashram Schools
- Bilingual primers (Tribal language and Hindi)
- Tribal area specific textbooks

One of the major parameters of the programme is that States would allocate project resources for tribal students at least in proportion to the share of the tribal population in the district population. For example, in Madhya Pradesh ₹ 197.63 crore is allocated for tribal districts of Madhya Pradesh out of total of ₹ 454.79 crore proposed for district level interventions. This comes to 40 percent of the funds which is higher than the proportion of tribal population.

Features of DPEP

A major initiative, entitled District Primary Education Programme, was started in 1993 in the area of elementary education to replicate what the Total Literacy Campaigns (TLCs) have been accomplishing in the field of adult literacy. The DPEP seeks to operationalise the strategy of decentralised planning identified by the POA, 1992 to be the main strategy for achieving UEE.

It builds upon the national experience in the pursuit of UEE as well the experience gained in the implementation of projects like the *Mahila Samakhya*, a programme of women's empowerment, the Bihar Education Project, the Lok Jumbish and the UP Basic Education project.

Central to DPEP are the following concepts

1. UEE is contextual. The contextuality varies widely across the country. Even in States like Kerala where participation is universal much requires to be done in respect of quality and achievement. In such States the pursuit of UEE would be mainly in the areas of quality, facilities and achievement. In other States participation and demand aspects need more attention.
2. Contextuality entails local area-planning with disaggregated targets and decentralised planning and management. Planning for UEE had hitherto been mainly at the national and state level. Barring some States and Union Territories, these entities are too large and heterogeneous for effective planning; they cannot provide contextuality. Ideally the planning should be from below, right from the village upwards but given the objective conditions, a beginning has to be made with the district as the unit of planning. The district plans are to be prepared through an intensive process of interaction with the local bodies, teachers and NGOs so that it is "owned" by all who are to be associated in implementation and it reflects the ground-level realities.
3. Resources are an important but not sufficient condition for achieving UEE. A host of measures both financial and non- financial, both on the supply side and on the demand side, need to complement higher allocation of resources.
4. The strategies for UEE have hitherto emphasised mainly access in terms of construction of class rooms and appointment of teachers. This has been inadequate and needs to be augmented by:
    - a holistic planning and management approach which goes beyond implementation of a disjointed set of individual schemes, perceives the task of UEE in its totality, integrates all the measures needed for achieving UEE in the specific context of the district;
    - this holistic planning should incorporate a gender perspective in all aspects of the planning and implementation process and be an integral part of all measures needed to achieve UEE.

- addressing the more difficult aspects of access, particularly access to girls, disadvantaged groups and out of school children;
- improving school effectiveness;
- strengthening the alternatives to schooling, particularly the non-formal education system;
- stressing the participative processes whereby the local community facilitates participation, achievement and school effectiveness;
- toning up teacher competence, training and motivation;
- stressing learning competence and achievement;
- stressing the need for improved teaching/learning materials; and
- checking of planning and management in respect of both routine and innovative areas.
- convergence between elementary education and related services such as ECCE and school health.

The programme would be implemented in a mission mode. A National Management Structure is being set up on the lines of NLMA which would oversee the implementation of the programme throughout the country and provide the necessary technical support to states and districts.

Implementation at the State level would be through registered autonomous societies with CMs as ex-officio Presidents of the General Council and Chief Secretary/Education Secretary as the Chairman of the Executive Committee. NGOs, Teachers, Educationists and Women are represented in these Committees. VECs play a key role in the implementation of the programme at the village level.

The loftiness of the objectives, the nature and intensity of the planning process, the integration of professional inputs, participative planning and management, and the emphasis on capacity building have together rendered DPEP an exciting idea not only in the country but all over the world.

DPEP has broken new paths in international cooperation, in that it belongs to the new genre of developmental cooperation which emphasises sustainability, equity, local ownership and execution and is supportive of national policies in the education sector.

DPEP is a home grown idea, in keeping with CABE guidelines, and its distinctiveness lies in that in spite of diversity of sources of funding, it is a national programme intending to achieve UEE in a contextual manner with emphasis on participation and capacity building.

The programme has been developed in 42 districts of the States of Madhya Pradesh, Assam, Haryana, Maharashtra, Karnataka, Tamil Nadu and Kerala.

The objective is to gradually expand the coverage of the programme to all districts which satisfy the twin criteria of:

- Educationally backward districts with female literacy below the national average; and
- Districts where TLCs have been successfully leading to enhanced demand for elementary education.

Five districts each in West Bengal and Andhra Pradesh are in the process of developing their district plans and would be ready for programme appraisal shortly.

The District Primary Education Programme has generated interest amongst several multilateral and bilateral funding agencies. The European Community has already committed approximately ₹ 585 crores (150 million ECUs) as programme support for DPEP. Negotiations have been completed with the World Bank/IDA for a credit agreement amounting to US $ 260 million for six States.

The ODA of United Kingdom has pledged support for DPEP in Andhra Pradesh and West Bengal. In fact, DPEP appears to be emerging as the main vehicle in the development of elementary education in the country and is likely to develop at the national level as an intermediary technical and resource organisation for primary education development in the country.

Sarva Shiksha Abhiyan (SSA) / Education for All Movement

SSA, a programme with a clear time frame (from 2000-2001 year onwards) for universal elementary education. A response to the demand for quality basic education all over the country. An opportunity for promoting social justice through basic education. It's an effort at effectively involving the Panchayati Raj Institutions, school management committees, village and urban slum level education committees, PTA's, MPTA's, Tribal Autonomous councils and other grass root level structures in the management of elementary schools. An expression of political will for universal elementary education across the country. A partnership between the central, state and the local government. It's an opportunity for states to develop their own vision of elementary education.

Background of SSA

Constitutional, legal and national statements for universalization of elementary education

1. Constitutional mandate, 1950 - The Directive Principles of State Policies postulates "The State shall endeavour to provide, within a period of ten years from the commencement of this Constitution, for

free and compulsory education to all children until they complete the age of 14 years."

2. National Policy of Education, 1986 - "It shall be ensured that free and compulsory education of satisfactory quality is provided to all children up to 14 years of age before we enter the twenty first century".
3. Unnikrishnan Judgement, 1994 - "Every child/citizen of this country has a right to free education until he completes the age of fourteen years." due to low attendance mid day meal was introduced

Basic Features of SSA

SSA is an effort to universalize elementary education by community-ownership of the school system. It is a response to the demand for quality basic education all over the country. The SSA programme is also an attempt to provide an opportunity for improving human capabilities to all children, through provision of community-owned quality education in a mission mode.

Aims of SSA

The SSA is to provide useful and relevant elementary education for all children in 6-14 age group by 2010. There is also another goal to bridge social, regional and gender gaps, with the active participation of the community in the management of schools.

Useful and relevant education signifies a quest for an education system that is not alienating and that draws on community solidarity. Its aim is to allow children to learn about and master their natural environment in a manner that allows the fullest harnessing of their human potential both spiritually and materially. This quest must also be a process of value based learning that allows children on opportunity to work for each other's well being rather than to permit mere selfish pursuits.

SSA realizes the importance of Early Childhood Care and Education and looks at the 0-14 age as a continuum. All efforts to support pre-school learning in ICDS centers or special pre-school centres in non ICDS areas will be made to supplement the efforts being made by the department of women and child development.

Objectives of SSA

- All children in school, education guarantee centre, alternate school, 'Back-to-School' camp by 2003.
- All children complete five years of primary schooling by 2007.
- All children complete eight years of elementary schooling by 2010.

- Focus on elementary education of satisfactory quality with emphasis on education for life.
- Bridge all gender and social category gaps at primary stage by 2007 and at elementary education level by 2010.
- Universal retention by 2010.

Interventions

There are fifteen interventions in SSA

1. BRC (Block Resource Centre)
2. CRC (Cluster Resource Centre)
3. AIE - Alternative and innovative education (AIE) is one of the major interventions of SSA to provide access for all children to primary education. Various strategies has been developed for ensuring participation of children of marginalised and deprived groups in tribal and coastal areas.
4. Civil works- The civil works component is important under SSA. Under this component, there is massive investment up to the limit of 33% of the total project budget. Provision of school infrastructure helps in providing access to children, and also helps in their retention, both of which are important objectives of the SSA. Provision of infrastructure for Resources Centres at sub-district levels helps in creating academic support, which acts as a catalyst towards quality improvement. The following constructions are under taken under civil works.
5. Free text books
6. Innovative activities - The innovative programmes implemented in schools are acting as a catalyst in the process of achieving useful and relevant elementary education for all children in the 6-14 age group and to bridge social, regional and gender gaps in the active participation of the community. The programmes are successful in creating interest in students on education and helped to retain their studies. The schemes implemented under Innovative Schemes are: Early Childhood Care and Education, Girls Education, SC/ST Education and Computer Education
7. Integrated Education for the Disabled Children (IEDC)
8. Management & MIS
9. R&E (Research and Evaluation)- This intervention consists of Research, Evaluation, Supervision and Monitoring. The norms propose an amount of ₹ 1,500/- per school for the development of capacities and supervision through resource/research institutions on an effective EMIS. There are provisions for regular school mapping/

micro planning for updating of household data. The funds can be utilised for both government and government aided schools. Following activities are proposed under the intervention. (1) Creating a pool of resource persons for effective field based monitoring, (2) Providing regular generation of community based data, (3) Conducting achievement test, evaluation studies, (4) Undertaking research activities, (5) Setting up special task force for low female literacy districts and for special monitoring of girls, SC, ST etc. (6) Incurring expenditure on Education Management Information System (7) Undertaking contingent expenditure like charts, posters, sketch pen, OHP pen etc. for visual monitoring systems (8) Conduct cohort studies.

10. School grant- School grant at ₹ 2,000 each was given to schools under the project. Out of the school grant ₹ 1000 was given to improvement of school library facilities. The rest was utilized towards making the nonfunctional equipment functional, school beautification, repair and maintenance of furniture, musical instruments and over all environment development of schools.
11. Teacher grant- In order to improve the class room transactions and preparation of teaching aids grant at ₹ 500 is given to all LP/UP teachers. The teachers utilized the grant to produce and procure TLM for effective classroom transactions. During 2007-2008, 547590 teachers both LP/UP were benefited.
12. Teacher Training- The quality education is the most important goal of SSA. The various strategies to improve the training are: (1) Training and retraining of teachers, (2) Familiarisation training on new curriculum and text books, (3) Familiarisation training on National Curriculum Frame Work (NCF 2005), (4) Examination reforms, (5) Training on grading system and assessment on the impact of grading system, (6) Scholastic and non-Scholastic areas improvement, (7) Training of teachers on Inclusive Education for children with special needs, (8) Planning and implementation of quality education measures, (9) Resource groups are strengthened at all levels (separate Resource Groups for each subjects) 300-350 Resource Person per district) Follow up activities, on-site support and review meetings are ensured. DIETs identified training needs - hard spots and develop training modules. This process helped to improve the quality of training. Training for Trainers and Block Programme Officers was conducted.
13. Remedial teaching
14. Community mobilisation

15. Distance education - The Distance Education Programme (DEP) is a National component of SSA, which is sponsored by Ministry of Human Resource Development, Government of India. It is being implemented by Indira Gandhi National Open University (IGNOU) in collaboration with all States/ Union Territories of India. The DEP-SSA will be an important input in the in-service education of teachers and other personnel in the area of elementary education. It will supplement the face-to-face training by using Multi-media packages like audio-video programmes, radio broadcast, teleconferencing etc. The Distance mode of training would not only help address a larger number of individuals, but also would provide uniformity in training inputs and reduce the transmission loss, which is generally experienced in the face-to-face cascade model of training.

Activities

- Civil infrastructure developments and improving
- Teacher training

Achievements

This program made significant achievements at village levels. In 2004 many villages in India were covered and preliminary education centers opened. In the south Indian state of Tamil Nadu, a village called Sattanathapuram (Town: Sirkazhi) located in Nagapattinam district, is one of the first village to implement this program successfully. Afternoon meal schemes for poor kids in support of state government combined with education for all programs made significant progress in literacy rate. Non-governmental organizations donated generously the lands for poor people and the construction of schools completed by Village Panchayats.

The Right of Children to free and Compulsory Education Act or Right to Education Act (RTE) 2009

"The Right of Children to Free and Compulsory Education Act 2009" (popularly called Right to Education Act or RTE Act) was legislated in August 2009, which comes into effect on April 1, 2010. This act is a detailed and comprehensive piece of legislation which includes provision related to school teachers and specific divisions of duties and responsibilities of different stakeholders. Important features of the Act are: Every child from 6 to 14 years of age has right to free compulsory education in a neighbourhood school till completion of elementary education; Private schools must take in quarter in their class, strength from weaker section and disadvantaged groups sponsored by the government; No child shall be subjected to physical punishment or mental harassment; no child will be held back or expelled till completion of elementary education; All schools except government schools are required to be recognized by meeting specified norms standards within three years to avoid closure. However, there are lots of lacunae in this bill. Firstly, this bill excluded children below six years of age from the provision of fundamental right to free early childhood care and pre-primary education. It also restricted the fundamental right of even the 6-14 year age group by placing a conditionality in the form of phrase "as the State may, by law, determine" as this gave the state the instrumentality to arbitrarily restrict, dilute and distort the fundamental right given through

The right of children to free and compulsory education act or right to education act (RTE) 2009 which was passed by the Indian parliament on 4 August 2009, describes the modalities of the provision of free and compulsory education for children between 6 and 14 in India under Article 21A of the Indian Constitution? India became one of 135 countries to make education a fundamental right of every child when the act came into force on 1 April 2010.

What is the act about?

- Every child between the ages of 6 to 14 years has the right to free and compulsory education. This is stated as per the 86th Constitution Amendment Act of 2002. The right to education act seeks to give effect to this amendment
- The government schools shall provide free education to all the children and the schools will be managed by school management committees (SMC). Private schools shall admit at least 25% of the children in their schools without any fee.

The National Commission for Elementary Education shall be constituted to monitor all aspects of elementary education including quality.

The salient features of the act

- Free and compulsory education to all children of India in the six to 14 age group;
- It clarifies that 'compulsory education' means obligation of the appropriate government to provide free elementary education and ensure compulsory admission, attendance and completion of elementary education to every child in the six to fourteen age group. 'Free' means that no child shall be liable to pay any kind of fee or charges or expenses which may prevent him or her from pursuing and completing elementary education
- No child shall be held back, expelled, or required to pass a board examination until completion of elementary education;

- A child above six years of age has not been admitted in any school or though admitted, could not complete his or her elementary education, then, he or she shall be admitted in a class appropriate to his or her age; Provided that where a child is directly admitted in a class appropriate to his or her age, then, he or she shall, in order to be at par with others, have a right to receive special training, in such manner, and within such time limits, as may be prescribed: Provided further that a child so admitted to elementary education shall be entitled to free education till completion of elementary education even after fourteen years.
- Proof of age for admission: For the purposes of admission to elementary education, the age of a child shall be determined on the basis of the birth certificate issued in accordance with the provisions of the Births, Deaths and Marriages Registration Act, 1856 or on the basis of such other document, as may be prescribed. No child shall be denied admission in a school for lack of age proof.
- A child who completes elementary education shall be awarded a certificate;
- Calls for a fixed student-teacher ratio;
- Will apply to all of India except Jammu and Kashmir;
- Provides for 25 per cent reservation for economically disadvantaged communities in admission to Class One in all private schools;
- Mandates improvement in quality of education;
- School teachers will need adequate professional degree within five years or else will lose job;
- School infrastructure (where there is problem) to be improved in three years, else recognition cancelled;
- Financial burden will be shared between state and central government
- It prohibits (a) physical punishment and mental harassment; (b) screening procedures for admission of children; (c) capitation fee; (d) private tuition by teachers and (e) running of schools without recognition,
- It provides for development of curriculum in consonance with the values enshrined in the Constitution, and which would ensure the all-round development of the child, building on the child's knowledge, potentiality and talent and making the child free of fear, trauma and anxiety through a system of child friendly and child centered learning
- It provides for rational deployment of teachers by ensuring that the specified pupil teacher ratio is maintained for each school, rather than just as an average for the State or District or Block, thus ensuring that there is no urban-rural imbalance in teacher postings. It

also provides for prohibition of deployment of teachers for non-educational work, other than decennial census, elections to local authority, state legislatures and parliament, and disaster relief.)

- It lays down the norms and standards relating inter alia to Pupil Teacher Ratios (PTRs), buildings and infrastructure, school-working days, teacher-working hours It makes provisions for a non-admitted child to be admitted to an age appropriate class.
- It specifies the duties and responsibilities of appropriate Governments, local authority and parents in providing free and compulsory education, and sharing of financial and other responsibilities between the Central and State Governments
- RTE Act has come into effect from 1st of April, 2010 across India except in the state of Jammu & Kashmir.
- Children in the age group of 6-14 years have the right to free and compulsory, quality elementary education up to Class 8
- The Act contains 38 sections in 7 chapters which are mandatory.
- For implementing the provisions of the Act, RTE Rules have been formulated.
- Child is the focal point of this Act.

The Functions of the Right to Education Act 2009

- Makes education Free and Compulsory and responsibility of the state
- Curriculum as per Constitutional Values
- Ensures Quality of Teachers
- Defines Norms for Schools
- Pushes for Social Reform
- Protects child
- Makes procedures more simple
- Puts power in hands of people
- Removes the oppression of Exams
- Govt. not liable for Free Education when parents admit child to private school.

Role of Stake holders

- Each agency – Central / State Governments, Local Self Government Institutions (LSGI), Parents, Other Depts., Schools, Head Teacher & Teachers, have well defined roles and responsibilities under this Act.
- One of the major challenges is to sensitize people about this Act especially the beneficiaries

- Ensure quality elementary education to all children
- The role of State Govt./ LSGIs Dept., SCERTs and DIETs is clearly given in eighth rule of the Act.

Key concept

Right to Free and Compulsory Education is to students of Classes 1 to 8.

Full time Formal School

- No more 'Non Formal Education'
- No drop-in centres for working children
- No Govt./NGO centres — Only Regular 'schools'
- No detention, No failure, No expulsion, No corporal punishment, No mental harassment of pupils , No board examinations, Follow Continuous and Comprehensive Evaluation
- Age appropriate enrolment in Classes
- Admissions : No screening; No capitation fees
- Year round admission
- No documents, Easy availability of 'Transfer Certificate' for migration to another school

Jammu and Kashmir Education Act 2002

Jammu and Kashmir Education Act 2002 received the assent of the Governor on 21st April, 2002 and published in Government Gazette dated 23rd April, 2002. It is an Act to provide for achieving the goal of universalisation of elementary education and to provide for better organization and development of school education in the State. Be it enacted by the Jammu and Kashmir State Legislature in the Fifty-third Year of the Republic of India as follows:

1. **Short title, extent and commencement** —
   (1) This Act may be called the Jammu and Kashmir School Education Act, 2002.
   (2) It shall extend to the whole of the State of Jammu and Kashmir.
   (3) It shall come into force on such date [as the Government may, by notification in the Government Gazette, appoint].
2. **Definitions** — In this Act, unless the context otherwise requires,—
   (a) "academic year" means the year beginning on such date as the Government may specify with respect to any area or school,;
   (b) "aided school" means a private school which is recognized by and is, or has been receiving grant-in-aid from the Government;

(c) "Board" means the State Education Advisory Board constituted under section 22 of this Act;

(d) "child" means a boy or a girl who is in such age group not being less than 6 years and not more than 14 years at the beginning of the academic year;

(e) "competent authority" means any officer not below the rank of a District Education Officer appointed by the Government for carrying out the purposes of this Act and different authorities may be appointed for different areas;

(f) "educational agency" means any individual, Society, Trust or body of persons registered with the Government and permitted to establish, run or maintain any private school, under this Act;

(g) "existing school" means any Government school or Government aided or recognized school established before the commencement of this Act and continuing as such at the time of such commencement;

(h) "Government" means the Government of Jammu and Kashmir;

(i) "Government school" means a school run by the Education Department of the Government;

(j) "Parent" in relation to any child includes a guardian and any other person who has the actual custody of the child;

(k) "prescribed" means prescribed by rules made under this Act;

(l) "private school" means a school established, run or maintained by any educational agency and recognized by the Government;

(m) "recognized school" means a school recognized under this Act;

(n) "school" means an educational institution primarily meant for imparting education up to, and including, the higher secondary level and includes-

(i) such institutions as are meant for providing instructions and training for teachers;

(ii) lands, buildings, playgrounds, hostels and movable properties such as furniture, books, apparatus, map and equipment, owned by and used for the activities of the educational institution;

(o) "State" means the State of Jammu and Kashmir.

3. Application of the Act — The provisions of this Act shall apply to all schools in the State.

4. Compulsory education up to class eight — The Government shall provide for free and compulsory education for children up to the level of class eight throughout the State within a period of ten years from the commencement of this Act and for this purpose it shall take appropriate steps to provide the necessary facilities.

5. Establishment of schools — The Government may, for the purpose of providing adequate facilities for school education;

(a) establish and maintain schools; and

(b) permit any educational agency to establish and maintain private schools.

6. Manner for establishing and running Government schools— The Government shall, by notification in the Government Gazette, stipulate the manner in which Government schools shall be established and run.

7. Local Area Education Committee and its functions— (1) The Government shall, in such manner and for such period, as may be prescribed, constitute a Committee, to be called the Local Area Establishment Committee, for each Panchayat Halqa, Town Area, Notified Area and Municipal ward for implementation of the provisions of this Act regarding compulsory education up to the level of class eight.

(2) The functions of the Local Area Education Committee, shall be:-

(a) to cause to be prepared a list of children in the concerned Panchayat Halqa, Town Area, Notified Area or Municipal Ward, as the case may be, and the list revised at such intervals as may be prescribed;

(b) to take such measures as may be necessary to ensure the attendance of children in schools;

(c) to notify the parent of each child that he is under an obligation to ensure the attendance of his child at a school on and from the date specified in the notice; and

(d) to carry out such other functions as may be prescribed.

8. Obligation of guardian to send children to school — The parent of every child shall cause the child to attend a school, whether Government or private, and also ensure that such child completes the full course of elementary education up to class eight, unless there be a reasonable cause for his non-attendance within the meaning of section 10.

9. Warning for failure to discharge obligation and for interference— (1) When the Local Area Education Committee has reason to believe that the parent of any child to whom this Act applies and who is bound under section 8 to cause the child to attend a school, has failed to do so or that any person other than the parent is utilizing the time or services of a child in connection with any employment whether for remuneration or not, in such a manner as to interfere with the attendance of the child at a school, it shall warn him in writing to refrain from utilizing the time or services of the child as aforesaid and direct to ensure the attendance of such child at a school within one week from the receipt of warning.

(2) When a Local Area Education Committee is satisfied that the parent has failed to cause his child to attend school or that any person is interfering with such attendance of a child even after the warning mentioned in sub-section (1), such a Local Area Education Committee or any member authorised by it shall lodge a complaint against such parent or other person with the Judicial Magistrate having territorial jurisdiction over the area.

(3) If the Judicial Magistrate is satisfied that the complaint is well founded, he shall pass an order directing the parent or other person to cause the child to attend school regularly and to refrain from interfering with the attendance of the child, after a specified date. If the parent or other person fails to comply with such order he shall, on conviction, be liable to a fine not exceeding two hundred rupees for the first offence and five hundred rupees for every subsequent offence.

10. Exemption from attendance — The Government may prescribe the grounds on which a child may be exempted from attending school.

11. No private school to be established or run without permission — (1) No private school shall be established, run or maintained without permission, in writing, of the Government or the Competent Authority.

(2) The Government shall prescribe the procedure to be followed for the grant of permission to establish, run or maintain private schools.

12. Recognition of private schools — (1) Only such private schools as are recognized shall be permitted to function.

(2) Notwithstanding anything contained in the Jammu and Kashmir Board of School Education act, 1975, the Government shall, by notification, in the Government Gazette, appoint the 'competent authorities' for carrying out the purposes of this Act.

(3) The Government shall prescribe the procedure to be followed for the grant of such recognition.

(4) The Government shall prescribe norms and conditions for the functioning of recognized school.

(5) The Government shall, on or before the first day of May every year, by notification in the Government Gazette, publish a list of such private schools as are recognized under this Act together with such particulars, if any, as it may consider necessary.

13. Management of private schools— (1) No private school shall be managed and run by any person other than an educational agency. The Government shall prescribe the procedure for registration of educational agencies.

(2) Every educational agency shall appoint a Manager to look after day-to-day running an administration of the school managed and run by such educational agency.

14. Duties of Manager— The duties of Manager shall include the following:-

(i) he shall be responsible for the administration of the school in accordance with the provisions of this Act;

(ii) all the property, both movable and immovable shall be in the possession of the Manager who shall be responsible for maintaining them in proper condition;

(iii) he shall maintain the records and the accounts of the school in such manner as may be prescribed; and

(iv) he shall be bound to render assistance and facilities as are necessary for proper management of the schools.

15. Permission for starting new classes and their recognition — Every private school shall have to seek the prior permission of the competent authority before adding any higher classes. Any higher classes so added in a school shall require recognition by the Government. The Government shall, by notification in the Government Gazette, prescribe the procedure for the grant of such permission and recognition.

16. De-recognition of schools — (1) The Government may de-recognize any private school, if in its opinion, the functioning of such a school is not in accordance with the provisions of this Act and the rules made there under:

Provided that no such order of de-recognition shall be passed by the Government unless reasonable opportunity is provided to the educational agency in this regard. The orders passed by the Government shall be final and binding.

17. Restrictions on alienation of property of aided schools— (1) Not with standing anything contained in any law for the time being in force, no sale, mortgage, pledge or transfer of possession in respect of any property of an aided school shall be made or created except with the prior permission of such authority as may be authorised by the Government in this behalf. No such permission shall be granted, if in the opinion of such authority, such permission will adversely affect the working of the school.

(2) Any transaction made in contravention of sub-section (1) shall be null and void.

18. Property to be in the name of the Educational Agency — Any property or assets owned, held or acquired by any person for or on behalf of any private school, shall, for the purposes of this Act, be deemed to be property of the educational agency notwithstanding that such property stands in the name of any individual.

19. Teaching and non-teaching staff in private schools — The academic and other qualifications of the teaching and non-teaching staff in the private schools shall not be lower than those prescribed for corresponding posts in Government.

20. Conditions of service of staff in private schools — All the private schools shall frame and notify their own terms and conditions of service of teaching and non-teaching staff including conditions relating to pay, gratuity, provident fund and age of retirement.

21. Grant-in-aid — The Government may give grant-in-aid to private schools. The Government shall frame rules prescribing manner in which grant-in-aid is to be given and the conditions to be fulfilled by the schools for the receipt of such grant-in-aid.

22. State Education Advisory Board: (1) The Government may, by notification in the Government Gazette, constitute a State School Education Advisory Board for the purposes of obtaining advice on matters pertaining to educational policy and administration.

(2) The Board shall consist of eleven members including the Chairman who shall be Education Minister of the State, Secretary to Government, Education Department, Chairman of the State Board of School Education and Directors of School Education shall be ex officio members of the Committee. The Government shall nominate the other members from among the eminent educationists, academicians, administrators and planners. The term of office of the non-official members of the Board shall be three years.

(3) The Government shall prescribe the procedure to be followed at the meetings of the Board and all other matters pertinent to be functioning of the Board.

23. Alteration in the designation of a Government Officer — Where any provision of this Act or the rules made there under refers to any officer of the Government by designation, then, if that designation is altered or the office held by such officer ceases to exist, the reference to that designation or office shall be construed as reference to the altered designation or, as the case may be, to such corresponding office as the Government may direct.

24. Indemnity — No suit, prosecution or other legal proceeding shall lie against the Government or any authority or officer in respect of anything which is in good faith done or intended to be done under any provision of this Act or the rules framed there under.

25. Courts not to grant injunction — Notwithstanding anything to the contrary contained in the Code of Civil Procedure, Samvat 1977 or in any other law for the time being in force, no court shall grant any injunction or make any interim order restraining any proceeding which is being or is about to be taken under this Act.

26. Delegation of powers — The Government may, by notification in the Government Gazette and subject to such conditions as it may specify, authorize any officer or authority subordinate to it to exercise any of the powers, except the power to make rules, exercisable by the Government under this Act.

27. Penalties — Whoever contravenes any of the provisions of this Act or rules there-under shall on conviction before the Judicial Magistrate be liable to a fine not less than rupees ten thousand for the first offence and rupees twenty thousand for every subsequent offence.

28. Power to remove difficulties — If any difficulty arises in giving effect to the provisions of this Act, the Government may by order, do anything not inconsistent with such provisions which appear to it to be necessary or expedient for the purpose of removing the difficulty:

Provided that no such order shall be framed after the expiry of two years from the commencement of this Act.

29. Power to make rules — (1)The Government may make rules for the purpose of carrying into effect the provisions of the Act.

(2) In particular and without prejudice to the generality of the foregoing provision, such rules may provide for all or any of the following matters, namely:-

(a) the provision of compulsory education;

(b) the establishment and maintenance of schools;

(c) the grant of permission to set up private schools;

(d) the recognition of private schools;

(e) the giving of grant-in-aid to schools;

(f) the levy and collection of fees in private schools;

(g) the manner in which accounts, registers and records shall be maintained and the auditing of the accounts of private schools;

(h) the returns, statements and reports to be submitted by schools;

(i) the inspection of schools;

(j) the constitution and functioning of the Local Area Education Committees;

(k) the standards of education and courses of study;

(l) the procedure for admission of students in schools; and

(m) any other matter, which is or may be required to be prescribed under this Act.

30. Repeal and saving — (1) The Primary Education Act, Samvat 1986, the Jammu and Kashmir Private Educational Institutions (Regulation and Control) Act, 1967 and the Jammu and Kashmir Education Act, 1984 are repealed.

(2) Subject to the provisions of sub-section (5) of section 12, the aforesaid repeal shall not affect the previous operation of the Acts so repealed.

Conclusion

One of the gravest failures of development policy in post-independence India has been the inability to ensure that all children attend school. The gaps in respect of provision of adequate schooling facilities and in respect of the proportion of children who continue to be out of school are particularly high in rural India. Official statistics on school education have been extremely misleading, and some of the agencies involved in the collection of these data have done great disservice to the cause of universalisation of school education by providing misleading statistics. Data on school education in India are collected at the school level and the household level. The data collected from schools, which form the basis for official estimates of school enrolment, provide hugely inflated estimates of the proportion of children regularly attending school. Such statistics have been used to underplay the problem and to underestimate the resources required to ensure free schooling for all children (Ramachandran, Rawal, and Swaminathan 1997). Over-reporting of school enrolment at initial levels of schooling results in overestimation of drop-outs, when most of the children recorded as drop-outs have actually never attended school. Such distortion of data results in inappropriate policy formulation with little focus on identifying out-of-school children and bringing them to school.

Another important limitation of the school-based statistics is that they cannot be used to separately study the access of rural children to schooling. Since a substantial number of rural children attend schools located in urban areas, rates of school attendance among them must be measured through household surveys and not through school-based statistics.

In view of the above, it is clear that household survey-based data from the Censuses of India and NSSO surveys should form the basis for official estimates of rates of school attendance and the number of out-of-school children.

A comparison of data on school attendance ratios for children aged 6–14 years from the Censuses of India and various rounds of NSSO surveys suggests that although there has been considerable improvement in school attendance rates, a very substantial lag remains among rural children. According to the 66th round NSSO Survey on Employment and Unemployment, about 2.2 crore children in this age group did not attend school. Of these out-of-school children, about 1.8 crores were rural children. It is worth noting that this estimate of the number of out-of-school children is about three times the estimate of out-of-school children under the Sarva Shiksha Abhiyan.

In terms of attendance rates, these data show that about 14 percent of rural children aged 6–14 years were not attending school. The Gross Attendance Ratio among rural children was 97 percent and the Net Attendance Ratio, 85 percent. In respect of the Net Attendance Ratio among rural children, the worst performing States in India were Bihar, Jharkhand, Rajasthan, Arunachal Pradesh, and Meghalaya. The gap between attendance ratios among rural boys and rural girls was highest in Rajasthan.

While the usefulness of school-based statistics for measurement of participation in schooling is limited, they are of great use in estimating gaps in availability of schooling facilities. It may be argued that collection of data on schooling facilities (including physical infrastructure, teaching aids, and human resources) should be the main focus of the District Information System on Education (DISE) and the All India School Education Survey (AISES). The annual coverage of DISE has expanded to over 13 lakh schools. This needs to be further expanded, particularly in some States, to ensure near-complete coverage. At the same time, to avoid duplication and wastage of resources, AISES needs to be restructured as a sample survey that will provide a useful check on the reliability of DISE statistics. The field operations for such a sample survey should be conducted by a competent agency like the National Sample Survey Organisation.

Some of the highlights of the educational data for 2008–09 are as follows.

- About 57 percent of rural elementary (primary and upper primary) schools in India had less than four classrooms. The proportion of rural schools that do not have one classroom per grade is substantially higher.
- About 13 percent of rural elementary schools in India did not have drinking water facilities.
- About 16 percent of rural elementary schools in India did not have any toilet facilities.
- About 49 percent of rural elementary schools in India did not have separate toilets for girls.
- About 70 percent of rural elementary schools in India did not have electricity.
- About 14 percent of all rural primary schools in India had only one teacher.

The data presented above show that there continue to be substantial gaps in schooling facilities and access of rural children to elementary schooling in India. The absolute levels of lack of adequate schooling facilities and the number of out-of-school children are seriously underestimated in school-based statistics. However, school-based statistics provide useful proportional estimates of gaps in facilities. Household survey-based data provide a more accurate picture of school attendance rates than data collected from schools. Household survey-based data also provide useful disaggregated estimates of school attendance rates among rural and urban children.

Model Questions

Very Short Answer type Questions. Each question carries 1 Mark. To be answer in about 20 words each.

1. Enlist any four objectives of Elementary Education.
2. Enlist the main objectives of OBB scheme.
3. What are the main features of SSA?
4. Why we depend on data collected through household surveys than data collected from schools for Statistics on Education?

Short Answer type Questions. Each question carries 2 Marks. To be answer in about 150 words each.

5. Discuss the salient features of RTE Act 2009.
6. Describe the provisions of J&K Education Act 2002.
7. Write a note on Elementary School Infrastructure in India.
8. Why UEE continue as a dream in India?

Multiple Choice Questions. Each Question carries 1 Mark.

9. In which year DPEP was launched?
   (a) 1986
   (b) 1992
   (c) 1994
   (d) 2001
10. Which one is the goal of SSA.
    (a) Universalisation of Pre-School Education
    (b) Universalisation of Elementary Education
    (c) Universalisation of Secondary Education
    (d) Universalisation of Higher Education
11. Universalization of Elementary Education refers to:
    (a) Universal Provision
    (b) Universal Enrolment
    (c) Universal Retention
    (d) All of the above.

12. Which one is the worst performing State on School Electrification.
    (a) Bihar
    (b) Uttar Pradesh
    (c) J&K
    (d) Jharkhand

Answer Key

9: C 10: B 11: D 12: A

References

Krishnan, D.K., & Thamarasseri, I. (2013). *Contemporary Issues in Indian Education.* New Delhi: Kanishka Publishers

Thamarasseri, I. (2007). *Education in the Emerging Indian Society.* New Delhi: Kanishka Publishers

Thamarasseri, I. (2008). *Early Childhood and Elementary Education.* New Delhi: Kanishka Publishers

Thamarasseri, I. (2011). *Current Developments in Indian Education.* New Delhi: Kanishka Publishers

Thamarasseri, I. (2014). *Issues and Challenges of Indian Education.* Agra: Shri Vinod Pustak Mandir

Thamarasseri, I., & Bhat, M. S. (2018). *Elementary Education*. Agra: Shri Vinod Pustak Mandir

Jammu and Kashmir School Education Act, 2002. retrieved on 10-3-2018 from http://www.bareactslive.com/JK/JK012.HTM

UNIT - 2

Administration of Elementary Education

Scope and Characteristics of Successful Elementary School Administration

Elementary School administrator is responsible for recruiting teachers, day to day running of the institution, setting goals and objectives of the institution. The scope of Educational Administration is very wide. It takes into its grip all types of activities that take place in the field of teaching and learning. To provide good and appropriate education to the learners involves all steps of educational activity that is the concern of the Educational Administration. It is good administration that provides excellent education. The basic point to be noted is that administration must first conceive "all round development" of education and then ensure the maximum developmental programme of education. The scope of administration extends through all the activities of education that start from planning:

1. **Planning:** This is the key factor in all types of education. It is commonly understood as an activity which leads to future course of action. Chinese proverb justifies; "If you plan for a year, plant a grain, if you plan for 10 years plant a tree and if you plan for 100 years plant men". Planning is not an independent activity. It is part of the whole process of administration. To avoid wasteful efforts efficient planning is needed. To execute activity proper planning is essential. Planning ensures (i) recognition of goals (ii) proper use of resources (iii) prevention of wastage, overlapping and haphazard efforts (iv) definiteness and orderly execution in any enterprise. In India Educational planning is required at four levels (I) central level (II) state level (III) local level and (IV) school level.
2. **Budgeting:** In smooth running of an institution budgeting is an essential element. Administration has to plan the first essential component that of budgeting. Organisation and administration involve well considered budgeting. It is a process of giving an estimated

account of revenues and expenditure as educational institution need financial security.

3. Organising: Organisation is a very important aspect of administration. It deals with systematic arrangements so that the purpose of entire programme can be achieved. Broadly organisation deals with two aspects (i) Material equipment and (ii) Human equipment. Material Equipment involves buildings, furniture, libraries, laboratories, workshops, museums, gymnasium, art galleries, playgrounds, farms, audio-visual aids, computers, T.V's etc. All these things should be properly organized so that this entire material element supplements learning. This entire material element otherwise used for entertainment only will not enhance learning. The task of administration is to schedule time as well as use of all that material systematically, psychologically and scientifically. Arrangement and organisation of Material equipment in fruitful and purposeful manner is the responsibility of the administration.

Human Equipment implies arrangement of all persons involved in teaching and learning situations. Educational Administration while planning the activity has scope to organize, budget and schedule time etc. in such a manner as all human elements involved in the activity be able to contribute towards teaching and learning. Human element involved in educational process are Students, Teachers, head of the institution, Ministerial staff, Account's wing staff, organizers as well as Management. Educational Administration has to plan the task in such a way that every person involved in the activity is well knit to the whole orbit and be knit and led to contribute according to its talent and best of the capacity. Educational Administration has a wider scope in:

- preparing curriculum for the different classes according to their diverse abilities and diverse aptitudes.
- preparing appropriate time table.
- organising systematic co-curricular programme.
- organising and distributing work among staff accordingly.
- establishment of laboratories and libraries.
- organising health and physical camps.
- establishing canteen and hostel facilities.
- organising examination schedules and yearly calendars of the institutions.
- Organising guidance and counselling cells within the institutions to provide guidance services to the students.
- Programs to establish relationship between school and community, school and parents and school and government.
- Providing various auxiliary services like mid-day meals, school uniforms, textbooks, etc if possible.

- Financing and Budgeting and finally administer safely all the programmes so that the institutions function properly in a healthy manner.

Characteristics of Successful Elementary School Administration

- **Instructional Vision**: Ensures that instructional practices are guided by a common, research-based instructional vision that articulates what students do to effectively learn the subject.
- **Continuous Improvement of Instruction:** Aligns resources (i.e., professional development, allocation of teacher time, budget decisions), policies, and procedures (i.e., school improvement plans, teacher evaluation) toward continuous improvement of instructional practice guided by the instructional vision.
- **High Expectations:** Sets high expectation for all students academically, behaviourally, and in all aspects of student wellbeing.
- **Constructive School Culture:** Establishes a safe, collaborative, and supportive school culture that places high priority on ensuring that students are successful in school and in life.

School administrators are essential to the success of any school district. They work twelve months a year and their tasks while on the job can range from developing curriculum content all the way to disciplining wayward students. Since school administrators are so critical to the success of the school district, it is important that they possess the leadership attributes needed to have a positive impact on the students and faculty members.

- **Responsibility:** A strong sense of responsibility is critical in administrative work. This is especially true since it is common for the principal to make decisions that will affect thousands of people, such as their students, the parents of those students and the teachers and faculty at the school. School administrators need to be aware of what is happening in the school and they should be very involved in the education process. This extra involvement can help an administrator to better understand the needs of the school and how his or her decisions are affecting the community.
- **Planning Ahead:** School administrators need to always be planning for the future and the years ahead. After all, the goal of education is to prepare children and young adults for their own futures. Having a solid plan for the future can help to increase efficiency and will set up administrators for a much smoother year. A good plan will generally involve some innovative ideas that can move the school forward and solve any problems the school might have. It is vital that a school administrator makes a strong effort to always be learning about new ways to improve the curriculum for the school.

- **Personal Involvement:** School administrators have a large volume of paperwork at their desks so it is understandable that they cannot be walking around the school all day long. This is not a good excuse for never leaving the office, since walking around the school can be a great way to increase communication with the faculty and the students. While walking around the school, in between getting some paperwork done, a school administrator can take the opportunity to get a feel for what is going on in the classrooms and throughout the halls at the school. This can also be a great opportunity to discover and solve some problems as they pop up. A large number of people attempting to earn their masters of higher education hope to one day be school administrators, but simply earning your masters in education is not enough to be a great school administrator. A great school administrator takes responsibility for his or her school and has a vision for the future. The school administrators who are heavily involved in the school, walk around, and get to know the faculty and students are the ones who really make a difference in their schools. It is this sense of personal responsibility that sets them apart and makes them truly progressive school administrators who can positively affect change in the students at their schools.

Characteristics of A Good Elementary School Administrator

(1) **A sense of purpose**: The values of an organization must be clear, members of the organization should know them, and they should exemplify and uphold them in their own actions.

(2) **Justice**: Everyone in an organization should be held to common standards, with rules and procedures that are clear, firm, fair, and consistent.

(3) **Temperance**: A leader must strive to maintain a proper balance of emotions; It did not mean that leaders should be dispassionate. Quite the contrary- but there are time for passionate advocacy and times for quiet reflection and reconsideration. Balance is the key.

(4) **Respect**: The dignity of each individual is the concern of any leader, and this is preserved by treating all members of the organization with respect and ensuring they treat one-another similarly, regardless of differences.

(5) **Empowerment**: Leaders are just that- leaders. Most of what happens in organizations is carried out by individuals other than those in formal leadership positions. Therefore, the more skilled they are, the more they feel confident in their abilities and competent to make decisions, raise questions, see new possibilities, and disagree respectfully with others at all levels of the organizational hierarchy, the stronger and more successful the organization will be.

(6) **Courage**: Leaders are paid to set direction, not wait for direction to emerge. They have to be willing to follow their convictions and bring their organization to new places. In education, this is most sorely needed in response to the test-based regimen that has taken over our schools at the expense of true education and social-emotional and character development.

(7) **Deep Commitment**: Leaders must not be polishing their resumes, but rather should have deep commitment to their organizations, the advancement of the organizations' missions, and the wellbeing of everyone in them. It is this deep commitment that makes leadership in schools so challenging, because it requires a commitment to every employee, student, and parent.

The performance of a leader must be judged by his/her skills and the character of his/her performance in the many and complex roles that leadership demands. Using the seven cornerstones of leading with character, is a tool for both evaluating and improving leadership competencies along both moral and performance dimensions.

Principles of Democratic School Administration

Democratic leaders offer guidance to group members, but they also participate in the group and allow input from other group members. It's hard to order and demand someone to be creative, perform as a team, solve complex problems, improve quality, and provide outstanding customer service. The style presents a happy medium between over controlling (micromanaging) and not being engaged and tends to be seen in organizations that must innovate to prosper. This type of leadership may be emphasized throughout the organization. It encourages decision making from different perspectives.

Kurt Lewin's study found that participative (democratic) leadership is generally the most effective leadership style. Participative leaders encourage group members to participate, but retain the final say over the decision-making process. Group members feel engaged in the process and are more motivated and creative.

- **Democratic education** is an educational ideal in which democracy is both a goal and a method of instruction. It brings democratic values to education and can include self-determination within a community of equals, as well as such values as justice, respect and trust.
- **Administrative structure**: Democratic schools often have meetings open to all students and staff, where everyone present has a voice and sometimes an equal vote. Some include parents. These school meetings can cover anything from small matters to the appointment or dismissal of staff and the creation or annulment of rules, or to

general expenditure and the structure of the school day. At some schools all students are expected to attend these meetings, at others they are voluntary. The main school meeting may also set up sub-committees to deal with particular issues, such as conflict resolution.

- **Conflict resolution**: Within the purview of democratic values, there is wide scope for how conflicts are resolved. There may be a formal system, with due process and the rule of law. There may be rules but no punishments. Other possibilities include, but are not limited to, a consensus process, mediation, and informal dialogue.
- **Finance:** Some democratic learning environments are parent-funded, some charity-funded. Schools may have a sliding scale based on family income. Publicly funded democratic schools exist in many countries.
- **Size:** Democratic schools vary in size from a few students to a few hundred. Even an individual unschooled can be described as learning democratically, if they are treated with democratic values.
- **Age range:** Age mixing is a deliberate policy in some democratic schools. It may include very young children, even babies. Some democratic schools only enrol older students.
- **Location:** Democratic education is not limited to any particular setting. Settings for democratic learning communities include in an office building, on city streets, and in a rural area.

Effect on quality of education

The type of political socialization that takes place in democratic schools is strongly related to deliberative democracy theory. Claus Offe and Ulrich Preuss, two theorists of the political culture of deliberative democracies argue that in its cultural production deliberative democracy requires "an open-ended and continuous learning process in which the roles of both 'teacher' and 'curriculum' are missing. In other words, what is to be learned is a matter that we must settle in the process of learning itself."

The political culture of a deliberative democracy and its institutions, they argue, would facilitate more "dialogical forms of making one's voice heard" which would "be achieved within a framework of liberty, within which paternalism is replaced by autonomously adopted self-paternalism, and technocratic elitism by the competent and self-conscious judgment of citizens."

As a curricular, administrative and social operation within schools, democratic education is essentially concerned with equipping people to make "real choices about fundamental aspects of their lives" and happens within and for democracy. It can be "a process where teachers and students work collaboratively to reconstruct curriculum to include everyone." In at least one conception, democratic education teaches students "to participate in consciously reproducing their society, and conscious social reproduction." This role necessitates democratic education happening in a variety of settings and being taught by a variety of people, including "parents, teachers, public officials, and ordinary citizens." Because of this "democratic education begins not only with children who are to be taught but also with citizens who are to be their teachers."

Preparation for life in a democracy

The "strongest, political rationale" for democratic education is that it teaches "the virtues of democratic deliberation for the sake of future citizenship." This type of education is often alluded to in the deliberative democracy literature as fulfilling the necessary and fundamental social and institutional changes necessary to develop a democracy that involves intensive participation in group decision making, negotiation, and social life of consequence.

Civic Education

The concept of the hidden curriculum includes the belief that anything taught in an authoritarian setting is implicitly teaching authoritarianism. Thus civic education, if taught in a compulsory setting, undermines its own lessons in democracy. A common belief in democratic schools is that democracy must be experienced to be learned. Another common belief, which supports the practice of compulsory classes in civic education, is that passing on democratic values requires an imposed structure. Arguments about how to transmit democracy, and how much and how early to treat children democratically, are made in various literatures concerning student voice, youth participation and other elements of youth empowerment.

Criticism based on political theory

Attachment parenting claims that a child needs to be on the lower end of a hierarchical relationship in order to have emotional health and healthy development.

Economic Theory

Core features of democratic education align with the emerging consensus on 21st century business and management priorities. Such features include increased collaboration, decentralized organization, and radical creativity.

Curriculum theory

While democratic schools don't have an official curriculum, what each student actually does might be considered their own curriculum. Democratic schools may not consider reading, writing and arithmetic to be the real basics for being a successful adult. A.S. Neill said "To hell with arithmetic." Nonetheless, there is a common belief that people will eventually learn "the basics" when they develop internal motivation.

DEMOCRATIC EDUCATION IN PRACTICE

A striking feature of democratic schools is the ubiquity of **play**. Students of all ages - but especially the younger ones - often spend most of their time either in free play, or playing games. All attempts to limit, control or direct play must be democratically approved before being implemented. Play is seen as activity every bit as worthy as academic pursuits, often even more valuable. Play is considered essential for learning, particularly in fostering creativity. Reading, writing and arithmetic: Interest in learning to read happens at a wide variety of ages. Basic principles of democratic educational administration are:

- Principle of democratic leadership.
- Principle of cooperation.
- Principle of scientific method.
- Principle of coordination.
- Principle of flexibility.
- Principle of planning.
- Principle of evaluation.

Education in a Democratic Society

Matthew Arnold investigated popular education in France and other countries to determine what form of education suited a democratic age. Arnold wrote that "the spirit of democracy" is part of "human nature itself", which engages in "the effort to affirm one's own essence...to develop one's own existence fully and freely."

During the industrial age, John Dewey argued that children should not all be given the same pre-determined curriculum. In Democracy and Education he develops a philosophy of education based on democracy. He argues that while children should be active participants in the creation of their education, and while children must experience democracy to learn democracy, they need adult guidance to develop into responsible adults.

Amy Guttmann argues in Democratic Education that in a democratic society, there is a role for everyone in the education of children. These roles are best agreed upon through deliberative.

The journal Democracy and Education investigates "the conceptual foundations, social policies, institutional structures, and teaching/learning practices associated with democratic education." By "democratic education" they mean "educating youth...for active participation in a democratic society."

DECENTRALIZATION IN DEMOCRATIC SCHOOL ADMINISTRATION

Decentralization is delegation of authority in the hands of lower management. It is lower management's systematic control of major policy making authority. The degree of Decentralization rests on the discretion and authority of the managers and the nature of the decisions they make at each level of the organization. It thrives under four conditions: (a) When the number of decisions made lower down in the managerial hierarchy, increases. (b) When the importance of decisions made lower down in the managerial hierarchy, increases. (c) When the number of functions affected by lower level decision, increases. (d) When the independence of lower level managers increases. Authority delegated among central hands and committees means decentralization of powers. There are no hard and fast rules about much to decentralize. Decisions can be made by lower department or managerial committees according to their situation, working conditions, activities and work environments. With the change in pattern of Govt; there is always change in patterns of organisation and administration. More organizations today are decentralized but to a limited degree. Present work force demands greater authority. Decentralization gives top level managers freedom to do what they are supposed to do; within the limits of complexity in technology and surrounding work environment.

In the field of education the pattern of decentralization has hard tasks to do in comparison to other industries. Industries deal with raw material and that raw material processed through hard and soft machine produce planned and finished goods as desired. In educational industry it is human being as input and trained and educated human beings as products. It is very difficult to be accurate planner, decision maker or processor as for as human life is concerned. Human being with full balanced self to be processed is as difficult as to put, Sun into a cage. But still decentralization pattern of administration provides changes of planning programs framing curricula, scheduling time and fixing evaluation programs into the hands of base level administrator and executors. Base level officers and committees of teachers as well as subject specialists plan such programs that can make top level managers nearer the targets. Group decision making techniques are being adopted. Face to face interchanging and interacting takes place which are applicable to high ratio of population. Managing committees, electronic meeting, open discussions, transparent studies through media, brain storming activities of experts are involved in decentralized pattern of administration. Expert view from trained and skilful teachers in matters of executing some new pattern and policy are taken into view, the prime need of course is the role to be played by creative and talented persons who can prove to be the real assets in their respective fields. In decentralized pattern of administration, problems are understood by all participants and decisions are taken by all members after good deal of discussions. Members/committees meet as a group decide policies clearly and reach the final with highest aggregate ranking. Schools and colleges are staffed by professionals. This has implication for the nature of management in educational institutions because professionals seek a measure of control over their working environment. As Handy (1984) suggests, schools are, "organizations of professionals who in the manner of professionals like to manage themselves." In practice teachers usually are too busy with their pedagogic activities to be able to devote much of their time to management. Most of the management responsibilities are exercised often by the head of the institution, on their behalf.

NATIONAL COUNCIL OF EDUCATIONAL RESEARCH AND TRAINING (NCERT)

The National Council of Educational Research and Training (NCERT) is an autonomous organisation set up in 1961 by the Government of India to assist and advise the Central and State Governments on policies and programmes for qualitative improvement in school education. The major objectives of NCERT and its constituent units are to: undertake, promote and coordinate research in areas related to school education; prepare and publish model textbooks, supplementary material, newsletters, journals and develops educational kits, multimedia digital materials, organise pre-service and in-service training of teachers; develop and disseminate innovative educational techniques and practices; collaborate and network with state educational departments, universities, NGOs and other educational institutions; act as a clearing house for ideas and information in matters related to school education; and act as a nodal agency for achieving the goals of Universalisation of Elementary Education. In addition to research, development, training, extension, publication and dissemination activities, NCERT is an implementation agency for bilateral cultural exchange programmes with other countries in the field of school education. The NCERT also interacts and works in collaboration with the international organisations, visiting foreign delegations and offers various training facilities to educational personnel from developing countries. The major constituent units of NCERT are located in different regions of the country. They are enlisted and briefly described below:

National Institute of Education (NIE), New Delhi

Departments

- Department of Education in Arts and Aesthetics [DEAA]
- Department of Elementary Education [DEE]
- Department of Education of Groups with Special Needs [DEGSN]
- Department of Educational Psychology and Foundations of Education [DEPFE]

- Department of Education in Science and Mathematics [DESM]
- Department of Education in Social Sciences [DESS]
- Department of Education in Languages [DEL]
- Department of Gender Studies [DGS]
- Department of Teacher Education [DTE]
- Department of Curriculum Studies [DCS]

Divisions

- Publication Division [PD]
- Library And Documentation Division [LDD]
- International Relation Division [IRD]
- Planning and Monitoring Division [PMD]
- Division of Educational Research [DER]
- Educational Survey Division [ESD]
- Division of Educational Kits [DEK]

Cells

- RMSA Project Cell
- Hindi Cell
- Public Relation Cell [PRC]

Central Institute of Educational Technology (CIET), New Delhi

Central Institute of Educational Technology (CIET), a constituent unit of NCERT, came into existence in the year 1984 with the merger of Centre for Educational Technology and Department of Teaching Aids. CIET is a premiere national institute of educational technology. Its major aim is to promote utilization of educational technologies viz. radio, TV, films, Satellite communications and cyber media either separately or in combinations. The institute undertakes activities to widen educational opportunities, promote equity and improve quality of educational processes at school level.

Pandit Sundarlal Sharma Central Institute of Vocational Education (PSSCIVE), Bhopal

The Pandit Sunderlal Sharma Central Institute of Vocational Education (PSSCIVE), Bhopal is a constituent unit of National Council of Educational Research and Training (NCERT), which is an autonomous organization under the Ministry of Human Resource Development (MHRD), Government of India. The Institute advises and assists the Central and State Governments on policy planning and implementation of vocationalisation of education and vocational education and training. It develops competency based curricula, courseware and e-learning materials for vocationalisation of education in schools. The

Institute has six Departments, namely (i) Agriculture and Animal Husbandry, (ii) Business and Commerce, (iii) Engineering and Technology, (iv) Health and Paramedical, (v) Home Science and Hospitality Management, (vi) Humanities, Science, Education and Research. The Centre/Cell includes the following: (i) Curriculum Development and Evaluation Centre, (ii) Centre for International Relations, (iii) Programme Planning and Monitoring Centre, (iv) National Skill Qualification Framework (NSQF) Cell. The PSSCIVE is functioning as the UNESCO-UNEVOC (International Project on Technical and Vocational Education) Centre in India.

Regional Institute of Education (RIE), Ajmer

Regional College of Education, Ajmer was set up in the year 1963. Later it was renamed as Regional Institute of Education (RIE), Ajmer in the year 1995. It looks after the educational interests of Northern Region comprising the states of Haryana, Himachal Pradesh, Jammu & Kashmir, Punjab, Rajasthan, Uttarakhand, Uttar Pradesh, the National Capital Territory of Delhi and the Union Territory of Chandigarh. Ajmer is well-known all over India as a historical and religious place of pilgrimage as well as an educational centre. It owes this reputation partly to the Regional Institute of Education (RIE). The Institute is situated six km. away from the Ajmer Railway Station in midst of idyllic surroundings with the historic Anasagar Lake in front and the Aravali hills all around. It is almost equidistant from the world famous Dargah of Khawaja Moinuddin Chisti beyond the lake and the holy place of Hindu pilgrimage, Pushkar, at the back. This Institute, with its spacious buildings, playgrounds, gardens, lawns and farm is spread over 110 acres. It is affiliated to the M.D.S. University, Ajmer and its courses are recognised by the NCTE, New Delhi. It is controlled and managed by the NCERT. The management committee, chaired by the Vice-Chancellor of the affiliating university performs the advisory role on matters of academic interest.

Regional Institute of Education (RIE), Bhopal

RIE Bhopal is a constituent unit of NCERT, New Delhi. The Institute looks after teacher education and other educational requirements of the States of Chhattisgarh, Goa, Gujarat, Madhya Pradesh, Maharashtra and UTs of Dadra and Nagar Haveli and Daman and Diu. The Institute is located at Shyamla Hills and is 7 Kms away from both Bhopal and Habibganj.

Regional Institute of Education (RIE), Bhubaneswar

Regional Institute of Education, Bhubaneswar a constituent unit of NCERT, New Delhi, caters to the educational needs of teachers of Eastern Indian region. It provides academic and technical support to the state of Odisha, West Bengal, Bihar, Jharkhand, Assam, Arunachal Pradesh, Sikkim, Manipur, Mizoram, Meghalaya, Tripura, Nagaland and Andaman and Nicobar Islands.

The institute act as a regional resource centre for all areas of education, especially school education. UNESCO Bangkok has declared Regional Institute of Education, Bhubaneswar as a resource centre for ICT.

Regional Institute of Education (RIE), Mysore

The Regional Institute of Education Mysore (Formerly Regional College of Education) founded on 1st August, 1963, is one of five such institutions established by the NCERT, New Delhi. Regional Institutes were started with main the objective of qualitative improvement of school education through innovative pre-service and in-service teacher training programmes and relevant research, development and extension activities.

The Regional Institute of Education, Mysore has established itself as an institute of repute in the area of school and teacher education. The institute has endeavoured to shoulder the responsibilities and challenges generated by changes in the educational scenario of the country and the southern region. The Institute has been functioning as Regional Institute of Education since 1995, following a major shift in its focus from pre-service education to in-service education. The pre-service teacher education programmes of the institute are affiliated to the University of Mysore and cater to the needs of south Indian states namely Andhra Pradesh, Karnataka, Kerala, Tamil Nadu, and Union Territories of Pondicherry and Lakshadweep. A Demonstration Multipurpose School (DMS) is attached to each RIE at Ajmer, Bhopal, Bhubaneswar and Mysore as a laboratory for trying out innovative practices in school education and teacher education. These are also used for practical training for the trainees of the institutes.

North-East Regional Institute of Education (NERIE), Shillong

The history of inception of North East Regional Institute of Education dates back to the year 1982. The 'Task Force' of National Council of Educational Research and Training (NCERT) headed by Madhuri Shah made a recommendation to set up a Regional Centre for NCERT in the north east. It was felt that the Regional College at Bhubaneswar was in no position to look after the needs of the north east which are not only unique but require priority attention in the context of socio-political situation. However, it is in the year 1995 that the idea of creating a separate Regional Institute of Education for the north east was mooted by amalgamating the then Field Units of NCERT at Guwahati and Shillong. At this juncture the Council appointed a One-man Committee under the Chairmanship of Prof. C.L. Anand, former Vice Chancellor, Arunachal University to prepare a "Blue Print" in connection with the setting up of a Regional Institute of Education (RIE) of the NCERT for the North East at Shillong.

The North East Regional Institute of Education (NERIE) is a constituent unit of NCERT, New Delhi. NERIE was set up at Shillong in 1995 to cater to the educational needs of the North Eastern states, viz., Assam, Arunachal Pradesh, Manipur, Meghalaya, Mizoram, Nagaland, Sikkim and Tripura. NERIE aspires to provide academic and technical support system to assist and advise the governments of the above mentioned states on policies and programmes on all aspects of school education and reshape the State curricula.

It primarily aims at capacity building of the state and district level resource institutions/teachers education institutions and State Boards of Secondary and Higher Secondary Education located in the region in undertaking research, development and training. The Institute will try to engage itself in (i) the promotion and support of the programmes of the Government of India and the NCERT, (ii) development of school education in the North- East, and (iii) development of a different kind of professional identity in the areas of language in education, science and mathematics education in the light of NCF 2005, teachers' professional development, research on sociological and cultural dimensions of education, etc.

The programmes of NERIE focus on development of interventions for the special problems of school education in the region such as the problems of under qualified and untrained teachers, high rates of school dropouts, low levels of pupil achievement and high rates of unemployment among school leavers/school dropouts.

The programmes of NERIE also focus on research, development and training in the areas of national priority concerns such as universalization of elementary education, vocationalization of secondary education, increased educational accessibility for girls, SCs and STs and the physically challenged, improvement of science and mathematics education, computer education and educational technology.

In view of the special demographic, geographical, and other features of the region, a distinguishing characteristic of the NERIE will be its functioning modality marked by distance mode of learning and training in addition to the conventional face to face system of education and training. This could be a step towards decentralization of delivery of training by making it accessible to a large number of clienteles. The Institute will network with Indira Gandhi National Open University (IGNOU) and CIET, NCERT, New Delhi for the purpose. The Institute will make all efforts to preserve the ethnic/cultural identities of the people of the NE region.

Since the programmes of the Institute will be formulated on the basis of the specific needs of the NE states, most of the programmes will be organized in the concerned states in collaboration with the state departments of education, SCERTs or Boards of Education except the common regional programmes. Keeping in mind the repeated requests from the Madrassa Board, the NERIE will also make efforts to improve the content and pedagogy of teaching secular subjects in the Madrassa schools of the region.

The long term role of the NERIE would be to facilitate development of human resource in the NE region so that the states are able to provide quality inputs in all aspects of school education. It is worth mentioning here that when the NERIE came into existence there were so many pre-service teacher training institutions operative in the region. This makes the NERIE different from the other RIEs. Keeping the aforementioned in mind, the NERIE will focus its attention on in-service teacher training programmes in the region.

Since the most important goal of the NERIE is to strengthen the functioning of the SCERTs and the DIETs in the NE States, it may start part time/ correspondence M.Ed., certificate courses in ECCE/ICT for the in–service faculty members of the SCERTs and DIETs in couple of years from now, and pre-service teacher training programmes as and when the Institute is ready for the same.

NCERT undertakes the following programmes and activities.

- **Research:** The NCERT performs the important functions of conducting and supporting educational research and offering training in educational research methodology. Different Departments of the National Institute of Education (NIE), Regional Institutes of Education (RIEs), Central Institute of Educational Technology (CIET) and Pandit Sunderlal Sharma Central Institute of Vocational Education (PSSCIVE) undertake research programmes on different aspects of school education and teacher education. NCERT also supports research programmes of other institutions/organizations by providing financial assistance and academic guidance. Assistance is given to scholars for publication of their Ph.D. theses. Research fellowships are offered to encourage studies in school education to create a pool of competent research workers.
- **Development:** Developmental activities in school education constitute an important function of the NCERT. The major developmental activities include development and renewal of curricula and instructional materials for various levels of school education and making them relevant to changing needs of children and society. The innovative developmental activities include development of curricula and instructional materials in school education in the area of pre-school education, formal and non-formal education, vocationalisation of education and teacher education. Developmental activities are also undertaken in the domains of educational technology, population education, and education of the disabled and other special groups.
- **Training:** Pre-service and in-service training of teachers at various levels; pre-primary, elementary, secondary and higher secondary,

vocational education, educational technology, guidance and counselling, and special education are the areas of training in which NCERT works. The pre-service teacher education programmes at the Regional Institutes of Education (RIEs) incorporate many innovative features. The RIEs also undertake the training of key personnel of the states and of state level institutions and training of teacher educators and in-service teachers.

- **Extension:** Various Departments of the NIE, RIEs, CIET and PSSCIVE are engaged in various ways. Constituents of NCERT work in close collaboration with various agencies and institutions in the states. Several programmes are organized in rural and backward areas in order to reach out to the functionaries in these areas where special problems exist and where special efforts are needed. Special programmes are organized for the education of the disadvantaged sections of the society. The extension programmes cover all States and Union Territories of the country.
- **Publication and Dissemination:** NCERT publishes textbooks for different school subjects for Classes I to XII. It also brings out workbooks, teachers' guides, supplementary readers, research reports, etc. In addition, it publishes instructional materials for the use of teacher educators, teacher trainees and in-service teachers. These instructional materials, produced through research and developmental work, serve as models to various agencies in States and Union Territories. These are made available to state level agencies for adoption and/or adaptation. The textbooks are published in English, Hindi and Urdu. For dissemination of educational information, or the NCERT publishes six journals: *The Primary Teacher* is published both in English and Hindi and aims at giving meaningful and relevant educational inputs to primary school teachers for direct use in the classroom; *School Science* serves as an open forum for discussion on various aspects of science education; *Journal of Indian Education* provides a forum for encouraging original and critical thinking in education through discussion on current educational issues; *Indian Educational Review* contains research articles and provides a forum for researchers in education; and *Bharatiya Adhunik Shiksha*, published in Hindi, provides a forum for encouraging critical thinking in education on contemporary issues and for dissemination of educational problems and practices. Besides these, a in house journal called *NCERT Newsletter / Shaikshik Darpan* is also published in English and Hindi.
- **Exchange Programmes:** NCERT interacts with international organizations such as UNESCO, UNICEF, UNDP, NFPA and the World Bank to study specific educational problems and to arrange

training programmes for personnel from other countries. It is one of the Associated Centres of APEID. It also acts as the Secretariat of the National Development Group (NDG) for Educational Innovations. The NCERT has been offering training facilities, usually through attachment programmes and participation in workshops, to educational workers of other countries. The NCERT acts as a major agency for implementing the Bilateral Cultural Exchange Programmes entered into by the Government of India with the governments of other countries in the fields of school education and teacher education. Educational materials are exchanged with other countries. On request, the faculty members are deputed to participate in international conferences, seminars, workshops, symposia, etc.

STATE COUNCIL OF EDUCATIONAL RESEARCH AND TRAINING (SCERT) / STATE INSTITUTE OF EDUCATION (SIE)

The State Council of Educational Research and Training or State Institute of Education (SIEs) was established during the mid-sixties in the country to work for qualitative improvement of elementary education through organization of in-service training for teachers and supervisors, execution of research and extension activities, and development of instructional materials.

SCERTs- Development and Present Status

The Government of India initiated a scheme for setting up the State Institute of Education in different states as far back as 1963 for qualitative improvement of school education in general and elementary teacher education in particular. Though initially only major states started these institutions, many other followed suit in view of the need for such academic institutions to co-ordinate all academic projects in every state or union territory.

Subsequently, in the course of time, in some states, specialized institutes/ agencies/units were established in some other specific areas like Science education, English language teaching, educational technology, vocational guidance and counselling etc. In 1973, the Ministry of Education and Social Welfare recommended that all such existing institutions or various units in the State Education Department be merged into a single organization and designated as the State Council of Educational Research and Training (SCERT). In some states the nomenclature of SIEs remained the same but with increased functions and responsibilities.

SCERTs/SIEs have been set up in almost all the states/Union Territories (UT's) in the country. Four the UTs namely Pondicherry, Daman and Diu, Dadar and Nagar Haveli and Lakshadweep have neither an SCERT not SIE. However the academic functions in these UTs are being looked after by the academic wings of State Education Departments or State Training Centres, of these some have be recently upgrades as DIETs.

The academic activities and programmes is an SCERT are carried out by its various departments/Units/Wings. Generally, the SCERT is headed by a Director who is assisted by the officers and subject specialists/Technical Assistants. The question of providing autonomous status to the SCERTs are envisaged in the scheme, is being pursued in many states/UTs.

The Changing Role of SCERT's

NPE 1986 and POA envisaged additional role and functions for the SCERT's. SCERTs is expected to guide support and assist the state education department in its mission to improve the quality of school education and teacher education. It will also function as the state resource institution to provide academic support to all stages of school education from pre-primary to senior secondary stage of education. SCERT's have the mandate to supervise and support DIET's in order to facilitate their operationalization and effective functioning.

Types of Activities and Programmes of SCERT's

Research: The staff members are expected to conduct research studies related to the significant educational problems of the state to improve the quality of elementary, secondary and teacher education. Besides they are conduct status studies and educational surveys to get benchmark data and develop information system related to school education and teacher education in the state policy planning and management.

Development: The development of curricular policies, syllabi and instructional material, print and non-print both for formal and non-formal education system and come under the purview of the SCERT's. The SCERT's/ SIE's may under take the task of developing criterion for inspection and supervision of elementary schools at block level.

Training:

- Continuing education of teachers, supervisors, and other educational personnel.
- Plan, implement, monitor and evaluate all pre-service and in-service teacher education, particularly at elementary level in the state.
- Short/long duration in-service training/orientation programmes for school teachers, master trainers and resource persons with the help of DIET's.
- Familiarize the DIET faculty with the latest technology for organizing in-service education of teachers.

Extension: SCERT is expected to function as a think-tank of the State Department of Education to promote innovations and action research for improved practices in school education and teacher education. For this, the SCERT should organize workshops for school teachers and the DIET faculty to guide them to design action research projects and evolve/replicate innovative practices to improve classroom teaching and other institutional programmes. In house staff development activities-seminars, talks, conferences research colloquia, panel discussions, extension lectures on latest developments and emerging problems in education by eminent academicians and scholars may be organized.

Dissemination: SCERT's/SIE's bring out reports of research studies, newsletters, journals/magazines, annual reports etc. They also disseminate important data, information, significant research findings through their newsletters/magazines and annual reports to the concerned institutions.

Linkage of SCERT with other Institutions: In the field of elementary education the Directorate of Education, Department of Adult and non-formal education and DIET's are the main Institutions with which the SCERT should have close relations and co-ordination. In the area of pre-school education SCERT is expected to prepare guidelines for organizing the activities at the child play centres, Anganwadis, Balwadis, etc. Integrated Child Development services (ICDS) run by the Social Welfare Department mainly dealt with health and nutrition components.

DISTRICT INSTITUTE OF EDUCATION AND TRAINING (DIET)

District Institute of Education and Training (DIET) as derived from National Policy of Education (NPE-1986) and Plan/Programme of Action (POA-1992). Elementary education is very crucial for developing human resource which in turn promotes the growth of economy. One of the road block, which impedes our march towards the goal is high dropout rate at elementary level. The NPE (1986) envisaged setting up thc DIET's in the country with a view to improving the quality of elementary education. It was envisaged the DIET's would provide pre-service as well as in-service education to all the elementary teachers in the district. The functioning of a DIET involves providing academic and resource support to achieve Universalization of Elementary Education (UEE) and improve quality of elementary education, non-formal education and adult education and strengthening elementary teacher training, both pre-service and in-service.

The DIET has the following major functions to perform.

- Conducting Training
- Providing academic and resource support to the elementary and adult education system in the district.

- Conducting action research and experimentation to deal with specific problems relating to universal elementary and adult education.

As per the guidelines of MHRD, a DIET would have the following seven academic branches.

(1) *Pre-Service Teacher Education (PSTE) Branch:* This Branch is to organize a regular full time two years teacher's training programme for 50 students.

(2) *In-service Field Interaction and Innovations Co-ordination (FIC) Branch:* DIET will regularly organize in-service teacher orientation programmes for teacher to equip them to meet the changing demands of the profession.

(3) *Work Experience (WE) Branch:* This branch identified locally relevant work experience areas and works for their inclusion in the curriculum of elementary schools.

(4) *Educational Technology (ET) Branch:* The primary functions of this branch are to:

  - equip the institute with a variety of educational gadgets for enriching the quality of education and teacher training,
  - develop different programmes of media intervention as input for quality schooling: and,
  - prepare teaching/learning material for pre-service and in-service teacher training and Non-formal education and Adult Education workers.

(5) *Planning and Management (P & M) Branch:* This unit of DIET plays the role of a nodal agency for assessing, planning, advising and meeting over all education needs and aspirations of the district covering primary education.

(6) *Curriculum, Material Development and Evaluation (CMDE) Branch:* The role and responsibility of the branch is to develop curriculum and learning materials for elementary education, teacher education, adult education and non-formal education.

(7) *District Resource Unit (DRU):* Primary responsibility of this unit is to assist in planning, co-ordinating and organizing programmes for adult and non-formal education personnel on a continuing basis.

The concept of grass root planning and development has been gaining ground in the country for quite a while. The getting up of institutions like the DIETs at the District Level seems to be a positive step in this direction

FUNDING AND FINANCING OF ELEMENTARY EDUCATION

The contribution of education is not restricted to economic returns only. Its significant effect on reduction in poverty and improvement in income distribution, improvement in health and nutritional status of the population, its negative relationship with fertility and population growth and positive association with adoption of family planning methods, and its positive relationship with general social, political and economic development and overall quality of life are well recognized. All this has contributed to the rapid growth of education in India, though it is still not adequate.

The National Policy on Education (NPE) 1968 and the NPE 1986 have laid special emphasis on the fulfilment of the Constitutional Directive of universalization of elementary education (UEE). Five Year Plans have repeatedly promised to take the nation towards achieving this goal. Elementary education was also included in the 'National Programme of Minimum Needs' in the Five Year Plans, and this inclusion has significant implications for allocation of resources.

There are three important aspects relating to allocation of resources to education:

- Allocation of resources to education vis-a-vis other sectors, i.e. inter-sectoral allocation,
- Intra-sectoral allocation of resources within education, i.e. allocation to different levels, and
- Inter-functional allocation of resources to different activities such as teaching, administrative, and welfare. Yet another important dimension of allocation of resources to education, that is important in a federal system like India, is allocation by the Union government to the states.

These aspects are briefly discussed here, surveying the existing scanty literature, and with the help of some important indicators using the recent data available. At the outset it may be noted that despite recognizing the contribution of education to economic growth and development, the pattern of allocation of resources to education is still far from satisfactory.

Inter-sectoral Allocation of Resources First, what is the priority given to education in the national development framework? This question is generally answered in terms of a few select indicators such as the share of education in Gross National Product (GNP), share of education in government expenditure, share of education in Five Year Plan outlays, etc, some of which are discussed below.

Share of Education in GNP

The share of education in GNP is the most standard indicator of national efforts on the development of education in a given society. This reflects the relative priority being accorded to education in the national economy. It is also found to be superior to several other indicators. On the recommendation of the Education Commission (1966), the Government of India (1968) quantitatively targeted investing 6 per cent of national income in education from the public exchequer by 1986.

As the goal has not been realized so far, it has repeatedly been reiterated that it will soon be fulfilled. Now the goal is set to be achieved by the end of the Ninth Five Year Plan, i.e. by 2002. Presently 3.6 per cent of GNP is invested in education in India (1997-78). Compared to the very low level of 1.2 per cent in 1950-51, this marks very significant progress. However, it needs to be underlined that this proportion is less than;

(i) the requirements of the education system to provide reasonable levels of quality education to all the students presently enrolled

(ii) the requirements of the system to provide UEE for eight years to every child in the age group 6-14, and consequent growth in secondary and higher education, as UEE in a comprehensive sense includes universal provision of resources, universal enrolment, and universal retention,

(iii) the recommendations of the Education Commission (1966), the resolve made in the NPE 1968 (DoE 1968), reiterated in the NPE 1986 (DoE 1986), and the revised policy (1992) to invest 6 per cent of GNP in education,

(iv) the proportion of GNP invested in education in many other developing, leave alone developed, countries of the world, including Africa, and

(v) finally the proportion invested in India before the Jomtien conference (1990). For instance, 4.9 per cent of Gross Domestic Product (GDP) was invested in education in India in 1990-91. But ever since, it has been consistently declining. It should be noted that it would be a stupendous task to reach a level of 6 per cent of GNP by the end of the Ninth Five Year Plan, as promised by the government, from the current level of 3.6 per cent. Among the countries of the world on which such data are available, India ranked 115th with respect to this indicator of national efforts on education, and amongst countries with a population of 100 million or more, India figures at the bottom, except Bangladesh.

The Education Budget

Perhaps a more important gauge of what is actually happening is the priority accorded to education in the government budget. Unfortunately there is no 'education budget' per se in India. To arrive at an education budget, one has to look at the education components in the union budget, and more importantly in the budgets of all the states and union territories (UTs). Only then can a complete picture of the education budget in the country be presented. We do not have such an 'integrated budget presentation' in our country.

The Union Budget fails to provide any significant idea, as its contribution is relative to the state budgets for education is very small. Further, in the budget framework, resources flow from the government in two forms - in the revenue account of the budget and in the capital account. While in the revenue budget the share of the education sector is reasonably large, in the capital budget the share of education is infinitesimally small, the net result being the pushing down of the share of education in the total budget. If central and state budgets are considered, in terms of both revenue and capital accounts, the total budget resources available for education formed around 11 per cent in 1995-96.

Resource Requirements for UEE

Finding resources to finance UEE is an urgent as well as, contrary to popular fears, an entirely achievable task. On the basis of the recommendation of the high powered "Saikia Committee (1997), a group of experts was constituted to estimate the financial requirement for making elementary education a fundamental right in the Constitution. Based on a detailed estimation of costs of each item/programme the group of experts has estimated that UEE requires additionally Rs 136.9 thousand crore during the next ten years. While this figure may seem awesome, certainly being much higher than the Rs 40 thousand crore for a five-year period estimated by the Saikia Committee, it has to be noted that additionally it means only Rs 14 thousand crore a year on average, or additionally 0.7 per cent of GDP (if the GDP grows at a modest rate of growth of 5 per cent per annum). This should easily be achievable.

According to the Committee's estimates, this would provide for a reasonably good pupil-teacher ratio of 1:30, improved physical access to schools, provision of instructional material, other necessary incentives, and on the whole a tolerable minimum level of quality of education to every child in India, by the end of the first decade of the twenty-first century. The expert group also felt that if the government is serious about the allocation of 6 per cent of GDP to education, the task becomes much easier 6 per cent of GDP would not only provide the needed resources for UEE, but it also allows provision of additional resources for growth of secondary and higher education. Further, the group showed that increasing of total allocation to education to reach 6 per cent of GDP is not at all difficult, given;

(i) the economy is likely to grow at a rate of growth of above 5 per cent,

(ii) the likely increase of tax/GDP ratio from 16 per cent to 18 per cent, and

(iii) the likely increase of the non-tax-revenue/GDP ratio from about 3 per cent to 5 per cent during the next ten years. The group also attempted to clear two absurd propositions that are in circulation: (i) that we cannot achieve UEE because it is too costly; and (ii) that the only way to achieve it is to divert funds to it from higher education.

Mobilization of Resources for Elementary Education

In the process of review of NPE 1986, the Government of India (1990) for the first time referred in detail to some of the methods that are nowadays being discussed to generate additional resources for education. These methods largely refer to the higher education sector. Prominent among the several measures that are discussed presently include:

(i) raising fees discriminately,

(ii) revitalization of the national loan programme for students,

(iii) special taxes such as graduate taxes,

(iv) corporate donations through liberal tax concessions, and

(v) self-financing by the education sector.

Most of them are relevant only in the case of higher education and to some extent secondary education, but not in the case of elementary education, and they are thus not discussed here.

As elementary education can be treated as a public good, and as UEE is, more than anything else, a Constitutional obligation, and as the Constitution desired that it be provided free to all, very few in India and even in other countries, argue for raising non-governmental resources for elementary education substantially. The argument instead is for using existing resources more efficiently, for strengthening the base for local finances, and for generation of voluntary community resources to supplement governmental efforts. The role of local bodies is being expected to be vital in not only generating more resources but also in the context of decentralized planning and management of school education. The 73rd Constitutional Amendment on panchayati raj (local self government) institutions may result in more demands on panchayats.

Financing of Private Schools

The private sector is slowly but steadily growing in size, though its present size is still very small. It is interesting to note that voluntary contributions to government institutions have quite significantly come down, and at the same time the number of profit-making private institutions has increased. These trends reflect a shift from motives of philanthropy and charity on the part of private enterprise to profit and greed.

Lastly, the size of private sector is very small, though it is causing significant distortions in the pattern of financing education. At the same time, its relative size cannot increase significantly, as the benefits attached to private schooling are mostly due to scarcity of places in private schools, and get reduced with expansion of the private sector. It has also been found that the private sector has already reached 'optimum' levels in India, the 'optimum' levels being defined in terms of the share of the private sector in developed countries like the USA.

The new economic policies initiated in 1991 that involve short-term stabilization and long-term structural adjustment policies in India will, it is feared, lead to immediate cuts in public budgets for education, as happened in several developing countries that adopted these policies, as these policies clearly involve reduction in public expenditures and deficits, and in the long run they may result in a drastic change in public policies on financing of education. The higher education sector in India has already experienced drastic budget cuts. It is feared that primary and elementary education might also suffer. However, the DPEP, being launched with external assistance in several states, it is hoped will provide some sort of protection to primary education from the budget squeezes. Nevertheless, the financial crisis in education is transparent, and it is forecasted to continue.

The need for strengthening the resource base for education is obvious. However, the choices seem to be limited as far as school education is concerned. Given the Constitutional Directive, and other considerations, the government should continue to take on complete responsibility of financing elementary education, and other sources can only supplement governmental efforts. There is need to improve the overall allocation pattern in financing education in India.

Conclusion

The Government of India and State Governments initiated a number of programmes to achieve the goal of Universalisation of Elementary Education under which concerted efforts have been made towards strengthening the Educational Management Information System in case of elementary level of education. Sporadic attempts were made in the past to develop a computerized educational management information system in India. Though the overall achievement in elementary education has shown some positive indicators in terms of increasing enrolment rates for boys and girls as well as increasing literacy rates the qualitative aspect seems to have gone ignored. The limited achievement have been the result both of reluctant increase in resources allocated to education and also due to programmes and schemes that focus on some of the specific lacunae in the educational infrastructure and the educational system. One cannot remain contended by the mere numbers of achievement alone.

MODEL QUESTIONS

Very Short Answer type Questions. Each question carries 1 Mark. To be answer in about 20 words each.

1. What you mean by Budgeting.
2. Enlist the characteristics of a good elementary school administrator.
3. Enlist the major constituent units of NCERT.
4. What are the functions of DIET.

Short Answer type Questions. Each question carries 2 Marks. To be answer in about 150 words each.

5. Discuss the scope and characteristics of successful elementary school administration.
6. Describe the types of activities and programmes of SCERTs.
7. What are the features of decentralized and democratic school administration?
8. Illustrate the funding and financing of elementary education in India.

Multiple Choice Questions. Each Question carries 1 Mark.

9. ———— leaders offer guidance to group members.
   (a) Autocratic
   (b) Democratic
   (c) Aristocratic
   (d) Laissez Fair
10. Who is the author of the book "Democracy and Education"?
   (a) Vygotsky
   (b) Tagore
   (c) Froebal
   (d) Dewey
11. ———— is delegation of authority in the hands of lower management.
   (a) Centralisation
   (b) Administration
   (c) Decentralization
   (d) Supervision
12. NCERT deals with:
   (a) Higher Education
   (b) School Education
   (c) Vocational Education
   (d) Adult Education

Answer Key

9: B 10: D 11: C 12: B

References

Krishnan, D.K., & Thamarasseri, I. (2013). *Contemporary Issues in Indian Education.* New Delhi: Kanishka Publishers

Thamarasseri, I. (2007). *Education in the Emerging Indian Society.* New Delhi: Kanishka Publishers

Thamarasseri, I. (2008). *Early Childhood and Elementary Education.* New Delhi: Kanishka Publishers

Thamarasseri, I. (2011). *Current Developments in Indian Education.* New Delhi: Kanishka Publishers

Thamarasseri, I. (2014). *Issues and Challenges of Indian Education.* Agra: Shri Vinod Pustak Mandir

Thamarasseri, I., & Bhat, M. S. (2018). *Elementary Education*. Agra: Shri Vinod Pustak Mandir

Tilak, J.B.G. *Financing Elementary Education in India*. retrieved on 10-03-2018 from http://birbhum.gov.in/DPSC/reference/9.pdf

UNIT - 3

Problems and Issues in Elementary Education

INTRODUCTION

The constitution of India clearly states that elementary education is a fundamental right of children in the age of 6-14 years. In order to meet the demands of the growing population, India has about 688,000 primary schools and 100,000 secondary schools. If the statistics are taken into account, then two third of the children, of the school-going age, are admitted to schools. But the reality of the situation is that most of them leave school halfway or do not attend regularly. So, even though the government is trying its best to uphold basic education for all, some issues remain unsolved.

ACCESS

Universal Access means School facilities should be provided to all the children between the age group 6 to 14 years in the country. The schools be easily accessible within the walking distance of the child. We must provide at least one lower primary school within a radius of one km and one upper primary school within a radius of 3km. The ratio of lower primary and upper primary schools must be 3:1.

Even though the number of schools have increased we could not provide schools within the walkable distance of students in some rural areas. As per the 6th all India educational survey, there are 8,22,486 schools in the country of which 5,70,455 are primary, 1,62,805 are higher primary. In all these schools, totally there are 17,30,166 primary teachers. There figures indicate the remarkable growth in the number of schools and in the number of teachers in our country. But even though we have to improve a lot to attain 100% universal access.

The Seventh All India Educational Survey (AIES) conducted by the National Council of Educational Research and Training (NCERT) provides an overview of the availability of schooling facilities in 2002 in India (NCERT,

2005). In 1993-1994 according to the Sixth AIES, 83.4% of habitations in the country had primary schooling facilities within a distance of one km (NCERT, 1998). The percentage of habitations served by upper primary schools at a distance of up to 3 km was 76.2 % of the country. By 2002, around 87 % of habitations had a primary school within a distance of one km, while 78% of habitations had an upper primary school within 3 km (NCERT, 2005). This suggests that physical access to school has continued to improve over the years, although at a relatively slow pace. The Seventh AIES reveals that among the major states in India, numbers of habitations with access to primary schools within walking distance, varied between around 94% in Andhra Pradesh; 75% in Himachal Pradesh and 77.2% in Jharkhand (which has a large tribal population). The survey also shows that the percentage of habitations having primary schools within the habitation was less than the national average in 2002 in states such as Assam, Jharkhand, Orissa and Rajasthan, where educational indicators are also often lower. With respect to the availability of upper primary schools, Jharkhand comes at the bottom of the table, with only 61.4% of habitations having access to upper primary schools within a distance of 3 km. Having said this, the Seventh AIES data shows an increase of more than 50% in primary schooling facilities in Assam, and a more than 30% increase in Chhattisgarh, Jammu & Kashmir, Madhya Pradesh, Punjab and Uttarakhand during the period 1993-2002. During the same period, substantial numbers of primary and upper primary schools were closed down in Kerala, probably due to demographic changes. The growth of schools remained slower generally in states with lower educational indicators. Having said this, studies indicates a phenomenal growth of the total number of schools in the country as a whole, with a rapid increase in student enrolment and numbers of teaching staff at the primary and upper primary levels in recent years. Available data shows that in 2005-2006, 107,539 schools were constructed and another 42,144 were under construction, and as many as 309,005 additional rooms were also constructed, while 270,581 more were under construction (GoI, 2007).

The rapid increase in the number of schools, teachers and students seems to be attributed, to a great extent, to an increase in single-room and single-teacher schools which invariably have inadequate physical and academic infrastructures (Blum and Diwan, 2007). For instance, the Seventh AIES (NCERT, 2005) shows that 15% of all primary schools in the country are single teacher schools. The share of single teacher schools is much higher in rural areas than in urban areas. Barring a few states such as Tamil Nadu and Kerala, all major states have a substantial number of schools in this category. The occurrence of these small schools seems most prevalent in Jharkhand and Bihar, followed by states like Maharashtra, Orissa and Karnataka. In terms of absolute numbers, Uttar Pradesh has the highest number of such small schools in rural areas, followed by Andhra Pradesh, Madhya Pradesh and West Bengal. These states also have a large number of small schools in urban areas.

Are there children who never enrol in primary school? What proportion of children in India fall in this category? These are difficult questions to answer. Regular datasets collected by the Education Department in India do not provide this information, as educational statistics published at national or state level focus either on Gross Enrolment Ratios (GER) or Net Enrolment Ratios (NER). These figures do not identify children who are never enrolled in school. Thus, the answer to this question has to be located in specially conducted surveys that try to identify if children have been to school or not. Findings of some of these surveys are discussed here. The National Sample Survey Organization (NSS) in its survey conducted in 2004 (GoI, 2006) asked whether respondents had ever been enrolled in school. The findings of the survey showed that 35% of individuals between the ages of 5-29 years old had never attended an educational institution (although in the case of younger children, there is a possibility that some of these would subsequently enrol). It is found that boys were more likely than girls never to enrol because they had to contribute to household income; this was more pronounced in the older age groups. Girls were more likely than boys never to enrol because they were engaged in domestic chores. Whether education was considered necessary was an important reason for non-enrolment of rural children in particular, i.e. 23% of never enrolled 5-14 year old rural girls; 22% of never enrolled rural boys. This is compared to 15% of never enrolled urban girls and 12% of urban boys.

Earlier surveys also pointed out that a considerable proportion of children never attended school due to their engagement in work either at home or in order to support household income. Some children found it difficult to attend school due to financial constraints.

The National Family Health Survey (NFHS II) in 1998 of 6-17 year old children reported costs of schooling as the main reason for the largest proportion of boys and girls never enrolling in school. 29% of never enrolled urban boys and 26% of rural boys; 30% of urban girls and 24% of rural girls cited this as the main reason for never attending school. Other important reasons included boys (both rural and urban) not being interested in education; and girls (particularly rural) being required to work either in the home or outside; this was also high for rural boys.

It is observed that in almost all the states of India, there has been an increase in gross enrolment ratio (GER) at the primary level across all social groups between 2004–5 and 2007–8. The net enrolment ratio (NER) at the primary level also increased from 84% in 2005–6 to 96% in 2007–8 for the country as a whole (Planning Commission, 2011). This is primarily the result of a number of initiatives undertaken by the Government of India in recent years aimed at achieving UEE. One of the major schemes introduced by the government in the year 2002 was the **Sarva Shiksha Abhiyan (SSA)**. It aims at providing basic education to all children in the age group 6–14 years while trying to bridge the social, regional, and gender gaps existing within the country, without any compromise in the quality of education. Another major step in this direction is the **Right of Children to Free and Compulsory Education (RTE) Act 2009** which came into force from April 2010. With the enforcement of this Act, education has now become a fundamental right of every child in this country. However, it is to be noted that for India as a whole, 19 per cent of the children in the age group 6–17 years are still out of school (Planning Commission, 2011). Retention rate poses another major challenge to the school education system in India. At the all-India level, average dropout rate at the primary level was 9.11% (9.35% for boys and 8.86% for girls) in 2008-09 (NUEPA, 2011). The high incidence of dropout in primary grades is also evident from the fact that the ratio of Grade V enrolment to Grade I enrolment was 71.86% in 2008-09. Moreover, mean years of schooling for the country as a whole was only 4.2 years in 2007-08 (Planning Commission, 2011). This is a matter of concern because children who do not complete at least five years of schooling are unlikely to retain literacy and numeracy skills in their adulthood thus adding to the pool of illiterate adults.

A combination of factors affects retention rates in schools. These include distance from home, quality of teaching, school facilities, economic costs, etc. Among the various reasons for discontinuation or dropping out, the three most important reasons identified in the NSS 64th Round Survey (NSSO, 2010) are lack of interest on the part of parents, lack of interest on the part of children, and financial constraints. These three factors together accounted for at least half of the cases of discontinuation or dropouts across all social groups. Among these, financial constraint was identified as the predominant factor for discontinuation/dropping out. Widespread poverty coupled with extremely low levels of public expenditure on education (especially on elementary education) makes this an obvious reason for dropout. Here it may be pointed out that the Post-occupancy Review Of Buildings and their Engineering (PROBE) (1999) survey (De et al, 1999) argues that it is a completely wrong perception that parental indifference is a major factor that keeps children out of school. The survey found a high and growing demand for good quality basic education even among the poorest and socially disadvantaged communities. If parents seem disinterested in sending their children to school, it is largely because many schools are dysfunctional and little teaching-learning takes place there.

Although school facilities have been improving over time, much still remains to be done in this area. Close to half of all primary schools in India are still being run either in one or two classroom buildings (NUEPA, 2011). Although the RTE Act 2009 stipulates one classroom per class, India seems quite far from that goal. Lack of adequate sources of drinking water and poor sanitation facilities (particularly for girls) are the other major concerns for school infrastructure. Teacher shortage poses another major challenge to our school education system. The desirable pupil-teacher ratio (PTR) is 30:1. But nearly 12% of all schools have a PTR of more than 60 students per teacher (NUEPA, 2011). The problem is compounded by the existence of a large percentage of untrained teachers and high rates of teacher absenteeism in schools. In fact, the PROBE Revisited Survey (De et al, 2006) highlights lack of teaching input and inadequate contribution of teachers who are appointed as one of the most important challenges facing the school education system. Poor infrastructural facilities in schools and little teaching-learning activity result in high rates of student absenteeism. For the country as a whole, net attendance ratio (NAR) during the year 2007-08 at the primary and upper primary levels was 82% and 60% respectively (NSSO, 2010). Poor attendance rates adversely affect learning outcomes of students because regular attendance is one of the prerequisites of achieving a desired level of learning.

Poor quality of learning in schools is perhaps the most serious challenge facing the primary education system in India. Kingdon and Banerji (2009), based on a survey undertaken in Bihar and Uttar Pradesh, argue that the current level of learning attainment among children is a cause for serious concern. The paper observes that Grade IV students who had very low learning levels at the start of the school year (i.e. who had not mastered even Grade II level basic skills when they entered Grade IV) had little gain in learning throughout the year. The paper emphasizes the need to build strong foundations of basic learning in the early grades. The study also identifies factors like extremely low rates of attendance among enrolled children, high rates of teacher absenteeism, worrying levels of teacher competence, etc. as some of the major factors behind low learning levels of students. Similar conclusions have been reached by Govinda and Bandyopadhyay (2011) based on a survey of 88 schools of Madhya Pradesh and Chhattisgarh. They contend that poor learning level is one of the major factors behind exclusion from school education. Another important change in India's school education system that has taken place during the past one-and-a-half decade has been the growing presence of private educational institutions. During the period 1995-96 to 2007-08, the proportion of students attending private-unaided institutions increased by 8 percentage points at both the primary and upper primary levels (Planning Commission, 2011). This has given rise to a debate regarding the quality and cost-efficiency of government schools vis-à-vis that of private schools.

Kingdon (2007) suggests that the popularity of fee-charging private schools in India is explained by their superior quality. Muralidharan and Kremer (2006), based on a nationally-representative survey of rural private primary schools conducted in 20 states of India in 2003, also argue that children in private schools have higher test scores, even after controlling for observable family and school characteristics. They also find that private schools are more common in areas with poor public school performance. However, some studies argue that private schools are unaffordable to the poorer sections of society (Harma, 2011) and may not always be qualitatively superior (Chudgar and Quinb, 2012; Bangay and Latham, 2013). These findings raise issues for serious policy deliberations. On the one hand, transforming education from a merit good to a market good might lead to increased efficiency; but, on the other hand, it might result in inequitable access to primary schooling for the children.

It is, thus, observed that increasing school enrolment does not ensure that children will learn in school and progress to higher levels of education. Specific measures are necessary to ensure that good quality education is imparted in primary grades.

EQUITY

Society and the State employ education to achieve several national goals. Promotion of equality among the people and excellence in economic, social, civic and cultural spheres of life are two significant goals for which education is employed. As of now, a process of globalisation of life has begun everywhere. Indian society is also in the thick of globalisation. To make a mark in this globalising world, there is a need to maintain quality and standards and be in the forefront of competition. Pursuit of excellence is a value in this direction. Just as India marches ahead, there is also a need to carry all cross-sections of society in this globalising universe. Otherwise inequalities in society may increase leading to social tensions and disintegration. A peaceful march towards progress and prosperity is possible with the pursuit of excellence and should be directed along with the pursuit of equity. A student of Education should know as to what it means to achieve these ends and how it is done through education.

The Constitution of India is a blueprint for the creation of a new society that has been nomenclatured as 'Democratic Socialism'. This implies a movement wherein individual interests are treated as of supreme value. Articles of the Constitution guarantee fundamental rights to all individuals. The envisioned society is founded on four fundamental values viz; Justice, Equality, Liberty and Fraternity. Several policies and strategies have been adopted by the Indian State for promotion of equality. Distribution of land to landless persons, provision of special incentives in agriculture, irrigation, power supply and housing to disadvantaged population, a nation-wide scheme of public distribution of cereals, pulses, oil and kerosene at subsidised rates, fertiliser subsidies, progressive taxation, concession to industrial entrepreneurs in backward regions are illustrative of these policies/strategies. Even educational policies and strategies in India are geared towards the promotion of equality. In fact, education is one of the chief instruments for heralding a new society as visualised by the Constitution. It is a non-violent, peaceful and enlightened strategy for creation of a society based on and leading towards the four fundamental Constitutional values.

Freedom or liberation is the goal of an individual and fraternity is the goal of a society. There is an age-old definition of education in Sanskrit which is stated as 'Sa udya, Ya Vimukhthaya' which means that education is that which liberates a person, makes him free from all types of bondage, ignorance, superstitions, prejudices, unscientific and irrational beliefs and takes him towards knowledge, truth and wisdom. For example, all human beings have the same divine, self-propelling spirit in them and hence all are equal as sparks of the divine is a fundamental truth of life which realisation dawns on an individual through the right type of education. Such a knowledge and understanding sets a human being free from ignorance and bondage. Fraternity can be a reality in a society where all individuals are equal and free. Creation of a society of equals and free individuals who live in harmony and peace is the Constitutional goal of Indian society. Education is the chief tool in realisation of these goals.

Indian society has been characterised by inequality for centuries. This inequality is both nature created and society contrived. Regional disparities in developmental levels are largely due to asymmetrical distribution of natural resources as well as apathy of organised society towards the same. However, there are several inequalities created and perpetuated by human society. They are related to caste and class. The belief that human beings and groups are hierarchically endowed in regard to their abilities, that those who have superior abilities should enjoy status and wield power over the rest has led to inequalities. Discrimination in regard to deprivation of privileges, special facilities, access to and other resources is borne out of such a belief. Deprivations in regard to ownership of property, control of administration, acquisition of learning, marriage relationships, participation in civic public life have led to unfair and unjust treatment of several groups of human beings in preference to others. It has, in sum, led to injustice in societal organisation and treatment of individuals/ groups. This is the society that we inherited at the time of independence and adoption of the Constitution. There is a conscious, deliberate, planned effort on the part of the Indian State to regulate, re-channelise and reform this in-egalitarian social structure and lead it towards 'Democratic Socialism'.

One sad feature of the in-egalitarian Indian society is the asymmetric distribution of learning levels, exposure to schooling, mean educational levels, access to opportunities and attainments in general as well as technical and vocational skills in the general population. This asymmetry is distinctly observed across caste and sub-caste groups, rural and urban populations, slum and non-slum population in cities and across various regions in the country. The inequalities arising out of this asymmetry is further accentuated in case of girls across all groups and regions. The case of education of girls is one of inequality within inequality. Provision of schooling and other educational facilities for the whole of the Indian population, 'Education for All', is expected to drastically reduce inequalities at least in regard to one basic need of life.

Universalisation of elementary education of a given standard and quality all over the country by 2010 AD is a commitment of the State in India under a nation-wide programme called the *Sarva Shiksha Abhiyan*. Universal elementary education is a human right and an obligation of a civil society that can be achieved in near future. This achievement may offset the imbalances in social status among the Indian people and facilitate a more refined day-to-day life. It is noteworthy that universalisation of secondary education is also on the agenda of the State in India.

Education is both an indicator as well as an instrument for the promotion of equality in a society. Literacy level in a society is a crude indicator which is universally employed as an indicator of the spread of education in a society as well as for the comparison of national and sub-national systems of education. Other indicators which are popular are mean level of education, enrolment rates at various levels, retention rates, attainment levels, manpower stocks, teacher-pupil ratios and the like. Differentials between the sexes on all these indicators are used to examine Gender Empowerment Measure. Literacy and school education, even the elementary ability to register one's signature, elevate the human spirit and endows the ability and feeling to experience the value of equality in daily life. Education liberates a person from bondage. Ignorance, superstitions, poverty, disease, squalor, slavish mentality are all bondages. Freedom from bondage leads to an experience of equality. Inequality is characterised by fear, subjugation, submission, unquestioning loyalty, blind respect for hierarchy and authority, passive acceptance of discrimination and in sum, a loss of freedom. Freedom on the other hand means self-regard, frankness, fearlessness, questioning frame of mind, responsibility and self-discipline. As such freedom presupposes equality. Equality can be there only where there is Justice in society. It is in such a society where there is established Justice, Equality and Freedom that there can be harmony, peace and brotherhood. In this way, education ploughs its path for the promotion of an egalitarian society and creation of democratic socialism through its movement from Justice and Equality towards Freedom and Fraternity. Social change implies changes in group culture and individual mind-sets which value equality. Achievements in regard to physical quality of life can flow from such reformed mind-set or enlightenment. Education mediates this change. It is the chief instrument for a society in transition from traditional to egalitarian values. National policy statement in education, the National Policy on Education, 1986, reflect the egalitarian concerns of the State.

Distinction between Equality and Equity

The difference between equity and equality is quite clear but those who are not aware of the nuances of English language often confuse between these two words. The difference is not very large but is based upon the fact that not everyone has been created equally by the almighty and has requirements different from others. Some are tall, while some are short. Some people are overweight, while there are thin people also. Do you expect all of them to eat the same quantity or amount of food? No? Therein lies the difference between equity and equality.

Let us see by an example. If you are the teacher of a class and have been given the task of distributing chocolates to all the kids equally, what you will do is to divide the total number of chocolates you have by the total number of students in your class and arrive at the number to be given to each child. This is what is denoted by the concept of equality.

But if you ask all your students to take off their shoes, mix them up and then throw two shoes at each student, though you have done no injustice and given two shoes to each child thereby following the concept of equality, you find every child complaining. Why, because no shoe is now fitting the feet of the children. Some have large feet and have got smaller shoes while those having small feet have got bigger shoes causing discontent among them.

Thus it is clear that though equality is a good thing and needs to be followed across genders and religions, there is a concept called equity which states that everyone has different needs and requirements and should be treated accordingly.

Again, in a business, do you divide profits equally among the labour and officer class? Or divide the profits among the partners equally, or according to their share of ownership? This explains the concept of equity.

Equity is a principle that is based upon justness and fairness, while equality demands everyone be treated at the same level. Of course as a teacher of a class, you have to distribute pencils and erasers equally among the students, but when it comes to giving marks to them, you have to assess the ability of every child and give him or her numbers accordingly. This is known as the concept of equity.

Do you give the same amount of food to your toddler as you give to your husband? Obviously not, as you know that their requirements are different. Here the principle of equity is at work, but if you have two kids, you ought to divide cookies or pastries equally among them to avoid any altercation between them. This is the concept of equality. There are situations when people demand equality, to be treated as equals, and indeed this is how any government needs to treat his subjects, irrespective of religion, caste, creed, or gender. But then there are situations, such as when appointing people on merit in jobs, or distributing financial aid among the needy. This is when any government has to apply the principle of equity, and not equality.

While equality is a value, equity refers to the strategies adopted to realise the value of equality. It is through concrete, transparent, physically observable strategic interventions of equity that the value of equality can be realised. For example, if all children in a school should be treated in a fair, just and humane way is a statement of equality and a value therein, the attention given to individual differences in attainment levels by the classroom teacher of school is a school strategy for equity and the organisation of Remedial Instruction for slow learners is a programme under this strategy. The figure 3.1 will clarify the distinction between Equality and Equity.

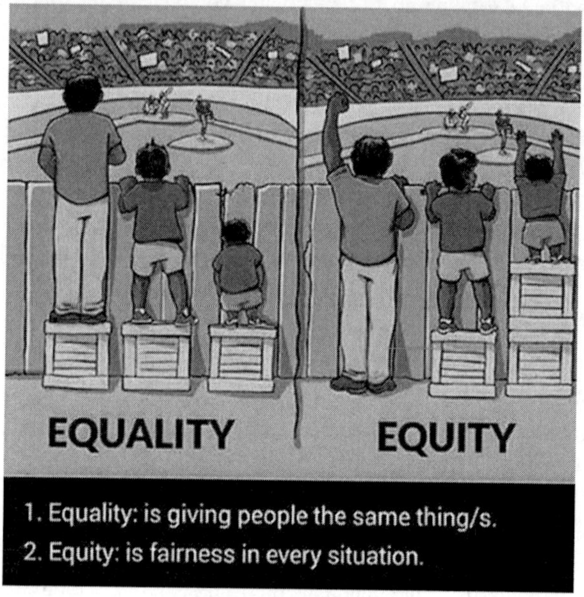

Figure 3.1: Equality and Equity

Strategies for Equity in Education

Equity in education cannot be divorced from equality. In other words equality cannot be meaningful without equity. They are intimately related to each other. We cannot talk of equity isolating it from equality. Therefore, it is essential to talk equity with equality. Here, it must be emphasized that when we talk of equality and equity we talk in consonance with constitutional framework.

Equality is a value of democracy. It is based on the assumption that the planet earth and its resources belong to all its inhabitants and they are entitled to a proportionate share of these resources. The consumption, utilisation and absorption of these resources may depend upon various factors including individual abilities which are distributed in a skewed measure across individuals. But there should be no discrimination in regard to the opportunities to access and enjoy these resources.

Even by 2000 AD, as per an estimate of the National Sample Survey Organisation (NSSO), 25 per cent of Indians, 250 million are below the poverty line of income. There is an observed strong association between poverty, illiteracy, non-enrolment in schools and drop-out behaviour. Demand for schooling is very low among Scheduled Castes, Scheduled Tribes, Minorities and girls among all groups. The Government of India/ States of the Union have been offering special educational facilities and incentives to disadvantaged sections of society to realise the objectives of universalisation of primary education. Attendance scholarship to children in the form of free uniforms, free textbooks and work-books, mid-day lunch for children, school bags, raincoats in coastal areas, hostel facilities, etc; are given to children to attend schools. Special scholarships are given even to the physically challenged persons.

Need and importance of Equality and Equity in Education

The following points highlight the need of equality and equity in education:

- *Human right:* Education has been considered as a Universal Human Right. The idea of equality and adequate opportunity to all was highlighted in the Universal Declaration of Human Rights, adopted by the General Assembly of the United Nations on December 10, 1948. As a sequel to this, the principles of "non-discrimination" and "right to education" were strongly advocated. These two principles inherited the concept of "equality of opportunity in education." Therefore, depriving any person of education on the bases of religion, race or class will be deprivation of Human Right.
- *Essential for democracy:* India is a democratic country. Democracy is based on the principle of equal freedom and equal rights for all its members, regardless of race, religion, sex, occupation or economic status. Democracy can be achieved through liberty, equality, fraternity and justice. In a democratic society equal rights and equality of opportunities are provided. Hence equality and equity in education are needed because it is through the education to all the people in a democracy that the success of democratic institutions is assured.
- *Egalitarian society:* Equality and equity in education are needed for the establishment of an egalitarian society - a society in which equality and social justice should be the norms.
- *Economic development:* Equality and equity in education are needed for the economic development of the nation. The desired success in economic development cannot be achieved without providing equality and equity in education.
- *Nations Advancement:* Equality and equity in education will ensure a rapid advancement of a nation. Education is now an investment. If

the people have equal opportunities to get education they will have a chance to develop their natural talent and thus enrich the society.

- *Search of Talent*: Equality and equity in education will extend the search of talent among all the people of nation. There will thus be available people with specialized talents for specialized jobs in a large number and the society will be benefitted.
- *Closer Link:* Equality and equity in education will develop a closer link between the moreover needs of a society and the availability of the skilled personnel.
- *Socializing Pattern of Society:* Equality and equity in education can help in bringing about silent revolution in the process of establishment of the socializing pattern of society.
- *Modernization:* Equality and equity in education are needed for accelerating the process of modernization in social, economic, political and education field.

Achieving Equality and Equity in Education

The following are the ways and means for achieving equality and equity in education:

To stop wastage and stagnation: There is huge wastage and stagnation at the primary stage. The constitutional directive of compulsory and universal education cannot be realized till the problem of wastage and stagnation is effectively solved. The causes of wastage and stagnation have to be found and removed. The following suggestions are given for reducing wastage and stagnation:

- Financial assistance has to be given.
- Parents will have to be educated.
- Part-time education will have to be provided.
- Social orthodoxies like indifference towards girls' education and narrow outlook towards co-education have to be removed.
- The school distance should be reduced.
- Maximum number of schools will have to be opened.
- School environment should be improved
- Curriculum should be improved. It should be child-centred, activity-centred, experience-centred, life-centred and community-centred.
- Play-way techniques of teaching should be introduced.
- Facilities for educating the children of underprivileged and backward sections of the society have to be increased.
- Entry will have to be regularized.
- Multiple entries should be allowed.
- Non-formal education has to be provided.

Provision of compensatory education: The concept of 'compensatory education' for the culturally deprived and socially disadvantaged is now universally recognized as a necessary condition of equality and equity in education. By compensatory education is meant provision of such special training and incentives as would compensate for the initial disadvantage experienced by the children of the socially and economically weaker sections and the culturally deprived groups. A person may not receive education or his education may remain incomplete due to poverty, child labour, low culture, poor hygiene, malnutrition, over-crowded homes, social environment and backwardness. Children from the lower socio-economic classes experience great difficulty in positively responding to school education unless their initial disadvantages are compensated and they are brought on level with others.

In India compensation has taken the form of special facilities and incentives. Article 15 (4) and Article 46 of the Constitution have made provision for special advantages for the socially and economically backward classes, particularly for the scheduled castes and scheduled tribes. Several concrete measures that have been taken in this direction. Some of them are as follows:

- Institution of scholarships.
- Reservation of seats in institutions of higher learning and quota system for jobs.
- Relaxation of requirements for admission to higher education.
- Remedial education and special coaching classes.
- Health care and mid-day meals.
- Provision of free school uniform, text-books and stationery.
- Lump sum grants.
- Expansion and school facilities like building and equipment, appointment of more teachers and special trained teachers.

Common School System: A very vital component of the overall strategy for securing equality and equity in education is the Common School System. These schools will be open to all children irrespective of caste, creed, community, religion, economic conditions or social status. In these schools access to good education, in terms of enriched curriculum, will depend not on wealth or class but on talent. No tuition fee will be charged in these schools. These schools would meet the needs and aspirations of the middle and lower classes, without unduly taxing them. Concrete steps for translating the concept of Common School System into action have to be taken. In order to achieve this objective, the existing Government, Local Body and Government-aided schools have to be transformed through quality improvement into genuine neighbourhood schools. Private schools also should be similarly transformed in course of time by making them freely accessible.

Selection on merit: Higher education by its nature is something which has to be earned. There is nothing like a 'right' to higher education in the absence of possession of the abilities required to profit from such education, nor can there be any compulsion for it. Higher education should be equally accessible to all on the bases of merit, ability or talent irrespective level of higher education can be taken to mean provision of opportunities for everyone who possesses the 'merit' required for it.

Equality and equity in education as suggested by Kothari Commission (1964-66)

Kothari Commission suggests that for equality and equity in education the following measures may be adopted :

- *No tuition fee:* The country should work towards a stage when education should be tuition free. Tuition fees at the primary and lower secondary stage should be abolished. At the higher secondary and university stage tuition free education should be extended to all needy and deserving students.
- *Reducing private costs:* Free text-books and writing materials should be provided at the primary stage. Book banks should be established in secondary schools and institutions of higher education. The libraries of secondary schools and institutions of higher education should contain an adequate number of sets of text-books so that the students can have an easy access to them. Grants for purchase of books should be given to talented students in educational institutions *i.e.,* the universities, affiliated colleges and secondary schools.
- *Scholarships:* There should be liberal schemes for scholarships at the primary, secondary and university stages. At the level of higher education the Government of India should assume the bulk of such responsibility. At the school stage this responsibility should vest in the State Government. The scheme of National Scholarships, University Scholarships, Scholarships in Vocational Education, Scholarships for Study Abroad and Loan Scholarships should be expanded.
- *Other forms of student aid:* Transport facilities should be provided imaginatively to reduce the cost on hostels and scholarships. Day study centres and lodging houses should be provided on a liberal scale. Facilities for students to earn and pay a part of their educational expenses should be developed. In all programmes of scholarships, preferential consideration should be given to the needs of girls.
- *Handicapped children:* There should be at least one institution for the education of the handicapped children in each district. There

must be adequate Teachers Training programmes for the education of handicapped children.

- *Regional imbalances:* Regional imbalances should be reduced to the minimum. Wider programmes for reducing the imbalances in the socio-economic development of the different states and districts in the country should go side by side.
- *Education of women:* The education of women should be regarded as a major programme in education for some years to come and bold and determined efforts should be made to face these difficulties involved and to bridge the existing gap between the education of men and women in as short a time as possible.
- *Education of backward classes:* The existing programme for the education of the scheduled caste should continue and be expanded. Greater efforts are needed to provide educational facilities for the nomadic and semi-nomadic groups. Hostels should be provided for the children of backward communities.
- *Education of the tribal people:* The education of the tribal people deserves great emphasis and attention. at the primary stage provision of facilities will have to be improved and Asharam Schools will have to be established in sparsely populated areas. The medium of instruction for the first two years should be tribal language and then the regional language. At the secondary stage, provision of schools, hostel facilities and scholarships have to be greatly expanded. In higher education, the administration of the scholarships programme will have to be decentralised and made more efficient provision for special tuition will have to be made both at the secondary and university stages. It is essential to develop cadres of persons who will wrote themselves to the service of the tribal people.

Equality and equity in National Policy of Education (1986)

National Policy on Education (1986) lays special emphasis on the removed of disparities and to equalize educational opportunities by attending to the specific needs of those who have been denied equality so far. In the National Policy on Education the following provisions have been made in order to achieve the target of equality and equity in education:

- *Women Education:* Education will be used as an agent of basic change in the status of women. The National Education System will pay a positive role in the empowerment of women. Under the New Education Policy, the expansion of women education has been emphasized. Eradication of women's illiteracy will receive top-priority. Major emphasis will be placed on women's participation in technical, vocational and professional courses at different levels.

Thus the age old gap between technical and vocational curriculum of boys and girls will be removed and they will be provided opportunities for technical, vocational and professional education on the basis of equality and equity.

- *Education of Scheduled Castes and Scheduled Tribes:* The central focus in the scheduled castes and scheduled tribes educational development is their equalization with the non-scheduled castes and non-scheduled tribes population at all stages and levels of education, in all areas and dimensions. The measures contemplated for this purpose include provision of free equation, free food, free clothes, scholarships and hostel facilities. Non-formal and adult educating programmes may also be arranged for such cases.
- *Other educationally backward sections and areas:* Suitable incentives will be provided to all educationally backward sections of society, particularly in the rural areas. Hilly and desert district districts, remote and inaccessible areas and islands will be provided institutional infra-structure.
- *Education of Minorities:* Some minority groups are educationally deprived. Greater attention will be paid to the education of these groups in the interests of equality and social justice. This will include the constitutional guarantees given to them to establish and administer their own educational institutions, and protection to their languages and culture.
- *Education of the Handicapped:* Mentally and physically handicapped children will be encouraged to get education so that they may effectively participate in the activities of the community. Children with motor handicaps and other mild handicaps will be imparted education with that of others. They will also be given vocational education. Provision of special schools and hostels will be made for the severely handicapped children. There will be reorientation of teacher-training programmes to deal with the special difficulties of the handicapped children.
- *Promotion of adult and continuing education*: The whole nation must pledge itself to the eradication of illiteracy, particularly in the 15-35 age-group. A vast programme of adult and continuing education will be implemented through various ways and channels like the following:
    - Strengthening the existing programmes of adult and continuing education.
    - Setting up continuing education centres especially in rural areas.

- Education of workers through their employers, trade unions and concerned agencies of government.
- Using radio, television and films, as mass and group learning media.
- Creation of learners' groups organizations.
- Providing post secondary educational institutions on a large scale.
- Providing books, libraries and reading rooms on a large scale.
- Publishing useful books and distributing them property.
- Organizing vocational training programmes based on need and interest.

Thus, Education has been considered as a universal human right. Equality and equity in education is directly related to democratic development, establishment of egalitarian society, socialistic pattern of society, economic development, nation's development and to accelerate the process of modernization. Free, Compulsory and Universal Education, Operation Black Board, Diversification Curriculum and Vocationalistion of Education, access to higher education on the basis of merit, DIET, Navodaya Vidyalayas, Distance Education, and Continuing and Adult Education, Open Universities, National Literacy Mission, Education through Radio and Television are efforts to bring equality and equity in education. Moreover, provisions and programmes for education for equality namely education for women's equality, education of scheduled castes, scheduled tribes, and other educationally backward sections and areas, education of minorities, education of the handicapped, and adult and continuing education will be helpful in achieving the target of equality and equity in education.

DROPOUT

Although most states in India have done well in enrolling more children in recent years, the inability of schools to retain those children has continued to be a serious problem. The highest reduction in dropout rates seems to have been achieved 1980-1991, both at primary and upper primary stages. Only marginal change was recorded in the following decade, 1991 to 2001, even though there was an unprecedented level of developmental action in primary education, through programmes such as Operation Blackboard and DPEP.

The situation seems to have improved in recent years showing a reduction of 10.5 percentage points from 39.0% in 2001-2002 to 28.5% in 2004-2005. It is most impressive for girls over the same period, where dropout rates declined by 14.5 percentage points. While dropout rates for girls was higher than boys up to and including 2001-2002, the trend reversed thereafter, with lower dropout rates for girls (25.4%) than for boys (31.8%) in 2004-2005.

Having said this, dropout rates in primary schooling in India remain high. This raises many questions about the efficiency and effectiveness of the schooling system.

Dropout rates among Scheduled Caste (SC) and Scheduled Tribe (ST) girls continued to be higher than that of the SC and ST boys. Similarly, the dropout rates of SC/ST girls in particular is higher than dropout rates of non SC/ST children. Even with substantial reductions in dropout rates, the situation with respect to SC/ST children is alarming. Indeed, less than two thirds of SC children enrolled at school complete five years of primary education. The situation is worse for ST children. Recent figures (2004-2005) show the survival rate among ST children is around 58% at the lower primary stage and only around 30% survive to reach the upper primary cycle. There is, however, no significant difference in the dropout rates for boys and girls among ST children.

After examining the data from the field, the National Sample Survey 52nd Round concluded that, 'drop out is a serious phenomenon in our educational system' (GoI, 1998). The situation continues to be serious. Reasons for dropping out of school were explored in the NFHS-2 (IIPS and ORC Macro, 2000). It was found that the predominant reason mentioned both in rural and urban areas was children not being interested in studying. Children being engaged in wage labour and home-based work was another major reason.

The 61st NSS (2004-2005) (GoI, 2006) shows the problem of drop outs continues. Data shows physical access to school is only a minor reason for dropping out. A substantial number of children were found to be dropping out because education was not considered necessary, they had to support household income (especially urban boys) or they had to attend to domestic chores (girls in particular).

Almost all data sources indicate that dropout rates among older children (11-14 years) is much higher than among lower age groups. The situation at the upper primary level (grades 6-8) is quite alarming as around half of the children who enrol in upper primary schools do not complete the upper primary cycle. Time series data given in the government's Selected Educational Statistics, 2004-05 (GoI, 2007) shows that over a period of 45 years dropout rates have decreased substantially, from 78.3% in 1960-1961 to 50.8% in 2004-2005, but this is far from satisfactory. The decrease is essentially due to the improved retention of girls in the school system, as between 1990-2005 the dropout rate reduced by nearly 15 percentage points for girls. Gender disparities have therefore practically disappeared in drop out / retention rates at the upper primary level.

The situation is particularly serious with respect to socially under-privileged groups. The rate of drop out of SC children, which was 67.8% in 1990-1991, came down to 57.3% in 2004-2005. There has also been considerable decline in the dropout rates of ST children over the same period

(78.6% in 1990-91 to 65.9% in 2004-2005). It remains clear that much still needs to be done to retain SC and ST groups in upper primary education. That said, it is also encouraging to note that dropout rates for SC and ST girls have declined steadily at the upper primary stage, although the rates continue to be higher than SC and ST boys.

Why do children drop out from elementary schools? The data indicates that boys aged 10-14 were more likely than girls to drop out in order to support household income, while girls are more likely to drop out in order to carry out domestic chores. In contrast, a smaller proportion of children in the 6-11 year age group were found to be leaving school for those same reasons. Apart from this, a large proportion of girls of 10-14 years old had to leave school due to 'other' reasons, which could include socio-cultural factors such as early marriage.

The number of out-of-school children has declined steadily since 2001. The number of out-of school children in the age group 6-14 years was estimated at 32 million in 2001 (Census 2001). This represented 28.2 per cent of the population in the age group 6-14 years in 2005-06. A national level study commissioned by the Ministry of Human Resource Development (MHRD), Government of India through an independent agency Indian Market Research Bureau (IMRB) conducted in 2005, estimated the number of out-of-school children at 13.45 million during the year 2005-06. According to this survey, the number of out-of-school children accounted for 6.94 per cent (4.34 per cent in urban and 7.8 per cent in rural areas) of the total number of children in the age group 6-14 years in 2005-06. The IMRB survey conducted in 2009 indicated that the number of out-of-school children declined from 13.45 million in 2005-06 to 8.15 million in 2009-10. These surveys indicated that the percentage of out-of-school children to total population in the age group 6-14 years has decreased from 6.94 per cent in 2005-06 to 4.28 per cent in the year 2009-10. A study to assess the number of out-of school children was commissioned in 2013-14.

There has been a decline in the percentage of out-of-school children across gender and all social categories such as Scheduled Castes, Scheduled Tribes and Muslim. The results of the surveys conducted in 2005 and 2009 indicated that the percentage of out-of-school girls to total girls in the age group 6-14 years decreased from 7.9 per cent in 2005 to 4.6 per cent in the year 2009. The percentage of out-of-school SC children to total SC population in the age group 6-14 years decreased from 8.1 per cent in 2005 to 5.9 per cent in the year 2009; the percentage of out-of-school ST children to total ST population in the age group 6-14 years decreased from 9.5 per cent to 5.2 per cent during this period, while the percentage of out-of-school Muslim children to total Muslim population in the age group 6-14 years decreased from 10 per cent in 2005 to 7.7 per cent in the year 2009.

One of the goals of the Sarva Shiksha Abhiyan (SSA) has been to achieve universal retention by enabling children enrolled in Class I to complete eight years of elementary education. The investment made in terms of expansion of schooling facilities, bridging gender and social category gaps in elementary education, and quality improvement initiatives, including improved school infrastructure, enhanced teacher availability, sustained academic support, Mid-day meal programme, awareness generation, increased community participation, curricular reforms and a rights-based approach, have contributed substantially to reduction in drop-out rates and improved retention rates in primary, upper primary and elementary education. Overall drop-out rate in primary education (Classes I-V): Available data relating to drop-out rates indicates that during the period 2000-01 to 2008-09, the over-all drop-out rate for Classes I-V declined by 15.8 percentage points. The decline in drop-out rates for girls (19 percentage points) was higher than that for boys (13 percentage points).

Drop-out rate in elementary education (Classes I-VIII): The drop-out rate for Classes I-VIII declined by 11.4 percentage points during the period 2000-01 to 2008-09. The decline in drop-out rates for girls (18.8 percentage points) was higher than that for boys (5.4 percentage points).

Drop-out rates in primary and elementary education (SC students): During the period 2000-01 to 2008-09, the overall drop-out rate for SC students at primary stage (Classes I-V) declined by 18.5 percentage points. The over-all drop-out rate for SC students at the elementary stage (Classes I-VIII) declined by 12.8 percentage points during this period.

Drop-out rate in primary and elementary education (ST students): During the period 2000-01 to 2008-09, the over-all drop-out rate for ST students in primary education (Classes I-V) declined by 21 percentage points. The over-all drop-out rate for ST students in elementary education (Classes I-VIII) declined by 10.4 percentage points during this period.

Decline in drop-out rates: During the academic year 2009-10, 9.1 per cent of pupils at the primary stage of education (Classes I-V) had dropped out. The annual drop-out rate was higher in Class I (10.2 per cent) and in Class V (15.9 per cent). There has been a steady decline in dropout rates in primary education since 2009-10. Between 2009-10 and 2012-13, the annual average drop-out rate in primary education declined to 4.7 per cent. The annual drop-out rate was higher in Class I (5.4 per cent) and in Class V (6.4 per cent). The dropout rate, though declining from year to year, still remains a major challenge.

WASTAGE AND STAGNATION

While clarifying the meaning of the word **wastage** in education Hartog Committee (1929) remarked the following: "By wastage we mean premature withdrawal of children from schools at any stage before completion of the primary courses". This statement does not mean there is no wastage in the Secondary Course and Higher Course. Any student, who receives education at any stage, is expected to complete his education with the prescribed period. If one withdraws from the course before completion, then that individual or individuals are deemed to be wastage to the course. In Primary Education, the main objective is the attainment of stable literary through five year schooling. If a child entering school leaves it or is withdrawn from school before completing class V, it leads to wastage in education. So wastage is premature withdrawal of children from schools. A rough and ready method to measure wastage is to compare diminution in enrolment from class to class in series of years. Such students do not complete the study of their curriculum and consequently the time, money and energy expended on such students prove to be sheer wastage. Hence the most popular use of the word "Wastage" in education means the wastage of time, effort and money.

Stagnation

The students at every stage of education are expected to pass the examination after finishing the whole course. But it has been found that in general practice many students are not able to pass the examinations in one class or in more than one class within the prescribed period. Thus, they fail and remain in the same class. These failed students repeat the same class and course whereas their other colleagues pass that class and study in the next upper class. This process has been called the process of stagnation. Thus by stagnation it is meant the stay of students in a particular class for more than one year.

So the word 'Stagnation' in education means the detention of a student in a class for more than one year on account of his unsatisfactory progress. The Hartog Committee reports, "By stagnation we mean the retention in a lower class of a child for a period of more than one year. Of course stagnation always means wastage". Really it was the Hartog Committee (1929), which for the first time pointed out that the "massive wastage and stagnation are taking place in primary education. Primary Education is ineffective unless it at least produces literacy".

No child who has not completed primary course of at least 4 years will become permanently literate. The investigation conducted by *Gokhale Institute* showed that literacy could be obtained before it could lapse. That is because, pupils acquire stable literacy only after they complete at least class IV. As in the case of primary education, the wastage and stagnation were also eating the vitals of the secondary education. The tremendous loss that is caused because of the problems of the wastage and stagnation will be clear by looking at the results of High School Final every year.

University education everywhere in the country is also not free from the ghost of wastage and stagnation. Probably, the problems of wastage and stagnation exist in a greater degree at this stage of education. It has been remarked that great 'wastage' of public money is taking place every year in the University Education. What is more regrettable is the fact that there is some indifference towards the serious loss of public money. Also no less indifference is shown for the wastage of time, money and energy of the students, their parents or guardians and their ambitions and aspirations in life.

The **causes of wastage and stagnation** are of three categories: economic, social and educational.

- **Economic Causes:** Studies conducted on the subject show that 65% of wastage is due to poverty. According to Kothari Commission Report, "A child is sent to school between 6-9 years of age because at this age he is a nuisance at home than a help. At the age of 9 or 10, the child becomes an economic asset, because he can work at home or earn something outside. This is especially true of girls who have to assist the over-worked mother at home. The child is withdrawn from the school and thus he becomes a wastage case". Parents mostly involve their children in domestic work and this leaves no time to child for study. Financial handicap is responsible for wastage and stagnation. Out of poverty some parents utilize the service of their children to supplement earning. In many cases poor parents find it almost impossible to lose the assistance of children. Poverty of Indian people is miserable that they find themselves unable to meet other expenses connected with the education even against the provision of free education of their children during harvest time; children cannot afford to go to school as they are required in the farm. Again, out of poverty children lack minimum diet and are unable to stay for long in schools.
- **Social Causes:** Class and caste distinctions prevail in India, the former in urban areas and the latter in rural areas. Especially in the case of girls custom of early marriages or betrothals stands a bar. There is an opposition to send grow-up girls to schools especially to the mixed schools without women teachers. Even in the case of boys some parents due to caste restrictions do not want their children to mix with power caste boys and girls. Co-education of boys and girls in some places is looked with suspicion. And as there is no separate provision of education for girls, deprivation of girls from schools leads to much wastage.
- **Educational Causes:** Only educational causes are responsible for another 30% of wastage. Government of India admits this in the following words: "The educational institutions being ill-equipped,

poorly housed and with dull and depressing environment unfortunately could not exercise effective counter-acting influence". Uncontrolled fresh admissions without consideration of age or time have no permanency. That is, admissions are made of under-aged and over-aged children. Again admissions are done throughout the year. So there is more of wastage and stagnation. That is because under-aged children lost interest in classes, whereas over-aged children remained away from school out of shame.

Lack of adequate accommodation, too much of over-crowding schools with high pupil-teacher ratio become the main causes of wastage and stagnation. Again, increased number of single-teacher schools, inefficient teaching, lack of teacher-pupil contact, frequent transfer of teachers and plural class-teaching disturbed the quality of instruction which ultimately cause much wastage and stagnation. In short, dull and unattractive schools, incomplete schools, inefficient and poor quality of teachers, defective examinations, uninteresting curricula, lack of proper parental attitude, absence of school health services and school mid-day meals are responsible for much of wastage and stagnation in schools. Sometimes children in schools suffer from diseases of serious kinds and they are withdrawn for a long period causing wastage. Death of one of the parents or both causes much hardship to children. Orphan children drop-out from school without completing education, and so the wastage.

Remedial Measures

Statistics indicate huge wastage at the Primary stage. Of every 100 pupils that enter class I only 40 reach class V and only 20 reach class VIII. So steps are required to be taken for fighting against such alarming wastage those 80 students out of every hundred leave school before they complete age of 14.

- Stagnation and wastage can be reduced by concentrating on quantitative improvement by (a) Universal provisional and (b) Universal retention. Again attempts should be made for qualitative improvement of pupils.
- Qualified teachers should be appointed to create better quality in the instructional programme to attract children.
- Fresh admissions should be made at the beginning of the school session within two months from the date of commencement of school year. And it should not be done throughout the year.
- As far as possible provision should be made for starting of Pre-Primary Schools to admit children below 6 years of age. So that it will be a sort of pre-registration and preparation of the pupils to get admitted in schools. It will avoid the enrolment of under-aged over-aged children.

- The curriculum may be made modest, simple and interesting so that it can be implemented most efficiently.
- Improvement, of the Professional competence of teachers may be made by providing training facilities, both pre-service and in-service. Necessary guide books for teachers and work books for students and other literature should also be provided.
- Adequate and attractive school buildings should be provided. Necessary equipment and teaching aids should be supplied for making education more interesting and effective.
- Teacher-pupil ratio may be maintained at such a level as to ensure adequate individual attention to be paid to each individual in every class particularly in class-I. As far as possible only trained and competent teachers should remain in charge of class I.
- As master of policy it has been adopted that children from class-I may be liberally promoted to class-II and the like without any detention at any stage.
- Provision of part-time schooling may be made for the benefit of children who cannot attend the school during regular hours on account of domestic and economic disabilities.
- Effective supervision and inspection may be provided in schools.
- Best possible use may be made of the existing resources, both human and material. The schools may be graded according to efficiency and standards. This will provide ground for qualitative improvement of schools, which ultimately will go to reduce wastage and stagnation.
- Special provision should be made for educating the mentally retarded children by opening special institutions in each State or district level.

To reduce wastage and stagnation in a bigger way, pupils may be given nutritious diet by introduction of mid-day meals under the School Health Service Programme. Existing mid-day meals system should be carefully regulated.

CHILD LABOUR

The issue of linkage between child labour and elementary education has received enormous attention during the last two decades. The issue received increased focus with the publication of Myron Weiner's seminal work: "The child and the state in India." (Weiner, 1990). Now after more than fifteen years, the situation is still not satisfactory as large number of children continue to languish as child workers instead of attending school regularly. The practice of employing child labour is persisting in every corner of the country. According to the MICS (2000) conducted by UNICEF (UNICEF, 2004) there are more than 12 million (5.2 per cent) child labourers and the Census of 2001 estimated the number to be 11.28 million. Poverty is invariably quoted as the reason for the perpetuation of child labour and consequent exclusion of the children from school education.

However, many scholars have blamed the Government for non-implementation of *Child Labour Act* with seriousness and also for failure in providing equitable and universal access to education to all the children of eligible age group. This, it is argued has resulted in swelling of the number of child workers who had no other option except joining labour force. Although some observers suggest that changes in labour market because of globalisation and liberalization contributes to the problem of child labour, it is generally argued (Burra, 2003) that in India, the problem of child labour "lies largely in the collusion between government officials, local politicians, big landlords and industrialists in ensuring the perpetuation of child labour." (Kabeer, 2003). Bajpai (2006), examining the cases of child labour, argues that child labour legislation is inadequate in its understanding of the situation. A large number of activities in which children are engaged remain untouched by legislations since it has listed certain activities as hazardous and gave legal protections to the children who are engaged in hazardous works. Children engaged in domestic work or such other activities are not protected by this law as it is not recognized as hazardous work even though many child domestic workers are abused, exploited by employers and do not attend schools. Moreover, since legal framework and National Policy and Child Labour Act, 1986 allow child labour in non-hazardous occupations, a large number of child workers remain out of purview of laws governing child labour. Whether poverty is the cause for child labour or not, experience and all evidences indicate that it is the children of poor parents who always face difficulty in attending school. Many studies also suggest a strong relationship between poverty, development and child labour, use of traditional technology, agricultural impoverishment, availability of nonfarm activities in nearby areas, nature and pace of economic development etc. determining the practice of child labour at large scale.

One cannot deny the fact that the economic status of a family is a powerful force shaping its behaviour in many aspects of life including the engagement of their children in productive labour thus restricting their participation in schooling. However, recent trends in enrolments clearly indicate that poor parents are increasingly sending their children to school, even private fee charging schools. Further, Government has had to launch several supplementary measures to educate the children, particularly of older age group, who could not attend schools earlier as they have been engaged in work. Based on field studies of organizing such programmes, Sinha (2006) argues for arranging residential bridge course camps and motivation centres for children currently engaged in labour, providing them with appropriate educational inputs, and subsequently mainstreaming in a gradual manner to formal schools after completion of their courses.

According to Census 2001, there has been a sharp decline in proportion of child main workers from 4.3 per cent in 1991 to 2.3 per cent in 2001, but at the same time number of marginal workers increased from 2.2 million to 6.89 million; in effect, the total number of child workers increased to 16.35 million in 2001 from 12.86 million in 1991. Most of these children were engaged in agricultural activities on part time basis. Burra (2006) refers to a substantial decrease in number of child workers combined with increase in school enrolment and reduction in percentage of out of school children. According to the figures given by Burra (2006) there has been dramatic change in the situation in Andhra Pradesh, in addition to Kerala and Tamil Nadu, with regard to participation of children in workforce and school as well. In contrast, percentage of child workers increased from 5.5 per cent in 1991 to 8.6 per cent in 2001 in Himachal Pradesh, even while school enrolment improved. MICS (A survey conducted in 2000) by UNICEF (2004) also throws light on the state level situation of child labour and school participation.

According to MICS the proportion of child labour presently is more than 15 per cent in Rajasthan (20.3 percent), A.P. (25.2 per cent), Tamil Nadu (21.6 per cent), Chattisgarh (19.2 per cent), Jharkhand (20 per cent), Orissa (15.4 per cent), Arunachal Pradesh (23.3 per cent), Sikkim (16.4 per cent). In Maharashtra, Karnataka and Chhattisgarh, Manipur their proportion is varying between 5-15 per cent. According to the same UNICEF report (2004), over 20 per cent of India's working children are from Uttar Pradesh, most of whom work at odd jobs, in factories and in the carpet industry for meagre wages. They are found in some of the districts like Bhadohi, Mirzapur, Jaunpur, Varanasi, Allahabad and Sonbhadra that account for over 85 per cent of the country's total carpet exports. One of the main reasons for the high prevalence of child labour in these areas is the burden of debt, which forces families to send their children to work and low literacy rates further compound the problem (UNICEF, 2004). Drawing reference from different researches Bhatty (1998) has argued that poverty is a highly inadequate explanation of regional variations in educational achievements. While some parts of the country despite economic prosperity are still lagging behind in terms of educational progress, in some other parts even abject poverty could not stop parents from sending their children to school. For instance, states like Haryana and Punjab which are considered economically progressive have still lot to do to achieve the goal of UEE.

Dreze and Gazdar (1997) found that despite showing economic prosperity literacy rate and school participation of children in western Uttar Pradesh are far from satisfactory. Further, refuting the traditional argument, Bhatty (1998) based on a review of many studies (Maharatna, 1996: 16; Unni Jeemol, 1996: 8; 135, Majumdar, 1997; Jabbi and Rajyalakshmi, 1997) points out that the opportunity costs do not forbid schooling and many unschooled children are also found not working anywhere. In fact, children start participating in workforce after attaining certain age. For example, the study of Kanbargi and Kulkarni (1991) reveals that "working for wages is significant among children in the 12-14 age groups." Thus, Bhatty found that "labour driven dropout rates are more likely to be low in the early grades and to rise significantly around the ages when children become more productive." This is a significant observation as largest proportion of drop out takes place in the early grades of lower primary cycle. It is clear from the discussion that more studies are required to establish the interconnection between poverty, child labour and schooling. Studies have to explore the question of how much poverty compels children to work and whether only working children are not being able to attend school or dropping out is caused only when children start working.

In the opinion of many scholars, the direct cost involved in educating children is one of the important reasons for non-attendance and drop out. Being unable to meet this 'direct' cost many poor parents withdraw their children from school (Mehrotra, 1995; Sinha and Sinha, 1995; 42nd Round NSS 1986-87, Tilak, 1995; Panchmukhi, 1990). Based on all these evidences, Bhatty (1998) has stressed that instead of putting exaggerated emphasis on child labour and inadequate motivation among poor parents as the major obstacles to universalisation of primary education, it is necessary to consider the direct costs of schooling that reduce the child's chances of participating in education. The discussions above highlight the complex relationship between poverty, child labour and exclusion from schooling. While some poor households may withhold their children from school, some others with similar conditions ensure education for their children. Child labour which effectively blocks school participation is indeed a complex issue, dependent on extraneous factors such as implementation of adult wage labour policies and not so much on the conditions and intentions of the children and their family. In all these, school related factors also play a critical role influencing the parents to decide in favour of or against continuation of their children in schools as they reach an age when they could be effectively engaged in remunerative work. While macro level data on the issue of child labour and poverty can be found, very little empirical evidences are available on the underlying interaction between, family economic circumstances, engagement of children in remunerative work and exclusion from schooling.

MEDIUM OF INSTRUCTION ISSUE

Language use in education depends on the linguistic situation of a country. Co-existence of many languages has been the essence of Indian heritage. Language uniformity is considered necessary for the economic development. Language is significant, not only as a medium of instruction but also as a determinant of societal access. An inclusive society is the foundation of a knowledge society. Today, a command over the English is a most important determinant of higher education and employment. English has been part of our education system for more than a century. Yet, English is beyond the reach of most of our young people. This makes for highly unequal access. There are many debates regarding the medium of instruction in India since independence. The *Three Language Formula* was first devised by the Central Advisory Board of Education in 1956 and formalized by the Education Commission (1964-66). The Constitution of India adopted many provisions about languages. It was claimed that, there should be one language which will be known throughout the length and breadth of the country and that Hindi which is prescribed as the official language at the Centre should be studied compulsorily. But still Hindi is not a communication device for many southern Indian states due to several reasons. As a result of historical causes, English has come to be the one language that is widely known among the educated classes of the country. Much of the national unity in political and other spheres of activity has been brought about through the study of English.

In India there are five distinct groups, of languages which have to be taken into consideration. That is;

(i) the mother-tongue;
(ii) the regional language when it is not the mother-tongue;
(iii) the official language of the Centre, more commonly called the Federal Language;
(iv) the classical languages-Sanskrit, Arabic, Persian, Latin, etc.; and
(v) English which has come to be recognised as an international language.

In those areas where the mother-tongue and the regional language are the same, the number of languages to be taken into consideration will be limited to four and in those areas where the regional language, the mother-tongue and the language of the Union are the same; the number of languages to be taken into consideration will be limited to three. So far as the Federal language or the official language of the Centre is concerned we feel that the areas in the different parts of the country may be divided into three regional groups:

(i) regions where Hindi is the mother- tongue, and therefore, is the regional language as well as the language of the Centre;
(ii) regions where although it is not the mother-tongue, Hindi is spoken by a large number of people of the region;
(iii) regions where Hindi is neither the mother tongue nor the regional language nor spoken or understood by the vast majority of the people. These are generally spoken of as non-Hindi speaking areas.

Languages and the Indian Constitution

The Constitution of India lays down that the official language of the Union shall be Hindi and that for a period of 15 years from the commencement of the Constitution, English language shall continue to be used for all the official purposes of the Union. Under Article 345 of the Constitution it is stated that "the Legislature of a State may by law adopt any one or more of the languages in use in the State or Hindi as the language or languages to be used for all or any of the official purposes of the State; provided that until the legislature of the State otherwise provides by law, the English language shall continue to be used for those official purposes within the State for which it was being used immediately before the commencement of this Constitution".

It also lays down that "the language for the time being authorised for use in the Union for official purposes shall be the official language for communication between one State and another State and between a State and the Union; provided that if two or more States agree that the Hindi language should be the official language for communication between such States, that language may be used for such communication. The President may, if he is satisfied that a substantial proportion of the population of a State desire for use of any language spoken by them to be recognised by that State, direct that such language shall also be officially recognised throughout that State or any part thereof for such purpose as he may specify". Under the special directives, it is stated that "it shall be the duty of the Union to promote the spread of the Hindi language to develop it so that it may serve as a medium of expression for all the elements of the composite culture of India and to secure its enrichment by assimilating without interfering with its genius the forms, style and expressions used in Hindustani and in the other languages of India specified in the eighth schedule, and by drawing whenever necessary or desirable, for its vocabulary primarily on Sanskrit and secondarily on other languages."

Regarding primary education in mother tongue, Article 350 (A) states that; "It shall be the endeavour of every State and of every local authority within the State to provide adequate facilities for instruction in the mother-tongue at the primary stage of education to children belonging to linguistic minority groups; and the President may issue such directions to any State as he considers necessary or proper for securing the provision of such facilities". Above we seen the provisions of the Constitution, as time and again we found that witnesses had diverse views on what was envisaged in the Constitution and the manner in which education should be developed. From a careful study of the provisions in the Constitution it may be inferred that two objectives were kept in view. Firstly, that Hindi will eventually be used by the Union Government in all official correspondence with the States, and for communication between one State and another, or between a State and the Union. Secondly, Hindi should be developed so that it may serve as a medium of expression for all the elements of the composite culture of India.

Secondary Education Commission (1952-03) on Study of Languages

The Secondary Education Commission (Muthaliar Commission) was greatly impressed with the amount of interest evinced in all States in the study of language at the school stage. In view of the development of regional languages in the different parts of the country and the languages spoken in such areas, it may not be practicable or desirable to attempt to lay down a uniform policy for the whole country. On the contrary some witnesses were strongly of the opinion that there should be some uniformity in regard to the study of the languages and that there was need for a definite policy to be laid down on an all-India basis. It was claimed by some that there should be one language which will be known throughout the length and breadth of the country and that Hindi which is prescribed as the official language at the Centre should be studied compulsorily.

Study of Hindi in the States

The States had taken different steps to make Hindi a subject of study at the school stage. They are:

- in some States Hindi is not merely a compulsory subject of study but it is also made the medium of instruction and examination throughout the school stage;
- Hindi is a compulsory subject of study at the school stage and it is a subject of examination but the medium of instruction is the regional language;
- in others Hindi is a compulsory subject as one of the languages to be studied, but although a test is provided, the result of the test is not taken into consideration for promotion; and
- in a few States the provisions for the teaching of Hindi is compulsory in all schools but Hindi as a subject of study is optional so far as the pupils, are concerned, and it is not regarded as a subject for examination.

In certain areas, the introduction of the study of Hindi as a compulsory subject had provoked opposition, and steps had to be taken to modify the rules framed there under. When, however, it was made optional, study of Hindi was taken by a large number of students.

Position of English in the Schools

In most States prior to 1937, English was not only a compulsory subject of study but also the medium of instruction in the secondary schools; the languages to be studied by the pupil were two, English and the mother-tongue or regional language or a classical language. Subsequently the medium of instruction was changed and at present in practically all States the medium of instruction is either the mother-tongue or the regional language. English is, however, a compulsory subject of study at the Secondary stage in practically all the States. In this connection it may be pointed out;

(i) that English is allowed to be the medium of instruction in schools where the students admitted are largely those whose mother-tongue is English,

(ii) in view of the difficulties experienced by a certain number of pupils who had to migrate from one part of the country to the other and who could not easily take to a new regional language, English was allowed to be continued in some schools as the medium of instruction and as a language of study.

The Position of Linguistic Minorities

The Central Advisory Board of Education considered in 1949 the case of pupils belonging to certain minority groups, whose mother- tongue was different from the regional language, and passed the following resolution: "That the medium of instruction in the Junior Basic (Lower Primary) stage must be the mother-tongue of the child and that where the mother- tongue was different from the Regional or State language, arrangements must be made for instruction in the mother tongue. This Regional or State language where it is different from the mother-tongue should be introduced not earlier than Class 3, not later than the end of the Junior Basic stage. In order to facilitate the switch-over to the Regional language as medium of instruction in the Secondary stage children should be given the option of answering questions in their mother-tongue for the first two years after the Junior Basic stage."

"If, however, the number of pupils speaking a language other than the Regional or State languages is sufficient to justify a separate school in any area, the medium of instruction in such a school may be the language of the pupils. Such arrangements would, in particular, be necessary in metropolitan cities or places were large population speaking different languages live or areas with a floating population of different languages. Suitable provision should be made by the provincial authorities for the recognition of such schools imparting education through a medium other than the Regional or State language."

Muthaliar Commission has received a communication from the Chairman of the Inter- State Board for Anglo-Indian Education, inviting the attention of the Commission to certain special guarantees that have been given in Article 337 of the Constitution and also to the Fundamental Rights, guaranteed under Article 30 of the Constitution. Article 30 states: "All minorities whether based on religion or language, shall have: the right to establish and administer educational institutions of their choice." "The State shall not, in granting aid to educational institutions, discriminate against any educational institution on the ground that it is under the management of a minority, whether based on religion or language." These provisions being obligatory, we have no doubt that the governments at the Centre and the States will adopt necessary steps to see to the fulfilment of such obligations as are laid upon them by the Constitution.

Muthaliar Commission has given in brief the present position in regard to study of languages in the different States. In most of the schools in the States, the present position is that either the mother-tongue or the regional language has been adopted as the medium of instruction. Where minorities exist provision is made to give instruction in the mother- tongue, if the minimum number of pupils is available.

Place of Hindi

The importance of learning Hindi has been stressed, since it has been adopted in the Constitution as the official language of the Centre. Hindi will be eventually the language used for purposes of all official correspondence between the Centre and most of the States and as a large number of people speak this language, it may also become the language of communication for other than official purposes. In other words, it is expected to become the lingua franca of the country. It is therefore stressed that Hindi should be made a compulsory subject of study in the school course as otherwise those who do not study Hindi may be handicapped at a later stage if they wish either to enter service or to communicate more freely with those parts of India where the language is commonly used. It is also stated that a common language like Hindi if known all over the country, would promote national unity and solidarity. Language necessarily promotes unity. Even though, many other countries where different languages have been recognised as State languages. For instance, in Switzerland four languages, German, French, Italian and Latin are recognised as official languages of the State and all correspondence is sent in the four languages. In Canada, English and French are recognised as official languages; while in South Africa, Africans, Dutch and English are the three languages accepted.

Place of English

A great deal of controversy also exists about the place of English in the scheme of studies. As a result of historical causes, English has come to be the one language that is widely known among the educated Indians. Much of the national unity in political and other spheres of activity has been brought about through the study of English language and literature and modern thoughts by all educated Indians. It is also stated that the present position of India in the international sphere is partly due to the command that educated Indians have acquired over English. Many eminent educationists and scientists have, therefore, expressed the opinion that under no circumstances should we sacrifice the many advantages that we have gained by the study of English. They hold that in matters pertaining to education, sentiment should not be the ruling factor and that what was most urgently needed was that our youth acquire knowledge from all sources and contribute their share to its expansion and development. In the attainment of this objective, study of English was bound to play an important part. On the other hand, some of the critics have pressed the view that it is unnatural and inconsistent with the present position of the country to prescribe a foreign language as a compulsory subject of study. They have also drawn our attention to the greater importance given to English in the past and the consequent neglect of other languages and other subjects of the curriculum. They feel that the whole position of English in the educational system needs to be re-examined in the new set-up particularly at the Middle and High school level. They are definitely opposed to the introduction of English at the basic stage, i.e., the first 7 or 8 years of a child's education.

Place of Classical Languages

The classical languages have always exercised great attraction though for a relatively small proportion of the educated people of any -country. To the bulk of Indians, Sanskrit which is mother of most Indian languages has always appealed both from the cultural and religious point of view. In the present state of affairs and in the light of the controversies that have been raging round the languages to be studied, many have deplored the fact that the classical language is being completely ignored. The number of persons that take to classical studies is diminishing rapidly and if this continues it is felt that the study of the classics which is of such immense value may eventually be completely neglected. There is a great deal to be said in favour of the view that the study of this language should be promoted and that those who wish to take to it should be given every encouragement possible. What has been stated about Sanskrit may also be said about the other classical languages. Those who have delved deep in the classical languages of Arabic and Persian or the few who have taken to Latin or Greek have likewise a feeling that these studies may not find a place in the future unless due provision is made for their study at the school stage.

Concluding remarks of Secondary Education Commission (1952-03) on Language Education

Secondary Education Commission recommended that English should be an optional subject of study at the Middle school stage. Others, however, feel that under present conditions and taking due note of the development of the regional languages and the official language of the Centre, it is necessary that a sound knowledge of English should be considered a pre-requisite to studies at the higher levels of learning. For this reason, it is stated that English should be a compulsory subject of study in the Secondary school beginning from the Middle school stage.

It is suggested that no student should be handicapped by ignorance of a language which will ultimately determine the career that he should choose. It should also be recognised that even in regard to many of the diversified courses of instruction as matters stand at present, knowledge of English will be extremely useful for understanding the subject better and for further study of the same subject. All these considerations lead to the conclusion that a study of English should be given due position in Secondary schools and facilities should be made available at the Middle school stage for its study on optional basis.

As regards the study of Hindi, it is felt that in view of its becoming the official language of the Centre and of some States, every pupil at the Secondary stage should be given an opportunity of acquiring a basic knowledge of the language and it be left to him to develop it according to his needs. From this point of view it is stressed that Hindi should be taught during the Middle school or the Senior Basic stage. As regards the classical language, it is felt that provision should be made for students desiring to take to these studies to have the necessary opportunity to do so either at the High school or Higher Secondary school stage.

Summary of Recommendations of Secondary Education Commission (1952-03) on Language Education

- Mother-tongue or the regional language should generally be the medium of instruction throughout the Secondary school stage, subject to the provision that for linguistic minorities special facilities should be made available on the lines suggested by the Central Advisory Board of Education.
- During the Middle school stage (Upper Primary), every child should be taught at least two Languages. English and Hindi should be introduced at the end of the Junior Basic (Lower Primary) stage, subject to the principle that no two languages should be introduced in the same year.
- At the High and Higher Secondary stage, at least two languages should be studied, one of which being the mother-tongue or the regional language. (Mudaliar Commission Report, 1953)

The Education Policy and Languages

The Education Policy of 1968 had examined the question of the development of languages in great detail. The policy observes that, Good translations of foreign books into Indian languages will be supported. Besides the promotion of the link language, programmes will also be launched to increase substantially the translation of books from one language to another and to publish multi-lingual dictionaries and glossaries. The young will be encouraged to undertake the re-discovery of India, each in his own image and perception.

Views of National Knowledge Commission (NKC 2005-2008)

NKC observed that, the time has come for us to teach our people - ordinary people- English as a language in schools. NKC recommendations broadly deal with the modalities of introducing English in schools from Class I, teacher training, language pedagogy and resource support for language teaching and learning. (NKC Report to the Nation, 2006)

The NKC has emphasized the importance of an inclusive society as the foundation for a knowledge society. NKC has also recognized the significance of language, not only as a medium of instruction or a means of communication but also as a determinant of access. An understanding and command of over the English language is a most important determinant of access to higher education, employment possibilities and social opportunities. School-leavers who are not adequately trained in English as a language are always at a handicap in the world of higher education. More often than not, teaching is in English. Even if it is not, in most subjects, books and journals are available only in English. And those who do not know English well enough find it exceedingly difficult to compete for a place in our premier educational institutions. This disadvantage is accentuated further in the *world of work*, not only in professional occupations but also in white-collar occupations overall.

The middle income or lower-income households spend a large proportion of their modest income on sending their children to relatively expensive English medium schools. Such educational opportunities for children are a priority that is almost at par with health care for the family. But there are a very large number of people who simply do not have the resources for such investment. The outcome is exclusion. It is believe that inclusion is possible through public provision.

There is an irony in the situation. English has been part of our education system for more than a century. Yet English is beyond the reach of most of Indian young people, which make for highly unequal access. The time has come for us to teach our people, ordinary people, English as a language in schools especially at the State run schools. Early action in this sphere would help us build an inclusive society and transform India into a knowledge society. In just 12 years of schooling, it would provide the country's school-leavers with far more equal access to higher education and, three to five years thereafter, much more equal access to employment opportunities.

The NKC recommends that the teaching of English as a language should be introduced, along with the first language (either the mother-tongue or the regional language) of the child, starting from Class I in school. This phase of language learning should focus on using both languages to create meaningful learning experiences for the child without disproportionate emphasis on grammar and rules. Many states and Union Territories already introduced English as a compulsory subject at different stages in primary school, by Class V at the latest. However, the implementation is slow and the quality of English language teaching is simply not good enough. The support systems, such as the number of teachers or materials for teaching, are neither adequate nor appropriate. NKC is recommending a fundamental change that seeks to introduce, nationwide, the teaching of English as a language from Class I onwards. This is not meant to be a stand-alone, add-on subject, but is meant to be integrated into the school curriculum.

Language learning cannot be separated from, and must be integrated with, content learning. Therefore, English should also be used to teach some non-language, content subjects, starting from Class III in school. The choice of subjects for this purpose can be left to schools depending on the proficiency of teachers and availability of materials. This would, in effect, create multi-medium schools. It would also help reduce the divide between English medium schools and regional language-medium schools. The pedagogy of language learning as well as teaching should be suitably contextualized, to lend meaning to real situations and daily lives. Yashpal Commitee report (*Learning Without Burden* - 1992-93) also expressed same views on English language education at school level. Moreover, assessment should be based on proficiency rather than achievement or rote learning.

In order to meet the requirement for a large pool of English language teachers, graduates with high proficiency in English and good communication skills should be inducted without formal teacher training qualifications. They could be selected through an appropriate procedure developed by the National Testing Service and then given a short–term orientation. The nearly four million school teachers all over India, regardless of their subject expertise, especially teachers at the primary level, should be trained to improve their proficiency in English through vacation training programmes or other short-term courses. Most teacher training programmes are not based on a real assessment of needs of teachers. Thus, the entire teacher education system caters to pre-service and in-service training that exists today, including training for language teaching, needs to be thoroughly reviewed, recognizing the centrality of language in the curriculum. A multiplicity of English textbooks should be made available to address the diversity of English language environments in the country. However, to ensure that certain standards are maintained, benchmarks may be laid down for the content of textbooks at each stage. Since language learning takes place not only through direct instruction but also through assimilation from the environment, the classroom needs to be equipped with appropriate supplementary audio-visual and print material.

Language learning opportunities should also be created outside the classroom through specific bi-lingual radio and TV channels, which could be introduced for formal and informal teaching and learning of English. State governments would need to be equal partners in the implementation of this idea. (NKC Report to the Nation, 2006)

What is the Purpose of Language Study? The question has often been raised as to the number of languages that can be learnt by pupils in the schools and at what stages the study of these languages should be commenced. While considering this problem, take into account the purpose which is to be served by the study of languages. There should be a clear' perspective of the purpose of study of each of these languages. It is ordinarily accepted that the mother-tongue is the most suitable language as a medium of instruction for the child beginning its study. If the same advance had taken place in regional languages as has taken place in many foreign languages, mother-tongue or regional language would have been the medium of instruction at all stages of the educational ladder. As the regional language is likely to be the language used by the majority in the region it is desirable to acquire knowledge of this language. Further, Hindi need to be promote as a link language among all peoples of the country. English language education will reduce the gap between different social classes and it also help to build of an inclusive and just Indian society. English occupies a special place in the domain of education. We are gradually moving towards an indigenous standardized Indian English.

CURRICULUM ISSUE / TEXT BOOKS

Curriculum includes all experiences which are provided to children either inside the school or outside the school, to achieve the objectives of education. Every child gets a number of experiences in the school, some of which are based on the prescribed syllabi and textbooks while some others are based on the co-curricular activities organized by the school. The process of curriculum development in India lies in between the two extremes of centralization and decentralization. It is seen that model exemplars of curriculum are provided by the centre which are utilized by the different boards of education in India. Muthaliar Commission (1952-53) and the Kothari Commission (1964-66) have provided such points. The central government formulated the National Policy on Education, 1986, which includes broad guidelines regarding the content and process of education of different stages. Based on this the NCERT has formulated the curriculum framework in 1988. **National Curriculum Frame Work** for elementary and secondary education brought out in 1988, has the following social, cultural, political, economic and pedagogical parameters.

- All the citizens of the country should enjoy equality of opportunity to pursue education. The curriculum should be an instrument to meet the special needs of disadvantaged sections of the society.

- To familiarize children with the cultural heritage of country.
- The citizen must be aware of their duties as also the ideals and principles of the constitution of India to ensure socio-economic and political progress of the country.
- Promotion of international understanding and peace should also be the objectives of curriculum.
- In view of the serious problems of population explosion, population related concepts ought to be integrated in the curriculum of different subjects.
- Other major objectives are the following:
  - Preparation of children for future life.
  - Total development of child's personality.
  - Child centered education
  - Develop creative thinking ability among students
  - Develop scientific temper among children
  - Work should be used as a medium of education.
  - Evaluation should be comprehensive and continuous one and made as an integral part of teaching learning process.
  - For effective curriculum transaction mass media and educational technology should be utilized.

The national curriculum framework has recommended certain areas of education and their time weightages at the primary and upper primary stages of school education.

Table 3.1: Time Weightage to Various Subjects Schooling

Primary Stage	**Time Allocation**
Mother tongue	30%
Mathematics	15%
Environmental Studies	15%
Health and Physical Education	10%
Arts	10%
Work Experience	20%
Upper Primary Stage	
Three language	32%
Mathematics	12%
Social Sciences	12%
Science	12%
Health and Physical Education	10%
Arts	10%
Work experience	10%

The proposed curriculum aims at the balanced development of child's personality. The cognitive aspect of personality is taken care of by the curricular areas like language, mathematics science and social science, while health and physical education and work experience take care of psychomotor aspects. Arts contribute to the development of affective domain of personality. The National curriculum frame work has recommended some core elements which should be taught compulsorily in all parts of the country. These include:

- History of India freedom struggle.
- Constitutional Obligation
- Content essential for development of national identity
- Common cultural heritage of India
- Democracy, secularism, socialism
- Gender equality
- Environmental issues
- Removal of social barriers
- Small family norms
- Development of scientific temper

Present Primary Curriculum

- Std I & II: Integrated curriculum
- Std III & IV: Mother tongue, English, Maths, Environmental studies, Health and Physical Education, Arts, work experience

Upper Primary Stage

- Three languages – mother tongue, English, Hindi.
- Mathematics
- Social Science
- Health and Physical Education
- Arts
- Work experience

Aims of Primary Curriculum: The primary curriculum aim to achieve the following.

- To acquire basic skills and processes.
- To develop critical thinking abilities and problem solving abilities.
- To enable the child both access and understand relevant information, critically examine it and be able to apply it meaningfully in day to day situation
- To prepare the child to live, work and play with others as a member of a group/team/community.

- To provide children opportunities and experience which help them acquire the capabilities of learning to live together with others in the community.
- To develop a positive attitude towards labour and to find the importance of dignity of labour.
- To enable the child to accept values and beliefs different from one's own and treat them democratically.
- To acquire skill in participating in group activities and develop communication skills to transact in groups.
- To develop attitude in participating societies and nations political processes.
- To acquire concepts and abilities for emotional and physical fitness.

Aims of Lower Primary Curriculum

- The child learns to read and write mother tongue
- Various concepts can be assimilated through hearing, reading and observations.
- The child acquire knowledge of nature, environment, social institutions around him etc through his lower primary classes.
- The child must recognize birds, animals, plants, agriculture, soil, metal etc around him.
- The child observe and study rivers, hills, trees, geographical peculiarities around him.
- Truthfulness, equality in sex, social manners, cooperativeness dignity of labour etc can be acquired at this stage.
- The child's enquiry capacities, mental power, knowledge skills etc should regid during the lower primary stage.

Aims of Upper Primary Curriculum

- To enable the child to communicate effective in mother tongue, appreciate literature, write fluently in mother tongue. Also able to communicate in English and Hindi.
- To give practice in observing nature and society.
- To know natural laws, social and political institution, etc.
- To give essential awareness about health, hygiene, environmental education, technological discoveries, scientists who affects human history.
- To give proper attention to personality development at this stage and develop creativity among children.

Different Types of Primary Curriculum

- **Child Centred Curriculum:** This is learn oriented subjects should chosen and taught keeping in view the social, emotional and intellectual needs of children as well as their capabilities and developmental status. Here children construct their own knowledge from their experiences and interactions with the world around them.
- **Activity-Centred Curriculum:** In activity-centred curriculum subject matter is translated in terms of activities and knowledge is gained as an outcome and product of those activities. Activity is used as the medium for imparting knowledge, attitudes as well as skills.
- **Integrated Curriculum:** Children at the primary stage are at a developmental level where the learning is meaningful only if the content is prevented in a holistic manner. Their observations and understanding of the things and happenings around are based on totality. Taking this characteristics of children into consideration, ideally the children at primary stage should not be expected to study different subjects in isolation from each other i.e., the total curriculum should be integrated into one whole.
- **Spiral Curriculum:** The whole curriculum is spread over a number of years. A general treatment of almost all the topics are attempted at the beginning and it is developed in successive years or in the same year at different units according to the mental development of the pupils. In the beginning of the course the whole aspect is given to pupils in a simplified way. Later more and more details of its part are added.
- **Curriculum Based on Constructivism:** Constructivism emphasizes the careful study of the processes by which children create and develop their ideas.

Cognitive Constructivism

According to the constructivist point of view, children literally construct their knowledge of the world and as a result, their level of cognitive functioning. Constructing knowledge and intelligence involves processes of self-directed and self regulated activity. These processes play major roles in children's assimilation of new information and experiences and accommodation to form new mental schemes. As a result, children continuously structure and restructure experiences in relation to existing schemes of thought. Experiences provide a basis for constructing schemes. Basically stated, "constructivism refers to the fact that knowledge is built by activities children from the inside rather than being transmitted through the senses". Constructivism has two branches: Cognitive constructivism and social constructivism. Cognitive Constructivism is based on Piaget's "Genetic epistemology" and Bruner's Inquiry/Discovery learning. **Social Constructivism** theory is the major theme of Vygotsky's theory. Vygotsky believes that social interaction plays a fundamental role in the development of cognition.

Theoretical Bases of the present elementary school curriculum is Constructivism (Piaget, Bruner, Vygotsky) and Multiple Intelligence Theory (Howard Gardner, 1983). Gardner argued that we do not have one underlying general intelligence, but instead have multiple intelligence each being controlled by an independent system in the brain. Gardner has identified eight intelligence.

- Linguistic Intelligence
- Logical Mathematical Intelligence
- Spatial Intelligence
- Bodily-Kinesthetic-Intelligence
- Musical Intelligence
- Interpersonal Intelligence
- Intrapersonal Intelligence
- Naturalistic Intelligence

According to Gardner each person has unique profile of these intelligences, with strengths in some areas and weakness in other.

Emotional Intelligence (Daniel Goleman - 1995) is a unitary ability (related to, but independent of standard intelligence) helpful in knowing, feeling and judging emotions a close cooperation with one's thinking process to behave in a proper way, for the ultimate realize of the happiness and welfare of the self in tune with others.

Constructivism in Primary Education

- Emphasizes learning rather than instruction
- Learning considered as a process.
- Priority to 'How to learn' than 'what to learn'.
- Nurtures the learners instinctive curiosity
- Encourages the spirit of inquiry
- Accepts the role of exploring and experiences in learning
- Mental models of learners taken in to consideration
- Support co-operative learning
- Encourage dialogue and communication among pupils and teachers
- Encourage learning through life situations.
- Strong foundation of cognitive theories
- Performance is given importance in evaluation

- Teacher as a facilitator, co-learner, diagnostician, democratic leader, continuous learners, planner, researcher, organizer, evaluator, produces, social connecter, and collector.

Salient Features of Present Primary Curriculum

- Learner centred- activity oriented
- Individualized learning – multiple learning
- Importance given to process and product of learning
- Continuous and comprehensive evaluation
- Co-operative learning as a major strategy
- Grading in evaluation
- Strategies like projects, seminars, debates, field trips, assignments, club activities etc are usual for to transact curricular objectives effectively.
- Integrated approach
- Spiral approach
- Wake up activities
- More importance to activity
- Importance of fantasy
- Importance give to home learning environment

Figure 3.2: A diagrammatic presentation of the sequential steps in a strategy for effective curriculum transaction (Cognitive learning)

New Curricular Material

Analyse each unit into graded sequential components category wise, specify expected outcomes appropriate to the learner as well as to the nature of the material.

Identify all the pre-requisites needed for easy assimilation of the new curricular material of the unit analysed

Search for the pre-requisites needed for the unit, in the existing cognitive structure of the learners, with a pre-diagnostic test covering the pre-requisites

Identify the deficiencies and gaps, diagnose and fill in the gaps by taking remedial steps and providing compensatory experiences

(*Contd...*)

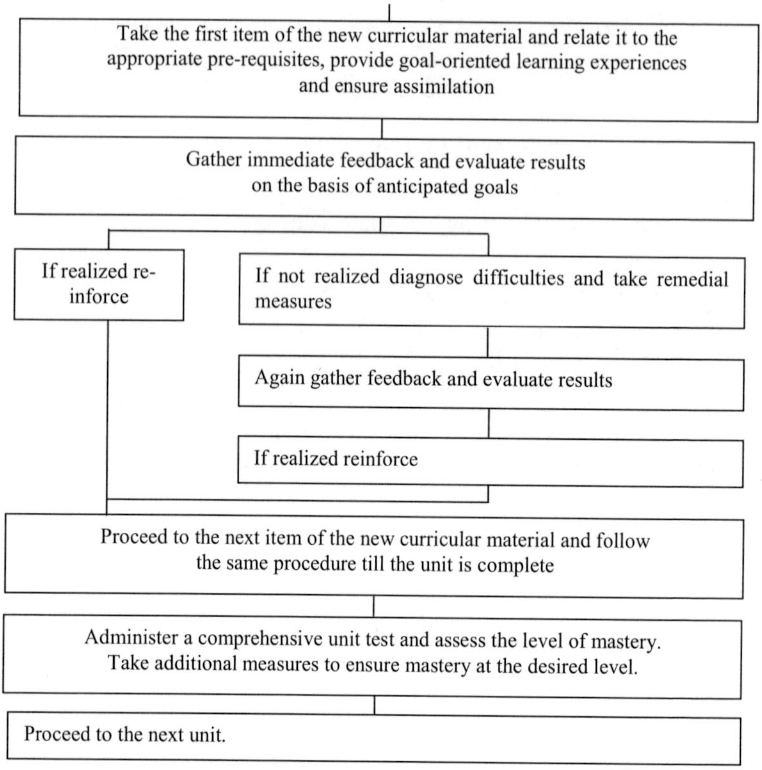

General Objectives of School Curriculum

School curriculum, on the whole, should aim at enabling the learners to acquire knowledge, develop concepts and inculcate skills, attitudes, values and habits conductive to the all-round development of their personality and commensurate with the social, cultural, economic and environmental realities at national level. School curriculum should, therefore, help to promote development in learner of:

- Language abilities and communication skills needed for social living and further learning:
- Competencies that facilitate mathematical operations and their applications in day-to-day life.
- Knowledge, attitudes and habits necessary for keeping physically fit and strong in conformity with normal developmental pattern.
- Qualities that make a man socially effective and happy in various social settings, such as friendliness, co-operativeness, compassion, self-discipline, self-criticism, self-control, humour, courage, commitment, to social justice and equality of sexes.

- Moral and character values such as honesty, truthfulness, dependability, courtesy, fearlessness, compassion, etc.
- Pre-vocational/vocational skills, willingness to work hard, entrepreneurship and dignity of manual work necessary for increases productivity and job satisfaction.
- Ability to appreciate and discover beauty in various life situations and integrate it with understanding of the environment and its limited resources and the need of conservation of natural resources and energy.
- Appreciation of various consequences of large families and over population and need of checking population growth.
- Understanding of the diverse cultural and social systems of people living in different parts of the country and the country's composite cultural heritage.
- Knowledge of scientific methods of enquiry and its use in solving problems, along with scientific temper characterized by spirit of enquiry, courage to question and objectivity leading to elimination of obscurantism, superstition and fatalism.
- Divergent and independent thinking necessary for self learning and for life-long learning leading to creation of a learning society.

Organization of Curriculum at Elementary Stage

The basic features and main thrusts of the new curricular framework could be visualized as follows:

- Emphasis on the development of human resources to put the young men and women of India on the fore front of development for the realization of the national goals of education, prosperity and social cohesion
- Broad- based general education to all learners at the elementary (5 years of primary and 3 years of UP) and secondary (2 years) stages.
- A broad-based common scheme of studies for the elementary and secondary stages with emphasis on the skill of "learning how to learn"
- The 1976 addition to the constitution of India laid down some fundamental duties which exhorted all Indian citizens to (a) abide by the constitution and respect its ideals and institutions, the National Flag and the National Anthem (b) Cherish and follow the noble ideals that inspired our national struggle for freedom (c) Uphold and protect the sovereignty unity and integrity of the country. (d) Defend the country and render national service when called up on to do so.

(e) Promote harmony and the spirit of common brotherhood among all the people of India. (f) Renounce practices derogatory to the dignity of women.

- The common core components comprise: (a) The history of India's freedom movement (b) The constitutional obligations (c) Content essential to nurture national identity (d) India's common cultural heritage (e) Egalitarianism, democracy and secularism (f) Equality of sexes (g) Protection and preservation of the environment (h) Removal of social barriers (i) Observance of the small family norm (j) Inculcation of scientific temper.
- Emphasis on ensuring to minimum essential level of acquisition of knowledge, understanding and skill in all subjects at all stages.
- Provision of flexibility in terms of selection of content/components and learning experiences.
- Emphasis on learner centred and activity based processes rather than the teacher-centred content-based approach during curriculum transaction.
- Recasting of the examination system and introduction of continuous and comprehensive evaluation that incorporates both scholastic and non-scholastic aspects of education.
- Provision of remedial teaching as well as counselling services for carrying out the diagnosis of learning problems.
- Setting up an appropriate system of National Testing Service (NTS) for the selection and development of norms of comparable competence across the nation.
- Applicability of the curriculum to all learners irrespective of their modes/channels of learning.
- Provision of essential facilities or the minimum conditions for learning through effective transaction of curriculum in all schools.

MID-DAY MEAL SCHEME

The Mid Day Meal is the world's largest school feeding programme reaching out to about 12 crore children in over 12.65 lac schools/EGS centres across the country. Mid Day Meal in schools has had a long history in India. In 1925, a Mid Day Meal Programme was introduced for disadvantaged children in Madras Municipal Corporation. By the mid 1980s three States viz. Gujarat, Kerala and Tamil Nadu and the UT of Pondicherry had universalized a cooked Mid Day Meal Programme with their own resources for children studying at the primary stage By 1990-91 the number of States implementing the mid day meal programme with their own resources on a universal or a large scale had increased to twelve states.

- With a view to enhancing enrolment, retention and attendance and simultaneously improving nutritional levels among children, the National Programme of Nutritional Support to Primary Education (NP-NSPE) was launched as a Centrally Sponsored Scheme on 15th August 1995, initially in 2408 blocks in the country. By the year 1997-98 the NP-NSPE was introduced in all blocks of the country. It was further extended in 2002 to cover not only children in classes I -V of Government, Government aided and local body schools, but also children studying in EGS and AIE centres. Central Assistance under the scheme consisted of free supply of food grains @ 100 grams per child per school day, and subsidy for transportation of food grains up to a maximum of Rs 50 per quintal.
- In September 2004 the scheme was revised to provide cooked mid day meal with 300 calories and 8-12 grams of protein to all children studying in classes I – V in Government and aided schools and EGS/AIE centres. In addition to free supply of food grains, the revised scheme provided Central Assistance for (a) Cooking cost @ Re 1 per child per school day, (b) Transport subsidy was raised from the earlier maximum of Rs 50 per quintal to ₹ 100 per quintal for special category states, and Rs 75 per quintal for other states, (c) Management, monitoring and evaluation costs @ 2% of the cost of food grains, transport subsidy and cooking assistance, (d) Provision of mid day meal during summer vacation in drought affected areas.
- In July 2006 the scheme was further revised to provide assistance for cooking cost at the rate of (a) Rs 1.80 per child/school day for States in the North Eastern Region, provided the NER States contribute Rs 0.20 per child/school day, and (b) Rs 1.50 per child/ school day for other States and UTs, provided that these States and UTs contribute Rs 0.50 per child/school day.
- In October 2007, the scheme has been further revised to cover children in upper primary (classes VI to VIII) initially in 3479 Educationally Backwards Blocks (EBBs). Around 1.7 Crore upper primary children were included by this expansion of the scheme. From 2008-09 i.e w.e.f 1st April, 2008, the programme covers all children studying in Government, Local Body and Government-aided primary and upper primary schools and the EGS/AIE centres including Madarsa and Maqtabs supported under SSA of all areas across the country. The calorific value of a mid-day meal at upper primary stage has been fixed at a minimum of 700 calories and 20 grams of protein by providing 150 grams of food grains (rice/wheat) per child/school day.

- During the year 2009 the following changes have been made to improve the implementation of the scheme:-
  - Food norms have been revised to ensure balanced and nutritious diet to children of upper primary group by increasing the quantity of pulses from 25 to 30 grams, vegetables from 65 to 75 grams and by decreasing the quantity of oil and fat from 10 grams to 7.5 grams.
  - Cooking cost (excluding the labour and administrative charges) has been revised from ₹ 1.68 to ₹ 2.50 for primary and from ₹ 2.20 to ₹ 3.75 for upper primary children from 1.12.2009 to facilitate serving meal to eligible children in prescribed quantity and of good quality .The cooking cost for primary is ₹ 2.69 per child per day and ₹ 4.03 for upper primary children from 1.4.2010.The cooking cost will be revised by 7.5% from 1.4.2011.
  - The honorarium for cooks and helpers was paid from the labour and other administrative charges of ₹ 0.40 per child per day provided under the cooking cost. In many cases the honorarium was so little that it became very difficult to engage manpower for cooking the meal. A Separate component for Payment of honorarium @ ₹ 1000 per month per cook- cum-helper was introduced from 1.12.2009.Honorarium at the above prescribed rate is being paid to cook-cum-helper. Following norms for engagement of cook-cum-helper have been made: (i) One cook-cum-helper for schools up to 25 students. (ii) Two cooks-cum-helpers for schools with 26 to 100 students . (iii) One additional cook-cum-helper for every addition of up to 100 students. More than 26 lacs cook-cum-helper at present are engaged by the State/ UTs during 2010-11 for preparation and serving of Mid Day Meal to Children in Elementary Classes.
  - A common unit cost of construction of kitchen shed @ ₹ 60,000 for the whole country was impractical and also inadequate .Now the cost of construction of kitchen-cum-store will be determined on the basis of plinth area norm and State Schedule of Rates. The Department of School Education and Literacy vide letter No.1-1/2009-Desk(MDM) dated 31.12.2009 had prescribed 20 sq.mt. plinth area for schools having up to 100 children. For every additional up to 100 children additional 4 sq.mt plinth area will be added. States/UTs have the flexibility to modify the Slab of 100 children depending upon the local condition.
  - Due to difficult geographical terrain of the Special category States the transportation cost @ ₹ 1.25 per quintal was not adequate to

meet the actual cost of transportation of food grains from the FCI godowns to schools in these States. On the request of the North Eastern States the transportation assistance in the 11 Special Category States (Northern Eastern States, Himachal Pradesh, Jammu & Kashmir and Uttarakhand) have been made at par with the Public Distribution System (PDS) rates prevalent in these States with effect from 1.12.2009.

- The existing system of payment of cost of food grains to FCI from the Government of India is prone to delays and risk. Decentralization of payment of cost of food grains to the FCI at the district level from 1.4.2010 will allow officers at State and National levels to focus on detailed monitoring of the Scheme.

8.41 crore Primary children and 3.36 crore Upper Primary children i.e a total of 11.77 crore children were estimated to be benefited from MDM Scheme during 2009-10. 11.04 crore children were covered under MDM Scheme during 2009-10. During 2010-11 11.36 crore children i.e. 7.97 crore children in primary and 3.39 Cr. children in upper primary are expected to be covered in 12.63 lacs institutions. Today, Mid day Meal scheme is serving primary and upper primary school children in entire country.

SPECIAL TRAINING PROGRAMME OF OUT OF SCHOOL CHILDREN

The Article 45 of the Constitution of India states, "The State shall endeavour to provide, within a period of ten years from the commencement of the Constitution, for free and compulsory education for all children until they complete the age of fourteen years." Education was included in the Directive Principles of State Policy and not in Fundamental Rights. Remaining in the domain of Directive Principles of State policy, education could not be acclaimed as a Right and was not justifiable. Education being in the concurrent list, Govt of India, State Govt. /UTs has tried to promote Elementary, Secondary and Higher education, but Universalisation of Elementary Education (UEE) continues to remain a distant goal for many states and UTs. Efforts from educationists, academics and civil society groups that focused on a Right based approach finally yielded results in 2002, when the 86th Constitutional Amendment was passed by Parliament and Article 21A, which makes right to education a Fundamental Right, was included in the Constitution in the chapter on Fundamental Rights. In doing so, it put the Right to Education on par with the Right to Life stated in Article 21.

Article 21A states: "the state shall provide free and compulsory education to all children of the age of 6 to 14 years as the state may, by law determine". As a sequel to this, Right to Free and Compulsory Education Act (RTE) was drafted and passed by Parliament on August 27, 2009, notified on February

16, 2010 to come into effect from April 1, 2010. This Act is called the Right of Children to Free and Compulsory Education Act 2009 (RTE). Right to Education Act 2009 implies that every child of 6-14 age groups has a right to elementary education of satisfactory and equitable quality in a formal school which satisfies certain essential norms and standard. The new law makes it obligatory on part of the state governments and local bodies to ensure that every child gets education in a school in the neighbourhood. The RTE Act also aims at reaching to the unreached and disadvantaged groups with providing specific provision of Free and Compulsory Education for every child who is above six years of age and has not yet been admitted to any school or though admitted, could not complete his or her education up to elementary level, then, he or she shall be admitted in a class appropriate to his or her age. To accomplish this task, there is a provision for Special Training in RTE Act for such children to bring them at par with their peer groups in the class.

Generally majority of out of school children belongs to disadvantage communities: i.e. Scheduled Castes, Scheduled Tribes, Muslims, Migrants, Children with Special Needs, Urban Deprived Children, working children, children in other difficult circumstances for example, those living in difficult terrain, children from displaced families and areas affected by civil strife etc. The reasons for Dropout and never enrolled children in schools are: i. Apathy of parents towards education. ii. Lack of awareness among parents about the necessity of education. iii. Financially weak parents. iv. Some of them may have dropped out to work or to get married. v. Seasonal migration of the family for work. vi. Unfavourable environment of the schools. vii. Not showing a desired level of achievement.

The Out of school children are identified, enrolled and Special Training is provided through the following interventions:

- Non–Residential Special Training Centres
- Non –Residential Special Training Centres run by NGOs
- Residential Special Training Centres run by NGOs
- Direct admissions
- Residential Hostel run by NGOs/Govt.

Under the RTE Rules, following provision of Special Training has been made for the out of school children - (1) The School Management Committee of a school owned or managed by the Government or the local authority shall identify children requiring special training and organize such training in the following manner, namely: The special training shall be based on specially designed, age appropriate Learning material, approved by the academic authority specified in sub-section (1) of section 29 of the Act The said training shall be provided in classes held in the premises of the school or in classes organized in safe residential facilities The said training shall be provided by teachers working in the school, or by teachers specially appointed for the purpose The duration of the said training shall be for a minimum period of three months which may be extended, based on periodical assessment of learning progress, for a maximum period not exceeding two years.

Out-of-school children: Who are they?

The National Policy on Education (1986) identifies universal access, universal enrolment and universal retention as the major targets to achieve the long cherished goal of Universalization of Elementary Education (UEE). Since then, many programmes and mission mode projects have been launched from time to time to accomplish the goal of UEE. But still, wide gender disparities remain across the country with regard to access, enrolment, retention and quality education in schools. The various programmes and policies of Government of India and various State Governments have significantly contributed to bring a paradigm shift in the elementary education system. The RTE Act has added momentum to all the earlier efforts of the country to universalize elementary education. There are significant developments during the last decades in terms of enrolments and gender and social category gaps in enrolments narrowed down considerably. Expansion of school infrastructure and facilities significantly increased access to schooling, and incentives and child entitlements, such as textbooks, mid day meal and uniforms started reaching to considerably larger number of children. Still, the issue of drop-outs continues to remain a major concern at the elementary stage. Out-of School children may be those who are non-enrolled in any school or dropped out at any stage before completing elementary education There is a great heterogeneity among children who are out-of-school. Various categories of 'out-of-school' children may include children living or working in urban slums, in streets, on railway platforms or construction sites. They may be found engaged as domestic workers, child labourers, tending cattle, working for wages in *dhabas*, mechanic shops, and rag pickers and as shoe shine boys.

Other categories may be those children who are involved in sex trade and migratory children whose parents migrate from area to area in search of work employments, usually may belong to SC, ST category. Children with special needs, who may belong to any of these categories, need to be identified. Those children who have a "disadvantage owing to social, cultural, economic, geographical, linguistic, gender or such other factors are also to be identified and brought into mainstream education. Besides these, children who get their education in minority communities run *Maktabs* and *Madarsa* learn religious texts and get little or no input on mainstream curriculum. Similarly, there may be adolescent girls, who have never attended school or may have dropped-out from school during early years. Children living in disturbed areas or in difficult circumstances, who are not attending school, also need to be identified and admitted in neighbouring school. Such diverged category of children need special training to bridge their learning gaps and mainstreamed in age appropriate classes.

A strategy for mainstreaming of these categories of children is a challenge; it needs to be worked out carefully taking into account all aspects which are related with educational developments of such children to fulfil the mandate of RTE Act. Reasons for dropouts of such categories of children need to be explored. Dropouts may be due to parents' illiteracy and lack of awareness, child labour, lack of quality, lack of professional competency and commitment in teachers, quality of curriculum and textbook, lack of physical facilities and infrastructure, lack of supervision and monitoring are some of the major reasons of drop out. Hence, this calls for urgent and strategic intervention of educational activities which would motivate such children to come to school again, participate in learning activities and remain in school till completion of elementary stage of education. Special training is significant in many ways in the context of bringing Out of School Children in school. As such, implementation of special training is a complex activity. There may be several issues and concerns which may vary from state to state. These need to be addressed as par state specific circumstances. At the same time, curricular and pedagogical approaches have to suitably moulded for learning enhancement of such children which is also a challenge and concern, deserve priority attention in the whole exercise of special training programme for its effective implementation.

Issues and Concerns: Keeping in view the different categories and various backgrounds of Out-of-School Children, organizing Special Training involves critical issues and concerns which need to be resolved in order to achieve the very purpose of special training stated in RTE Act. These issues and concerns are related with regard to identification of Out-of-School, assessment of entry level knowledge and skill, development of teaching and learning material/ Bridge Course, training of teachers involved in special training and other activities. Some of the other related issues are, mainstreaming of such children in age appropriate classes after special training, tracking of children after mainstreaming to find out if the children are coping with new environment in the school and to find out whether they need additional academic assistance to sustain their retention and continue till completion of elementary stage of education. Other issues and concerns may be as under:

- Identification of the procedures for assessment of competencies of Out of School Children enrolled in schools.
- Evolving a workable plan for organization of special training and ensuring quality education for Out of School Children within the stipulated time frame.
- Evolving monitoring and supervision mechanisms for realizing the objectives of special training.

- Ensuring roles and responsibilities of Head Teacher/ Teachers in organizing special training.
- Development, procurement and timely availability of Special Learning Support Materials (SLSMs) in all schools/ special training centres.
- Ensuring equitable social environment so that no child is subjected to caste, class, religious or gender discrimination in the school/ centre.
- Ensuring continuous comprehensive evaluation (CCE) of children to record progress for maintaining individual profiles and finding ways for appropriate and timely corrective measures.
- Training for all functionaries at various levels from State level to School/ School Management Committee (SMC) level in order to meet the learning needs of out-of-school children. Suggestive strategies and interventions have been provided in the Guidelines to address some of these issues enumerated above.

Design of Special Training

As mentioned above, RTE Act 2009 states that where children not admitted to, or who have not completed elementary education, is directly admitted in a class appropriate to his or her age, then, he or she, in order to be at par with others, has a right to receive Special Training (ST). Mainstreaming of such children into formal schools is to be done through special training of varying durations, which would enable them to be at par with other children in the class and facilitate them in getting admission into age-appropriate classes to fulfil the goal of Special Training. In this endeavour the long cherished goal of Universal Elementary Education could also be realized. The purpose of the special training is to integrate the children with rest of the class academically and emotionally. ST should not be seen as only renaming of erstwhile Non-Formal Education (NFE) or Education Guarantee Scheme /Alternative and Innovative Education (EGS&AIE) centres which provided for Residential Bridge Courses (RBCs) and Non-Residential Bridge Courses (NRBCs) for dropouts/non-enrolled. As a matter of fact, ST is a specific intervention which aims at enabling admission of OoSC in age appropriate classes with comparable competencies enabling retention of such children and facilitates them to complete elementary stage of education. There are critical areas, which need to be taken into consideration in the whole process of implementation of special training, such as, assessment of entry level competencies of the children, the nature and duration of the special training, devising and developing curriculum and Special Learning Support Material (SLSM), location of the training, ensuring roles and responsibilities of various functionaries and their training. Transactional strategies for varied learning abilities of children, handling of heterogeneous group of children, coping with adjustment issues of children after their mainstreaming are other significant aspects need to be addressed during special training. Continuous and Comprehensive assessment of children along with Supervision and Monitoring of the whole process of special training at regular intervals need to be ensured for successful implementation of special training under special provision of RTE. Keeping in view the complexities and significance of the special training, it has to be designed in a way that it takes into account all such aspects, which have been mentioned above, each of these aspects has been explained in detail as given below:

- Duration of the Special Training Duration of special training shall be for a minimum period of three months extendable up to two years. There should be periodic assessment of learning progress made by such children on continuous basis in special training. The entry level assessment will determine the duration of special training in each case and placement in age appropriate class thereafter. The Head teacher/ teacher must ensure that a consolidated record of all children is maintained in the training centres for better traceability of learning outcomes for necessary interventions. The assessment of the children shall be done by the concerned teachers. Preferably, it should be validated by the Head teacher. The school shall maintain performance record of children, clearly indicating the progress made during the period of special training at regular intervals, stating the milestones accomplished for further action with regard to children's admission in age appropriate classes.
- Location Special training may be held on the premises of the schools, or through classes organised in safe residential facilities. It may also be organised in and around the locality as decided by the School Management Committee members (SMCs). Special training may be provided by teachers working in the school or by teachers specially appointed for the purpose. The help of NGOs/volunteers may also be taken.
- The Nature of Special Training may be residential or non-residential in nature: Residential – where out-of-school children are scattered, and who need residential facility such as in hilly areas. Non Residential – where out-of-school children are very much concentrated in an area and school is located within walking distance.
- Special Learning Support Materials (SLSM) As par sec 29, (I), RTE ACT the special training shall be based on specially designed, age appropriate learning material, approved by the Academic Authority, these may be referred as Special Learning Support Materials During training programme the teachers should be familiarized with the

special training support material in the context of pedagogy, as given below: The SLSM should be developed in such manner which enables learners to develop their knowledge and competency levels as per their age, by adopting a condensed curriculum. This will help the learners to bridge the learning gaps to be at par with their peers in short duration.

Recognizing the scale and time-bound nature of the task, innovative and flexible delivery of curriculum and suitable teaching learning strategies should be devised to enable children to be at par with other children and mainstreamed in a regular class suited to his/her age. Enrolment of out- of- school children can be made at any time during the academic session. Such children should be welcomed in the school and special attention should be paid for their mainstreaming through special training programmes. Special Learning Support Materials should be developed and designed in a manner, which will help in preparing out-of-school children to join formal schools and adjust with the school environment. Suitable teaching learning strategies should be adopted accordingly to enable the learners to achieve the competencies appropriate for their age in short period, during which the children are allowed to learn at their own pace. This prepares the children to cope with the demands of the formal school system. The curriculum transacted to the learners should be in a condensed form so that the learners achieve equivalence with their peers in the formal school and get admitted in the appropriate class. The SLSM should be based on specific requirements of multi-level teaching of children of different age-groups and abilities. It should be so designed that it is free from all biases. There should be flexibility for accommodating contextual and local specific requirements and learning contents. SLSM should be easy for teachers and enjoyable for children. While developing SLSMs, it is desired that the experts/ agencies/ institutions should adopt the strategies already tried out to be effective in schools under SSA (existing bridge courses), and several interventions made by different NGOs for the purpose. However, the spirit of these SLSMs should centre on the following objectives: (i) To unearth the hidden knowledge of children in order to assist them to progress further. (ii) To help and support teachers in learning enhancement of children enrolled for special training

ELEMENTARY CURRICULUM WITH REFERENCE TO NCF 2005

The National Curriculum Framework (NCF) 2005 prepared by the National Council of Educational Research and Training (NCERT) aims to bring about a significant shift towards schools and systems that are child-friendly and inclusive, and teaching-learning processes that are more based on a constructivist approach, responsive to each child's needs. The NCF-2005 has resulted in a series of initiatives for renewal of school education curriculum at the State level, revision of textbooks and other teaching-learning materials, changes in pedagogy and leaning assessment procedures. Across the country, States are being supported to design and implement comprehensive quality improvement programmes with a view to bringing about renewal of State curriculum keeping in mind the principles underlying NCF-2005, including redesigning of textbooks and other teaching-learning materials, reorientation of the teaching-learning process and learning assessment systems and institutionalization of quality monitoring systems in order to ensure improved student learning.

The NCF-2005 brings into focus the need to arrive at a relevant, balanced set of educational aims describing what the learners should learn. The NCF-2005, identifies educational aims as comprising the following: a commitment to democracy and values of equality, justice, freedom, concern for others' well-being, secularism, respect for human dignity and rights; a sensitivity to others' wellbeing and feelings, together with knowledge and understanding of the world which would form the basis of a rational commitment to values; a capacity to learn and willingness to unlearn and relearn as means of responding to new situations in a flexible and creative manner; and appreciation of beauty and art forms as an integral part of human life. The NCF-2005 lays down the broad principles for the development of curriculum by the States/UTs and for designing the detailed syllabus and textbooks and other teaching-learning materials. The syllabus for Classes I to VIII prepared by NCERT reflect some of the key principles which need to be taken care of while undertaking curriculum renewal at the State/UT level. These principles include: resonance of the values enshrined in the Constitution of India; sensitivity to gender, caste and class parity, peace, health and needs of differently-abled children; infusion of environment-related and work-based knowledge at all levels of school education and in all subjects of study; linkages between school knowledge in different subjects and children's everyday experiences;appropriateness of topics and themes for relevant stages of children's development and continuity from one level to the next; inter-disciplinary and thematic linkages between topics listed for different school subjects which fall under discrete disciplinary areas; and nurturing aesthetic sensibility and values by integrating the arts and India's heritage of crafts in every aspect of the curriculum.

The NCF-2005 envisages development of textbooks that facilitate construction of knowledge by learners through the understanding of concepts, by active exploration, reflective thinking, and by providing interactive opportunities for children to carry out activities in groups, with continuous and self and peer assessment of learning. Syllabus, textbooks, pedagogic practices and assessment frameworks based on the NCF-2005 have been developed at the National level to facilitate curricular renewal at the State levels. NCF 2005 recognises the diversity of contexts in India and recommends that instead of one textbook for all in a particular State, a menu of quality curricular packages be developed.

The period of elementary school (from Class I to Class VIII) is now also recognised as the period of compulsory schooling vide the constitutional amendment making education a fundamental right. The beginning of this period marks the formal introduction of the child to reading, writing and arithmetic, culminating in the introduction of the formal disciplines such as the sciences and the social sciences towards the end of elementary school. This period of eight years is one of tremendous cognitive development, shaping reason, intellect and social skills, as well as the skills and attitudes necessary for entering the work place. As the effort to achieve UEE is stepped up, the elementary school classes now cater to many children of school-going age coming from diverse backgrounds. Plurality and flexibility without compromising on standards need to become the hallmark of education for this period. Education during this period must be of an integrated character, enabling children to acquire facility in language and expression and to grow in self-confidence as learners, both within and outside school.

The first concern of the school is on the development of the child's language competence: issues related to articulation and literacy, and the ability to use language to create, to think and to communicate with others. Special stress is needed to ensure that there are maximum opportunities for those who wish to study in their mother tongue, including tribal languages and linguistic pockets, even if the number of students is small. The ability of the system to promote and nurture these options, along with working out mechanisms to ensure that future options remain open, should become a marker of its ability to provide for quality education. To achieve this, there must be a creative and concerted effort to maintain the multilingual genius of Indians and implement the three-language formula. While English may be taught during this period, it must not be at the expense of learning Indian languages. The development of mathematical thinking, beginning with learning numeracy and moving towards the enjoyment of and facility with more abstract ideas, needs to be supported with concrete experiences and work with manipulations. It is in the early years, up to Class IV, that efforts at diagnosing learning difficulties and addressing remedial work in language and mathematics must be directed. Such concrete experiences are also essential in the introduction to the integrated study of the environment through which children's intuitive knowledge of the world is integrated into school knowledge. Over the years, this study should move towards a more disciplinary approach, but with integrative themes, within which there are located opportunities to develop concepts and learn the vocabulary and methods of the discipline. The study of arts and crafts is essential for developing not only the aesthetic sensibility but also for learning how to manipulate materials and developing attitudes and skills essential for work. The curriculum must expose children to practical life skills and work experiences of varied kinds. Physical development through sports activities is also a must. A variety of activities at this stage of schooling should be made available, including participating in cultural programmes, organising events, travelling to places outside the school, providing experiences to develop socially and emotionally into creative and confident individuals sensitive to others, and capable of taking initiative and responsibility. Teachers with a background in guidance and counselling can design and lead activities to meet the developmental needs of children, thus laying the foundation for the necessary attitudes and perceptions towards the self and the world of work. They can also provide the needed support and guidance to children belonging to various strata of society for their sustenance through the elementary school years. The approach to the whole curriculum should be process oriented rather than outcome oriented. All these arenas of development should be made available to all children. Care must be taken to ensure that the curriculum does not reinforce stereotypes about preferences, choices and capabilities of different groups. In this context, the gradual inclusion of vocationally oriented skills as a part of exposure to work would be an important aspect of an inclusive curriculum.

References

Equity and Excellence in Education. retrieved on 30-04-2018 from http://egyankosh.ac.in/bitstream/123456789/8327/1/Unit-17.pdf

Expanding Access with Equity. retrieved on 30-04-2018 from http://www.create-rpc.org/pdf_documents/Paper_R.Govinda.pdf

Gargesh, R. (2006, June 8). language issues in the context of Higher Education in India. *Symposium on language issues in English-medium Universities across Asia*. Lecture conducted from University of Hong Kong.

Government of India, *Education and National Development the Report of Education Commission*, 1966. pp-149-151.

Government of India. *Education Commission* (1964-66). New Delhi.

Government of India. *National Policy on Education*, MHRD, New Delhi, 1986.

Government of India. *Programme of Action*, MHRD, New Delhi 1992.

Govinda & Bandyopadhyay (July 2008). *Access to Elementary Education in India: Country Analytical Review.* New Delhi: National University of Educational Planning and Administration (NUEPA)

Govinda & Bandyopadhyay. *Achieving Universal Elementary Education in India*

Gulati, S. *Education and Equity*. School of Open Learning. University of Delhi. retrieved on 30-04-2018 from https://sol.du.ac.in/mod/book/view.php? id=1449 &chapterid=1334

Krishnan, D.K., & Thamarasseri, I. (2013). *Contemporary Issues in Indian Education.* New Delhi: Kanishka Publishers

MacDonald, James B. *A Proper Curriculum for Young Children*, Phi Delta Kappa 50, No. 7, (March 1969): 406.

Main features of the RTE Act. retrieved on 30-04-2018 from http://ncert.nic.in/departments/nie/dee/publication/pdf/guidelines16.12.2013.pdf

Mukherjee, J. Elementary Education in India: Enrolment, Retention and Quality. *Arthaniti*. 13 (1-2) 2014/76. retrieved on 30-04-2018 from http://www.econcaluniv.ac.in/Arthanitiweb/book/2014/JM.pdf

Nedha (February 24, 2011). *Difference Between Equity and Equality*. retrieved on 30-04-2018 from https://www.differencebetween.com/difference-between-equity-and-vs-equality/

NUEPA (2014). *India - Education for All 2015: National Review*. retrieved on 30-04-2018 from http://unesdoc.unesco.org/images/0022/002298/229873E.pdf

Rawat, D.S. (1970) *Pre-Primary Teacher Education Curriculum*. New Delhi: NCERT.

Sharma, J. C. (2001). *Multilingualism in India*. retrieved on 25-07-2015 from http://www.languageinindia.com/dec2001/jcsharma2.html

Special Training for Out of school children- PAB (2015-16). retrieved on 30-04-2018 from http://edudel.nic.in/ssa/7.pdf

Srivastava, R. N. (1984). Linguistic Minorities and National Language. In F. Coulmas (ed.), *Linguistic Minorities and Literacy*. The Hague: Mouton

Thamarasseri, I. (2007). *Education in the Emerging Indian Society*. New Delhi: Kanishka Publishers

Thamarasseri, I. (2008). *Early Childhood and Elementary Education*. New Delhi: Kanishka Publishers

Thamarasseri, I. (2011). *Current Developments in Indian Education*. New Delhi: Kanishka Publishers

Thamarasseri, I. (2014). *Issues and Challenges of Indian Education*. Agra: Shri Vinod Pustak Mandir

Thamarasseri, I., & Bhat, M. S. (2018). *Elementary Education*. Agra: Shri Vinod Pustak Mandir

Thamarasseri, Ismail. (2014). *Issues and Challenges of Indian Education*. Agra: Shri Vinod Pustak Mandir

Tilak, J.B.G. *Financing Elementary Education in India*. retrieved on 10-03-2018 from http://birbhum.gov.in/DPSC/reference/9.pdf

UNIT - 4

Introduction to Secondary Education

Introduction

Secondary education is the stage of education that includes all the classes after the primary school and before university education is started. This stage is considered to be the backbone of the country's entire educational programme. This however, is also the stage which marks the completion of education for the large majority of pupils. Secondary education is also the basis of higher education which gives the desired direction to the nation's power. An inefficient system of secondary education therefore is bound to affect adversely the quality of education at all later stage. Secondary education is the stage of education following primary education. Except in countries where only primary or basic education is compulsory, secondary education includes the final stage of compulsory education and in many countries it is entirely compulsory. The next stage of education is usually college or university. Secondary education is characterized by transition from primary education for minors to tertiary, "post-secondary", or "higher" education (e.g., university, vocational school) for adults. Depending on the system, schools for this period or a part of it may be called secondary schools, high schools, gymnasia, lyceums, middle schools, sixth-form, sixth-form colleges, vocational schools and preparatory schools, and the exact meaning of any of these varies between the nations.

In India high school is a grade of education from Standards IX to XII. Standards XI and XII are also called Higher / Senior Secondary School. Usually students from ages 14 to 17 study in this section. These schools may be affiliated to national boards (like CBSE, ISC, and NIOS) or various state boards. Education is compulsory until age 14. Although most are stand-alone day schools, some popular schools are residential. Traditional second stage in formal education, typically beginning at ages 14-16 and ending at 16-18.

At the Secondary School level, there are two divisions, the junior and the senior. The junior stage of secondary schools is known in some cases as middle schools or lower secondary schools and in some as the Senior Basic Schools. It covers a period varying in different areas, between 3 and 4 years. In the majority of States, the pattern is one of three years. High Schools correspond to the senior school stage of secondary schools. In the large majority of cases this stage extends over a period of three years. In a few States the High School period is limited to two years, the Middle School being of four years duration. It is time that we recognise the rising levels of democratic consciousness and social aspirations among the young people in the age group of 14-18 years, particularly from the deprived sections of society including girls and the disabled, for a greater share in nation's political, social and techno-economic life. This pressure is expected to take a quantum jump consequent upon the anticipated progress in the UEE by 2010. In view of this, the Central and the State/UT governments must jointly initiate planning to implement the agenda of universal and free secondary education in the first phase by the year 2015 and then extend it to senior secondary education in the second phase by the year 2020.

The conventional expectation from secondary/senior secondary education lies in its role in creating the necessary base for generating technical person power, raising the potential of a society in contributing to the growth of knowledge and skills and hereby enhancing the nation's capacity to face the challenge of global competitiveness. That in itself constitutes a significant part of the vision. However, this is not all. The contemporary and additional expectation from secondary education is to build a democratic citizenship that is committed to the Constitutional goal of enabling India to move towards an egalitarian, secular and enlightened society while also being sensitive to India's rich cultural and linguistic diversity and its composite culture. In order to extend the access of secondary education to the hitherto marginalised sections of society, comprising almost two-thirds of the 14-18 year age group population, and make their participation at this level genuinely inclusive, it would become imperative that the long-overdue changes in the social, cultural and pedagogic character of the secondary/senior secondary school are not delayed any further. Indeed, such changes are expected to benefit even those sections that manage at present to participate in and survive through secondary education, in spite of its exclusionary character. This implies that universalisation of secondary education cannot be envisaged merely in terms of quantitative expansion of what we have today.

Secondary education should be determined by the needs of the society to be served, the character of the individuals to be educated, and the knowledge of educational theory and practice available. These factors are by no means static. Society is always in process of development; the character of the secondary-school population undergoes modification; and the sciences on which educational theory and practice depend constantly furnish new information. Secondary education, however, like any other established agency of society, is conservative and tends to resist modification. Failure to make adjustments when the need arises leads to the necessity for extensive reorganization at irregular intervals. The evidence is strong that such a comprehensive reorganization of secondary education is imperative at the present time.

Objectives of Secondary Education

Secondary Education, in fact, is that stage of education which helps children to become capable members of a modern society. It develops the individuals potential, his ability, his aptitudes, his interests & qualities of character. It enable the individual to enter in the life as a knowledge, active minded & sociable individual. According to Secondary Education Commission (1952-53) the main objectives of secondary education are as follows.

- Development of Demotic citizenship
- Development of Clear thinking
- Development of Scientific outlook
- Development of Clear and free expression
- Development of Social Co-operation
- Development of True patriotism
- Improvement of vocational efficiency
- Development of personality
- Education for leadership

Objectives of secondary education according to Kothari Commission (1964-66) are;

- Education and productivity
- Social and National Integration
- Education and Modernization
- Social, Moral and spiritual values

Secondary Education in India serves as a bridge between elementary and higher education and prepares young person's between the age group of 14-18 for entry into higher education or work situations. The population of children in this age group has been estimated to be 88.5 million as per Census, 2001. Enrolment figures show that only 31 million of these children were attending schools in 2001-02, which means that two-third of the population remained out of school. Given the liberalization and globalization of the Indian economy, the rapid changes witnessed in scientific and technological world and the general need to improve the quality of life, it is essential that school leavers acquire a higher level of knowledge and skills than what they are provided in the eight years of elementary education. The average earnings of secondary school certificate holders are significantly higher than those with primary school education.

Steps have been taken in the last few years to universalize elementary education. Towards that end Sarva Siksha Abhiyan (SSA) is being implemented all over the country in collaboration with the State Governments. Mid-day Meal Scheme is a part of this programme. As a result of these steps, the number of "out of school" children (6-14 years) has come down to less than 5% of the total population in that age group. The SSA at the elementary level to universalize elementary education for the age group 6-14 has already set the stage for an exponential growth of demand for secondary education. While the growth of enrolment in the secondary school, had increased at an annual rate of 2.83 per cent during 1990s, it increased at 7.4 per cent, per annum between 2000 and 2003. The full impact of SSA is likely to be reflected during the terminal years of the Eleventh Plan. If the goal of universal retention at the elementary level is achieved by 2010, steps will have to be taken to expand facilities for secondary education in a big way.

As a successful result of Sarva Skhiksha Abhiyan (SSA), the number of "out of school" children (6-14 years) has come down to less than 5 per cent of the total population in that age group, and thus the stage has been set for an exponential growth of demand for secondary education. Secondary Education is a crucial stage in the educational hierarchy, as it prepares the students for higher education and also for the world of work. With the liberalization and globalization of the Indian economy, the rapid changes witnessed in the scientific and technological world, and the general need to improve the quality of life and to reduce poverty, it is essential that school leavers acquire a higher level of knowledge and skills than is provided in the 8 years of elementary education.

General Aims and Objectives of Secondary Education

- Development of tolerance
- Development of sense of co-operation
- Development of patriotism
- Equal opportunities of thought, speech, writing
- Inculcation of values
- Character development
- Development of international understanding
- Intellectual development
- Appraisal of culture Conservation, preservation and transmission of culture

Today, the demand for secondary education worldwide is soaring due to progress towards universal primary school completion, large cohorts of young people searching for the key to a better life, and the global demand for an increasingly sophisticated labour force. This heightened demand for secondary education is accompanied by the need to respond to the twin challenges of "increasing access to" and, at the same time, "improving quality and relevance of" secondary education. These two overarching themes run through all other issues in secondary education. A key policy objective of the World Bank is to ensure that both access and quality are increased for those generally excluded by poverty, ethnicity, gender, and other factors.

Access

One of the main challenges for policymakers is to ensure that secondary education is accessible to young people. In many countries, inequity in access to secondary education is a major barrier to human development, and therefore to economic growth and poverty reduction. Despite significant growth in secondary school enrolments in recent years, developing countries still face enormous challenges. Whereas the primary school completion gap between rich and poor countries has diminished, the gap in the proportion of the population with secondary education has widened in the past 40 years. As secondary enrolment expands, gender differences in access become more apparent. Cultural factors that favour sending boys to school while keeping girls at home to do domestic work, combined with low expectations that girls will enter the job market, are often cited as the primary reasons for gender differentials. Affordability is another reason why many children do not attend school or drop out early. Many families depend on their children to contribute to the family income; others simply cannot afford the expenses associated with school attendance.

Quality and Relevance

As the demand for secondary education increases, there must be an accompanying emphasis on increasing the quality and relevance of that education. The demand for higher skilled workers to actively and effectively participate in the global economy is driving the push for quality and relevance. Policymakers and educators must re-examine every facet of the secondary education system to ensure that young people are gaining the skills and knowledge that they need to be successful in today's world. Only through increasing quality and relevance can secondary education truly serve as a catalyst to economic growth and poverty reduction. While many poor countries must struggle simultaneously with increasing enrolment and quality of education, many middle-income and transition countries, in particular those in Eastern Europe, Latin America, and East Asia, have already achieved high enrolment levels in secondary education. Their main challenge is to improve quality, relevance, and efficiency to better align their education systems with those in open democracies and to respond to the rapidly changing demands of increasingly globalized economies.

Curriculum

Within the context of the knowledge economy, changing work patterns are leading to radical new approaches in the way curriculum knowledge is selected, organized, and sequenced. In addition, greater emphasis on the democratization of access to knowledge and on the formation of social capital, as well as better understanding of youth issues and how adolescents learn, are greatly impacting curriculum design. Today, in many countries, adults and young people share a feeling that secondary education curriculum is profoundly inadequate. It is commonly asserted that there is a knowledge gap between the subject matter currently being taught and the knowledge and skills that are required if individuals and countries are to be competitive in the globalized world. There is a demand for a much closer intertwining of theoretical and practical learning, as well as general and vocational education, to prepare students to take full advantage of educational and employment opportunities.

Assessment

In the effort to expand secondary education and improve its quality the role of national examinations cannot be taken for granted. Examinations can be used to distribute opportunities for further education and as a condition for accessing labour markets. They are a powerful tool for influencing and shaping secondary school curriculum. Broadly speaking, entrance examinations to secondary education are disappearing or are being used for purposes other than competitive selection. On the other hand, concern about global competitiveness has sparked an increased interest in nationwide student achievement testing. Good assessment tools provide policymakers with critical decision-making information to evaluate the quality and cost-effectiveness of educational intervention.

Teaching

The teaching profession is charged with the immense task of building human skills and capacities necessary for economic growth, poverty reduction, social well-being, and individual development. It is no surprise that teachers are considered the most important element in education systems everywhere. Reform efforts in both developed and developing countries assume that the most direct and effective way of raising instructional quality is to introduce changes in teacher education and recruitment, improve the knowledge and pedagogical skills of teachers, and to ensure that organizational conditions promote effective instruction. Globalization and the shift to the knowledge economy have had a profound impact on teacher recruitment, training, and support. There is an increasing demand for teachers who are knowledge workers, designers of creative and relevant learning environments to help move students towards the growing opportunities in higher education and employment.

Technology

Globalization, the increased importance of knowledge as a driving force in economic development, and the skill-biased nature of technological changes in the workplace are putting additional pressures on national governments to modernize and revamp their secondary education systems in order to produce graduates who are well prepared to enter the work force or institutions of higher learning. Information and Communication Technologies (ICTs) are transforming teaching and learning processes in educational systems worldwide.

For some decades now technologies have been seen as tools for expanding access to education at reduced costs. Indeed, distance education has contributed to expanded educational access, particularly at the tertiary level. However, ICTs also introduce substantial and recurring new costs, as school systems struggle to stay current with technology. The mere presence of computers in classrooms does not guarantee that student learning will improve. Effective use of ICTs requires accompanying, and often difficult, changes in curriculum, teaching, and school organization. In addition, sophisticated technologies are not always introduced equitably, resulting in the exclusion of some students based on location, gender, income, or other factors.

Financing

The escalating demand for secondary education increases the pressure on national budgets in an already constrained financial environment. Significantly increasing access to secondary education requires new financial resources. There is little evidence, however, that increases in funding alone lead to improvements in the quality of education. The financial reality is that many developing countries and transition economies lack the capacity to raise the additional resources necessary to address the new challenges in secondary education. Nations must find new ways of increasing funding for secondary education through public, private, or community sources, and at the same time, maximizing efficiency and effectiveness in resource allocation and utilization.

Governance

In the 21st century, traditional modes of organizing and governing secondary education are no longer relevant. Long-established forms of governance based on a system of publicly authorized, publicly funded, and publicly operated schools supported by centrally defined norms and regulations are being replaced by an array of governance arrangements in which the central government continues to play a central role in steering and monitoring the system, but lower-level governments and private sector share in the funding and operation of schools. Countries that have had reasonable success in providing most of their young people with good secondary education share four common elements in governance: transparent, well-known regulations; a sharp definition of responsibilities; strong public management; and a precise definition of outcomes and measurement of results. Moreover, secondary education systems today must be flexible and responsive to the rapidly changing environment, balancing student needs with management issues in the global information age.

Curricular Structure and Course offerings at Secondary Level

Examining the situation prevailing in mid-1960's with respect to curricular structure at the secondary level, the Education Commission (1964-66) recommended its reorganization in the following words: "The first step in this direction would be the abandoning of the present higher secondary pattern in which specialization begins in class IX, and the institution of a new higher secondary course beginning in class XI." While recommending a nation-wide shift to 10+2+3 pattern, the Commission visualized that "the first ten years of schooling will provide a course of general education without any specialization." The Commission further clarified that "the system of 'streaming' in schools of general education, which now [i.e. in mid-1960s] begins in class IX, should be given up and no attempt at specialization should be made till after class X." This recommendation for a common curriculum until class X within the 10+2+3 framework was accepted in NPE-1968 and a major programme of shift with additional outlays was undertaken throughout the country. NPE-1986 reiterated this pattern of education as part of the National System of Education.

The National Curriculum Framework (1975) proposed a common curriculum for the ten-year school, to be followed by diversification beginning at class XI for the +2 stage. This basic principle is now practiced nation-wide. The National Curriculum Frameworks prepared successively in 1988, 2000 and 2005 have continued to follow this imperative of NPE-1986. It is in this background that the Committee examined the proposal from certain quarters that diversification should be pre-pone to class IX. The proponents of this view contend that "the most significant reason for mass scale failure in the tenth board examination is the common curriculum and course offerings . . . . . nearly 80 per cent of the candidates who fail in the board examination fail in mathematics, English and science . . . . besides significant wastage of the educational resources, it affects self-esteem and self-concept of the students." The solution offered by these proponents to the problem of "mass scale failure in the tenth board examination" and its adverse impact on the "self-esteem" of students consisted in "diversification of students into several streams of education beyond eighth standard" and offering them a "cafeteria approach" from class IX onwards. This view was debated by the Committee at length. In the view of the Committee, however, the root cause of "mass scale failure" is not the common curriculum offered until class X as per NPE-1986. Instead, the cause of the failure lies in the framework in which subject knowledge is conceived, the manner in which knowledge is transacted and the evaluation parameters and the assessment procedures adopted for examining students. The right to study and succeed in basic mathematics, science, social science and languages, including English, and other mainstream subjects is as much a fundamental right of a child as to have access to and complete secondary / senior secondary education. Keeping this in mind, the National Curriculum Framework - 2005 has made several radical proposals to revisit the very character of knowledge, shift to a new pedagogic approach and change the entire examination system. Such changes are urgently required in order to make sure that the nation is freed of this phenomenon of "mass scale failure" and widespread but apparent "under-achievement". Without such a paradigm shift, it would not be possible to universalize secondary education either. We need to be especially concerned about the prevailing practice of not offering science or mathematics at Plus Two stage in many rural schools/ urban slums or to SCs, STs, girls or the disabled (or not providing science labs at class IX-X level in backward areas), thereby forcing these children to go in for the so-called "softer" options. This practice has a significant negative impact on the aspirations of the masses for upward social mobility for their children.

Aims of Secondary Education according to Secondary Education Commission (1952-1953)

The first-ever statement on aims of education for democratic India was made by the Secondary Education Commission in its Report published in 1953. The Commission stated that education which is national in character must develop in its citizens' habits, attitudes and qualities of character and equip them to bear the burden of life in the changing economic structure.

- **Development of Democratic Citizenship:** It is a challenging responsibility with education to carefully train every citizen for democratic citizenship. Such training involves development of multi-sided qualities. A democratic citizen should have the understanding and the intellectual integrity to distinguish truth from falsehood and facts from propaganda. Education should train the young scholar to reject fanaticism and prejudices.
- **Improvement of Vocational Efficiency:** Education must aim at increasing the productive or vocational efficiency of young students. In order to achieve this aim, there should be much greater emphasis on crafts and productive work. Diversification of courses should be introduced at the secondary stage so that a large number of students may take up agricultural, technical, commercial or other practical courses which will train their varied aptitudes. This will also enable

them to take up vocational pursuits at the end of the secondary schools course.

- **Development of Personality:** Education should develop literary, artistic and cultural interests of the students. These are necessary for self-expression and for the full development of human personality. For this purpose subjects like art, craft, music, dancing etc. should be included in the scheme of studies.
- **Education for Leadership:** In order to make democracy function successfully, it is essential to inculcate the qualities of leadership in our youth. Education should train the youth to provide leadership in the social, political, industrial and cultural fields.

Kothari Education Commission and Educational Objectives

In its Report which appeared in 1966, the Kothari Education Commission observed that education must become a powerful instrument of social, economic and cultural transformation. For this purpose, the Commission suggested the following objectives of education:

- ***Education for Increasing Productivity:*** The Commission suggested that education must be related to productivity to increase national income. In order to create a link between education and productivity, the following programme has been suggested by the Commission:
    - o *Science Education.* In order to enhance productivity, science education "must become an integral part of school education, and ultimately some study of science should become a part of all courses in the humanities and social sciences at the university stage."
    - o *This will develop understanding of basic principles*, problem-solving attitude; promote the ability to apply these principles to problems of life and to encourage the spirit of enquiry and experimentation.
    - o *Work Experience.* According to the Commission, work experience implies participation in productive work in school, in the home, in a workshop, on a farm, in a factory or in any other productive situation. In the programme of relating education to life productivity, this work-experience must be introduced as an integral part of all education, general and vocational.
    - o *'Forward Look' in Work Experience.* Every attempt should be made to link work experience to technology and industrialisation, including agriculture. The education of a student is not held to be complete unless he participates in some type of work-experience in real life conditions. It is in this way that education can pay high dividends. This 'forward look' in work experience

is important for a country which has embarked on a programme of industrialisation.

- o *Vocationalisation of Secondary Education.* Every attempt should be made to give a vocational bias to secondary education and to increase the emphasis on agricultural and technological education at the university stage. This will surely bring education into closer relationship with productivity. This is of special significance in the Indian education where education has so far been training the youth for the so called white-collar professions.

- ***Education for Social and National Integration***. According to the Commission, social and national integration is an important objective of a national system of education. The Commission has suggested the following steps for strengthening the nation through education:
- ***The Common School System***. In the opinion of the Commission, "If our educational system is to become a powerful instrument of national development in general and social and national integration in particular, we must march towards the goal of a common school system of public education. (i) which will be open to all children irrespective of caste, creed, community, religion or social status; where access to good education will depend, not on wealth or class, but on talent; (ii) which will maintain adequate standards in all schools and provide at least a reasonable proportion of quality instruction (iii) In which no tuition fee will be charged; and (iv) Is which would meet the needs of the average parent". This system should effectively be implemented in a phased programme spread over 20 years.
- **Social and National Service.** The Commission felt that the existing educational system increases the sad gulf between the educated and the uneducated classes, between the intelligentsia and the masses. In order to eliminate this evil, the Commission, recommends that 'Some form of social and national service should be made obligatory for all students and should form an integral part of education at all stages. This can become an instrument to build character, improve discipline, inculcate faith in the dignity of manual labour and develop a sense of social responsibility." The Kothari Commission has suggested the following two main forms in which such service can be organised: (i) Encouraging and enabling students to participate in community living on the school or college campus; and (ii) Providing opportunities of participation in programmes of community development and national service.
- **Evaluation of Language Policy**. The development of a proper language policy can also assist in social and national integration.

- **Promoting National Consciousness.** According to the Commission, education must aim at promoting national consciousness by (i) Promoting understanding and re-evaluation of our cultural heritage; (ii) Creating a strong faith in future; (iii) Developing international understanding; (iv) Inculcating Democratic Values. The educational programme in schools and colleges should be designed to inculcate democratic values.
- **Education for Modernisation.** The present century has seen great advancement in scientific and technical knowledge as a result of exploration of knowledge. While the rest of the world is marching ahead in every field of human activity India cannot go limping behind. In order that India should keep pace with modernisation, the Commission has made the following suggestions: (i) Education should awaken curiosity, develop proper interests, attitudes, and build up such essential skills as independent study and capacity to think and judge for one. (ii) Education should create adequate and competent intelligentsia to meet the needs of the day.
- **Education for Social, Moral and Spiritual Values.** The national system of education should emphasise the cultivation of fundamental social, moral and spiritual values. For this purpose the Commission has suggested the following steps: *(a)* The Central and State Governments should adopt measures to introduce education in moral, social and spiritual values in all institutions under their control. This should be done on the lines recommended by the University Education Commission and Committee on Religious and Moral Instruction. The privately managed institutions should also follow on the same steps. *(b)* In order to develop social, moral and religious values, some periods should be provided in the time-table. Instruction of this type should be given by general teachers. *(c)* The University Departments of Comparative Religions should show special concern about this aspect of education. *(d)* It is necessary to promote a tolerant study of all religions so that its citizens can understand one another better and live together amicably

Core Objectives of Secondary Education

- The pupil learns to express himself comprehensibly, both orally and in writing.
- The pupil learns to adhere to conventions (spelling, grammar, use of words) and learns to appreciate the significance of these conventions.
- The pupil learns to use strategies to expand his vocabulary.
- The pupil learns to use strategies to acquire information from spoken and written texts.

- The pupil learns to find, arrange and assess information in written and digital sources, for himself and others.
- The pupil learns to participate in meetings, planning and group discussions.
- The pupil learns to give oral presentations.
- The pupil learns to read stories, poems and informative texts that are close to his sphere of interest and that help expand his perception of the environment.
- The pupil learns to structurally prepare and participate in language activities, such as speaking, listening, writing and reading.
- The pupil learns to reflect upon the way he carries out his language activities and, based upon these and the reactions by others, learns to draw conclusions in order to carry out new language activities.

EQUALITY AND SOCIAL JUSTICE

These two fundamental principles as enshrined in the Constitution imply equality and social justice towards secondary education, inside secondary education and through secondary education. It is only when the school curriculum empowers the child adequately to initially understand, then question and finally deal with that inequality and injustice, the child would be in a position to continue to seek equality and social justice in her life after the school. This is not all. We must draw attention to at least six dimensions of equality and social justice for which the school system will have to strive for viz. (a) gender; (b) economic disparity; (c) social i.e. SCs/STs; (d) Cultural (including the issues of religious and linguistic diversity); (e) disability (both physical and mental), and (f) rural-urban. All these dimensions need to be reflected with sensitivity in the curriculum such that the self-esteem of each child is built up. This is necessary for ensuring that all children are able to complete their secondary education. The issue has a structural dimension too. Almost 25% of the secondary schools today are private unaided schools whose clientele comes only from the privileged sections of society. This means that the children studying in such schools are deprived of the experience of knowing children of different social classes and diverse cultural backgrounds. It is inconceivable that such schools can inculcate a sense of equality or social justice among their students or even build up an appreciation of the composite culture and plural character of India. This anomaly can be taken care of only by including the private unaided schools in a Common School System, as recommended by the Education Commission (1964-66)

Relevance and Development:

No education today can be accepted as being relevant unless it helps in unfolding the full potential of the child; and plays the role of linking the development of the child with the society and its political, productive and socio-cultural dimensions. We would like to list five domains in which the developmental role of education can be envisaged:

- building up citizenship for a country that is striving to become a democratic, egalitarian and secular society;
- interdisciplinary approach to knowledge, concept formation (not just piling up information) and its application in daily life and attributes such as critical thought and creativity;
- evolving values in a plural society that is, at the same time, stratified and hierarchical;
- generic competencies that cut across various domains of knowledge as well as skills; and
- Skill formation in the context of rapidly changing technology which demands formation of multiple skills, transfer of learning and ability to continue to unlearn and learn.

A substantial proportion of parents send their children to schools with expectation that education will enable their children to face the 'world of work' with confidence and carve out a meaningful livelihood for themselves. For this purpose, it is essential that learning emerges from the child's social ethos and her productive experience, and at the same time ensures that the child will have access to global knowledge and challenges

Structural and Curricular Aspects

Curricular reforms cannot be delinked from structural reforms. There is a consensus today throughout the country with respect to the 10+2 pattern of school education, as recommended by the Education Commission (1964-66). The Education Commission had also advocated that a minimum of 10 years of common curriculum is required for building citizenship in a democracy and for linking the 'world of knowledge' with the 'world of work'. In this concept, diversified courses will be introduced only at the +2 stage. These recommendations related to curriculum could be implemented by all States/ UTs only because the Central Government enabled a nation-wide switchover to the 10+2 pattern. In contrast, the policy on vocational education of "diverting" at least 25% of the children enrolled at the + 2 stage to the vocational stream by the year 2000 has not found favour with students. According to the Ministry's Annual Reports, less than 5% of the enrolment at the +2 stage in the year 2003 was in vocational stream. One can infer that the children refused to be "diverted" and preferred the academic stream. The issue has been recently addressed by the National Focus Group on 'Work and Education', as constituted by NCERT, as part of the exercise of reviewing and revising the curriculum framework. The report of April 2005 recommends a two-pronged strategy with radical structural and curricular implications for the entire school education, including secondary education, viz. (a) Productive work must be introduced in the curriculum as a pedagogic medium for acquisition of knowledge, building values and skill formation from pre-primary stage to the + 2 stage; (b) A nation-wide programme of Vocational Education and Training (VET) must be built up in mission mode and be structurally and administratively placed outside the school system incorporating modular courses with lateral and vertical linkages. As long as the proposed two pronged strategy of simultaneous structural and curricular reforms is not institutionalized, it is inconceivable that the "world of work" can be meaningfully integrated with the "world of knowledge" and vocational education can become a significant and effective programme

The four guiding principles, namely universal access, equality and social justice, relevance and development, and structural and curricular aspects as guiding principles together imply a paradigm shift necessary for moving towards the goal of Universalisation of Secondary Education. This shift is expected to simultaneously impact at the level of access, socio-cultural character, developmental objectives and structural-cum-curricular provisions of secondary education - all at the same time and throughout the nation. We do not, however, envisage a change overnight but what is required is an unambiguous commitment to a policy framework that will be necessary for translating this vision on the ground. International Commission on Education for the 21st Century also mentioned human beings live in four planes namely physical, intellectual, mental and spiritual. Accordingly, future citizens of India should be physically strong and sound, intellectually competent, mentally/ emotionally matured and intelligent, and spiritually intelligent and enriched to be creative, innovative and exploring. To support education at four planes, the Commission identified four pillars of learning, namely, learning to know, learning to do, and learning to live.

VOCATIONALISATION OF SECONDARY EDUCATION

The Centrally Sponsored Scheme of Vocationalisation of Secondary Education at +2 / Higher Secondary level is being implemented since 1988. It provides for diversification of educational opportunities so as to enhance individual employability, reduce the mismatch between demand and supply of skilled manpower and provides an alternative for those pursuing higher education. The revised scheme is in operation since 1992-93. The Scheme provides for financial assistance to the States to set up administrative structure, area vocational surveys, preparation of curriculum, text book, work book curriculum guides, training manual, teacher training programme, strengthening technical support system for research and development, training and evaluation etc. It also provides financial assistance to NGOs and voluntary organizations towards implementation of specific innovative projects for conducting short-term courses. The Scheme, so far, has created infrastructure of 21000 sections in 9619 schools and creating a capacity of about 10 lakh students at + 2 level. The grants released so far since the inception of the scheme is ₹ 765 crore. Based on the recommendations of various Committees / Review Groups, the existing Scheme is being revised. The corner stone of the National Vocational Education Qualification Framework (NVEQF) is the close partnership and collaboration with the industry/ potential employers at all stages starting from identification of courses, content development, training and provision of resource persons, assessment, accreditation, certification and placement.

India's prospects of Vocationalization and Diversification of Education

In India, we believe that education is the key to the task of nation-building. It is also a well-accepted fact that providing the right knowledge and skills to the youth can ensure the overall national progress and economic growth. Combine the thought with the fact that India is a nation of young people - out of a population of above 1.1 billion, 672 million people are in the age-group 15 to 59 years - which is usually treated as the "working age population". It is also being predicted that India will see a sharp decline in the dependency ratio over the next 30 years, which will constitute a major 'demographic dividend' for India. In the year 2001, 11% of population of the country was in age group of 18-24 years which is expected to rise to 12% by the end of XI Five Year Plan. This young population should be considered as an invaluable asset which if equipped with knowledge and skills, can contribute effectively to the development of the national as well as the global economy. The vision is to realize India's human resource potential to its fullest in the education sector, with equity and inclusion. The Report of the Education Commission (1964-66) set a number of goals to be pursued. One of them was "to vocationalise secondary education." In the year 2007, Government of India announced that 1600 new industrial training institutes (ITIs) and polytechnics, 10,000 new vocational schools and 50,000 new Skill Development Centres would be opened to ensure that annually, over 100 lakh students get vocational training, which would be a four-fold increase. There are emerging shortages are there in the reservoir of skilled and trained manpower in a number of sectors. There is thus a need to expand the VET programmes to take advantage of the demographic dividend of the country and to fulfil the aspirations and right of the youth to gainful employment and contribute to national productivity.

System of Vocational Education and Training (VET) in India

The Technical and Vocational Education and Training system (TVET) in India develops human resource through a three-tier system:

- Graduate and post-graduate level specialists (e.g. IITs, NITs, engineering colleges) trained as engineers and technologists.

- Diploma-level graduates who are trained at Polytechnics as technicians and supervisors.
- Certificate-level for higher secondary students in the vocational stream and craft people trained in ITIs as well as through formal apprentice-ships as semi-skilled and skilled workers.

There are more than 17 Ministries/Departments of Govt. of India providing or funding formal/non-formal VET programmes. The total annual training capacity of VET programmes thus offered is estimated to be about 25 lakh. However there is a lot of variation among the various programmes in terms of duration, target group, entry qualifications, testing and certification, curriculum, etc. which has resulted in problems related to recognition of qualifications, equivalence and vertical mobility.

Need for Vocationalisation of Education in India

Vocational Education and Training (VET) is an important element of the nation's education initiative. In order for Vocational Education to play its part effectively in the changing national context and for India to enjoy the fruits of the demographic dividend, there is an urgent need to redefine the critical elements of imparting vocational education and training to make them flexible, contemporary, relevant, inclusive and creative. The Government is well aware of the important role of Vocational education and has already taken a number of important initiatives in this area. In India, skill acquisition takes place through two basic structural streams – a small formal one and a large informal one. Details of major formal sources are listed in table below;

Table 4.1: Details of major formal sources of skill acquisition

Type of Source	*Institute*	*Capacity*	*Quantity*
Mainstream Education system	Centrally sponsored Scheme of Vocationalisation of Secondary education run by the Ministry of HRD	Enrolling less than 3 % students at the Upper secondary level	9,583 schools offering about 150 educational courses of two years education
Training Institutions outside the school and university system	ITIs (Govt./Aided/Private)	Total seating capacity of 7.85 lakh	1922 Public & 3566 Private ITIs
Diploma Level	Polytechnics	1,244 Polytechnics run by MHRD with a capacity of 2.95 Lakhs	1,747 AICTE approved diploma programs with 294370 seats

Need for Strengthening Vocational Education Programmes

The major reforms proposed for bringing about necessary 'flexibility' in the offering of vocational courses and development of 'modular competency based curricula' in collaboration with industry to suit the needs of both target groups and the employers (industry) will be useful in reducing the shortage of skilled manpower. In addition the high dropout rate of students after Class X is significant and a cause of worry, as evident from the following statistics:

Table 4.2: Number of Schools and Students

Number of secondary schools (Class IX- X)	1,23,265
Number of higher secondary schools (Class XI –XII)	60,383
Number of students in secondary schools	2.89 crore
Number of students in higher secondary schools	1.66 crore
Projected population of 14-16 age group	4.84 crore
Projected population of 16-18 age group	4.86 crore

Source: Selected Educational Statistics (2008-09) – provisional data. Population projections are based on census data compiled by Registrar General of India.

It would be beneficial if these children, as also a large number of children who have the inclination, but are compelled to join formal secondary schooling, to be channelized into vocational education. This would lead to a system of education which is more meaningful and relevant in the local context. Gradually the ambit would be expanded to address the needs and aspirations of those engaged in traditional means of livelihoods too. The contribution of such educated youth would boost the state of the Indian economy through the thrust of the Government on universalization of secondary education, skill development and social justice through inclusive education and training.

CONTINUOUS COMPREHENSIVE EVALUATION (CCE)

NCF - 2005 has criticized that the procedures being implemented in our schools are actually suppressing the thinking capacity of children making them powerless creatures. It has raised a strong objection against the textbooks, the teaching learning procedures, and the examinations that have not been changed for years, and making the schools work with the aim of developing rote memorization. In the name of evaluation, the present examinations are testing how much information the student can retain but not his/her level of achievement of various competencies. The government have made the conduct of examinations is a very complex activity and it leads to mass copying and malpractices in the examinations as well as the results. In the view of that, NCF - 2005 has clearly stated that the aim of evaluation should be the attainment of the educational aims and goals, but not marks and ranks.

The Right to Education Act - 2009 has indicated that the government and the teachers should responsible for providing children learning experiences at school in order to improve their physical, morally ,emotional, mental, cognitive, social, and emotional development; and to achieve the academic standards specified for their class. Children's interests, attitudes and values should be developed along with school subjects. It has directed the teachers not to subject children to examination pressure, but to give them 'learning without burden', monitoring their progress through Continuous Comprehensive Evaluation, and thus work towards their all-round development. The curriculum gives equal importance to teaching learning experiences and the evaluation of the achievement of children. Evaluation conducted in schools evaluate not only the children's knowledge, but also their personality development, and is done on a continuous basis throughout the year, it is called Continuous Comprehensive Evaluation.

CONTINUOUS means not limited to any particular teaching learning process or any event or any situation, but to observe all components of learning on continuous basis. Evaluating children's physical and cognitive development in an orderly manner on a continuous basis in the school and outside the school without letting them know that they are being evaluated. By identifying the gaps in learning and by taking up remedial measures, the teacher as well as the student should be able to do self-assessment.

COMPREHENSIVE means 'All-round development' development in the children's physical, mental, ethical and cognitive domains means that treating arts, work, values, health and life skills on par with language, mathematics, science and social studies. Comprehensive evaluation gives importance to creativity, analytical skills and rational thinking in addition to knowledge, understanding and application.

Teachers, parents and the society as a whole commonly look at the evaluation from the examination point of view. The present examination system forcing the children to memorize the information given in the textbooks, making them write it in the examinations and finally awarding marks for that has become the main aim of education. This type of examinations instead of forming positive attitude towards learning and school, subject children to fear, anxiety and stress. The present evaluation system is teacher centred. Evaluation has become a examination programme that is conducted ignoring the children's interests, attitudes and competencies. In this mad race for marks, undesirable happenings are taking place giving way to meaningless competition leaving no scope for the children's emotional development and the achievement of life skills. The unit and terminal examinations conducted in the name of evaluation are only good for stamping children 'pass' or 'fail' but not to identify the learning gaps and to remediate them.

The information given in the name of 'progress cards' contains evaluation done on scholastic areas only. The co- scholastic areas and extracurricular activities like art education, work experience, value education, life-skills, moral education, peace education etc., are not given due importance. Teaching and learning is shifted away from rote methods and focusing on self-expression. There is need for the policy makers, educationalists and teachers to have a closer look at Continuous Comprehensive Evaluation and try to understand its true meaning. Children's progress should be assessed in the classroom with teaching learning processes through formative evaluation, and bid farewell to one time evaluation at the end of the year.

Since evaluation is to know children's level of achievement of academic standards, examinations should be conducted using the question papers prepared by the teacher only. Under any circumstances, teacher should not buy them or use the ones prepared at *mandal* level or school complex level. Teachers should observe and assess the children's performance while they read, write, do maths, work in groups, and participate in discussions. Teacher assesses children while they participate in teaching learning processes is called formative evaluation. When this is done comprehensively on a continuous basis, it is called Continuous Comprehensive Evaluation. All-round development means not just learning the information given in the textbooks - it is the children's physical, cognitive, emotional, social and cultural development. Present examination system is useful only to measure how much the children can remember but not to measure their competencies in various areas. Memory-based examinations will only subject children to intense stress, anxiety and depression. Since, there is a need to evaluate the children's development comprehensively on a continuous basis.

Aims and the objectives of Continuous Comprehensive Evaluation

Evaluation is not meant for memorizing information and reproducing it in examinations. It should assess the behavioural changes in children's cognitive, psycho-motor and affective domains which have been brought out by the learning experiences provided in the classroom, and help children to improve.

- To help develop cognitive, psychomotor and affective domains
- To lay emphasis on thought processes and de-emphasize memorization
- To make evaluation an integral part of teaching-learning process.
- To use evaluation for improvement of students' achievement and teaching-learning strategies, on the basis of regular diagnosis followed by remedial instructions.
- To use evaluation as a quality control device to maintain desired standards of performance.
- To determine social utility, desirability or effectiveness of a programme and take appropriate decisions about the learner, the process of learning and the learning environment.
- To make the process of teaching and learning a learner-centred activity.

Comprehensive Evaluation evaluates all components equally without maintaining the distinction between curricular and co-curricular areas. RTE has not only focused on the right to education but also on the quality of education too. RTE points out that child's knowledge, potentiality and talent, development of physical and mental abilities are to be evaluated at the fullest extent and learning through activities, discovery and exploration in a child friendly and child-centred manner. Making the child free of fear, trauma and anxiety and helping the child to express views freely. According to RTE no child shall be required to pass any board examination till completion of elementary education.

UNIVERSALIZATION OF SECONDARY EDUCATION (USE) IN INDIA

Universal implies creating universal access and opportunity for all children to receive secondary education. It is evident from the international experiences that secondary education becomes naturally universal once universal elementary education has been achieved. The transition rate from eighth to the ninth grades in India is almost 85 per cent and this transition rate is further improving. With the universalisation of elementary education through SSA, there will be universal demand for secondary education. What is important is to make good quality education available, accessible and affordable to all young persons in the age group of 14-18 years with special reference to economically weaker sections of the society, the educationally backward, the girls and the disabled children residing in rural areas and other marginalised categories like SC, ST, OBC and Educationally Backward Minorities. As stated earlier, the CABE committee on Universalisation of Secondary Education (2005) recommends universal secondary education by 2015; As per the report, the projection of enrolment, transition rate indicates full possibility of universal enrolment in secondary education by 2015. By 2020, the target should be universal enrolment, full retention and mastery learning in all kinds of learning tasks by more than 60% learners. Also, by 2020, there will be provision for universal senior secondary education and universal retention. This will be possible because of high transition rate from 10th to 11th standard and high retention rate in the senior secondary grades even now.

Secondary education serves as a link between the elementary and higher education, and plays a very important role in this respect. A child's future can depend a lot on the type of education she/he receives at the secondary level. Apart from grounding the roots of education of a child, secondary education can be instrumental in shaping and directing the child to a bright future. This stage of education serves to move on higher secondary stage as well as to provide generic competencies that cut across various domains of knowledge as well as skills.

Providing secondary education to all, both boys and girls, with a focus on quality education assumes greater meaning today, when we consider the emerging challenges in our society. For instance, rising levels of socioeconomic aspirations and also the democratic consciousness particularly among marginalized sections of population such as the *dalits*, tribals, OBCs, religious and linguistic minorities and girls seek space in the secondary education system for greater access, participation and quality. The recent significant development viz., Universal Elementary Education (UEE) being achieved through *Sarva Shiksha Abhiyan* (SSA) and also the impact of globalisation and rapid growth of new technologies have led to reassessment of India's preparedness to generate required technical manpower, develop new knowledge and skills, and remain competitive at global level. The secondary and higher secondary education system has a key role to play in enabling the nation to move towards these objectives.

Given the high transition rate of about 85% from class VIII to IX and the anticipated progress in UEE, which is now widely acknowledged, that the time has arrived for taking proactive measures to plan and provide for universal access to secondary education and senior secondary education in a phased-wise manner. A sub-committee of Central Advisory Board of Education (CABE), which is the highest deliberative and advisory forum on education in the country, was, therefore, constituted in September, 2004. This Committee (2005) was assigned with a responsibility of preparing a blueprint for the universalisation of secondary education consequent upon the attainment of universalisation of elementary education. Deliberating widely on the concerns and challenges of secondary education in India, the Committee submitted its report in June, 2005. Their major recommendations are as follows:

- The guiding principles of Universal Secondary Education should be universal access, equality and social justice, relevance and development, and structural and curricular considerations. There have to be norms for schooling. Such norms should be developed for each state with common national parameters as well as state specific parameters.
- Each state should develop a perspective plan for universal secondary education. Decentralised micro-level planning should be the main approach to planning and implementation of universal secondary education.
- Financial requirements for covering the cost of universal elementary and secondary education will form approximately 5.1 percent of the GDP which is not sufficient. The immediate allocation of 6 percent of the GDP for education and progressive increase in this proportion will be necessary to move towards universalisation of secondary education.

Guiding Principles of USE: For achieving the goal to provide quality education to all adolescents both girls and boys, up to the age of 16 by 2015 and senior secondary education up to the age of 18 by 2020, secondary education system needs to strengthen its preparedness for the coming plan periods allowing a paradigm shift in its conceptual design. The four guiding principles for creating the conceptual design of secondary education as visualized by this are reproduced under:

(1) ***Universal Access*****:** Access is to be envisaged in physical, social, cultural and economic terms – all interwoven in a common concept. This calls for a redefinition of some of the basic features of the Indian school. For instance, it is not sufficient to provide physical access to an orthopedically disabled child. It is equally critical that the disability of such a child is not seen in medical terms alone. The moment a barrier-free physical access is provided, this child's disability disappears and she/he becomes as capable as the rest of her/his peers. In this sense, the disability is a social construct and the matter does not end by solving the problem at the physical level alone but demands a change in the mindsets of her/his classmates, teachers and the curriculum planners or textbook writers. Similarly, in the case of a *dalit* child, access is as much a cultural question as it is one of a school being available in the neighbourhood. There are poignant accounts of how alienating and humiliating school experience can be for children of the deprived sections of society. This kind of alienation is equally visible in gender discrimination as it operates as a 'hidden curriculum' all the time as an extension of patriarchy embedded in society. In these circumstances, children don't just 'drop out' voluntarily, but either they are 'pushed out' or even 'walk out' in protest. It is only when the school is able to create a new cultural ambience and a child friendly curriculum that universal access would begin to mean more than just concrete, black boards or even computers.

(2) ***Equality and Social Justice:*** These two fundamental principles as enshrined in the Constitution imply equality and social justice towards secondary education, inside secondary education and through secondary education. It is only when the school curriculum empowers the child adequately to initially understand, then question and finally deals with that inequality and injustice, the child would be in a position to continue to seek equality and social justice in her life after the school. This is not all. We must draw attention to at least six dimensions of equality and social justice for which the school system will have to strive for viz. (a) gender; (b) economic disparity; (c) social i.e. SCs/ STs; (d) Cultural (including the issues of religious and linguistic diversity); (e) disability (both physical and mental), and (f) rural-urban. All these dimensions need to be reflected with sensitivity in the curriculum such that the self-esteem of each child is built up. This is necessary for ensuring that all children are able to complete their secondary education. The issue has a structural dimension too. Almost 25% of the secondary schools today are private unaided schools whose clientele comes only from the privileged sections of society. This means that the children studying in such schools are deprived of the experience of knowing children of different social classes and diverse cultural backgrounds. It is inconceivable that such schools can inculcate a sense of equality or social justice among their students or even build up an appreciation of the composite culture and plural character of India. This anomaly can be taken care of only by including the private unaided schools in a Common School System, as recommended by the Education Commission (1964-66).

(3) ***Relevance and Development*:** No education today can be accepted as being relevant unless it (a) helps in unfolding the full potential of the child; and (b) plays the role of linking the development of the child with the society and its political, productive and socio-cultural dimensions. We would like to list five domains in which the developmental role of education can be envisaged: (a) building up citizenship for a country that is striving to become a democratic, egalitarian and secular society; (b) interdisciplinary approach to knowledge, concept formation (not just piling up information) and its application in daily life and attributes such as critical thought and creativity; (c) evolving values in a plural society that is, at the same time, stratified and hierarchical; (d) generic competencies that cut across various domains of knowledge as well as skills; and (e) skill formation in the context of rapidly changing technology which demands formation of multiple skills, transfer of learning and ability to continue to learn. A substantial proportion of parents send their children to schools with expectation that education will enable their children to face the 'world of work' with confidence and carve out a meaningful livelihood for themselves. For this purpose, it is essential that learning emerges from the child's social ethos and her productive experience, and at the same time ensures that the child will have access to global knowledge and challenges.

(4) ***Structural and Curricular Aspects:*** Curricular reforms cannot be delinked from structural reforms. There is a consensus today throughout the country with respect to the 10+2 pattern of school education, as recommended by the Education Commission (1964-66). The Education Commission had also advocated that a minimum of 10 years of common curriculum is required for building citizenship

in a democracy and for linking the 'world of knowledge' with the 'world of work'. In this concept, diversified courses will be introduced only at the +2 stage. These recommendations related to curriculum could be implemented by all States/ UTs only because the Central Government enabled a nation-wide switchover to the 10+2 pattern. In contrast, the policy on vocational education of "diverting" at least 25% of the children enrolled at the + 2 stage to the vocational stream by the year 2000 has not found favour with students. According to the Ministry's Annual Reports, less than 5% of the enrolment at the + 2 stage in the year 2003 was in vocational stream. One can infer that the children refused to be "diverted" and preferred the academic stream. The issue has been recently addressed by the National Focus Group on 'Work and Education', as constituted by NCERT, as part of the exercise of reviewing and revising the curriculum framework. The above report (April 2005) recommends a two-pronged strategy with radical structural and curricular implications for the entire school education, including secondary education, viz. (a) Productive work must be introduced in the curriculum as a pedagogic medium for acquisition of knowledge, building values and skill formation from pre-primary stage to the + 2 stage; (b) A nation-wide programme of Vocational Education and Training (VET) must be built up in mission mode and be structurally and administratively placed outside the school system incorporating modular courses with lateral and vertical linkages. As long as the proposed two-pronged strategy of simultaneous structural and curricular reforms is not institutionalised, it is inconceivable that the "world of work" can be meaningfully integrated with the "world of knowledge" and vocational education can become a significant and effective programme. Hence, the four guiding principles, imply a paradigm shift necessary for moving towards the goal of universalisation of secondary education. This shift is expected to simultaneously impact at the level of access, socio-cultural character, developmental objectives and structural-cum-curricular provisions of secondary education - all at the same time and throughout the nation. For speedy change an unambiguous commitment to a policy framework is necessary for translating this vision on the ground.

SECONDARY EDUCATION: NATURE AND SCOPE

Education for the holistic development of the Adolescents

Secondary education spreads over the ages of 15 and 16, and then to 17 and 18 in the senior secondary grades. These are the years of adolescence, and late adolescence. These are the years of transition; indeed, most crucial years of life. There are steady and fast changes in the body structure transforming to adult form and image of life. At this age, the bodily changes take final shape and stabilise. This is also the stage of emotional transformation and maturity that swings between joy and trauma. Secondary education essentially has to be the education of the adolescence. Experiences in schooling have to be designed to be responsive to the needs of transition and stabilisation. Since large number of students is likely to transit from education to the world of work, it is also the stage of transition to work. Secondary education must foster skills of transition. Though both boys and girls experience transition, there is a special case for girls and it needs special attention. Because of prejudices, taboos and social stigma, phase of transition for girls is more difficult. Also, it will be necessary to develop a gender friendly curriculum. Contemporary secondary education concentrates primarily on learning a few subjects challenging the 'cognitive intelligence', that too largely the lower order cognition. This very approach to secondary education puts at disadvantage a large number of students because students with differential abilities and potentialities are unable to cope with the demands of the kind of education offered in secondary education; on the other hand, secondary education does not contribute and nurture children native wisdom and imagination that they bring with them to the school. For example, a child who is very good in sports is ridiculed for low scores in mathematics or geography. The future secondary education must be designed to nurture multiple abilities like linguistic or verbal ability, logical-mathematical ability, spatial ability, bodily kinesthetic or sports ability, musical ability, inter-personal ability, intra-personal ability and naturalist or environmental ability. The primary intention of designing secondary education with a purpose of holistic development of the adolescent is to ensure that a young person with musical ability can emerge as a musician, one with bodily and kinesthetic ability is able to emerge as a sportsperson, as much as the person with linguistic ability can unfold himself or herself as an orator, a writer, etc. Equally important is nurturing the logical-mathematical ability that can produce a scholar in mathematics and science and other such scholastic subjects. In absence of education designed to facilitate holistic development, children with abilities other than scientific and mathematical abilities are treated as weak and not fit for the employment market. This not only makes them underachievers but also demolishes their self-concept and self esteem. In essence, for universalisation, secondary education must offer adequate opportunity for unfolding the full potential in each student.

Curricular Structure and Course Offerings

The recommendation of the Education Commission (1964-66) for a common curriculum for until class X within the 10+2+3 framework was accepted in NPE-1968 and a major programme of shift with additional outlays was undertaken throughout the country. NPE- 1986 reiterated this pattern of education as part of the National System of Education. The National Curriculum Framework (1975) proposed a common curriculum for the ten year school, to be followed by diversification beginning at class XI for the +2 stage. This basic principle is now practiced nation-wide. The National Curriculum Frameworks prepared successively in 1988, 2000 and 2005 have continued to follow this imperative of NPE- 1986.

"However, there are views from many quarters that "the most significant reason for mass scale failure in the tenth board examination is the common curriculum and course offerings ...... nearly 80 per cent of the candidates who fail in the board examination fail in mathematics, English and science ... besides significant wastage of the educational resources, it affects self-esteem and self-concept of the students." The solution offered by these proponents to the problem of "mass scale failure in the tenth board examination" and its adverse impact on the "self esteem" of students consisted in "diversification of students into several streams of education beyond eighth standard" and offering them a "cafeteria approach" from class IX onwards. But actually the root cause of "mass scale failure" is not the common curriculum offered until class X as per NPE-1986. Instead, the cause of the failure lies in the framework in which subject knowledge is conceived, the manner in which knowledge is transacted and the evaluation parameters and the assessment procedures adopted for examining students. The right to study and succeed in basic mathematics, science, social science and languages, including English, and other mainstream subjects is as much a fundamental right of a child as to have access to and complete secondary/ senior secondary education." *(Report of the CABE Committee on USE, pg. no. 13)*

Keeping this in mind, the National Curriculum Framework – 2005 has made several radical proposals to revisit the very character of knowledge, shift to a new pedagogic approach and change the entire examination system. Such changes are urgently required in order to make sure that the nation is freed of this phenomenon of "mass scale failure" and widespread but apparent "under achievement". Without such a paradigm shift, it would not be possible to universalize secondary education either. We need to be especially concerned about the prevailing practice of not offering science or mathematics at Plus Two stage in many rural schools/ urban slums or to SCs, STs, girls or the disabled (or not providing science practical experiences at class IX-X level in backward areas), thereby forcing these children to go in for the so-called "softer" options. This practice has a significant negative impact on the aspirations of the masses for upward social mobility for their children.

Work and Education

The CABE Committee on USE expresses its deep concern with respect to the exclusionary character of education in general and secondary education in particular based upon the report (April, 2005) of the National Focus Group on Work and Education constituted by the NCERT as part of its exercise of National Curriculum Framework-2005. This is founded on the artificially instituted dichotomy between work and knowledge (also reflected in the widening gap between school and society). Those who work with their hands and produce significant wealth are denied access to formal education while those who have access to formal education not only denigrate productive manual work but also lack the necessary skills for the same. Accordingly, the Committee recommends the following two-fold strategy for a major curricular reform: (1) Productive work (and other forms of work as well, including social action and engagement) may be introduced as a pedagogic medium for *knowledge acquisition, developing values and multiple-skill formation.*

Common Core Curriculum

A common core curriculum incorporating work-centered pedagogy initially until Class X and, within the foreseeable future, up to Class XII for all children, should be the objective. A set of work-related generic competencies (basic, inter-personal and systemic) may be pursued and also inform the redesigning of evaluation parameters as well as the assessment system, including the public examinations. Generic competencies will include, among others, critical thinking, transfer of learning, creativity, communication skills, aesthetics, work motivation, work ethic of collaborative functioning and entrepreneurship-cum-social accountability. This will provide a firm foundation for building up a programme of '*Vocationalised Education*' (to be distinguished from '*Vocational* Education') at the secondary/ senior secondary stages. (2) Vocational Education and Training (VET) may be conceived as a *major national programme in the mission mode* and be structurally and administratively placed *outside* the school system.

VET in this new perspective will be built upon the *bedrock of 10-12 years of work-centred education in the school system*, unlike the prevailing notion of vocational education 'hanging' in vacuum. VET will include (a) flexible and modular certificate/ diploma courses of varying durations; (b) multiple entry and exit points with in-built credit accumulation facility; (c) vertical and horizontal linkages with the academic, vocational and technical programmes; (d) accessibility all the way from the level of village clusters to the Block and District levels, and also in urban areas; (e) provision for carving out 'work benches' in the neighbourhood out of the existing economic activities, production and technical centers; (f) scope for engaging local farmers, artisans, mechanics, technicians, musicians, artists and other service providers as Resource Persons or invited faculty; and (g) a decentralised accreditation and equivalence programme which will also recognise 'work benches' for the purpose of evaluating and certifying students." The Committee wishes to emphasise that the above proposal to institutionalise work-centered pedagogy in the school curriculum and building Vocational Education and Training as a programme of national significance for the adolescents and youth can be translated on the ground only if the necessary systemic changes are made. Let us not hesitate in fulfilling this historical expectation.

Common School System

The Education Commission (1964-66) had recommended a Common School System of Public Education (CSS) as the basis of building up the National System of Education with a view to "bring the different social classes and groups together and thus promote the emergence of an egalitarian and integrated society." The Commission warned that "instead of doing so, education itself is tending to increase social segregation and to perpetuate and widen class distinctions." It further noted that "this is bad not only for the children of the poor but also for the children of the rich and the privileged groups" since "by segregating their children, such privileged parents prevent them from sharing the life and experiences of the children of the poor and coming into contact with the realities of life. . . . . . also render the education of their own children *anaemic and incomplete*." The Commission contended that "if these evils are to be eliminated and the education system is to become a powerful instrument of national development in general, and social and national integration in particular, we must move towards the goal of a common school system of public education."

The 1986 policy, while advocating a National System of Education, resolved that "effective measures will be taken in the direction of the Common School System recommended in the 1968 policy." Taking into consideration these policy imperatives and the contemporary emphasis on decentralisation along with the necessary flexibility in the school system to be able to respond to the contextual curricular demands, the concept of the Common School System (CSS) has itself been evolving. Based upon the evolving public discourse on CSS, the following definition of CSS can be constructed:

- **Common school system** essentially means a national system of education which is based on the values and principles of the Constitution of India which provides education as a comparable quality to all children irrespective of their caste, creed, language, economic or cultural background, geographic location or gender. This is the perspective articulated by the National Policy on Education-1986 and further elaborated by the National Curriculum Framework-2005. Such a national system of education will be governed by certain minimum infrastructural, financial and curricular norms. For instance, in the context of the recruitment and working conditions of teachers, provision for basic resources, and structural flexibility and academic autonomy necessary for innovation are concerned with the spirit of National Policy on Education and the National Curriculum Framework 2005.

As per the report of the CABE committee on USE the guiding principles and basic characteristics of a successful programme of Universalisation of Secondary Education are fully consistent with the Common School System as defined above. The CABE committee report clearly mentions that the kind of paradigm shift discussed here can become sustainable only when it is implemented in all categories of schools, including the privately managed unaided schools, in the whole of the country within a declared timeframe, though a properly phased programme. This essential linkage between curricular reforms and systemic reforms must be understood, before it is too late. And such reforms would be feasible only within the framework of a Common School System.

Three-Language Formula

The *three-language formula* evolved out of a major political exercise and negotiations in the critical decade of 1950s and the early years of 1960s in response to the rising tensions with respect to different language regions of the country and the question of related cultural identities. In essence, this outcome reflected the federal spirit of our Constitution and the commitment to sustain and promote India's plural character. It is in this background that the 1986 policy made a commitment to implement the three-language formula "more energetically and purposefully".

NCF-2005 also reiterates this position and proposes to make a renewed bid to fulfil the commitment. While, as part of this formula, a crucial responsibility befalls upon the elementary stage of education to promote the mother tongue as a medium of education, it is the secondary/senior secondary stage of education that becomes the real testing ground of the more challenging aspects of the formula. The 1986 policy also acknowledged the "uneven" implementation of the formula. The Hindi-speaking states, with their substantial demographic spread, have a special responsibility in responding to this challenge, especially with respect to the concept of the third language as a modern Indian language from a non-Hindi speaking region. Concrete steps in this direction will provide a new thrust for the non-Hindi speaking states to make a fresh commitment to implement the language policy in letter and spirit. It is here that the political commitment made by the nation's leadership soon after independence to strengthen India's unity and integrity, promote intercultural dialogue and build an enlightened and articulate citizenship, will be redeemed. In this context, the Committee would like to urge upon the Central Government to take the initiative of setting up an effective and adequately funded structure and process for promoting inter-language translation of the highest quality material available in different languages of India. An active role of the States/UTs will be critical to the success of this central initiative. This process must also cover the word class material available globally in the languages of different countries and make it available widely in all major

Indian languages. India's capacity in the field of IT should prove to be of special asset in this respect, provided urgent political will addresses this issue.

It would be only appropriate if this inter-language endeavour would include Braille and computer-aided facilities for making quality material available to the disabled children also. Apart from enriching communication and understanding among different language regions of the country, the availability of such material in Indian languages will go a long way in enriching the quality of education not just at the secondary/ senior secondary education level but at the higher education level as well.

Teaching –Learning Processes

Curricular structure and course offerings are the necessary condition for quality secondary education. Instructional processes provide the sufficient condition for quality secondary education. Contemporary pedagogical practices are characterised largely by lectures where students are passive listeners. Such kind of processes contribute at best to lower order cognition, memorization and fragile learning; together, they make a grand nexus for large-scale failing in examination. Students lack problem-solving ability, higher order thinking and cognition, and creativity. Most importantly, they miss out on 'learning to know' or learning to learn. If the new generation secondary education sets its targets for students to be able to think critically, solve problems individually and collectively, be creative, teaching-learning must undergo a paradigm shift. Pedagogy must bring students at the centre of stage where they primarily learn to learn through peer interaction, problem-solving, experiential learning, etc. In this new learning scenario, teachers will be facilitators of learning. Research as a tool for learning is quite common all over the world; introduced even at the pre-primary stage. Indeed, by the time students are in the 9th and 10th standards they should become researchers to be able to crack problems, contemplate solutions, explore and experiments alternative and creative ways of problem-solving.

Student Assessment and Evaluation

Secondary education is the turning point for a large majority of students. Not only the certificate one earns after schooling but also the actual learning during schooling is the lifelong resource. Along with building dynamism in curricular framework as well as pedagogy, evaluation must undergo major changes. Conventionally, education system, particularly school education is guided and controlled by concern for results in examination irrespective of the quality of learning - whether fragile or sustainable. The competition, though artificial, for securing percentage of marks in the final examination creates unusual stress in the students leading often to mental break down and suicides. This must change. Change in the mechanics of examination will be too simplistic a solution, amounting to treating the symptoms, not the disease itself. Examination-stress is directly related to facing the challenge of examination with 'fragile' learning due to memorizing huge stock of information. In order to manage the stress factor in examination it will be necessary to ensure sustainable learning which the function of instructional processes is. Yet, it will be necessary to reconstruct and redesign examination system with attributes like flexibility where a student can achieve mastery learning in a flexible time frame and accumulate credits; eliminating power tests (fixed duration), adopt continuous and comprehensive evaluation. The practice of mark sheets indicating marks in certain subjects must be replaced by a portfolio that would accommodate a student's performance in a variety of domains like life skills, academic/non-academic and vocational subjects, personal qualities, etc. The portfolio should be comprehensive, revealing of the total being of the student.

Guidance and Counselling

In this context, it is extremely important to recognise the role that guidance and counselling play for meeting the needs of adolescent students going through the secondary and higher secondary stages of education. Provision for guidance and counselling is necessary in view of the fact that adolescent boys and girls are facing a fast process of socio-economic and cultural change, and quite often the traditional institutional frameworks provided by the family and community are not adequate for helping the adolescent to cope with the demands made upon him/her. In a society going through a rapid process of institutional change and modernization, facilities for guidance and counselling in every secondary school are necessary. Even as the secondary education system expands towards universalisation, staff for guidance and counselling will be required to ensure that first generation school goers receive adequate coverage in terms of their psychological and personality related needs. Financial allocation necessary for making guidance and counselling a common reality of every secondary school will need to be worked out, and institutional infrastructure necessary for making professional input for such a facility will have to be put in place.

Schooling Facility

There is a lot of disparity in schooling facilities in various regions of the country. There are disparities among the private schools, among private and government schools in the same state, between schools in central sector like Kendriya Vidyalayas (KVS), Navodaya Vidyalayas (NVS), Tibetan Schools, Sainik Schools, etc. Also, there are no specific norms for secondary schools. In view of providing universal quality secondary education, it is imperative that specially designed norms are developed at the national level and then disaggregated for each State/UT keeping in mind the geographical, socio-cultural, linguistic and demographic conditions of not just the State/UT but also, wherever necessary, of the Blocks. Also, the disparities among various categories of schools must be reduced. This will require planning of educational facilities, and management of educational services to be streamlined.

Rashtriya Madhyamik Shiksha Abhiyaan (RMSA)

As a follow-up of the recommendations of the CABE Committee report, the MHRD has launched a scheme for universalisation of access to and improvement of quality at secondary stage in the year 2009 and has brought out a "Framework of implementation of *Rashtriya Madhyamik Shiksha Abhiyaan*". The framework provides a detailed road map for the implementation of access and equity related components of USE and also deliberates upon quality components providing norms largely for infrastructure requirements. Hence, a need was observed by various stakeholders for a document, which provides a vision and multi-layer strategic guidelines on quality improvement of secondary education. The present document on "Vision and Multi-layer Strategic Guidelines for Quality Improvement in secondary education" begins with vision as already set by the CABE report and the RMSA framework and moves ahead to address the quality issues with suggested strategies and action plans.

SECONDARY EDUCATION IN INDIA – VISION

Since Free and Compulsory Elementary Education has become a Constitutional Right of Children in India, it is absolutely essential to push this vision forward to move towards Universalisation of Secondary Education, which has already been achieved in a large number of developed and several developing countries. In this context, the vision for secondary education as follows: ***The vision for secondary education is to make good quality education Available, Accessible and Affordable to all young persons in the age group of 14-18 years.*** (RMSA Framework, MHRD, 2009). This vision statement points out towards three A's i.e. Availability, Accessibility and Affordability of secondary education to the target group under the overarching objective of providing quality. India is emerging as the fastest-growing economy in the world. The success depends largely upon human resource development. If we look at the Indian higher education as provider of leadership-manpower in various sectors of economy, we need to tune our secondary education to emerge as the single largest provider of working people in all spheres of national productivity. Universalisation of secondary education will need to fulfil three major criteria, namely, universal enrolment in the 9th and 10th grades, universal retention achieving zero dropout rate, and universal performance with successful completion by all who are enrolled in the secondary education.

Initial questions that need to be resolved are: achieving universal access, equity and social justice. Whereas universal access may be possible to achieve through expansion of schooling facilities in the formal and unconventional modes, special efforts will be required for achieving equity, social justice and performance of all the diverse groups of learners. Although success in SSA will substantially facilitate the process yet it will take at least another 10 years of committed efforts, in a mission mode approach; universal secondary education should be targeted to be achieved by 2020 and the success in accomplishing this goal will be determined by the synergy among various stakeholders for planning, implementation and execution, political will and support.

CURRENT STATUS OF SECONDARY EDUCATION AT NATIONAL AND STATE LEVEL

Secondary education serves as a bridge between elementary and higher education and prepares young person's between the age group of 14-18 for entry into higher education. The population of children in the 14-18 age group (the age for secondary and senior secondary level education) has been estimated at 96.6 million, as projected by the National Sample Survey Organisation in 1996-97. However, enrolment figures show that only 27 million children were attending secondary schools, which means that two thirds of the eligible population remains out of the secondary school system.

The number of secondary schools in India increased from 7,416 in 1950-51 to 1,16,820 in 1999-2000. However, this number is not adequate to accommodate the out-of-school children and the growing number of upper primary school pass-outs. The impact of recent initiatives undertaken for the Universalisation of Elementary Education is resulting in an increased demand for the expansion of secondary education. There has been no fundamental change in the structure and organisation of the secondary and higher secondary education system during the Ninth Plan period since the initiation of the National Policy on Education (NPE), 1986. In the wake of the Policy, several centrally-sponsored schemes were launched and national level institutions for school education were established/strengthened. Ten centrally-sponsored schemes are in operation in the secondary education sector. The experience of the implementation of the programmes as well as various reviews and evaluation studies have highlighted the need to modify and strengthen these schemes. Against a budgetary allocation of ₹ 2,603.49 crore for the sector in the Ninth Plan, the expenditure incurred has been to the tune of ₹ 2,322.68 crore.

The focus in the Ninth Plan was on reducing disparities, renewal of curricula with emphasis on vocationalisation and employment oriented courses, expansion and diversification of the open learning system, reorganisation of teacher training and the greater use of information and communication technology. Hostel facilities for girls, integrated education for the disabled, free education for girls etc. have also received attention. During this period the various Central institutes/organisations like National Council of Educational Research & Training (NCERT), National Open School (NOS), Kendriya Vidyalayas and Navodaya Vidyalayas were further strengthened. The Table 4.3 gives details of the growth of the Secondary Education Sector over the Plan periods.

Table 4.3: Growth of the Secondary Education Sector

Number of High/Higher Secondary institutions, Students and Teachers (1950-2000)

Year	High/Higher Secondary Schools/Inter/ Pre-degree/ Junior Colleges	Students (in lakh)	Teachers (in lakh)
1950-51	7416	15.0	1.27
1990-91	79796	191.0	13.34
1995-96	90134	249.0	14.93
1998-99	112438	277.6	17.47
1999-2000	116820	282.1	17.20

Source: Selected Educational Statistics, MHRD, 1999-2000

While, in terms of absolute numbers, state financing of secondary education continued to grow (though it is still inadequate), financing of secondary and higher education has shown a declining trend in terms of percentage spending on education from the Sixth Plan onwards (Table 4.4). The share of elementary education in total spending has been increasing, reflecting the priority to implement free and compulsory elementary education.

Table 4.4: Expenditure on Education in the Five Year Plans

Expenditure on Education in the Five Year Plans

(Rs. lakh)

Five Year Plans	Elementary (%)	Secondary (%)	Higher (%)	Total Expenditure
I	85(56)	20(13)	14(9)	15,300
II	95(35)	51(19)	48(18)	27,300
III	201(34)	103(18)	87(15)	58,900
IV	239(30)	140(18)	195(25)	78,600
V	317(35)	156(17)	205(22)	91,200
VI	803(30)	736(25)	530(18)	2,04,300
VII	2,849(34)	1,829(22)	1,201(14)	8,50,000
VIII	4,006.6(47)	1,538(18)	1,055.8(12.4)	8,52,190
IX	16,364.88(65.7)	2,603.5(10.5)	2500.0(10.0)	24,90,850

Note: The figures in parenthesis indicate % to total allocation.
Source: Five-Year Plans, Annual Plans and MHRD Reports.

Participation of the private sector (including non-governmental organisations or NGOs) in the management of secondary schools with official recognition and, in many cases, with financial assistance, has also increased. Private organisations currently manage around 51 per cent of secondary schools and 58 per of higher secondary schools. In order to meet the educational needs of those who have not been able to enrol themselves in the formal system, opportunities have been provided through the National and State Open Schools, utilising contact centres and multi-media packages. Distance education in the school sector also got a fillip with the National Open School was started in 1989, identifying new vocational areas and providing on-demand examination. Improvements in the content, process and quality of education, particularly environment education, science, mathematics and computer literacy have been emphasised with central financial support available for schemes related to this. New initiatives taken after the National Policy on Education was revised in 1992 include the revision of the curriculum, setting up of resource centres for value education and a National Centre for Computer-aided Education etc. Several measures taken to enrich the school curriculum are being continued with added thrust. However, the scheme of vocationalisation of education has not appealed to the stakeholders because lack of industry-institute linkages, manpower demand surveys and various academic constraints. At present, only 10 per cent of the students are opting for the vocational stream, against a target of 25 per cent by 2000.

Educational development of children with special needs received an impetus with the enactment of the Persons with Disabilities (Equal Opportunities, Protection of Rights and Full Participation) Act, 1995. The Act entrusts the appropriate governments and the local authorities to provide children with disabilities access to education, employment, preferential allotment of land for certain purposes, non-discrimination in transport, financial incentives to Universities to enable them to undertake research etc. Programmes for attitudinal changes, capacity building among teachers and training institutions to educate children with special needs have been taken up.

Along with providing opportunities for equal access and ensuring a minimum level of learning achievement for all, it is equally important to nurture talented children especially those from the rural areas and those belonging to lower income group. There are several programmes for the development of talent. Residential Jawahar Navodaya Vidyalayas from Class VI to XII are established in the Seventh Plan as model schools and to provide quality education to talented children from rural areas selected on the basis of a common admission test. Each district is supposed to have one such school. Currently, there are 462 Jawahar Navodaya Vidyalayas with about 1,25,000 students on their rolls.

The National Council of Educational Research & Training (NCERT), New Delhi, conducts a National Talent Search Examination to identify talent.

International Chemistry, Mathematics and Physics Olympiads are held every year to identify talent in these subjects. India has been participating regularly in these Olympiads.

Talented students from rural areas are provided scholarships at the secondary stage in order to develop their potential by providing them access to good schools. A total of 38,000 scholarships have been awarded to students. Internal compulsions and international commitments are forcing the secondary education system to gear up to meet the ever-increasing demand for education. Initiatives such as the externally-aided District Primary Education Programme (DPEP), the Sarva Shiksha Abhiyan, increasing number of schools in the private sector and the drive for elimination of the gender gap in line with the Dakar Declaration on Education for All in 2000. Concerted efforts, backed by national consensus, are called for to meet these daunting challenges.

The major thrust in the Tenth Plan, thus, is to meet the increased demand for secondary education. The Government has to play a greater role to the encourage opening of new secondary schools, expansion of capacity of the existing schools including double shifts, upgrading of upper primary schools in backward, un-served and underserved areas, as also expansion and diversification of open schooling and distance education system. One of the many options being considered during the Tenth Plan is for the Kendriya Vidyalaya Sangathan to establish schools in partnership with voluntary agencies. It is proposed to set up 150 Kendriya Vidyalayas in addition to the present network of 854 schools. Another option is to provide a one-time grant/seed money to societies, trusts and not-for-profit organisations like the R.K. Mission, the Jesuits, the DAV Trust, which already run reputed schools to encourage them to set up more schools.

It is proposed to establish more Navodaya Vidyalayas to cover the districts which do not have one right now and also to strengthen these existing schools by providing them facilities for cultural activities, computers and sports facilities. It is also proposed to help the Central Tibetan School Administration (CTSA), which runs about 70 schools for children of Tibetan refugees, to set up more schools.

During the Tenth Plan, the National Open School (NOS) would intensify efforts to ensure that the open school system is to the under-privileged groups. A scheme to reimburse to the NOS the fees incurred on scheduled castes/scheduled tribe (SC/ST) students, girls and physically challenged students is also on the anvil. The NOS will also be restructured to affiliate regular schools/centres, which offer NOS curriculum as an alternative to the curricula of other school Boards. The nearly 1,200 study centres are proposed to be increased by around 15 per cent per year. New admissions, which are around 200,000 students a year, is likely to increase at 20 per cent per year. The NOS proposes to implement the schemes of 'On-Demand Admissions' and 'On-Demand

Examinations', which give flexibility to the students to take admissions and examinations during mid-session.

The scheme of providing boarding and hostel facilities for girls, initiated in 1993, has already been revised in order to increase the enrolment of girls at the secondary level. The scheme provides for financial assistance to eligible voluntary organisations to improve the enrolment of adolescent girls belonging to the rural areas and weaker sections.

In order to make secondary education more relevant in the current context, the NCERT will continue to emphasise modernisation and revision of curriculum, updating of courses and vocationalisation of education. The Council would operationalise the fifth Regional Institute of Education for the North-Eastern Region at Shillong. The NCERT is conducting the nation-wide All India Educational Survey in order to strengthen the database during the Plan period.

The Central Board of Secondary Education (CBSE) and the Council for the Indian School Certificate Examination (CISCE) conduct public examinations at the end of Classes X and XII. Both are self-financing bodies, which do not receive any assistance from the government. A total of 5,850 schools are affiliated to the CBSE as on 15 April 2001 and 1,119 schools to the CISCE as on 31 August 2001. The NOS is the third national-level body conducting equivalent examination at the secondary and senior secondary level. As part of the zero-based budgeting exercise and in order to bring in greater effectiveness in the implementation of the central sector and the centrally sponsored schemes, the schemes of secondary sector have been grouped under following four broad heads :

- **Quality Improvement in Schools:** This comprises the centrally sponsored schemes of Promotion of Sciences Laboratories, Environmental Orientation to School Education, Promotion of Yoga, as well as the central sector schemes of Population Education Project, International Mathematics/ Science Olympiad. The state governments would develop training modules for in-service training of teachers and provide infrastructure and research inputs for quality improvement in schools.
- **Information and Communication Technologies (ICT):** This will include the reworked centrally sponsored schemes - Computer Education and Literacy in Schools (CLASS) and Educational Technology (ET) – which seek to familiarise students with IT. Keeping in view the current demand for IT, a major thrust is to be given to this scheme. State governments would prepare Computer Education Plans (CEP) for computer literacy and education. The components of the merged scheme ICT in Schools would include

(a) funding support for CEPs; (b) strengthening and reorientation of the staff of the State Institutes of Education and Training (SIETs); (c) Digitalisation of SIETs' video and audio cassettes in partnership with NGOs; (d) web/internet-based education to be managed by the SIETs.

- **Access and Equity:** This scheme will comprise, among other components yet to be designed, the ongoing scheme of Strengthening of Hostel/Boarding Facilities for Girl students.
- **Integrated Education for Disabled Children (IEDC):** In the Tenth Plan, greater efforts will be made to expand inclusive education to cater to the needs of mentally and physically challenged students. The scheme will continue as a separate centrally sponsored scheme and will be redesigned. It will now focus on the following elements: (1) Convergence with the Integrated Child Development Services (ICDS) scheme for early interventions; with the DPEP and Sarva Shiksha Abhiyan for education of the mentally and physically challenged up to the elementary level; with the special schools under the Ministry of Social Justice and Empowerment. Other components of the scheme will be inclusive pedagogy and curriculum, training of teachers and preparation of teaching learning material; research and development (R&D), advocacy and evaluation; and funding through the PTAs/VECs/ management committees of the schools.

Conclusion

The impact of recent initiatives undertaken for the universalisation of elementary education is resulting in increased demand for expansion of secondary education. Unless steps are taken to expand the secondary education system, it would be difficult to accommodate the increasing number of upper primary pass-outs. While there has been an increase in the number of secondary schools, the spread has been uneven; there are regional disparities and variations in the socio-economic status of various states and Union Territories. The significant gender gap also has to be narrowed down. The on-going efforts in revision of curricula at the secondary education level, so as to make it more relevant, would continue in the Tenth Plan. The convergence of centrally sponsored schemes will help in imparting science, mathematics and, computer education as well as environmental and value education in a more focused manner. There is a line of thinking which believes that subsidising students through a 'voucher system', as is the practice in some of the Latin American countries, is more effective than 'subsidising' institutions. The students will enrol themselves in reputed schools, letting the market forces weed out the inefficient and poor quality institutions.

References

Krishnan, D.K., & Thamarasseri, I. (2013). *Contemporary Issues in Indian Education.* New Delhi: Kanishka Publishers

Thamarasseri, I. (2007). *Education in the Emerging Indian Society.* New Delhi: Kanishka Publishers

Thamarasseri, I. (2011). *Current Developments in Indian Education.* New Delhi: Kanishka Publishers

Thamarasseri, I. (2014). *Issues and Challenges of Indian Education.* Agra: Shri Vinod Pustak Mandir

Thamarasseri, I. (2014). *National Goals and Education.* New Delhi: Discovery Publishing House (P) Ltd.

UNIT - 5

Factors and Influences of National Education System

Introduction

A national system of education is often defined from the perspective of formal education system. This includes institutionalized formal education from early childhood education, primary education, secondary education, tertiary education and university education. The informal and non-formal education subsets are often assumed to be part of the formal education and if not ignored altogether, they are given little attention. However, it is important the national educational system should be wholly inclusive of all the subsets of the educational system, that is, formal, informal and non-formal education.

In light of this simple understanding of a national system of education, it is important to note that, behind every system of education, there are factors or features that determine or influence and hence shape each one of the system. However, the national character of a given system of education is never determined by one factor, but rather a combination and interweaving of several factors. Some factors are dominant in one particular system while in another system, they would be less dominant. Consequently national factors of a country are closely related with nationalism and national system of education. As such, in the study of comparative education we should study the factors which make the education of a country national. These factors include geographical, economic, social, cultural, historical, religions, political, language and technological. In this chapter we shall study some such factors.

IMPACT OF PHILOSOPHICAL FACTORS ON DEVELOPMENT OF EDUCATION SYSTEM

The education system of a country is influenced by the philosophy of the land. Philosophy influences life, therefore, its influence on education is quite natural. For example, in ancient Greece, Socrates, Plato and Aristotle based the educational system of the country on a particular philosophy of life and entrusted the administration of the country to philosophers. In China today, the educational system is based on communist philosophy.

In ancient India the *Gurukul* system of education was based on Vedic philosophy of life. The educational system in the Buddhist period as obtained in *Vihars* and monasteries based on Buddhist philosophy.

The Dayanand Anglo Vedic Colleges of modem India are based on the philosophy of life propounded by Swami Dayanand Saraswati. Similarly, there are some institutions based on Sri Aurobindo's philosophy.

In modern India, some people are advocating a special system of education based on the Sarovodaya philosophy of Gandhiji and Vinoba Bhave. Thus the philosophical factor is a very important factor in the study of comparative education.

Philosophy influences every aspect of education namely the aim, content, method and discipline. It is philosophy which determines whether the aim of education should be intellectual, spiritual, liberal, aesthetic, moral or vocational. For example, the Hindu philosophy in ancient India resulted in the evolution of the *Gurukula* system of education. The militant philosophy ancient Sparta gave rise to the regimental system of education. The Nazism of Germany gave rise to the Fanatic, anti-Jewish system of education.

Philosophy influences the methodology too. Naturalistic philosophy emphasizes child-centered methods, idealism emphasis Socratic and lecture methods while pragmatism emphasis the project method.

In the case of curriculum, naturalists start with present experiences and interests of children. Idealists stress the study of religion, culture ethics and literature. Pragmatists advocate the study of functional subjects which have utility value.

Philosophy influences the discipline in education. Autocratic philosophy leads to expressionism, idealism leads to impressionism, naturalism leads to emancipation and modern pragmatism leads to free discipline.

The teacher must possess a sound philosophy of life. He/she must be a lover of wisdom, a seeker of knowledge and man/women of virtues/values. Then only he/she can bring about desirable changes in his/her pupils.

Inter-Dependence of Philosophy and Education

The chief task of philosophy is to determine 'what constitutes a life worth living'. The chief task of education is 'to make life worth living'. Therefore the relationship between philosophy and education is very close. Philosophy tells the goal and essentials of good life. Education tells the means to achieve those goals and learn those essentials of good life. Philosophy deals with abstract; education deals with the concrete. All great philosophers are great educators. Fichte said that; "The art of education will never attain complete clearness without philosophy". James Ross said that; "Education is the dynamic side of philosophy". John Dewey: "Philosophy is the theory of education in its most general phases".

Philosophy and Aims of Education

Aims, goals, ends or objectives of education are the first essentials of any educational system. Without them the whole educative process would be meaningless. Aims of education depend on the philosophy that prevails at the time of determining the aims of education. That is why they have been charging with the changing philosophy of life. 'No System of education', says Acharya J.B. Kripalini, the noted Gandhian philosopher, "Can be properly appraised, and appreciated, unless it is studied in connection with the ideas and ideals which it represents".

Philosophy and Curriculum

The need of philosophy of education felt very seriously in the area of curriculum planning. The philosophical approach to life is the guiding factors in the choice of students to be included in the curriculum.

Philosophies of Education and Curriculum

Meaning of Curriculum: The curriculum is the sum total of the schools efforts to influence learning, whether in the classroom or in the playground, or out of school: K.G. Saiyidain; "The curriculum is primarily an aid in the process of adjusting the child to the environment in which he functions from day to day and in the environment in which he will have to organize his activities late". The concept of the curriculum differs with different schools of philosophy.

Philosophy and Methods

Methodology of teaching establishes a contact of the teacher, the taught and the subject. It raises many problems. All such questions and the problems that arise in the classroom techniques are satisfactorily tackled by philosophy. Sarvodaya- A socialist philosophy, is a culmination of Indian idealistic thought. Its foundation have deep roots in the Indian soil, but it is different from Indian philosophies. Our philosophies were individualistic. Sarvodaya, Its basis in the socio-economic conditions of the present day world, is aimed at the 'good of all' presents a synthesis of all good points in different Indian and western philosophies of life. "Correlation of studies" is the main principle of Sarvodaya method. It develop an integrated personality. **The philosophical method** is not absolutely different from scientific method. Philosophical problems have much in common with the scientific problems. The philosopher utilizes the same method of induction and deduction as used by scientist.

- *Induction*: The principles of different sciences are arrived at by means of inductive process. The philosopher utilizes concepts and propounds new theories. E.g. materialism, idealism etc. And then he tries to explain his experiences satisfactorily on the basis of these theories.
- *Deduction*: Deduction is the process to arrive at certain particular prepositions from a general prepositions.
- *Dialectical method*: This is the natural method of philosophical thinking. This is a common place experience that when we think over a problem we arrive at certain positive facts. That is *thesis*. Now after sometimes we came to know some facts which are contradictory to thesis that is *anti-thesis*. This thesis and anti-thesis cannot live together for a long, hence they are synthesized into a *synthesis*. This synthesis arrived through anti-thesis is more comprehensive than the original thesis. Thus knowledge grows in a dialectical process through thesisà anti-thesisà synthesis. This method was developed by Hegal.
- *Analysis*: Analysis means the process of distinction between different elements evolved in a particular state of experience, so that, they might be more clear. Realistic philosophers have emphasized this procedure while absolutists have advanced arguments against it.
- *Synthesis*: This method involves connecting together the scattered elements in a particular experience which brings into light new patterns and facts. The idealist philosophers have laid emphasis on synthesis.

Relationship of Education and various area of National Life and various Components of the System of Education

One of the most important contributions of the philosophy of education to the cause of education is the provision of criteria for deciding the relationship of state and education, economic system and education, curriculum, school organization and management, discipline etc. These problems have led to the evaluation of different philosophies of education. The criteria of judgment everywhere are determined by philosophy; therefore, philosophy of education provides the criteria for critical evaluation and judgment in these fields.

Philosophy of education of a Country performs various functions. They are discussed below:

- **Determining the aims of education:** Philosophy of education provides original ideas regarding all aspects of education particularly educational aims. It is said that educational philosophy gives different views, but this situation is not harmful, rather it helps in providing education according to the need of society. The difference in view of philosophy of education reflects the multiplicity and diversities of human life. Philosophy of education guides the process of education by suggesting suitable aims from the diversities of life and selecting the means accordingly.

- **Harmonizing old and new traditions in the field of education:** In the process of social development the old traditions become outdated for the people. They are replaced by the new traditions. But this process of replacement is not always smooth. It is faced with lots of opposition from certain orthodox sections of the society. At the same time it must be kept in mind that every 'old' is not outdated and every 'new' is not perfect Therefore, there is a need of co-coordinating the two in order to maintain the harmony between both. This function can be performed by philosophy of education.
- **Providing the educational planners, administrators and educators with the progressive vision to achieve educational development:** Herbert Spencer has rightly pointed that only a true philosopher can give a practical shape to education. Philosophy of education provides the educational planners, administrators and educators with the right vision which guides them to attain the educational goals efficiently.
- **Preparing the young generation to face the challenges of the modern time:** Social commentators have given many labels to the present period of history for some it is the information age and for others it is post modernity, later modernity, high modernity or even the age of uncertainty. One more addition to this list may be that 'present age is an age of Globalization as a phenomenon arrived on the economic scene in the 1990 in India. This watchword has had its implications in the social political, economic fabric of the country of which education is a part. Philosophy of education is a guiding, steering and liberating force that helps young people to and society at large to face the challenges of the modern time.

IMPACT OF RELIGIOUS FACTORS ON DEVELOPMENT OF EDUCATION SYSTEM

The influence of religion is very powerful as it penetrates the emotional depth of human nature. The *Brahmanic* system of education, the Buddhist education, medieval Islamic education were dominated by religion. In Europe the protestant countries were wedded to the education of the masses and the catholic countries to the education of the classes.

Religious loyalties also dictate aims, content and even methods of instruction in education. Indeed, religion and beliefs have also been known to influence and shape aspects in education system.

In Africa, European Christian Missionaries did influence and continue to influence the education system. The initiative taken by the Christian churches to extend education and their power to control development often explains many of the common elements which can be discerned in education systems in countries that were colonized by the Europeans. For examples schools days are from Monday to Friday and resting days are Saturday and Sunday. This is more so because some people have their worship days as Saturday and others on Sunday.

Religious organizations have also been and are still involved in educational development through building of educational institutions. For example, the catholic Jesuits succeeded in building up some of the greatest systems of secondary and higher education institution known in history. There is currently a catholic university establish in Kenya besides many catholic sponsored primary and secondary schools. The Muslim faithful also have their own establish institutions of learning as well as other religious groups such as the Hindus, Buddhists.

In Africa, the present systems of education have been influenced by the work which was initiated by European Christian missionaries who included Catholics, Protestant and Muslim. All these have influenced features in the education system in the areas, they occupied. Most current is that the primary and secondary curriculums have religious subjects being taught in schools in Kenya.

Religion has played an important part in the development of education ever since the beginning, even before the creation of schools. The first schools, which were monasteries, started around the Dark Ages, approximately 450 A.D.; Back then, education's only purpose was to people of the religious persuasion, especially Christianity. Christianity is the religion that has most affected education, and so was the case back then, too. The pope commanded more respect and authority than the king, the church taxed the people, and the church dictated the laws of the land.

Religion occupies a very important place in an individual's life. History is testimony of the fact that thousands of persons have sacrificed their lives for the sake of religion. The history of Europe is full of such examples. In a religious country, the public is generally conservative and resents any change in its old traditions.

Therefore in the organisation of an educational system we have to be careful about the religious sentiments of the people. In an industrialised country, due to scientific developments, old traditions usually begin to break-down and the society is re-constructed according to the needs of the time. Education has to pay a special role in this reconstruction.

But opposite to this, in an agricultural country, the public is conservative and views any change with suspicion and it wants to preserve its religious traditions intact. Accordingly the educational system has to be organised. Needless to remark that the religious sentiments of the people have to be honoured in any educational system.

Therefore, the religious factor cannot be ignored in the study of comparative education. Indeed, a comparative discussion of how different religious loyalties have given birth to various educational systems in different countries of the world will be very interesting.

Now we shall understand some such factors which may be regarded as results of scientific developments in the world. These factors are those of socialism, humanism, nationalism and democracy. The influence of these factors on education came to surface from the beginning of the modern age.

Religion and education, two of humankind's most ancient endeavours, have long had a close relationship. Historians and social scientists have written about this relationship and about how the two may influence each other. Religion is certainly not the only reason for this variance; many other factors may play an equal or greater role, including economic, geographic, cultural factors and political conditions within a country or region.

Looking to the past

Contemporary access to schooling – a solid pathway to educational attainment – depends on a country's educational infrastructure. In many instances, the foundations of that infrastructure are based on facilities originally built by religious leaders and organizations to promote learning and spread the faith.

In India, the most learned men and women of ancient times were residents of Buddhist and Hindu monasteries. In the Middle East and Europe, Christian monks built libraries and, in the days before printing presses, preserved important earlier writings produced in Latin, Greek and Arabic. In many cases, these religious monasteries evolved into universities.

Other universities, particularly in the United States and Europe, were built by Christian denominations to educate their clergy and lay followers. Most of these institutions have since become secular in orientation, but their presence may help explain why populations in the U.S. and Europe are highly educated.

Apart from their roles in creating educational infrastructure, religious groups were foundational in fostering societal attitudes toward education.

Islam

There is considerable debate among scholars over the degree to which Islam has encouraged or discouraged secular education over the centuries. The first word of the Quran as it was revealed to Prophet Muhammad is "Iqra!"

which means "Read!" or "Recite!". Muslims are urged to pursue knowledge in order to better understand God's revealed word. Early Muslims made innovative intellectual contributions in such fields as mathematics, astronomy, philosophy, medicine and poetry. They established schools, often at mosques, known as *Maktab* and *Madrasa*. Islamic rulers built libraries and educational complexes, such as Baghdad's House of Wisdom and Cairo's Al-Azhar University, to nurture advanced scholarship. Under Muslim rule, southern Spain was a center of higher learning, producing such figures as the renowned Muslim philosopher Ibn Rushd alias Averroes.

But other scholars contend that these educational attainments, and the regard that Muslims had for intellectual inquiry in realms outside religion, were gradually attenuated by a complex mix of social and political events over several centuries. These events included foreign invasions, first by the Mongols, who destroyed the House of Wisdom in 1258, and then by Christians, who pushed Muslims out of Spain in 1492. Some scholars argue that the educational decline began earlier, in the 11th and 12th centuries, and was rooted in institutional changes. In particular, contends Harvard University Associate Professor of Economics Eric Chaney, the decline was caused by an increase in the political power of religious leaders who prioritized Islamic religious learning over scientific education. Their growing influence helped bring about a crucial shift in the Islamic approach to learning: It became dominated by the idea that divine revelation is superior to other types of knowledge, and that religious education should consist of learning only what Islamic scholars had said and written in the past.

In the view of some historians, this shift severely constricted intellectual inquiry in the Muslim world as the natural sciences, critical questioning and art were downplayed. Education became primarily the study of established, traditional religious and legal canons. This change also tightened religious scholars' control over the education of Muslims in Africa and the Middle East – a hold that was not broken until colonial governments and Christian missionaries introduced Western-style educational institutions.

Some scholars argue that the decline in secular learning and the narrowing of intellectual inquiry among Muslims have been exaggerated, or did not take place. Columbia University history professor George Saliba writes: "In particular, the decline of Islamic science, which was supposed to have been caused by the religious environment … does not seem to have taken place in reality. On the contrary, if we only look at the surviving scientific documents, we can clearly delineate a very flourishing activity in almost every scientific discipline" after the 12th century. Nowadays, Islamic religious leaders and religious schools still have great influence on education in some Muslim-majority countries, but they compete with government and private schools offering secular topics.

Christianity

In the view of some scholars, the 16th-century Protestant Reformation was a driving force for public education in Europe. Protestant reformers promoted literacy because of their contention that everyone needed to read the Bible, which they viewed as the essential authority on doctrinal matters. Driven by this theological conviction, religious leaders urged the building of schools and the translation of the Bible into local languages – and Reformation leader Martin Luther set the example by translating the Bible into German.

Some scholars, however, argue that the "Second Reformation" of the German Pietist movement in the 17th and 18th centuries was even more influential in promoting literacy. Historians Richard L. Gawthrop of Franklin College and the late Gerald Strauss of Indiana University note that in addition to stressing the need for personal Bible reading, the Pietists persuaded German authorities to mandate Bible reading as "the chief instrument of religious instruction in primary schools, [which was] a powerful impetus to the spread of mass literacy."

In more recent times, religion was a prime motivator in establishing U.S. schools run by faith groups – including Quakers, Protestants and Catholics – that educated generations of immigrant families.

Historically, however, Christianity and science often have come into conflict with each other, as illustrated by the 17th century clash between astronomer Galileo Galilei and the Roman Catholic Church, as well as the condemnation by prominent religious leaders of Charles Darwin's 1859 theory of human evolution. The Scopes Monkey trial in 1925 further highlighted the rift between science and some branches of Christianity over the theory of evolution, a contentious relationship that endures even today.

In sub-Saharan Africa, meanwhile, scholars describe how religious missionaries during colonial times were the prime movers in constructing educational facilities and influencing local attitudes toward education. These missionary activities, the scholars conclude, have had a long-lasting positive impact on access to schooling and educational attainment levels in the region. Research by Baylor University sociologist Robert D. Woodberry, for instance, suggests that Protestant missionaries in Africa "had a unique role in spreading mass education" because of the importance they placed on ordinary people's ability to read scripture. As a result, they established schools to promote literacy wherever they went and translated the Bible into indigenous languages.

Harvard University economics professor Nathan Nunn, who contends that education was "the main reward used by missionaries to lure Africans into the Christian sphere," says that in addition to establishing schools, "missionaries may have altered people's views about the importance of education." Woodberry and Nunn conclude, however, that Protestant and Catholic missionaries had differing results. Except where they were in direct competition with Protestant missionaries, Catholic missionaries concentrated on educating African elites rather than the masses, Woodberry observes. And Nunn notes that Protestant missionaries placed greater stress than Catholics on educating women. As a result, Protestants had more long-term impact on the education of sub-Saharan African women.

Buddhism

Scholars of Buddhism note that Siddhartha Gautama, the religion's founder, often is called "teacher" because of his emphasis on "the miracle of instruction." He considered learning essential for attaining the Buddhist goal of enlightenment.

"In many ways, Buddhism is particularly dedicated to education because unlike many other religions it contends that a human being can attain his or her own enlightenment ('salvation') without divine intervention," writes Stephen T. Asma, a professor of philosophy at Columbia College Chicago.

Buddhism is "also extremely empirical in its approach, suggesting that followers try the experiment of dharma (i.e., Buddha's Four Noble Truths) for themselves to see if it improves their inner freedom," Asma notes, adding: "Because the philosophy of Buddhism takes this pragmatic approach favouring education and experiment, Buddhism has little to no formal disagreement with science (as evidenced by the Dalai Lama's ongoing collaboration with neuroscientists)."

This theoretical openness to scientific knowledge, however, did not always play out at the practical level within Buddhist communities, Asma contends. "Powerful Buddhist monasteries, especially in China and Tibet, frequently resisted modernization (including science) for fear of foreign influence and threats to entrenched Buddhist power structures," he writes.

Despite this tension between theory and practice, Buddhism has been a major influence on the educational systems of many places, especially India, Sri Lanka, Thailand, Myanmar, Cambodia, Laos and Tibet. From around the fifth century onward, Buddhist monasteries emerged as centers of education, not just for monks but also for laymen. Several monasteries became so large and complex that they are considered prototypes of today's universities. In India, the most famous of these educational centers – Nalanda, in what is now Bihar state – is said to have had 10,000 students from many different countries, and offered courses in what then constituted philosophy, politics, economics, law, agriculture, astronomy, medicine and literature.

In Thailand, monastic schools located in Buddhist temples were the main source of education for male children for many centuries, though they offered primarily religious education. When the Thai government introduced Western-style, secular education around the beginning of the 20th century, it used monastic schools as the vehicle for reaching the wider population. As of the 1970s, "almost 50 per cent of Thailand's primary schools [were] still situated in Buddhist monasteries." Similarly, in Japan the Buddhist monastic education tradition was so influential that one 19th-century scholar of Japan wrote that "Buddhism was the teacher under whose instruction the nation grew up."

Hinduism

For Hindus, education vanquishes a fundamental source of human suffering, which is ignorance, says Anantanand Rambachan, a professor of religion at St. Olaf College. As a result, education has been highly valued in Hinduism since the religion's inception in ancient times. Hindu scriptures urge adherents to seek knowledge through dialogue and questioning, and to respect their teachers. "Learning is the foundational stage in the Hindu scheme of what constitutes a good and a meaningful life," Rambachan says. Since ignorance is regarded as a source of human suffering, he adds, "the solution to the problem of ignorance is knowledge or learning."

The Hindu esteem for education is reflected in different ways. To start with, the most authoritative Hindu scriptures are the Vedas, a word that comes from the Sanskrit root word vid, which means knowledge, Rambachan says.

University of Florida religion professor Vasudha Narayanan says Hindus regard two types of knowledge as necessary and worthwhile. The first, vidya, is everyday knowledge that equips one to earn a decent and dignified life. The second, jnana, is knowledge or wisdom that brings awareness of the divine. This is achieved by reading and meditating on Hindu scriptures.

Historically, the caste system in India was a huge barrier to the spread of mass literacy and education. Formal education was reserved for elite populations. But in the seventh and eighth centuries, the vernacular language of Tamil began to be used for religious devotion in southern India, which led to greater access to all kinds of knowledge for a wider group of people. "That is when you start having men and women of different castes composing poems of praise for God, poems that are still recited in temple liturgy today," Narayanan says.

Later, in the 18th and 19th centuries, both secular and religious education came to be seen by Hindus as a universal right, and it gradually began to be extended to all members of the faith. Still, today, the vast majority of Hindus (98%) live in developing countries – mainly India, Nepal and Bangladesh – that have struggled to raise educational standards in the face of widespread poverty and expanding populations, which helps explain why Hindus have relatively low educational attainment compared with other major religious groups.

Judaism

High levels of Jewish educational attainment may be rooted in ancient religious norms, according to some recent scholarship. The Torah encourages parents to educate their children. This prescription was not mandatory, however, until the first century.

Sometime around 65 C.E., Jewish high priest Joshua ben Gamla issued a religious decree that every Jewish father should send his young sons to primary school to learn to read in order to study the Torah. A few years later, in the year 70, the Roman army destroyed the Second Temple following a Jewish revolt. Temple rituals had been a pillar of Jewish religious life. To replace them, Jewish religious leaders emphasized the need for studying the Torah in synagogues. They also gave increased importance to the earlier religious decree on educating sons, making it a compulsory religious duty for all Jewish fathers. Over the next few centuries, a formal school system attached to synagogues was established.

These developments signalled "a profound transformation" of Judaism, according to economic historians Maristella Botticini of Bocconi University and Zvi Eckstein of the Interdisciplinary Center Herzliya. Judaism became, they write, "a religion whose main norm required every Jewish man to read and to study the Torah in Hebrew and to send his sons from the age of 6 or 7 to primary school or synagogue to learn to do so. … Throughout the first millennium, no people other than the Jews had a norm requiring fathers to educate their sons."

This religious obligation meant that male Jews, to a greater degree than their contemporaries, were literate, which gave them an advantage in commerce and trade. Jewish scholarship was enhanced in the early Middle Ages, beginning in the late sixth century, by the emergence of Talmudic academies of Sura and Pumbedita in what is now Iraq. In the late Middle Ages, centres of Jewish learning, including the study of science and medicine, emerged in what is today northern Spain and southern France.

Until the early 19th century, however, most education of Jewish boys was primarily religious. That began to change with the *Haskalah*, the Jewish Enlightenment movement initiated by East and Central European Jews.

This intellectual movement sought to blend secular humanism with the Jewish faith and to encourage openness to secular scholarship among Jews. It revived Hebrew as a language of poetry and literature, which reflected the reformers' appreciation of their Jewish religious heritage. At the same time, they were strong proponents of reforming Jewish education by including secular subjects, such as European literature and the natural sciences. This educational project often brought the reformists into conflict with more orthodox Jewish religious leaders.

Scholars also have explored how religions' cultural norms and doctrines may affect educational attainment by determining which subjects are taught in schools, how much emphasis is placed on religious knowledge versus secular education, and if there is gender parity in educational attainment.

There has been considerable research on ways in which religious teachings on gender roles may be linked to women's educational attainment. Some scholars have noted that from the Reformation onward, Protestant groups encouraged educating women, with effects that still resonate today. "Martin Luther urged each town to have a girls' school so that girls would learn to read the Gospel, evoking a surge of building girls' schools in Protestant areas," write economic professors Sascha O. Becker, of the University of Warwick, and Ludger Woessmann, of the University of Munich. Looking at 1970 data for European countries, the two conclude that countries with higher shares of Protestants were "clearly associated" with greater parity between men and women in years of education.

Woodberry and Nunn, experts on missionary activity in sub-Saharan Africa, both highlight the Protestant missionaries' insistence that girls and women be educated. In the missionaries' view, "everyone needed access to 'God's word' – not just elites," writes Woodberry. "Therefore, everyone needed to read, including women and the poor."

By contrast, cultural and religious norms in Muslim societies often hinder women's education. Lake Forest College political scientist Fatima Z. Rahman examines how family laws in Muslim-majority countries can affect women's higher education. She finds that when a country's family laws closely conform to a strict version of *sharia*, or Islamic law, the share of women in higher education is smaller. This is not the case when family laws are based on more general Islamic precepts. The stricter laws "impose a limit on physical mobility which is typically required for pursuing higher education or a career," Rahman concludes. There are signs that this could be changing, however, as women make gains in higher education in some conservative Muslim countries in the Gulf Cooperation Council – including Saudi Arabia.

Some academic studies have probed ways a particular religion's attitude toward secular knowledge – whether it is seen as a necessity for spiritual growth or as a distraction from achieving personal salvation – can affect the pursuit of formal education. In this regard, sociologists Darren E. Sherkat, of Southern Illinois University Carbondale, and Alfred Darnell, a visiting lecturer at Washington University in St. Louis, find that "fundamentalist beliefs and conservative Protestant affiliation both have significant and substantial negative influences on educational attainment." Young followers of fundamentalist religious leaders, they add, "will likely limit their educational pursuits." They suggest that Christians who regard the Bible as inerrant – that is, as the error-free word of God – are less likely to enrol in college preparatory classes and "have significantly lower educational aspirations than other respondents."

While Darnell and Sherkat focus their research on Christians in the United States, their observations about how religious attitudes toward secular knowledge may affect attainment offer possible insights into attainment patterns seen in other religions and other parts of the world.

Some scholars, however, hypothesize that higher levels of religious observance and engagement produce greater educational attainment. They posit that religious involvement enhances an individual's social capital in the form of family and peer networks, which promote educational success. University of Texas sociologists Chandra Muller and Christopher G. Ellison, in a study of U.S. teenagers, find that there is "a positive influence of religious involvement on several key academic outcomes," such as obtaining a high school diploma. Similarly, in her study of women raised as conservative Protestants, University of Illinois economics professor Evelyn L. Lehrer observes that those who frequently attended religious services during adolescence completed one more year of schooling than their less observant peers.

Strong social capital also is proposed by Paul Burstein, a sociologist at the University of Washington, as a topic needing further research to explain the high educational attainment of Jews. Research focused on the social capital approach, Burstein argues, provides "a framework for showing how Jewish religious beliefs and practices, and the organizations created to sustain them, help Jews acquire skills and resources useful in the pursuit of secular education and economic success."

Burstein argues that previous studies looking at "beliefs or behaviours that are specifically Jewish," or at Jewish "marginality" – either from traditional Judaism or Western society in general – have not offered complete explanations for Jewish educational success.

Religion in Education

Religion seems to be avoided in schools, educators are reluctant to raising the topic of religion in the classroom. Understandably they worry about offending students, or favouring a belief for that matter. Addressing religion in schools is essential to learning, and can adequately provide students with a diverse connection to the world. It is legal to discuss and teach students about religion in an unbiased and academically correct way. Therefore it is the educator's choice whether to do so or not. Religion is an important factor in education for various reasons. Including religion in education will help decrease the amount of religiously motivated hate crimes. Along with making the student body more diverse, and enhancing the students education. Students have a First Amendment right to religious expression in school and should be able to exercise that right.

Religiously motivated hate crimes are on the rise, therefore to decrease this we should be teaching students about religion during school hours. Research shows that the percentage of hate crimes led by religion bias was about three times higher in 2012 than in 2004. Many of the violent hate crime leaders are school age. If educators encourage students to understand and respect people of different religious beliefs, it will immensely help lower the percentage of these hate crimes. Without teaching religion in schools some children feel that crime is acceptable, along with acting out because they aren't taught any better.

Today, our student bodies are much more diverse. Which means that students are going to come across students of different race, culture, and religions. Students need to learn how to be able to accept these differences, and not be judgmental. To ensure that students of less familiar cultures and religious backgrounds feel included and accepted in their learning environment, teachers need to begin providing different types of opportunities for all of the students to share unique features about themselves. As their classmates become more educated about these differences, the likelihood of exclusivity and bullying will largely decrease.

Religious literacy is key to a well-rounded education; this will enhance the student's education by teaching them more knowledge about different religions around the world. If students are going to function as global citizens, and be members of society; they will need to understand religion's impact on history, politics, society, and culture. Students should know basic religious facts and should be able to recognize the diversity that exists in each belief system that surrounds them. Students will also be encountering different types of people throughout their lives, and they are going to need to know how to deal with it and accept it.

Students have a First Amendment right to religious expression in school. With that being said, the U.S. Constitution contains two different types of clauses, known as the religion clauses. They are there to inform the relationship between religion and public schools. As government employees, public school teachers and administrators must follow these two clauses and are required to be neutral about religion while educating their students. Students have the right to believe in what they had like to believe, and say what they want to say. Students are allowed to express how they feel, and they do indeed have the right to religious expression.

Students who are taught about religion seem to have a better grasp on reality. Allowing them to have a better concept about what is going on in the world around us dealing with different religions, cultures, and values. Along with being more open minded about other peoples beliefs, instead of just focusing on their own and acknowledging others. Religious education is easily ignored when it comes to teaching it in schools. People feel that religion does not need to be discussed. That it is better to just keep to themselves, in fear that it could offend someone and their own beliefs. When religion is brought up in education we seem to ignore it, and not appreciate it the way that we should. Religion gets merged in with citizenship and social studies, instead of talking about it separately. Students should be taught about religion. It can teach them valuable ways of thinking, which can help them throughout life. Religion is a key concept and helps broaden people's knowledge about the world around us. There are so many different types of religions, which is why it is necessary for us to have an understanding and idea of the other religions that people are a part of and value.

IMPACT OF SOCIO-CULTURAL FACTORS ON DEVELOPMENT OF EDUCATION SYSTEM

Schools at large often and closely reflect the social patterns prevailing in a particular country. As such the education system is usually seen as a social factor which must reflect the ethos of the people that it serves. In this regard, it is the prime aim of education to ensure cultural continuity through fostering the growth and development of national characteristics that often act as stabilizing forces. In its simplest definition a culture of a society is the total way of life of the society. Every society consist of human beings and in whatever state they find themselves they always have some kind of educational system. This form of education of the society will always strive to perpetuate and protect its traditions and aspirations. As such a close study and analysis of each education system will always reveal the cultural concept and pattern of the community in question. Also the social patterns of the people in any particular community or country are reflected in its system of education.

It is important to realize that the culture of the people often changes at a slow pace. In each culture, there are certain values which are not affected by time and place, for example, faith in God, love for truth and non-violence and the ideal of universal motherhood and justice are the permanent values of many cultures of the world. However, radical reforms in a society may be slowed down or blocked at the level of implementation because of the cultural lag. In African the various projects for educational reform does indicate that there has been basic cultural charges in the life of a people from the colonial period into the post independence period. In many countries of the world today, changes have occurred in the attitude of the youngsters towards their elders, for example students do not show due respect to their teacher as students did some twenty five or thirty years ago. The teachers also now care more for the increments, in their salaries and other allowances then for teaching. In many meetings of teachers, there is more talk of groupism, backbiting and salaries, than of students' welfare. In some circles, guardians and parents also do not respect teachers as they did before. All these and others are a clear indication that the relations between parents and children, sisters and brothers, husband and wife, masters and servants and between many other units of society have undergone great changes. Thus, we have begun to discard many old mores and modes and are adopting more liberal attitudes. As such time and place have been changing many elements of culture and as a result it is being reflected in the education system in various ways.

Another view of cultural and social change is in the reshaping of the educational machinery to make for equality of educational opportunity for all. This has led to the widening of the school curriculum and increased emphasis on the importance of the right kind of technical educational for the new technological age. As a result, the old dichotomy between a liberal and a technical education is slowly broken down and the social distinctions which existed mainly because of that divide have become of no consequence and has been minimized with time. In this regard therefore, it is necessary to develop love for one's own culture through the education system because it strengthens nationalism. In order to make the country strong and prosperous, the spirit of nationalism must be nurtured. In each country there are various types of communities, classes, castes, and interests and due to the lack of national feelings many people ignore national interests. In many cases minorities are suspicious about the majority and in certain contexts this may be true of the majority as well. This makes it necessary to inculcate love for the country's culture and especially through the adoption of a national system of education.

Education reflects the social pattern of society. The tremendous explosion of science and technology has shaken the old leisurely outlook on life and has created intricate problems of social adjustment. A new emphasis has been placed on literacy. A growing interest is shown in re-organizing the curricula at all stages. The new forces in the social structure of the Indian society have provided a fresh incentive for educationists to pattern the educational system.

Education will be different in different kinds of society since total way of life of a society influence education. Even the same society, education provided at different time spans will be different. Although it is said that education is one of the causes in social change, it could be seen that in most cases educational change trends to follow rather than initiate social changes. Educational institutions and other organizations are inter-related with the rest of the social structure. A.K.C. Ottaway stated, "Education is an activity which goes on in a society and its aims and methods depend on the nature of the society in which it takes place".

Culture and education are initially and integrally connected. Hence the cultural pattern of a country conditions its educational pattern. E.g. A society based on the spiritual pattern of culture emphasis the attainment of moral and eternal values-truth, goodness and beauty- of life through education. At the same time a society based on materialistic pattern emphasis the attainment of material values through education. Culture influences aims of education, curriculum, methodology, discipline, and text books.

In each country a number of races exist. These races influence its educational system. The race which considers itself superior to others tries to rule over them. If it succeeds in this attempt, then it tries to strengthen its control on them by developing a particular educational system.

For example, the French and the British people established their colonies in Africa. Because they were 'white', these people thought that they were superior to the natives of Africa. So they developed a special kind of educational system to strengthen their control over the black natives.

Thus, in South Africa, the racial factor has been an effective element in the educational system of that country. Similarly, during the British rule in India, the English people introduced a type of educational system in order to produce a special type of workers to run their administrative machinery. They did this to strengthen their imperialistic control over the country.

Accordingly, English was made the medium of instruction and a particular type of curriculum was introduced. Their actions were prompted by the feeling that their culture and civilisation were superior to those of the Indian people. Needless to emphasise once again the importance of the racial factor in the study of comparative education.

Discrimination

Sometimes there are social or cultural factors that hold back poor countries. Discrimination is one of these. If there are certain people groups that are discriminated against, the country's overall productivity can suffer. This may be a tribe, a caste, a racial category or minority language group. Cameroon, which has both French speaking and English speaking regions. All the infrastructure happens in the French speaking part. French speakers in Canada complain of the opposite. Welsh speakers in Britain, or Catalans in Spain, have historically faced similar problems. Racial discrimination may be an issue, excluding certain groups from economic activity, either deliberately or not. Racial minorities regularly have poorer exam results and economic prospects than the majority. More serious forms of exclusion would be apartheid South Africa, or the Asian communities driven out of Uganda under Idi Amin, which was disastrous for Uganda's economy.

Another division may be the role of women. Jeffrey Sachs talks about this in *The End of Poverty*: 'Cultural or religious norms may block the role of women… leaving half the population without economic or political rights and without education, thereby undermining half of the population in its contribution to overall development.' If you don't believe that women should work, you have effectively halved the earning potential of your country.

Population

Closely linked to this is the population issue. If women see staying at home and bringing up children as their chief role, they will have more children than those who work. There is nothing wrong with having lots of children, as long as you can provide for them. Jeffrey Sachs again: 'With fewer children, a poor household can invest more in the health and education of each child, thereby equipping the next generation with the health, nutrition, and education that can lift living standards in future years.'

IMPACT OF ECONOMIC FACTORS ON DEVELOPMENT OF EDUCATION SYSTEM

Formal education is possible where production exceeds consumption. This may be the result of tremendous industrial development or favourable natural circumstances. This will depend upon the fertility of the soil, abundant mineral deposits and proper climate conditions for work. Such conditions provide men with leisure to pursue education. Where there is a subsistence economy, it is a far cry to afford time for formal schooling. This is the reason why poorer and undeveloped countries have a minimum education for their children while industrially advanced countries keep nearly all their children at school and for a longer time.

Education is the result of economic development. It is true in all its aspects. The quality of education is also decided by economic development of the society. A poor country cannot provide for all its citizens costly educational facilities. It is applicable in the case of a family also.

The type of education is also determined by the economic condition. The education needed by an agrarian and an industrialized communities/ countries will be different.

The type of education largely depends on the economic strength of any country. Also the economic factor determines the content and method of an education system. It is important to note that formal education is often possible where production exceeds consumption. In indigenous traditional education people were trained depending on the economic conditions and needs of the community. From an economic perspective, expenditure on education refers to the amount or percentage of national revenue spent on education by both individuals and the government. If the economic condition is poor, education becomes backward in many aspects while if the economy of a country is strong, then educational aims and the curriculum are given a special direction for making the country prosperous. For example, in the USA and Japan, education system is patterned so as to make the individual graduate, strong and capable enough to stand on his or her own feet after having received education. While in India, college and university graduate do not know where to go after completing their education and most of the students continue to stay on in the university as long as they can so that one can post pone for a few years the problem of the educated - unemployed.

Another economic influence on education is that, the poorer classes in communities tend to be content with minimum education for their children, and the richer classes are known to be able to keep their children longest at school because they can afford to meet the costs. In a subsistence economy, that is, one is which people are just able to make ends meet, educational systems tend to be informal occurring on the job. On the contrary, where there are enough grants in systems of education, minimum requirements are met and thus the quality of education is often high. For example, Britain, France, Japan and the USA among other strong economy countries, they provide enough grants that are allocated to their systems of education; actually they have enough funds to support all educational programmes in their education systems. Unlike the case of developing countries, where funds are very scarce, which affects even payment of teachers salaries, essential resource materials such as textbooks are not adequate and in some cases not even available. As such, this greatly affects the nature of the systems of education in terms of the content and methods in learning institutions and in essence the whole system of education.

In this regard, the growth of the capacities of individual citizens and national development is of great importance. In fact, the education system should be such that, it provides opportunities for the maximum development of each citizen. The aim here is to ensure that the wealth of the nation is not concentrated in the hands of a few capitalists who manage to attain some level of education. It is actually by developing individuals that the overall growth of the nation can be guaranteed. At the same time, there should be no-class distinction in the planning of education that should be permitted, because this results in neglect of the education of other more capable citizens. If this happens it often results in social disparities and in the long run weakens the nation. Proper planning of the education system also calls for the establishment of a proper national character, which if it lacks, then the necessary leadership and co-operation of the people will also be lacking. Lack of a proper national character, means that the national education system will not be able to realize its objectives. Consequently, with good leadership and people's cooperation, there is much that can be achieved even when adequate economic resources are wanting. Thus, there is evidence to show that there is a very close relationship between economic security and the national system of education of any country.

The educational system of a country is closely related with its economic condition. The aims and curriculum of education are framed according to the economic condition of the land. The belief about the economic system as adhered to by a country is inculcated in the citizens.

For example, under the socialistic economic system, the State is the owner of all property. Therefore at the very primary stage of education children are given the impression that all property belongs to the State and each individual has to protect it. In the democracies like U.S.A. and India the situation is quite different. In these two countries the individual property is recognised.

Therefore in the development of their educational systems full attention is paid to the lights of the individual. That is why in these countries "Public Schools" for the children of a few rich and higher class people are allowed to exist. Evidently, the economic factor is a very effective element and in the study of comparative education it occupies a special place.

Education, Skill Development impact on Economic Growth in India

Education is a process of facilitating learning - knowledge, skills, values, beliefs etc. So, education determines the country's future as it is having all the powers to change everything. We have come across so many philosophies like naturalism, realism, idealism, modern philosophies and philosophers like John Dewey, Aurobindo Gosh, Rabindranath Tagore, MK Gandhi who believed in traditional way of learning along with modern concepts and also Nehru had strong believe in Rationalism. Apart from these, we had older way of educational methodology like *Gurukuls*, where students have to stay and learn the mantras, Upanishad by storytelling, games, managing the battles, moral values, leadership skills etc taught by gurus. But the drawback of this methodology was it is only applicable for certain group of people like those who are from *Shatriyas* and other elite castes. The difficulties and struggle were felt from the olden period onwards, but still we did not achieve 100% in that. It should reach all people irrespective of age, sex, economic status, religion, language, cultures etc. "Education for All" Initiative must be followed. "A high rate of education is essential for countries to be able to achieve high levels of economic growth so that the developing countries should grow faster than rich countries because they can adopt cutting edge technologies already tried and tested by rich countries".

Strong Review Argument

Education contributes to economic growth by imparting basic attitudes, moral values and specific skills, which are necessary for variety of places. It contributes economic growth by improving health, reducing fertility, and political stability. Importance of educational system is to produce a literate, disciplined, flexible labour force via high-quality education. Adelunji et al. (2005) found that long run relationships between enrolments in primary and tertiary level as well the average years of schooling with output of workers. The results revealed that a well-educated labour force possessed a positive and significant impact on economic growth through factors accumulation and on the evaluation of total factors productivity. Aghion et al. (2009) conducted a study on casual impact of education on Economic growth's evidence from U.S. The hypothesis tested some investments in education raise growth. They find that exogenous shocks to research type education have positive effects in states fairly close to the technological frontier.

Denise Hawkes et al (2012) a meta analysis was done on relationship between education, skill and economic growth in Low– Income Countries (LICs). Objective of the study was to address the impact of education, skill on economic growth to the direct effect on human capital investments on growth in LICs. The search based on 43 LICs, 3,842 unique studies were screened. The results showed that investing in education skills promotes economic growth in LICs correct in general. Also, some gaps like improper measurements in education and skills were found.

The principle finding suggests that those national and transnational organizations who have invested heavily in human capital development in LICs are likely to see a return on this investment in terms of economic growth.

The Indian educational system is producing more graduates every year. But the graduates have lack of basic communication and problem solving skills. Those are essential for even the elementary level jobs. Today's education is seen only in earning money. Education is offered to earn good money and also the educational institutions have become more commercialised.

When we talk about present curriculum in India, it is out dated nearly 30 years old. Some institution sticks on an old curriculum. Few want the change and fight a long futile battle trying to change it. So there is a need of massive change in present and development of new curriculum along with administering the planned one. Vocational training should be mandatory alongside lots of practical work, as more importance has been given to theoretical classes rather than practical classes due to many issues like lack of facilities, lack of trainers etc.

The present day education system in India comprises of about 600,000 primary, 150,000 upper primary, 70,000 secondary school and higher secondary schools. The network of institution of higher education includes more than 7000 colleges of general education about 1000 professional colleges and number of specialised institutions in industrial, scientific, technical, social sciences and research. There are 150 million students who are enrolled with an employment of about 4 million teachers.

Significance of Education, Skill and its Impacts on Employability

Education is the backbone of each family that too women's education is very essential. Nowadays, the value of education is just earning a degree without a goal, why this happens? The reason is lack of reinforcement, loss of hope on employment. "Nation does not need pointless, goalless youngsters, instead need mindful, talented, skilful youth to compromise the dynamic society and improve the status of our country among others". So the government has the responsibility to bring the hope and set stage for the youngsters of India.

Each individual has to think and answer these questions like where we stand? What we have? Where has to go? What is our life time goal? How to bring the status in the society? This is not only for the people and also for the nation. The Nation also should set the goals on what we have? What must be taken initiative to improve the economic growth? What are all the sectors that need attention to improve the economic growth? So select that kind of areas and plan the strategies to implement the methodology which should contain need based education and skill development and plan for periodic monitoring.

Education alone is not needed. For proper execution, skill is necessary. In India, importance of skill is an unattended aspect except in few areas like Medicine, Engineering etc that too not everywhere. What about other areas of studies? The graduates are still struggling in communication, lack of boldness to present the presentations. India is composed by demographic dividend with multiple languages, cultures, religion etc. So teaching in common language is not possible like other countries, if we do it, other issues crop up.

Skill Learning

Having knowledge alone is not adequate to bring the changes, the need of skill to execute properly is important. Now the new ministry introduced "Skill India Mission" for the youth to meet their domestic demands and also for the betterment of economic growth of our nation. Through this mission, Jobless, school dropouts, graduated, uneducated, and women will be given training based on their knowledge and ability which will certify them to get the jobs. For the students it will be starting from the school to provide communication skill, entrepreneurship, problem-solving skills, etc.

The skill India mission has been introduced all over the India. It is not only for the schools, "SKILL FOR ALL" irrespective their education, sex, age etc. The central government has many vocational and professional skill-based training programmes. Apart from the courses the mission is planning to reach the rural India also. So the main aim of the mission is reach the outreach population. Training will be given to carpenters, black smith, masons, nurses, cobblers, welders, tailors, weavers etc. Importance will be given to the area where the government can improve the economic growth like real estate, construction, jewellery designing, tourism, banking, transportation, gem industry, textile etc.

It will improve the individual earnings and which directly influence economic growth of the nation. The mission also plans to bring the courses for specific age groups on language and communication skills, personality development skills, behavioural skills, life and positive thinking skills, including job and employability skills which will be conducted by group discussion, games, brainstorming, simulation, practical experiences and case studies etc. This will be managed by academic institutions, public and private sectors, Non-governmental organizations etc.

Quality of schooling institutions and Economic Growth

Micro economic evidence of productivity increasing the effects of education and skills, it is naturally extending the view to the macroeconomic perspective of long run economic growth of countries. It is same like education earning relationships. There are three mechanisms through which the education may affect economic growth.

First, education increases the human capital inherent in the labour force, which increases labour productivity and transitional growth towards equilibrium level of outputs. Secondly, education may increase the innovation capacity of the economy and the knowledge on new technologies, products, processes, promotes growth. Thirdly, education may facilitate the diffusion and transmission of knowledge needed to understand the process new information and to implement successfully new technologies devised by others, which again promotes economic growth.

Problems and Policies

Today, problems of identification are too high in India. For example, concentrating on teacher's salaries, class size, and institution benefits etc., secondary schooling literacy rates are low. There are encounter sporadic or nonexistent assessment of student education which is are important issues.

The shift of focus from year of schooling to cognitive skills has important policy implications because policies that extend schooling may be very different from best policies to improve skills. The policy conundrum is that student achievement has been relatively impervious to a number of interventions that has been tried by countries around the world.

- Improve and revise the health and nutrition policy which directly influences children's ability to concentrate and leads to gain in basic achievements.
- Create awareness about people involvement for support their children and provide path to develop their skills.
- Strongly need to change the structural changes in curriculum and school institutions.
- Recover school resources and skill-based education.
- Improve incentives for student's performance and strong accountability system that accurately measures a student's performance.

- Local autonomy that allows schools to make appropriate educational choices and competition in schools, so that parents can enter into determining the incentives that schools fare.
- The student autonomy also considered because parents should not impose to select the path.

Cognitive skills have powerful effects on individual earnings on the distribution of income and on economic growth. Changes in curriculum structure and measurements of tools which assess cognitive skill are needed to bring the better impact on economic growth, because economic growth is strongly influenced by the skills of labour force in India.

IMPACT OF GEOGRAPHICAL FACTORS ON DEVELOPMENT OF EDUCATION SYSTEM

The geography of any particular place is often natural, which means that it is undefined by man. Man in this respect ought to behave in accordance with the geography and nature in particular. In this regard the education system cum school system is influenced by the geography of the particular region. By and large the geography of a particular area dictates the type of building and equipment, means and methods of transporting children to school, school going age of pupils among others. However, there are three major geographical aspects that influence the educational system directly. These are, climatic conditions, population distribution and land configuration. In regard to climatic conditions they influence the system of education in terms of, content of education depend on the continental climate, for example, training of doctors in the tropics is likely to emphasize more on tropical disease like malaria.

Extreme low temperatures in Continental Europe, affects accessibility to school by young children. Temperatures also affect the time at which schools can reasonably begin in the morning and when they end. In Norway, for example, the sun does not rise during winter until ten o'clock in the morning and often temperatures fall to negative 20 degrees. Thus in the Scandinavian countries there are no infant schools or early childhood education departments in some schools because of extreme temperatures. Climatic conditions also influence the education system in relation to time of vacations. In North America and many countries in Europe take school vacations during cold winter and others during hot summer. In hot climatic conditions especially experienced in arid and semi-arid areas, learning often takes place during morning hours when it is cool. When it is hot in the afternoon very little learning takes place due to excessive heat.

In regard to population distribution, which is often as a result of geographical influence also affects the educational system. Generally worldwide, population is either concentrated in the urban centres, or scattered in the country side. For example Australia has two systems of education, that is, one for the urban areas and the other for rural areas. In the urban areas there are well-equipped schools with adequately qualified teachers and administrative personnel. While in the rural areas, schools are small with one teacher for ten up to forty students. This is because farms are far from the nearest schools and daily attendance is difficult. Therefore the central government is responsible for their administration and financing. The government also provides the means and organization of correspondence, tuition and travelling teachers. As such most students receive education through correspondence and occasional visits by the travelling education inspectors.

In regard to land configuration, this also influences the education system in terms of architectural structure of farm houses, school buildings, village location and also the whole way of life and thinking of people because of the rigours of the climate, in some cases, because of closeness of family ties, boarding schools for children are non-existence, except for the few who come from far and inaccessible places on daily basis. By and large land configuration determines settlement and location of schools.

The geographical position has its inevitable impact on the culture, civilisation and education of a nation. The various countries of the world have different geographical positions. Therefore, their modes of living, civilization, culture, social institutions and educational systems are also different.

The climate of a cold country is different from that of a tropical one. Therefore, ways of living and social organisation of the two types of countries are not the same. Serial systems influence the educational organisation.

An agricultural country emphasises agricultural education in its educational system, and an industrial country pays special attention to technological and industrial subjects in the organisation of its curriculum. In a cold country there is a long winter vacation and in a hot country a long summer vacation. Evidently, the educational structure of a country is conditioned by its geographical situation.

The physical and economic environment influences national character and so, indirectly, conditions a country's educational attitudes. At the same time, elements in the environment may have an immediate impact on school systems. Climatic conditions may hinder school attendance by young children, national economic poverty may delay the introduction of compulsory schooling and in industrialization may impose new demands for certain skills.

Climatic conditions typical of the whole of north western Europe are found in Belgium, Holland, Denmark and the Irish Republic. All have average January temperatures above 300F and only in Denmark does the January average fall below freezing-point. Average July temperatures in the four countries are between 58F. and 630F. These temperature conditions denote an equable type of climate. In addition, there is a high degree of uniformity of rain fall in these countries, except on the peripheral uplands of Ireland. Annual rainfall reaches

30 inches in most locations, with no great seasonal variation. Therefore, these countries have a common climate with certain local variations.

If this type of climate is capable of influencing patterns of education in the four countries, then the influence should be uniform rather than contrasting. In particular, adverse climatic conditions are likely to have most influence at the primary level, for example with regard to the onset of compulsory education and the length of the school day.

In Denmark and Holland, the law requires school attendance from the age of seven years, unless private tuition is given. In Belgium and Ireland, attendance is from six years of age. Major contrasts exist in the sphere of infant education, i.e., in school attendance by children not yet subject to the law. Holland and Belgium have seen major growths in infant education in the present century. In 1957, 85 per cent of Belgian children aged three to six years were at school while in Holland, 83 per cent of all children aged five to six years were at school.

Neither Denmark nor Ireland has developed a system of infant education comparable with that of Belgium or Holland. In Denmark, only 17 per cent of all children aged six years were at school in 1956 and, as in Ireland, there is a tendency for these young children to attend infant classes in primary schools rather than separate nursery schools.

There is no uniformity in the length of the primary school day in these countries. The school day in Denmark lasts from four to six hours, depending on pupil-age. Both Belgium and Holland have a five-hour day for most pupils while in Ireland, it usually lasts 4 to 41/2 hours. The school day in Belgium and Holland begins at about 9 a.m., in Denmark at 8 a.m., whereas in Ireland, many schools have assembly at 9:30 a.m., the first lesson starting at 9:50. Thus, with regard to the primary school day, Denmark and Ireland occupy extreme positions not explicable in terms of climate.

Winters in Denmark are slightly colder than in the other countries, yet the primary school day begins earlier. Average winter temperatures in Ireland are a little higher than in the other countries, yet the school day is shorter and usually starts later. One may conclude that in these countries direct climatic controls over education cannot easily be found. The northwest European climate does not exert a unifying influence over those sectors of the education systems most likely to be affected by climate. If climate does set educational limits, they are likely to be so wide as to be irrelevant; they are also incapable of assessment: "The influence of climate on man, direct or indirect, defies measurement.

- A temperate climate such as that experienced in north-western Europe is, in a sense, a neutral, permissive climate. It allows a wide range of educational practices in terms of school-attendance, length of school day and curriculum, and cannot be invoked as a factor accounting for particular aspects of school organization in the four countries. Nevertheless, it may be that other climates, for example, those with considerable temperature extremes or pronounced seasonal variations, are capable of exerting direct controls over education.

- Population distribution is a factor in the development of education systems by virtue of its effect on the size of the average school. Where population density varies considerably between urban and rural areas, there may be a corresponding division of schools into urban and rural types.
- A tradition of rural migration, as in Ireland, directly affects the demand for education, the rural school curriculum and educational attitudes.
- The relationship between agriculture and education in a country depends less on the type of farming practiced or its importance in the economy than on social factors such as the age-structure of the farming community, the system of land-ownership and prevailing attitudes to farming. Of crucial importance is the existence of farming associations.
- The important role of professional associations is seen, also, in the growth of technical education for industry. Where such associations have not emerged, as in Ireland, responsibility for the maintenance of technical standards devolves on the State.
- Belgium is a country with a highly diversified economy in terms of agriculture, industry and commerce. Belgium has a highly developed system of vocational guidance. Ireland has virtually no such system. In the Irish countryside, about one-half of the school-leavers enter farming, at least initially, and vocational guidance can play no part in the choice of occupation of such children.
- Education may be thought of as a process apart from, even alien to, economic production. If so, it follows that school aims need include no reference to the future employment of pupils, nor need the curriculum include specifically vocational subjects. To the Marxist, to whom reality exists only within the social and economic framework, such a view denotes an unacceptable dualism between education and economic production. The schools of north western Europe lean more towards the former view, towards the Aristotelian "education for leisure," hence the isolation of vocational education for agriculture and industry from the general school system.
- This isolation is becoming less evident, with the growth of multilateral secondary schools integrating general and vocational studies, and with the gradual replacement of part-time vocational training by full-time education. (Anderson, 1965).

IMPACT OF POLITICAL FACTORS ON DEVELOPMENT OF EDUCATION SYSTEM

"Education is the most important shared experience in our lives it is so important and so all-pervasive that it is almost impossible to define. Education will not supply all the answers to the problems that beset us, either as individuals or as a nation, but if we set about it the right way, it is the best single means of promoting intellectual, moral, physical and economic wellbeing" (Aldrich, 1996). Education teaches us the joy of learning and gives us the qualifications for employment, which builds confidence and self esteem and gives us the skills and values to meet the demands of a fast changing worlds and society. (Estelle, 2001). As education meet the demands of society so society is itself is a product of that knowledge or education which informs societal attitudes towards life and its problems, the value it attaches to the things of the world in general, the place of man in the universe in particular and the norm sets to which our thoughts and behaviour must conform.

Political ideologies go a long way in determining the aims and the system of education. Different political ideologies like totalitarian or fascist communist or socialist and democratic will call for different systems of education. Political philosophy of a nation has great influence on its education. Today we have different forms of political systems. They are totalitarianism, communism and democracy etc.

A totalitarian state will assume complete control of the educational system. The rulers will prescribe curriculum, syllabi, text books. Education will be directed to secure mechanical discipline, duty and unquestioned obedience. There will be no room for community participation. E.g. Education in ancient Sparta.

Communism conceives education as one of the principle instruments for economic advancement and social progress. State produce text books and they conduct training in order to attain the goal of socialism. Education will be a national concern. Individuals will have only limited freedom in educational sector. Education will be free at all levels.

In a democratic setup education is under the control of society. The powers and resources are distributed between central and state governments. The state provides educational facilities. A kind of participatory approach and de-centralized planning is adopted here. Universal education is a matter of social necessity in a democratic society. Education aims at improvements in vocational and practical efficiency. Significant place is given to the total development of each individual. The schools indicate respect for the national flag and National Anthem. Exceptional children/poor/disadvantaged are given special consideration. Education of ancient Athens ups to an end this kind.

The ruled nations had a different educational system than their rulers as they were being exploited by their rulers. The system of British education was implanted in this country from purely political motives.

History of a nation must influence the education of that country. History of a nation includes, its past politics, culture, social system, economy etc. Thus, influence of any of the above factors will influence education also. E.g. Still India following British system of education.

If a nation's history was full of wars, the education in that nation will give much importance to training of troops and developing modern Ammunitions/ weapons. If a nation was under the rule of some other nation, its education will be influenced by the culture, politics and social system of that ruling nation. Definitely education in present will be influenced by history.

The political philosophy which controls the government of a country often has its inevitable impact on education. The political factor dictates the kind of administration the system of education will have. They also underlie the features in education system and the functioning of the same. For example, the fundamental ideas of socialism as a political philosophy were about the exploitation of labour by capital and this resulted in class mass. As a political philosophy, socialism recognizes property as the basis of the economic structure of the state which results in the concentration of civil and legal power in the hands of the property owning class. Socialism advocates for the nationalization of the means of production; where owners of means of production do not work and workers who produce do not own anything. A change of such a social order can only be achieved with reform in education. This would be through a state mechanism with full control of education and the curriculum and this means that the citizens must be trained by the state, for the state and in state institutions. In such cases, the details of the curriculum are often decided by the state authorities and involve functional training of citizens. The curriculum may also involve scientific training for social utilization purposes.

Good examples of countries that have introduced a socialist system of education are Mexico, Bulgaria and Cuba. The common features of their education system include monopoly of the state control on education, secularism, physical and military training political indoctrination in and out of school and also more emphasis on science subjects. In these states, freedom of individuals and the idea of tolerance are not accepted. Unlike these countries, France has a centralized system of education based on its political philosophy. In France, everything to do with education is controlled from the centre (metropole) which is the central government. In the case of USA and Japan, their education systems are highly decentralized, and are often based on the democratic influence and the capitalistic political philosophy of these countries.

There is also a close relationship between the national character and the national system of education. For example, the national character of USA is democratic as such its education system is democratic in most of its aspects. Nationalism also as a political ideology influences the system of education in a country. Nationalism could be defined as a psychological feeling within a group which believes they have common outlook and traditions based on myth of common ancestry. These common ancestries include race, language, religion and territory and often strengthen the consciousness of nationality. The racial aspect which is often within the political ideology of a country may play a significant role in determining features in the education system. Race refers to a tribe, a nation or a group of nations. Modern population includes people of different racial origins. The British colonial policy was based on the principle of decentralization and on the building up of a commonwealth of nations each of which should be free to develop its own culture and national character. Hence there is a close relationship between national character and national system of education and the former has been universally accepted as an important basis of national system of education. Thus the political system of a country is closely related with its educational programme.

The Factor of Nationalism

For strengthening the sense of unity the spirit of nationalism is created in a country. This is evident in India particularly after 1947. Here there are various castes, religions and languages. Regionalism erodes the very foundation of our national life.

In spite of these differences, our attention is drawn to the social, cultural and political unity inherent in our country in order to strengthen the national spirit. Accordingly, in our aims regarding education and the curriculum, special attention is given to the development of this sense of unity in the children.

However, we have to note that the spirit of nationalism in a country may be helpful only when the international outlook is not forgotten, because then, one may become blind to the inadequacies of one's own country.

This tendency can ultimately make the nation weak. The examples of Hitler of Germany and Tokyo of Japan are eloquent testimonies to this. Evidently, the factor of nationalism influences the system of education and its study is important in comparative education.

The Democratic Factor

In democracy we find two forms, in one form political equality is emphasized and in another social unity. Within the first form come, U.S.A, Great Britain, France, India, Japan, etc. and in the other form China and North Korea may be mentioned. Because of its particular kind of democratic ideologies, each country has nurtured a special type of education.

The differences found in their educational patterns are because of their different democratic faiths which are quite evident in their different aims, organisations and contents of education. In the study of comparative education we have to note these differences in order to understand the underlying elements correctly.

The Factors of Socialism

The impact of socialism may be sensed in the various aspects of our life to-day. Plato's ideas had the seeds of socialism. He advocated the state control of rearing and bringing up the children. Accordingly, he stood for complete state control over the development of education of children.

This ideology influenced education in Greece for sometime in due course. Sir Thomas More of England in his book "Utopia" advocated socialistic principles in accordance with Plato's ideas. He held that the state must arrange for public education in order that the citizen may fulfil his duties to the state.

Rousseau, too, had advocated a socialistic pattern of society. He stood for universal education under the control of the State. Condorcet may also be mentioned in this connection.

Condorcet stood for equal opportunity of education for all citizens. Rousseau and Condorcet were supported by such writers as Saint Simon (1760-1825), Robert Owen (1771-1858), Charles Fouries (1772-1837), Etienne Cabet (1778-1856) and Louis Blanc (1811-1882).

Modem socialism has its origin in Marxism. Karl Marx (1818-1883) made Hegel's materialism as the base of his philosophy. Marx contended that the economic condition of a country is at the base of its social, political and spiritual process. According to socialism, the purpose of education is to develop the means of production for the welfare of the State.

We find an example of this type of socialism in China and North Korea. Religion has no place in this type of education. Thus the factor of socialism has an important place in the development of education - therefore the importance of this factor in the study of comparative education cannot be overlooked.

The Factor of Humanism

Towards the close of the middle ages humanistic ideas were spread in Europe with the view to make man free of blind superstitions and to base his life on scientific ways. This spirit ultimately wanted to give full scope for the development of an individual. Humanism keeps human welfare as its prime aim. Man is considered to be the measure of everything.

This idea in Europe took root from the beginning of the Renaissance. It penetrated the human mind so deeply that it ultimately resulted in the separation of the Church and State.

During the sixteenth and seventeenth centuries some humanists advocated the introduction of some such ideas in education that the impact of humanism on the educational systems of their lands can be very well understood. Comenius in his emphasis on sense-training expressed only the influence of humanism.

The effect of humanism on education was seen in France during the seventeenth century when education was separated from the Church and the State was made responsible for education of its citizens.

New methods of teaching were devised in Germany because of the influence of humanism. England felt its impact, in the form of changes in the curriculum. In various countries such subjects as geography, mathematics and science began to be taught in such a way as to make them useful in practical affairs of life.

Now attention began to be paid to the co-relationship between philosophy and science. In U.S.A., Thomas Jefferson and Thomas Panie supported the introduction of humanistic elements in the educational system.

During the third decade of the present century, John Dewey of U.S.A supported the incorporation of humanistic elements in education. In the present age, the impact of humanism may be clearly sensed in education.

Today we consider only that curriculum and method of teaching good which promotes the growth of the individual. Thus we find that the humanistic factor influences education and we cannot ignore it in the study of comparative education.

Impact of Politics and concerns with the Indian education system

India is the largest democracy in the world. India has the largest number of political parties, which take part in election campaign. In the 1996 national elections, almost 600 million people voted and an average of 26 candidates competed for each of the 543 territorial constituency seats. Elections are held at different levels in India. The two major election levels are at national level, after which the national government is established and at state level after which the state government is established. Elections are also held for city, town and village councils. Indian politics has different political issues. However these issues remain to be issues without any solutions for decades. Some issues are national level and some regional level. Some communities demand more economical and social rights for their communities, while others demand more autonomy for their cultures within the Indian states. Some demanded autonomous states within the Indian Union, while the others demanded to be independent from India. However, with all its problems India survives as a single state with democratic character. But a number of political problems still exist and remain unsolved in India. Education system is undoubtedly the foundation of a nation. Education makes man civilized and therefore the country. It makes the mankind literate in ethics and moral values. If we have a well nurtured and balanced education system, then half the task of the country's development is done. But when we look into the Indian context in India education system, it is suffering with many issues that needs to be addressed at the earliest, we have some very big problems and thus the challenges are tougher. The problem that we come across on a daily basis and in large scale is political corruption in the education system. Today is the age of innovation and specialisation. And with this fast moving techno-age, the Indian educational system seems to go nowhere. Though we are aware about the progressive minds of Indian students all over the world, we tend to overlook the fact that most of them find abode abroad in USA or Australia.

IMPACT OF LINGUAL FACTORS ON DEVELOPMENT OF EDUCATION SYSTEM

Many languages may be spoken in a country, but only one enjoys the status of a national language. In every country the national language occupies a special place. Also every government tries to ensure that every one acquires the capacity to express himself through the national language. Without one's own national language, no country can be said to be strong.

Language in itself is a symbol of the people. Each community or group has an original language of its own which often suits its environment and stage of cultural development. It is through language that individuals become members of a community and this is important in building the national character. Through the native language, the child has the first expression of himself/herself and the world. However, in the modern world today, there is increasing use of foreign language especially in the school system. This requires a child before entering school to learn the foreign language. In most cases, before entering school the child acquires proficiency in mother tongue or native language and in so doing builds up vocabulary covering most of the objects of sense, impression and daily activities. This means using a different and a foreign language in school system means superimposing on this basis a language of ideas expressed entirely in a foreign medium and this often poses a problem to the learners.

In East Africa, Kiswahili has slowly influenced features in the education systems in Kenya, Uganda, Tanzania, Rwanda and Burundi. Kiswahili is a compulsory subject in primary schools in Kenya and Tanzania. In Tanzania Kiswahili is used as a medium of instruction in all primary schools. In South Africa, there are two linguistic groups, the English speaking and the Africans speaking groups. After the colonization by the British, English was enacted as a medium of instruction in schools. The inhabitants spoke Afrikaans and had been used to the Dutch school system. The use of English failed and in 1914 Afrikaans was recognized also as a medium of instruction in school for African speaking children. As such, in a South Africa, a bilingual system of education came into being, where some schools use English, while others use Afrikaans or even both.

French as a language is also used in former French colonies like Cameroon, Tunisia, Madagascar, Senegal, Rwanda and Burundi. Cameroon also emerges as a bilingual country with two official languages and two systems of education, that is, the Anglophone to the West and Francophone to the East. Although the Cameroon government has been trying to put the two zones together it has proved to remain difficult. Interestingly the ex-British Anglophone system of education continues to produce local syllabuses with the aim of making secondary school examination; the ex-French francophone system still clings firmly on the old and move formal baccalaureate.

By and large in Africa colonialism influenced the language of instruction in schools. In the former British colonies, pupils were taught in their vernacular in the lower elementary or primary school curriculum. The French colonies put more emphasis on French as a medium of instruction. To date most of the inherited systems of education still suffer from the effect of the colonial masters in the school system and at large in the education system. Thus the place of national language in the development of a national feeling cannot be over-emphasized. As such in a national system of education, special emphasis is placed on the study of national language.

The individual has to learn the language of the group in which he is born. The culture and civilisation of a country are expressed through its language although there are other features as well which unmistakably point to its culture and civilisation.

However, the importance of the language cannot be denied. In the educational system of a country its language occupies a special place. We know that if the mother tongue is the medium of instruction, the people are generally of strong national character and if the medium is a foreign language the national character becomes weak.

It is true that there are many other factors that are responsible for moulding the national character, but the medium of instruction has its own special importance, in the educational system. Those educational problems of a country which are related with its cultural elements can be understood on the basis of linguistic factors.

Linguistic Policies in Multilingual India

In India there are five distinct groups, of languages which have to be taken into consideration. that is;

(i) the mother-tongue;

(ii) the regional language when it is not the mother-tongue;

(iii) the official language of the Centre, more commonly called the Federal Language;

(iv) the classical languages-Sanskrit, Arabic, Persian, Latin, etc.; and

(v) English which has come to be recognised as an international language.

In those areas where the mother-tongue and the regional language are the same, the number of languages to be taken into consideration will be limited to four and in those areas where the regional language, the mother-tongue and the language of the Union are the same; the number of languages to be taken into consideration will be limited to three. So far as the Federal language or the official language of the Centre is concerned we feel that the areas in the different parts of the country may be divided into three regional groups:

(i) regions where Hindi is the mother- tongue, and therefore, is the regional language as well as the language of the Centre (E.g. Uttar Pradesh);

(ii) regions where although it is not the mother-tongue, Hindi is spoken by a large number of people of the region (E.g. Maharashtra, Punjab);

(iii) regions where Hindi is neither the mother tongue nor the regional language nor spoken or understood by the vast majority of the people. These are generally spoken of as non-Hindi speaking areas (E.g. Kerala, Tamil Nadu, Karnataka).

Language use in education depends on the linguistic situation of a country. Co-existence of many languages has been the essence of Indian heritage. Language uniformity is considered necessary for the economic development. Language is significant, not only as a medium of instruction but also as a determinant of societal access. An inclusive society is the foundation of a knowledge society. Today, a command over the English is a most important determinant of higher education and employment. English has been part of our education system for more than a century. Yet, English is beyond the reach of most of our young people. This makes for highly unequal access. There are many debates regarding the medium of instruction in India since independence. The *Three Language Formula* was first devised by the Central Advisory Board of Education in 1956 and formalized by the Education Commission (1964-66). The Constitution of India adopted many provisions about languages. It was claimed that, there should be one language which will be known throughout the length and breadth of the country and that Hindi which is prescribed as the official language at the Centre should be studied compulsorily. But still Hindi is not a communication device for many southern Indian states due to several reasons. As a result of historical causes, English has come to be the one language that is widely known among the educated classes of the country. Much of the national unity in political and other spheres of activity has been brought about through the study of English.

What is the Purpose of Language Study? The question has often been raised as to the number of languages that can be learnt by pupils in the schools and at what stages the study of these languages should be commenced. While considering this problem, take into account the purpose which is to be served by the study of languages. There should be a clear' perspective of the purpose of study of each of these languages. It is ordinarily accepted that the mother-tongue is the most suitable language as a medium of instruction for the child beginning its study. If the same advance had taken place in regional languages as has taken place in many foreign languages, mother-tongue or regional language would have been the medium of instruction at all stages of the educational ladder. As the regional language is likely to be the language used by the majority in the region it is desirable to acquire knowledge of this language. Further, Hindi need to be promote as a link language among all peoples of the country. English language education will reduce the gap between different social classes and it also help to build of an inclusive and just Indian society. English occupies a special place in the domain of education. We are gradually moving towards an indigenous standardized Indian English.

IMPACT OF TECHNOLOGICAL FACTORS ON DEVELOPMENT OF EDUCATION SYSTEM

Technological changes cannot also be ignored in education. Technology and especially modern technology also influence the education system of the country. Historically, emphasis on industrial and technical education followed the industrial revolution. Technology affects the type of education as well as the means of instruction.

With the emergence of computer technology, internet technology, this has revolutionalised the whole education system especially in the developed countries. Through information communication technology, home learning has been made possible. Universities are also adopting e-learning. Today the influence of technology in education cannot be ignored. Indeed the challenge is for the educational administrators and policy makers to see to it that the right infrastructure is in place in order to allow the use of information communication technology fully and be able to reap its maximum benefits in the education system especially in the developing world.

The era of 21st century is often regarded as an era of technology. Technology, today, plays a very important role in our life. It is seen as a basis of growth of an economy. An economy which is poor in technology can never grow in today's scenario. This is because technology makes our work much easier and less time consuming. The impact of technology can be felt in every possible field one such field is Education.

What is technology ?

Technology is a term that refers to a body of knowledge. That is employed to generate tools, create skills, and choose materials for human use. Technology includes the use of materials, tools, techniques, and sources of power to make life easier or more pleasant and work more productive. Education in its general sense is a form of learning in which the knowledge, skills, and habits of a group of people are transferred from one generation to the next through teaching, training, or research.

Type of Technology used in Education.

- **Smart boards**: Smart board is an interactive white board that allows the teacher to project an image from a laptop to the front of the room and the teacher can then digitally draw on that image.
- **Classrooms PC**: They give them the option of recording their notes for long period of time. Most classes require student to do a lot of reports and presentations. You want a computer that will get this job done better than the rest. This allows for students to be more in tune with their learning by allowing them to have their own personal computer.
- **Projectors:** Projectors hook up to the teacher's laptop and projects the screen from the laptop to the white board in the front of the room. By doing this it allows students to see a larger version of what is on the laptop screen.
- **Television:** Televisions can be used to show instructional DVDs or to be able to watch important current events.

Positive Impacts Technology in Education

- **Enhanced Teaching and Learning**: Technological developments like digital cameras, projectors, mind training software, computers, PowerPoint presentations, 3D visualization tools; all these have become great sources for teachers to help students grasp a concept easily. It has to be understood that visual explanation of concepts makes learning fun and enjoyable for students. They are able to participate more in the classroom and even teachers get a chance to make their classes more interactive and interesting.
- **Globalization**: When schools in different parts of the state, students can "meet" their counterparts through video conferencing without leaving the classroom. Some sites, such as www.glovico.com are used to help students learn foreign languages online by pairing a group of students with a teacher from another country.
- **No Geographical Limitations:** With the introduction of online degree programs there is hardly any need of being present physically in the classroom. Even several foreign universities have started online degree courses that student can join. Distance learning and

online education have become very important part of the education system nowadays.

Negative Impacts

- **Declining Writing Skills:** Due to the excessive usage of online chatting and shortcuts, the writing skills of today's young generation have declined quite tremendously. These days, children are relying more and more on digital communication that they have totally forgot about improving their writing skills. They don't know the spelling of different words, how to use grammar properly or how to do cursive writing.
- **Increasing incidents of Cheating**: Technological developments like graphing calculators, high tech watches, mini cameras and similar equipment have become great sources to cheat in exams. It is easier for students to write formulas and notes on graphing calculators, with least chances of being caught.
- **Lack of Focus**: SMS or text messaging has become a favourite pastime of many students. Students are seen playing with their cell phone day and night or driving and very often even between lectures. Being ever-connected to the online world has resulted in lack of focus and concentration in academics and to some extent, even in sports and extracurricular activities.

Technology has a very positive impact on education and at the same time may also pose negative effects. Teachers, and students should take advantage of this in the good light and eliminate the drawbacks which are pulling back many of students as well as schools from achieving excellence. It is thus time for every country to introduce a more technologically equipped education sector in the future.

For over twenty five years now institutions of learning continue to invest in the constantly changing technology, nevertheless one question has remained unanswered all through, "is there any evidence that the use of technology in the learning of students leads to higher levels of the learning?" The need for an answer has increasingly become more urgent in the past few years because of two main factors: One, the need to improve on standards which is based on accountability and two, the organizational cost which is/ will be involved in the purchase and implementation of the technology (Protheroe, 2005).

It is good for any learner, educators, administrator, authority figures in education and the government at large to understand and accept the fact that technology is here to stay. We are living in the world where interacting with technology is inevitable; in fact the digital technology has become part of life, in that it's inseparable from man livelihood. Technology is used in almost all parts of the universe for gathering information, constricting knowledge, keeping records, distance learning, performing simulations, creating proposals, and collaborating lifelong learning and work globally (Margaret etal., 2005). The pervasive use of technology in all spheres of life that includes education, business, communication industry, industries, entertainment, transport, health among many other fields warrants an educator to employ more efforts in preparation of students so that they will play active roles in the technological world (Schacter, 1999). We do not refute the fact that the student will need technology in their day to day lives, but the question we ask ourselves is; will the students' learning be impacted by the employment of technology in their learning system.

We can't help it but seek the truth; policy makers, governors and legislators each year find themselves in a fix facing a difficulty of making a choice among diverse attractive options on educational improvement. The question of whether they should invest on reduction of size of a classroom, teacher's training, textbook addition, childhood education or employment of technology in the learning system so as to perk up the end product of education remains unanswered. Since advanced technology that is employable in the learning system is not very old the study of the impact of technology on the learning of students is still at infancy (Schacter, 1999)

The report from the CEO Forum (2001) has pointed out that there is a need for a student's achievement to be broadened so as to be inclusive of the 21st century skills that will inevitably be required for the student to thrive into the future. The report has argued that the same technology has been important in revitalization of economy, business and development it's equally applicable in enrichment of the education system. It's imperative to employ every arsenal that could play an important role in ensuring that students learning is boasted making the student a better candidate as well as a more productive worker in the future.

In order to raise a student's achievement it's imperative to equip the student with a solid and firm foundation of the basic skills as well as motivate them to learn. Technology can play an important role in facilitating the achievement of this goal. Technology engages students through firing of their imagination. Technology helps teachers to stimulate the minds of young learners in such a way that makes them to have profound and lasting transformation (Jonassen, Howland, Mara, & Crismond, 2006). There are numerous research studies that have been conducted on the impact of technology on the achievements of students in the learning process; the findings of these researches have demonstrated remarkable similarities of the results. This paper has done a review of the literatures on this concept and has revealed the following conclusions:

Learners, especially those who have some disadvantages in life (students with special needs), learn basic skills which include writing, reading and arithmetic faster and better if they get an opportunity to put the skills into practice through use of technology.

Technology manages to engage students; when students are using technology to learn, they tend to be hooked up to technology hence spending more time learning the basic tasks as opposed to the rest of the student who do not use technology (use more traditional methods).

Technology gives a teacher/ lecturer an opportunity to individualize the education curriculum and modify it so that it fits to the needs of an individual student; this helps the students to achieve their potential.

Students who gets opportunities to use technology are exposed to learning through technology portray an advanced level of learning comprehension and a higher likelihood of putting into practice what they learn in their lives (Middleton & Murray, 1999).

Through the exposure to technology in the learning process students are able to access a broader range of communication media in the expression of their ideas and in a more clear and powerful manner.

The exposure to technology makes students develop an attachment to education and learning and hence absenteeism and dropout rates are reduced to near zero. Students are motivated to further their studies and join colleges after graduating from high schools (Grabe & Grabe, 2004).

The self esteem of students is amplified if they learn from technological exposure. When they manage to put into practice what they learn, they feel motivated to share that knowledge and seek further knowledge. They gain greater confidence and abilities in their approach to challenges (Jonassen et al., 2006).

In short, technology is here to stay. In the world that we live in almost all sectors have employed technology in the endeavour to improve their output; sure enough the benefits of technology are clear enough. In the education system there has been little progress in the employment of technology in students learning (Middleton & Murray, 1999). The reason behind little application of technology has been lack of enough evidence to clarify whether technology if employed in the learning of students has any impact. There are contrasting views relating to this question. The various stake holders in education (educators, government, legislators, governors) have over time wondered whether investing in technology in institutions of learning is the most appropriate thing to do in the endeavour of improving the learning system. The employment of technology in the learning system has great positive impact on the learners learning process (McDonald et al., 2008).

According to the secondary data that have been gathered through literature review, the employment of technology in the learning process has immense impact in enhancing the learning of students. The studies conducted have identified that students who are exposed to technology in their daily leaning activities have an increased average performance in their standardized test as opposed to their peers who uses traditional methods to study. The studies have also identified that the students exposed to technology understands concepts more easily and are able to put into practice that which they learn (Grabe & Grabe, 2004). Consequently their self esteem is boosted and they are able to do even better. Technology exposure makes students to develop more attachment to learning hence absenteeism and dropout rates are reduced. Learning becomes more independent and students spend more time studying, and even gaining wider knowledge.

In the world that we currently live in, technology is a very vital factor. With each passing day a new software or gadget is being brought into the market that serves to improve our lives in one way or another and make it much easier and also to advance an already existing software or gadget. However, it is important to note that despite the fact that technology plays a big role in making our lives easier, it is not the only role it has.

Technology is increasingly growing its **importance in the education** sector. The more technology advances, the more benefits it provides for students at every education level.

Technology that is made use of in the classroom is very beneficial in helping the students understand and absorb what they are being taught. For instance, since there are a number of students who are visual learners, projection screens connected to computers could be put in classrooms to let the students see their notes as opposed to simply sitting down and listening to the instructor teach.

There is a number of very good software that can be used to supplement the class curriculum. The programs make available to students quizzes, tests, activities and study questions that could help the students continue with the learning process when they are out of the classroom.

Today, technology has been incorporated into a good number of curriculum even those that do not belong to the technology and computer classes. Students make use of computers to come up with presentations and also make use of the internet to carry out research on a variety of topics for their essays and papers.

Students also get to know how to use the technology available in the world today through the tech and computer classes. This gives the guarantee that following their graduation, the students will not have any difficulties with using technology when they are out there in the work place, which might serve to make them more competitive compared to an individual who has no access to a certain software or technology in school.

With the continuing advances in the technological world, students are getting improved access to such educational opportunities. Every time something 'better' and 'new' is brought into the market, the price of the existing technology is decreased which makes it much more accessible in the educational setting even to those schools that might not have a lot of financial resources available to them.

Technology has greatly grown to the point that it is also available today to assist those kids who are yet to begin school. There are a number of educational systems and video games for the small children that assist them in getting ready for school and in a number of situations also give them a head start on their education.

MODEL QUESTIONS

Very Short Answer type Questions. Each question carries 1 Mark. To be answer in about 20 words each.

1. How of Philosophy and Education intervene each other?

2. What is the impact of Hinduism on Ancient Indian Education?

3. How the Monastic schools located in Buddhist temples acted as a main source of education?

4. "Religious obligation for education gave Jew community an advantage in commerce and trade". Substantiate.

Short Answer type Questions. Each question carries 2 Marks. To be answer in about 150 words each.

5. Illustrate the influence of socio-cultural factors on aims of education, curriculum, methodology, and text books.

6. "The quality of education in country is decided by the economic development of that Country". Justify.

7. How Socialistic and Democratic educational systems are vary.

8. Why educational structure of a country is conditioned by its geographical situation?

Multiple Choice Questions. Each Question carries 1 Mark.

9. A ____________ State will assume complete control of the educational system.

(a) Communist

(b) Totalitarian

(c) Democratic

(d) Socialist

10. In Denmark and Holland, the law requires school attendance from the age of seven years only. It is due to :

(a) Political reasons

(b) Philosophical factors

(c) Geographical factors
(d) Economic factors

11. Which religion have a major influence on the educational systems of Sri Lanka, Thailand, Myanmar, Cambodia, Laos, Tibet and Japan :
(a) Christianity
(b) Islam
(c) Hinduism
(d) Buddhism.

12. Under socialistic economic system, who is the owner of educational institutions.
(a) Edupreneur
(b) State
(c) Principal or Head Master
(d) Municipal Corporation

Answer Key

9: B 10: C 11: D 12: B

References

Abiogu, G. (2014) Philosophy of Education: A Tool for National Development?. *Open Journal of Philosophy*, 4, 372-377. doi: 10.4236/ojpp.2014.43040.

All Answers Ltd. (November 2017). Social And Political Factors That Shape Education Available Education Essay. Retrieved from https://www.ukessays.com/essays/education/social-and-political-factors-that-shape-education-available-education-essay.php?vref=1

All Answers Ltd. (November 2017). *The Impact of Technology on Students Education*. Retrieved on 10-03-2018 from https://www.ukessays.com/essays/education/the-impact-of-technology-on-students-education-essay.php?vref=1

Anderson, D. (1965). Geographic and Economic Factors and the Development of Educational Systems in Western Europe. *Comparative Education Review, 9*(2), 147-154. Retrieved on 10-03-2018 from http://www.jstor.org/stable/1186030

Borah, R.R. Impact of Politics and Concerns with the Indian Education System. *International Journal of Educational Planning & Administration*. Vol. 2, No. 2 (2012), pp. 91-96 retrieved on 10-03-2018 from https://www.ripublication.com/ijepa/ijepav2n2_06.pdf

Chakraborty, A.K. (2003). *Principle and Practice of Education*. Meerat: R. Lal Book Depot.

Factors influencing National Systems of Education. retrieved on 10-03-2018 from http://camponotes.blogspot.in/2013/01/factors-influencing-national-syastems.html

How religion may affect educational attainment: scholarly theories and historical background. (2016). retrieved on 10-03-2018 from http://www.pewforum.org/

2016/12/13/how-religion-may-affect-educational-attainment-scholarly-theories-and-historical-background/

Inder, M. (May 9, 2014). *Impact of Technology on Education*. retrieved on 10-03-2018 from https://www.slideshare.net/maninmax/impact-of-technology-on-education-34470659

Mahendran, A. (Sep. 16, 2015). Education, Skill Development impact on Economic Growth in India. *The Hans India*. retrieved on 10-03-2018 from http://www.thehansindia.com/posts/index/2015-09-16/Education-Skill-Development-impact-on-Economic-Growth-in-India-176280

Manjari, A. *11 Importance Factors Responsible For the Growth of Comparative Education*. retrieved on 10-03-2018 from http://www.shareyouressays .com/knowledge/11-importance -factors-responsible-for- the-growth-of-comparative-education/ 115574

McLaughlin, E. (March 25, 2015). *Religion in Education*. retrieved on 10-03-2018 from https://www.hastac.org/blogs/emmamclaughlin22/2015/03/25/religion-education

National Academy of Sciences Washington (2001). Contextual Forces that Influence the Education System. retrieved on 10-03-2018 from https://www.nap.edu/read/10023/chapter/9.

Taneja, V.P. (2003). *Educational Thought and Practice*. New Delhi: Sterling Publishers (P) Ltd.

Thamarasseri, I., & Bhat, M. S. (2014). *Comparative Education*. New Delhi: Kanishka Publishers

Thamarassseri, I. (2008). *Education in the Emerging Indian Society*, New Delhi: Kanishka Publishers (P) Ltd.

The Effect of Religion on Education Essay. retrieved on 10-03-2018 from https://www.bartleby.com/essay/The-Effect-of-Religion-on-Education-FKSCHSZVC

The Importance of Technology in Education. retrieved on 10-03-2018 from http://myessaypoint.com/the-importance-of-technology-in-education

Williams, J. (July 1, 2007). Cultural and social factors that affect development. retrieved on 10-03-2018 from https://makewealthhistory.org/2007/07/01/cultural-and-social-factors-that-affect-development/

UNIT - 6

A Critical Study of the Educational Programmes

UNIVERSALIZATION OF ELEMENTARY EDUCATION IN SRI LANKA

Sri Lanka is a lower-middle income country with a per capita income of approximately US$ 2,400, and a population of around 20 million people. Sri Lanka's high rate of literacy is due to its sustained growth through the twentieth century. Primary education spans the first five grades of schooling, grades 1-5. Student's progress automatically to lower secondary education for four years of education in grades 6-9 and then on to upper secondary education in grades 10-11 for a two year course that culminates in the **General Certificate of Education Ordinary level examination (GCE O-L).**

The curriculum for primary education is designed separately from those for subsequent stages of education. The primary education curriculum stage is encapsulated in a primary curriculum framework that derives from extensive debate during the 1990s in connection with the recommendations in 1997 of the national education commission, the work of the technical committee on primary education appointed by the presidential task force and detailed implementation work by the primary education unit of the national institute of education. Since 2003 the National Educational Research Centre (NEREC) based at the University of Colombo has administered tests in first Language, Mathematics and English to grade 4 children in a sample of schools country-wide. In the 2009 assessments a cut-off percentage of 80 percent rather than 50 percent were 48 percent in First Language, 53 percent in Mathematics and just 19 percent in English. The budget of the national Ministry of education includes a separate budget line for primary education but this money is allocated only to the primary sections of national schools. Province, zone, division and school budget do not separate allocations and expenditure for primary and secondary. There is no reason in principle why separate budget lines could not be created for most types of expenditure.

Several external agencies have supported the education system and Education for All (EFA) strategies in Sri Lanka. UNICEF continues to provide long term assistance in promoting early childhood care and development of literacy centres, and quality improvement of primary education.

Education has been a major field of state and volunteer activity in Sri Lanka almost throughout her entire history. The Buddhist *pirivenas* modelled on the great Indian institutions of *Taxila* and *Nalanda* and the Brahmin Guru tradition provided both religious and secular education required by the rulers, the priests and the professional classes. Vocational education was provided in the apprenticeship mode while the majority benefited from informal education based on the mores of society. Until the advent of the sea-faring Western invaders the royalty and the nobility had extended their patronage to the founding of historic institutions of learning benefiting both the clergy and the laity, and the production of great religious, literary and professional works, both in prose and in verse. However, with the invaders gaining control over the whole of the country even the few great monastic educational institutions that had not been destroyed in the fighting, fell into abeyance and the flood of religious, literary and professional treatises ceased.

After gaining independence in 1948 successive governments continued with the policy of democratization of educational provision. The progressive increase in enrolment of pupils in schools and the rise in literacy indicate the achievements in this field.

Until 1960 the state schools and state-aided private schools continued to exist side-by-side resulting in a duality of control in the educational system. This dualism operated to the disadvantage of the poor: "The combined effect of these dualities was that educational provision was unplanned, unevenly distributed, wasteful of human and financial resources and that above all access to a quality education was by and large denied to the mass of the rural population and the urban poor." With the take-over of assisted schools for state management in 1960 this duality of control in education was also done away with.

In the 1960s government expenditure on education reached a very high level. It averaged 4.5 per cent of the GNP and 16 to 20 per cent of the annual government budget. Much of this expenditure was incurred on the payment of salaries to the teaching staff and provision of building facilities. But a small percentage was used for quality improvement, e.g., preparation of curriculum material and in-service training of teachers. The extension of science teaching to a large number of rural schools during this period could be described as an attempt to meet the social demand for equality of educational opportunities.

Quantitative expansion of education without a parallel thrust to align the system with the socio-economic needs of the country resulted in a relatively high incidence of educated unemployment. The system's output mainly prepared students for white collar jobs and administrative careers, far exceeding the demand of the economy. The educational reforms introduced in the early part of the 1970s gave "first priority to the task of formulating a new structure that will be well fitted to the needs of the country over the years ahead." These reforms introduced an 'integrated' curriculum laying emphasis on pupil participation and activity-based learning in the primary grades and a common curriculum including science, mathematics and pre-vocational subjects in the junior secondary grades.

Certain modifications in the system, with regard to the grade structure of the school system, was introduced in 1978. The supply of free school books is another progressive step that helped to retain a larger number of pupils in the system. The importance of non-formal education as a means of providing vocational and technical training opportunities for school drop-outs as well as continuing education and personal fulfilment courses for adults was recognized and several projects were inaugurated to benefit the target population.

The Constitution of Sri Lanka in its chapter on Directive Principles of State Policy and Fundamental Duties, states that the state is pledged to establish in Sri Lanka a democratic socialist society of which one of the objectives is "The complete eradication of illiteracy and the assurance to all persons of the right to universal and equal access to education at all levels." Thus the principle of universal and compulsory education is enshrined in the Constitution.

The size of schools in Sri Lanka varies from less than 50 pupils to over 4000 pupils. The small schools are situated mostly in the remote rural areas and the plantation districts while the large schools are situated in densely populated cities. A large number of schools in Sri Lanka are co-educational. But there are a few single-sex schools in the cities. Most of these are assisted schools established during the colonial era. Of the 9521 schools, 149 are boys' schools and 210 are girls' schools while 9162 or 96 per cent are mixed. According to enrolment figures in the primary cycle male enrolment is slightly higher than female enrolment. However in the junior secondary and senior secondary cycles the females outnumber the males.

The present school system in Sri Lanka can be described as mainly a state-controlled system. The system that existed during the colonial period was characterized by a dual management: the government system of schools and the assisted school system run by various religious denominations with government assistance. Following the take-over of the assisted schools in 1960 only 62 schools remain outside the state system. Of these 62 schools 25 schools receive financial assistance from the government for the payment of teachers' salaries. All schools have to follow the national policy on education as enunciated by the government.

There are other educational institutions called *Pirivenas*, which are run by the Buddhist clergy mainly for the purpose of imparting the training necessary for those aspiring to enter the Buddhist priesthood and the lay students over 14 years of age who wish to be trained in a religious atmosphere. Some of these institutions are well known centres of oriental learning in the tradition of the ancient Buddhist institutes of learning. About 330 institutions are financially supported by the government.

The Education Ministry does not directly conduct pre-education centres. As the lower limit of school age is fixed at five years it is believed that the activity-based, environmentally-based instruction given in the kindergarten is adequate preparation for formal education. However a large number of voluntary organizations and private individuals are engaged in running pre-school centres. In the rural areas the *Sarvodaya Movement*, the rural development societies and village development councils (Gramodaya Mandalayas) have organized such centres. In the plantation sector, such centres are organized by the state plantation co-operatives. The Ministry of Local Government and the Ministry of Social Services assist voluntary organizations to set up pre-school institutions. In the urban areas there are many efficiently-managed private nursery schools. Although the Education Ministry does not run pre-school institutions, the Ministry is exploring the possibility of providing facilities such as training of pre-school teachers and regulating management of preschools run by various organizations and individuals.

The adult education programmes were reorganized in the 1970s to meet the needs of out-of-school youths and adults in the country. A technical and vocational training programme for school drop-outs was launched to train them in skills which would help them to enter the job market or establish self-employment. In 1978 a general adult education programme was started to provide life enrichment courses for the adult population. Adult education officers were appointed on an electorate basis to organize this programme. In 1981 the Ministry organized literacy centres on a pilot basis to provide an alternative structure to the formal school with a view to realizing UPE. The non-formal education programmes have close linkages with the formal system and often use the resources of the formal system. Programmes such as literacy centres facilitate the re-entry of their clients into the formal system. The universities and tertiary educational institutes are administered by the Ministry of Higher Education.

In the decade of the nineties activities under the Education for All programme appear to have been enriched and accelerated by Sri Lanka's own reform agenda. The Report of the Youth Commission (SP I of 1990) carried a recommendation for the appointment of a National Commission for Education Policy "which would aim at achieving a consensus with regard to education policy". Acting on this recommendation the government appointed a National Education Commission in 1991 with members whose appointment was approved both by the government and the opposition. This Commission in

1995 presented a set of proposals aimed at extending educational opportunity and quality improvement in education in schools. A Presidential Task Force and twelve technical committees working under the Task Force were appointed in December 1996 to prepare policy proposals for implementation.

With the acceleration of the pace of implementation Compulsory Education Regulations that came into operation in January 1998 and the Grade I Primary Education Reforms were implemented in the Gampaha district in 1998 and introduced islandwide in 1999. The same procedure was adopted in implementing the Grades 2-5 Primary Education Reforms too, first in the Gampaha district, in grade order, and islandwide in the following year in the same order. (NEC 2003 PP. 16-17)

The compulsory Education Regulations passed by Parliament as part of these reforms apply to children in the age group 5 to 14. Parents are required to ensure admission of their children to school and their continuous attendance thereafter. (General Education Reforms: 3.1.1) All obstacles that hitherto stood in the way of admitting children to school were cleared. For instance, in cases where parents were not able to submit birth certificates of their children, Heads of schools were instructed to accept affidavits or a letter from the *Grama Niladhari* (Village Administrative Officer) as proof of a child's age.

In addition to textbooks, further incentives such as clothing, stationery and school needs were to be provided according to need, to families requiring such assistance. Voluntary organizations and non Governmental Organizations were encouraged to help in these programmes. In order to encourage and enable girls of school-going age to attend school they were to be released from the domestic responsibility of looking after their younger siblings at home by the establishment of crèches and day care centres under the Early Childhood Development Programme.

During the five years of primary education the child was expected to attain the following goals of education:

- Being knowledgeable and well informed
- Being practically skilled
- Being disciplined
- Being refined
- Being able to speak well

Under these reforms a competency-based curriculum was to be implemented. A "competency" was defined as a combination of knowledge, skills, attitudes and values. It was expected that during the primary school years the child would acquire the following five basic competencies related to,

- communication
- the natural, social and artificial environment

- ethics and religion
- the use of leisure, enjoyment and recreation
- learning to learn.

The primary stage of education was to consist of three Key Stages as follows:

- Key Stage One: Grades 1 and 2
- Key Stage Two: Grades 3 and 4
- Key Stage Three: Grade 5

In order to attain the EFA goals the following targets, among others were to be considered:

- To ensure the initial enrolment of all boys and girls in school at the official primary school entry age of 5+ by 2004.
- To increase the levels of learning achievement by all pupils in the Key Stages of primary education by 2004. (General Education Reforms, Chapter 4)

Sri Lanka joined the Monitoring Learning Achievement Project in 1994 and in the same year carried out a sample survey of learning achievement. Students who completed the primary cycle of education (Grade 05) in 1993 formed the target group of this study. The study highlighted the following unsatisfactory features that prevailed throughout the country:

- Poor performance levels in Literacy, Numeracy and Life Skills.
- Wide disparities in performance among (a) districts and (b) school categories.

In order to remedy the above defects and raise the quality of primary education the following steps were taken:

- Awareness programmes were conducted to bring to the notice of everyone concerned the state of primary education in the country as a whole and within the different districts/regions.
- The structure of the Year Five scholarship Examination coming at the end of the primary cycle was changed so as to ensure a beneficial backwash effect on the classroom.
- Essential learning levels that all students should acquire at the end of each year, in the two subject areas, Language and Mathematics were identified.
- Attempts were made to bring about an attitudinal change in primary school teachers by de-linking them from teacher centred learning and guiding them towards child-centred learning.
- Quality improvement projects were implemented in districts that had registered poor student achievement.

Several measures are being taken to broaden opportunities for education in information and Communication Technology (ICT) for schools in remote areas (Central Bank of Sri Lanka, 2010, p. 75). Basic strategies identified under Primary the Education Reform were.

- The Extension of Education Opportunities
- Quality Improvement of Primary Education
- Professionalization of Teachers
- Management of Education and Provision of Resources

These strategies exhibited a high degree of congruence with the goals of Dakar Framework for action under EFA. The launch of initial reforms was guided by short - term action plans developed by PTF in 1997. These strategies gave considerable force to the initiation of reforms. The Ministry of Education, realizing the need for long - term plans to ensure the sustained implementation and institutionalization of the reforms, has taken timely action to develop a National Level Five Year Plan for Primary Education with the involvement of all major stake-holders in primary education both at National and at Provincial Level. The programme was sponsored by the Department for Intentional (DFID, UK, n.d.).

The ministry of Education has identified 150 schools as "Isuru Schools" with the objective of developing these schools to the level of national schools for secondary education in selected divisional secretariat areas to ease the high demand for admission into national schools. it is expected to increase the number of "Isuru Schools" to 325 by end 2012 Further, the government has taken measures to develop 1,000 full-fledged secondary schools island wide, with the establishment of a primary school network as a measure to ensure quality education for all. Measures are being taken to establish "Teacher Villages" for teachers to facilitate their livelihood in remote areas so as to effectively address the shortage of teachers in those areas.

The Education Sector Development Framework and Program - ESDFP (2006 -2010) also was organized under four main policy themes, with the intention of introducing the quality education to the system. These are: Theme 1: Promoting equitable access to basic and secondary education; Theme 2: Improving the quality of primary and secondary education; Theme 3: Enhancing the economic efficiency and equity of resource allocation; and Theme 4: Strengthening education governance and service delivery.

Under these reforms the disparities in the primary sector among the schools were limited to certain extent. But, there is a lack of access to quality of education largely visible due to the factors such as; disparities in the distribution of facilities and resources, inadequate teachers deployment to rural areas, uneven distribution of skills among teachers, inadequate cost recovery in tertiary education, lack of accountability, effective supervision, monitoring, and evaluation, and lock of linkages within and outside the educational system.

Lack of resources and teacher shortages are worse for smaller schools mostly situated in rural areas, particularly schools in conflict-affected North and East, in remote plantations, and in less developed provinces. Linked to frequent changes in the organization and management systems, political influence over resource allocation and personnel appointments, and centralized decision-making.

Sri Lanka views education as a fundamental right of every individual. The acceptance of this view by every political party in the country is a manifestation of the importance which the country as a whole attaches to democratization of education. The pre-eminent position given to education in the country's value system has led to the enshrinement of the principle of universalization of education in the country's constitution which is the fundamental law of the land. Provision of a legal basis for compulsory education, expansion of educational facilities and enforcement of compulsory attendance requirements are different dimensions of an endeavour to bring education within reach of all individuals. This multi-dimensional approach was adopted in the past to achieve the ideal of universal education. However, experience has clearly demonstrated that neither the expansion of facilities or the enforcement of compulsory attendance was sufficient to achieve universalization. Utilization of educational facilities is a function of the socio-economic status of the people and their attitudes. Improvement of socioeconomic conditions would lead to a higher rate of participation.

Participation in education is determined not only by the educational opportunities that are provided but also by the degree to which such opportunities are used. Provision of a wide network of schools is no guarantee that educational opportunities are within the reach of the intended target group. It has been observed that socio-economic factors keep a certain proportion of children of school-going age away from school. Several measure:, have been adopted by the state to reduce the cost of education to parents and to induce them to send their children to school.

The supply of free textbooks has contributed to increased retention of pupils within the system, The fact that the books were supplied to all pupils without considering the financial capacity of parents prevented a social stratification of pupils within the school. Provision of free 'snacks' to all children in the lower grades of the primary cycle of selected schools in another positive measure taken to provide some degree of relief to the more economically depressed. The free mid-day meal programme is implemented In collaboration with the CARE. Scholarships enable talented pupils from disadvantaged homes to continue education in better-equipped secondary schools. Children in the last grade of the primary cycle who perform well at the scholarship examination are entitled to financial assistance from the state if the income levels of their parents are low.

Nearly 30 per cent of the pupils who enter the school system leave before completing the primary cycle. One of the reasons for the failure of the system to retain all pupils until completion of the primary cycle is the fact that the curriculum and the instructional methodologies often fail to stimulate and sustain interest. The promotion of activity-based methods, particularly through environmental studies and creative activities, is a major objective of quality improvement in primary education. The Ministry seeks to improve pupil performance through specialized primary teacher training, curriculum revision, textbook writing and the development of a minimum learning continuum. Assessment of pupil performance will be part of the teaching activity.

The decision taken by the Ministry to deploy graduate teachers in the primary grades is part of a system of innovations aimed at improving the quality of primary education. The open school. The Ministry is committed to a policy of expansion of non-formal education based on the philosophy of continuing and recurrent education. Implementation of a proposal contained in Education Proposals for Reform will lead to the establishment of an island-wide network of open schools.' The open school will provide a variety of courses including personal enrichment courses, vocational courses and courses facilitating re-entry into the formal education system. The drop-outs from the formal system and the disadvantaged who have never gone to school will be offered opportunities for further development. Different types of non-formal education programmes will be offered using the facilities of a cluster of schools. One important function of the open school will be to function as a support centre for the large majority who leave school to enter the world of work.

School zoning and rationalization of the school network: A main weakness of past strategies was the emphasis placed on the development of individual schools in the endeavour to democratize educational opportunities. Development of a network of schools to meet the educational needs of identified geographical areas.

One of the objectives of the school zoning and rationalization plan is UPE. School facilities will be used to benefit as large a proportion as possible of the school-age population. Regional education authorities will prepare a three-year rolling plan for the educational development of each zone taking into consideration the likely enrolments in each cycle of education. The zoning plans will be integrated into a three-year rolling plan for the educational development of the whole district/region.

Although Sri Lanka has achieved a high level of participation in primary education, the country is likely to progress toward universalisation rather slowly. Participation in education is a function of a multiplicity of factors and the mere provision of teachers and classrooms is unlikely to significantly affect the enrolment ratio. Many children in disadvantaged environments do not attend school even when facilities are available within easy reach. Strategies for improved participation must take into consideration both the needs of deprived localities and the need to optimize the use of available resources.

The policy objectives underlying the present efforts and the strategies employed for achieving UPE may be summarized as follows:

- Reduction of inter-district and intra-district disparities to bring about democratization of education;
- Positive discrimination in providing facilities to bring education within reach of disadvantaged groups;
- Enrichment of the primary curriculum to provide stimulating experiences for growing minds;
- Enhancement of the internal efficiency of the system through reduction of repetition and drop-out rates;
- Rationalization of the school network to optimize the use of resources in the endeavour to provide equal educational opportunities;
- Development of formal and non-formal programmes with cross linkages to facilitate the flow of pupils between the two systems;
- Employment of non-formal modalities to meet the educational needs of school drop-outs and non-participants;
- Development of management capabilities for principals of schools to increase the efficiency of the system;
- Provision of incentives to retain the school-age population within the school system; and
- Integration of educational and rural development activities at the grass-roots level.

For more than fifty years Sri Lanka has consistently adhered to a policy of democratization of education. Implementation of this policy has resulted in a relatively high level of participation. However, the country has to progress further to achieve UPE. Improvement of socio-economic conditions, especially in the disadvantaged localities; improvement and further expansion of the school network within the formal system; and the adoption of alternative structures for the education of those who have not benefited from the formal system will hasten the process of universalization.

UNIVERSALIZATION OF ELEMENTARY EDUCATION IN BANGLADESH

Bangladesh has one of the largest primary education systems in the world with an estimated 16.4 million primary school aged children (6 to10 years). There are 365,925 primary school teachers (approximately 53% of teachers and 23% of head teachers are women), working in more than 82,218 schools (with ten different types of schools, including Madrasahs). The Primary

Education Compulsory Act passed in 1990 made primary education free and compulsory for all children up to Grade 5.

Bangladesh is now at a crossroads, given its educational development and growth pattern. With a large and relatively young population – 155 million people in 2012, and 31 percent of them below the age of 15 - the country is poised to earn a considerable demographic dividend, provided these young people get the opportunity of quality education and skills development resulting in gainful employment. The headway Bangladesh has already made in education as well as in other social sectors is globally recognized, but there are still a number of formidable challenges that need to be correctly identified and tackled with utmost efficiency and commitment. It consists of three Policy Notes (PNs) focused on Access and Equity, Education Quality, and Skills Development.

Bangladesh has a good track record in enhancing access and equity in education, with remarkable achievements in widening access to primary education, attaining gender equity at the primary and secondary education levels, marked reduction in repetition and dropout rates, and attaining reasonably high levels of completion in primary education. Gender equity in primary and secondary education has been achieved well ahead of the Millennium Development Goal target set for 2015. But on the debit side, enrolments of the poor are still lagging. About five million children are still out of school, either because they did not enrol in school or dropped out very early, mostly due to poverty. The repetition rates are still high despite the notable decline in recent years. The transition rates are low across various levels of education. Children living in urban slums suffer from both demand and supply-side limitations to education. What needs to be done now is to target the remaining, hardest-to reach population groups so that they have access to universal primary education. Quality early childhood development should be pursued and the efficiency level in the utilization of funds substantially improved. Budgetary allocations for secondary and higher education also have to be increased considerably.

The Bangladesh education system is large, catering to over 30 million students, involving many stakeholders (for example, there are 13 types of providers in primary education; 10 examination boards at the secondary level; and about 98 percent of secondary institutions are private, mostly supported through public subsidies). The country has experimented with some of the most innovative models of demand-side financing and public-private partnerships. There are two ministries managing education - the Ministry of Primary and Mass Education (MoPME), which covers primary education (grades 1–5), non-formal education, and literacy; and the Ministry of Education (MoE), which is mandated to oversee secondary education (grades 6–12), technical and vocational education and training, higher education, and *madrasah* education.

With regard to quality of education, Bangladesh has already taken some bold steps to assess the health of the education system. Some major projects are now being implemented to address the quality question at the primary, secondary and tertiary levels. However, the challenges for improving the quality of the education system are daunting and multi-faceted. They include low learning levels, inadequate acquisition of non-cognitive skills, inequitable learning among students, a high degree of variation between schools, low teacher motivation, low time on task, weak examinations and teacher development systems, limited incentives for performance compared to much fewer disincentives for poor performance, and low levels of accountability in properly using public finance. The Quality PN seeks to diagnose the maladies, and suggest policy options that may raise the levels of education quality. One of its important messages is that issues in education quality improvement are neither linear nor uni-dimensional, and that they require simultaneous interventions on several fronts.

The Government of Bangladesh recognises education as a means of reducing poverty and improving the quality of life for children. As a signatory to the Convention on the Rights of the Child, the Government of Bangladesh, with assistance from development partners, has made positive steps towards fulfilling children's rights to education, according to the Education for All and Millennium Development Goals. As a result, the country has made significant progress towards achieving universal primary education and gender parity in schools.

In 2003, Bangladesh prepared a national action plan for 'Education for All' with a specific set of goals to be achieved by 2015 and took the Dakar Framework of Action, 2000 as the basis of that work. The plan embraces all the goals of EFA for making education accessible to all and provided for all. The country has prepared 'Primary Education Development Program-II' (PEDP-II) on the basis of Dakar framework and national Plan of Action. The main objectives of PEDP-II are to increase primary school access, participation and completion in accordance with government policy related to EFA and other commitments and to improve the quality of student learning and performance outcomes.

Equitable Access: The aspect of equitable access to primary education coincides with the perception of human rights across the gender identity and disadvantaged groups. Current conception of human rights includes a variety of attributes, such as economic rights, and cultural rights; all these aspects are related to equal access to education provision for all. Article 3 of the World Declaration on Education for All pointed out that: Basic education should be provided to all children, youth, and adults. To this end, basic education services of quality should be expanded and consistent measures must be taken to reduce disparity (UNESCO, 1990:3). The declaration further reiterated that for basic education to be equitable, all children, youth and adults must be given the opportunity to achieve and maintain an acceptable level of learning. The most urgent priority was given to ensure access to, and remove every obstacle that hampers their active participation. An UNESCO study entitled Salamanca Declaration and Salamanca Framework for Action emphasized that, Schools should accommodate all children regardless of their physical, intellectual, emotional, social, linguistic or other conditions (UNESCO, 1994: Article 3:6). In line with this roadmap Bangladesh pursued a comprehensive policy in the provision of access to quality education for primary school aged children including girls' through numerous interventions. The Primary Education Compulsory Act, which was passed in Parliament in 1993, underlined that: "No child be deprived of education for lack of teacher, learning materials and adequate space and No child be subject to disparities of access to primary education arising from gender, income, family, cultural or ethnic differences and geographic remoteness" (JS-Legislation, 1990:2). As part of this policy thrust, a separate ministry for primary education has been established in 2003, and primary education became free for all children in government run schools. Textbooks at the primary level are free for students in all government and registered non government schools, stipend programs and incentives are given for the purpose of equitable access to primary education. The Directorate of Primary Education (DPE) is currently (2003-2008) implementing Primary Education Development Program-II (PEDP-II) with an overall investment cost US$2.6 billion, which is a sector-wide effort undertaken by the government (Baseline Report, 2005:11). Fundamental to the PEDP II is the concept of a coordinated and integrated sub sector approach, assisted by multiple donors, but run by the Government of Bangladesh (GOB) through Ministry of Primary and Mass Education (MOPME) and the DPE, with the basic aim of improving the quality of the primary education provision for all children in Bangladesh (PEDP II, 2003:1). Due to these policies and programs, Bangladesh has achieved a phenomenal change in the past ten years; especially in terms of achieving MDGs and equitable access to primary education.

Issues of UEE in Bangladesh

Despite many achievements during the past decade, major improvements are still needed in order for all children to receive the benefit of quality education. The major challenges include: poor quality of education; high dropout rates; promotion of equity and accessing education; decentralization of education administration; and special needs education. In terms of access, the high enrolment rates achieved for both boys and girls do not yet equate to covering ALL the children in Bangladesh. It is currently estimated that there are more than 3.3 million out-of-school children throughout the country. Schooling opportunities are also very limited for some specific groups such as working children, disabled children, indigenous children and those in remote areas or living in extreme poverty. The UNICEF 2006 Multiple Indicator

Cluster Survey reports that only about half of the children living in urban slums attend school compared to a national average of 81% net attendance ratio, and about 24% of slum girls never enrol in any form of formal or non-formal school. Even for those who are enrolled, completion of the primary education cycle is a critical issue. Only 55% of children eventually reach Grade 5.

Access of girls and boys to primary education is no longer an issue. However, equity is a major concern in the aspects of gender and inclusiveness for disadvantaged children. While more girls are currently enrolled in primary school compared to boys the number of girl students significantly decreases through secondary school. The school environment is far from fully inclusive. Disadvantaged children (such as children with disabilities or from ethnic minorities) are particularly vulnerable to exclusion from educational opportunities. For example, it is estimated by the Bangladesh Bureau of the Census that approximately 10% of the children of preschool and primary-school age (3-10 years) are disabled. Currently 77,488 children with special needs of various types are enrolled in primary schools. Contrary to the overall and general trend of girls' enrolment in schools being higher than that of boys, the enrolment of girls with special needs is significantly lower than boys. There are many children who are not going to school but who could attend if schools were more inclusive using child friendly.

The quality of the teaching learning process, the school environment and children's learning achievements are also major challenges. Poor qualifications and lack of teacher motivation are major challenges. Approximately 24% of Government Primary Schools and Registered Non Government Primary Schools teachers are untrained. The traditional and dominant way of teaching in most schools tends to focus on memorizing facts. There is little emphasis on developing analytical, practical or vocational skills. This results in several issues such as low achievement rate, high dropout and high repetition rate. Currently, it takes an average of 8.6 years (8.7 for boys and 8.5 for girls) for a child to complete the five-year primary school cycle.

Contact hours are an essential component of learning. Unfortunately, contact hours in Bangladesh average about half of the international standard of 900-1000 per year. 90% of schools are double shift, meaning that student in Grade 1 & 2 attend in the morning (2 hours) and Grade 3 to 5 in the afternoon (3.5 hours). Coupled with high student absenteeism rates of 19%, the actual average contact hours could be even lower.

Improved toilets and water supply are also a priority area for improvement in primary schools. Access to quality facilities is directly associated with quality of retention and attendance rates of students. The number of toilets in schools has been increasing however, an acute shortage remains. In 2008, 5% of schools reported having no toilet and another 14%7 of schools reported the use of only one toilet. On average, in primary schools, there are 150 pupils to each toilet. Similarly, poorly functioning tube-wells and access to water, including water free from arsenic, continue to challenge schools and impact on the retention and dropout rates of children. As a result of all these factors, children's achievement levels are far below the national targets. Only about half of the primary school graduates achieve the minimum national curriculum competencies.

Hossain (1978) conducted a study on the problems of introducing universal primary education system in Bangladesh to identify the different problems from various areas; namely, economic, social, environmental, geographical, religious, administrative and political. The study is mainly descriptive in nature and it used survey method. It finds that the programmes of universal provision, enrolment, and retention effected by socio-economic, geographical, religious, administrative and political factors. Besides these, poverty of parents as well as state creates problem to introducing the universal primary education system in Bangladesh.

Impact of UEE in Bangladesh

During the past decade, Bangladesh has made great progress in improving the primary education situation. The number of enrolled students increased from 12 million in 1990 to over 16 million in 2008, and net enrolment rate was boosted from 60% in 1990 to 90.8% in 2008. Equality has also improved as girls' primary school enrolment has increased and surpassed boys in primary education. Similarly, the percentage of female teachers has been steadily increasing. In 2008 about 53% of teachers in GPS and RNGPS were female, up from 21% in 1990. The proportion of female head teachers, however, remains low with only 23% female posts in 2008 (up from 18% in 2005). Below is a summary of a range of improvements to the quality of teaching and learning in the classrooms:

- SLIPs are empowering head teachers and teachers and strengthening their professional motivation, thereby enhancing their sense of ownership of in schools. Like many decentralization reforms, the School Level Improvement Plans (SLIP) initiative is strengthening the participation of teachers, School Management Committees, parental and community involvement in schools.
- There is improved awareness of education among parents and teachers encouraging students to enrol and take part in and stay in school.
- School level planning processes are encouraging better links among teachers, parents and School Management Committees. The community and School Management Committees have become

more involved in school management and supervision through school planning exercises.

- Decentralized management of the school calendar has brought improved school administration in rural areas where attendance ratios link directly to agricultural and storm seasons.
- 64 million free textbooks were provided to pupils. In 2008, 91% of primary students received their textbooks within the first two month of the academic year.
- A large number of training programmes have been carried out to improve the quality of education. In 2008, 74% of Government Primary Schools (GPS) and 77% of Registered Non-Government Primary Schools (RNGPS) of primary school teachers had the Certificate in Education, 41% of GPS and 45% of RNGPS teachers received subject based training to refresh and enrich their classroom teaching techniques and 25% of GPS and 28% of RNGPS teachers received basic in-service training.

Bangladesh has improved **access and completion** at all levels of education, especially at the primary level. As a result of massive expansion of supply, targeted stipends to bring the poorest and girls into schools, and continued investments in education, Bangladesh achieved almost universal access in primary education. Primary and secondary gross enrolment rates (GERs) have reached 101 percent and 63 percent in 2010, increasing from 91 and 52 percent in 2000, respectively. The primary net enrolment rate (NER) is most recently reported as 93 percent. Enrolment in pre-primary is low at 23 percent (2009). Primary, lower secondary, and secondary education completion have systematically increased over time. Thirty-six percent of people aged 41–50 in 2010 have completed primary education; whereas that same share among people aged 15–19 is 76 percent, indicating that the share of primary school completers has more than doubled in 30 years.

Bangladesh has achieved **gender equity** in both primary and secondary education, well ahead of the Millennium Development Goal target set for 2015. Females are ahead of males in primary and junior secondary, but behind them in higher secondary and tertiary completion rates. Between 2000 and 2010, the primary NER increased from 67 to 80 percent for females and from 64 to 74 percent for males. Girls outnumber boys in secondary education - the NER increased from 44 to 55 percent for girls and from 32 to 45 percent for boys. In higher education, however, just 40 percent of the enrolled students are female. At the primary and junior secondary level, completion rates of females are 8 to 9 percentage points higher than those of males in 2010, and the gender gap in completion at the junior secondary level has reversed between 2000 and 2010, favouring toward females. However, at the secondary and higher education level, men have 5 to 7 percent higher completion rates than women, although the gap is decreasing. Only about 45 percent of tertiary students are female. The number of female students is even lower for public and private universities, at around 26 percent.

Other National Efforts of Bangladesh

In response to the initiative arising from the World Conference on Education for All and the advocacy efforts in the wake of the World Summit for Children, the Bangladesh government established a National Committee on Basic Education for All, which is headed by the Minister of Education and consists of representatives of government ministries and NGOs. The Committee's task is to help identify national policy and strategic options, promote coordination and review progress. A Steering committee headed by the Secretary of Education also has been set up at the working level to support the work of the National Committee.

In addition with the participation of the Prime Minister and the Executive Director of UNICEF, the government initiated a social mobilization programme in 1992. The objectives of this initiative are to generate and sustain national awareness and of commitment to education for all at all levels. The programme is expected to implement several strategies: develop a consensus among politicians, planners and administrators, activate community bodies such as school managing committees and parent-teacher groups, remove gender bias in all education materials, and promote coordinated involvement of the government, NGOs and other allies.

Bangladesh is fortunate in having a fairly widespread network of institutions for education. Basic education facilities fall into two broad categories:

- Government financed and controlled primary schools (approximately 38,000 directly managed by the government and 8,000 government recognised but privately managed). These schools follow a standard curriculum and have boys and girls in the proportion of roughly 60 to 40 percent.
- Community supported religious educational institutions: (a) about 60,000 (maketabas, vihars) for religious education of young boys and girls in about equal proportion, (b) about 20,000 primary level lbtedayee Madrassas (IM) with about 63,000 teachers and 1. 7 million students.

Bangladesh is one of the poorest countries of the world, which has failed to provide educational facilities to all the children belonging to the relevant age-group. In this context, the role of the non-governmental and voluntary organizations can be of great help, particularly in the field of primary education, where the government has failed to do so.

Enrolments of the poor are lagging in Bangladesh

Inequity in primary enrolment because of household poverty has been reduced by half between 2000 and 2010. For example, the gap in the primary NER has declined from 16 to 6 percentage points between 2000 and 2010. However, secondary GER among the poor (45 percent) is substantially low compared to 76 percent for the non-poor. In tertiary, NER for the non-poor increased from 9 percent to 11 percent between 2000 and 2010, while NER for the poor remains at the same level as 10 years ago, thereby widening the gap between the two groups.

Repetition and dropout rates have declined, but they are still high; combined with low transition rates across various levels of education, these imply low levels of learning in Bangladesh. Seven percent of grade 1 students repeat the grade, raising concern about the readiness of new entrants to primary education. Ten percent of grade 5 students repeat grade 5, suggesting that many are not ready to complete primary education. In addition, although the primary school dropout rate of government primary schools (GPSs) and registered nongovernment primary schools (RNGPSs) has declined from 47 to 40 percent between 2005 and 2010, the dropout and repetition rates for GPSs and RNGPSs (45 and 12 percent in 2009, Bangladesh Primary Education Annual Sector Performance Report [ASPR] in 2011) are significantly higher than the national average of 6 and 5 percent in 2009, respectively. A significant percentage of children aged 6–17 drop out of school very early; 6 percent of children stop at the pre-primary level, another 6 percent complete only grade 1, and 24 percent complete grade 5 but never enrol in secondary education. Given the level of repetition and dropout rates in 2009, it is estimated that out of 10 primary students who enter school, only about 7 to 8 students reach grade 5; 6 to 7 students transit to grade 6; 5 students reach grade 10; and 3 to 4 students complete higher secondary without any repetition.

About 5 million children are still out of school, either because they did not enrol in school or dropped out very early, mostly due to poverty. This is the population of children who are most difficult to bring to school and most difficult to retain until the completion of the primary cycle. About 16 percent of children aged 6-14 are out of school (2010) and 13 percent of children never enrol in or never complete grade 1 (HIES, 2010). Parents' education and household income are two of the most significant risk factors for children being out of school. The poorest children (coming from the poorest 20 percent of families) are 12 percent more likely to be out of school, and this difference is mostly due to them having a lower chance of ever enrolling in or completing grade 1, compared to the richest 20 percent. Having a mother with more than a secondary education reduces the chance of being out of school by about 8 percent, compared to having a mother with no education, after taking into account other risk factors. Geographically, children in the Sylhet, Dhaka, and Chittagong divisions have a higher risk of being out of school. Disabled children and those with learning difficulties are pretty much out of reach of the education system in the country at present.

Children living in urban slums are suffering not only from demand but also supply-side limitations to education. The primary GER in the slums is 91 percent, compared to 101 percent nationwide. Similarly, the NER is 62 percent in the slums compared to the national rate of 77 percent (2010). For secondary education, the current GER and NER in the slums are comparable to the 1995 national rates. Twenty five percent of secondary school-aged children of poor households in the slums attend secondary school, while the number is 49 percent among the non-poor slum households. There is a gender gap in enrolment, favouring females. A gap of 18 percentage points is observed between the primary school GER of extremely poor households versus the non-poor in slums, while for secondary education; the gap is even wider (24 percentage points). Although 60 percent of slum primary students attend government and NGO schools and about 70 percent of slum secondary students attend non-government schools, evidence points to a shortage of accessible schools for slum children, especially at secondary level, and the availability of NGO schools is one of the strong supply factors associated with increasing enrolment for slum children. Children whose households migrated recently to the slums are more likely to drop out. The largest share of education spending for slum children goes to private tutoring, both in primary (21 percent) and secondary (31 percent) education.

Although low by international and regional standards, the government of Bangladesh is the largest contributor to education financing in the country. The amount Bangladesh spends on education has remained relatively stable in the last 10 years, oscillating between 2.2–2.5 percent of the gross domestic product (GDP) over 2000–2008, while countries like India and Nepal have had ratios ranging from 3.1–4.4 percent and 3.0–4.6 percent, respectively, in the same period. The average public education spending of low-income countries is also consistently higher than that of Bangladesh over the last decade, at around 3.2–3.7 percent. Almost all government schools - secular and religious - are funded by public resources, both in primary and secondary education in the form of Monthly Pay Orders (MPOs) to cover teacher salaries, and they provide free tuition and a stipend to rural female students. Teacher salaries—which represent more than 90 percent of the total education budget, both in government and non-government schools—essentially come from the revenue budget. This leaves little room for operational expenditures. According to the benefit incidence analysis, the poorer households are receiving more public education spending at the lower education levels, but the higher education spending is directed more toward the richer population.

Policy directions towards UEE in Bangladesh

Target the remaining, hardest-to-reach population groups to attain universal access in primary education. Reaching the goals of universal access in primary and higher enrolments in secondary will be important to help Bangladesh get closer to its goal of reaching middle-income status. This could be pursued through: (i) identifying the remaining hard-to-reach population and developing specific policies and programs to address their needs; (ii) developing a program to address the educational needs of children in urban slums; (iii) scaling up successful stipend schemes, and (iv) working in close partnership with the non-government sector.

Pursue quality early child development. Early child development (ECD) has shown a lot of promise in terms of equalizing learning outcomes, such as enrolment, retention, and cognitive development among children from diverse backgrounds. The learning gains have been highest for children from the poorest backgrounds. In Bangladesh, remaining inequities—which seem to start early and continue throughout the lifetime—are large. And, enrolment in early child development is quite low at present. It is therefore recommended that Bangladesh attempt to provide high-quality ECD to all of its children. Since the non-public sector has been a principal provider of these services, attempts should be made to work closely with them, facilitating expansion of their services through public financing of these NGO-run programs.

Enhance efficiency. High levels of inefficiency indicate that increasing expenditures will not necessarily result in better outcomes, and the chances for underutilization of funds, or misuse of funds, remain. To reduce repetition and dropout rates and improve transition rates in the education system, it requires a two-pronged approach—improve the quality and relevance of education, as well as support for disadvantaged children to lessen the negative impact of demand-side constraints (such as poverty and learning difficulties). In Bangladesh, both areas need to be prioritized. Demand-side constraints can be tackled through some of the aforementioned initiatives, but improvements in the system's quality and relevance will determine, to a large extent, the usefulness that families see in education.

Increase allocations of the national budget for secondary education, and support resource mobilization in higher education. Bangladesh has achieved steady GDP growth over the last 10 years, but has kept the amount of GDP allocated to education at 2.2–2.5 percent, which is relatively low compared to countries with a similar GDP per capita. In secondary education, dealing with the task of enhancing access and improving the quality of learning requires more resources than are currently available. A formula-based funding mechanism should be initiated to ensure more efficient use of public resources. For higher education, increasing autonomy, decentralization, and resource mobilization of colleges and public universities could enable expansion with quality. Allocating scholarships and student aid and deploying adequate student loan schemes to enable access to tertiary education for students from disadvantaged backgrounds is also necessary.

Although Bangladesh has succeeded in providing greater educational access to its populace, learning is low and unequal. An assessment of literacy and numeracy in grade 5 indicates that only 25 percent of grade 5 students master Bangla, and only 33 percent master Mathematics competencies. At the grade 8 level, competencies in Bangla, English, and Mathematics are respectively 44, 44, and 35 percent. Regional differences exist in students' learning outcomes. Dhaka and Chittagong are performing better than the national average, but performance in Rajshahi and Sylhet is lagging significantly behind. Students in GPSs perform better than students in RNGPSs. The performance difference that appears in grade 3 becomes more severe by the end of the primary education cycle, particularly so in the Barisal and Sylhet divisions. Students from poor households across the nation perform generally lower than students from wealthy households. It is estimated that the children from poor families are at least three-fourths of a school year behind their richer counterparts in Bangla, and half a school year behind in Mathematics.

Learning inequalities begin early, and continue throughout a student's lifetime. Low levels of learning appear to exist even in the lower grades - 50 percent of the students in grade 3 already fail to meet the competency target for Mathematics, and 33 percent fail to meet the same in Bangla. These students are most at risk of dropping out before completing primary education, and are most likely to join the informal labour market. In contrast, a student with a better foundation of skills who performs better in primary or secondary school, from a more privileged background, is more likely to move further into higher education, increasing his/her chances of obtaining a job that requires higher skills and pays a higher wage.

An important determinant of learning within the school is the quality of the teacher. In fact, several international studies have confirmed that an effective teacher is the single most important school-related factor responsible for better learning. From a review of international impact evaluation studies in developing countries, the programs that address the problem of weak teaching are empirically proven to be the most effective programs. Although teachers are one of the principal resources available to the education system, it appears that they are not being utilized in the most effective manner in Bangladesh. The current system does not attract, constitute, and retain the best professionals, and once recruited, it provides little incentive to keep them motivated. Teachers' lack of their subject knowledge is negatively affected with students' learning, and they are not encouraged to be innovative with their pedagogical approaches or to learn from their peers through any learning networks. Additional years of experience in teaching also are not correlated with higher student learning, mostly due to low motivation levels.

UNIVERSALIZATION OF ELEMENTARY EDUCATION IN INDIA

Education is a lifelong process. Education is helpful in developing a power of thinking and also improves the power of rationality towards life. Education makes peoples educated and introduced them with needful skills. Education enhances our knowledge, learning skills, developing attitude and values etc. Education can also bring desirable changes in the behaviour of the learner. Education is being provided to the learner at different levels or stages like primary stage, secondary stage and higher stage. Primary education is the stage where education touches at every point. At this level the child curiosity, creativity and activity should not confined by a rigid and unattractive methods of teaching and learning. The Constitution had resolved in Article 45 under the Directive Principles of State Policy that the 'State shall endeavour to provide within a period of ten years from the Commencement of this Constitution for free and compulsory education for all the children until they complete the age of fourteen.' The government of India has made education a fundamental right and it has been a birth right for every one living in the country. Since independence, the central and the state governments have been expanding the provision of primary formal and non-formal education to achieve the goal of Universalisation of elementary education (UEE). The achievement of target of free and compulsory education is the great challenge and many efforts have been done to achieve this goal.

The role of Universal Elementary Education (UEE) for strengthening the social fabric of democracy through provision of equal opportunities to all has been accepted since the inception of our Republic. With the formulation of NPE, India initiated a wide range of programmes for achieving the goal of UEE through several schematic and programme interventions.

Universalisation of elementary education has been long accepted as a pre-condition to socio-economic and political development of any society.

Although this has been recognized as a need of an individual, this need has been given an expression of fundamental right in Article 28 of the Convention on the Rights of the Child. The Constitution of India does not recognize right to education as a fundamental right but has placed it explicitly in Article 45 under the Directive Principles of the State Policy. This Article places an obligation on the State to endeavour to provide for free and compulsory education to all Children up to the age of 14 years. The International Instruments which have been ratified by India including the convention on the Rights of the Child and the International Covenant on

Economic, Social and Cultural Rights explicitly provide for Right to Education up to the elementary level or up to 14 years of age.

The National Policy on education also emphasizes the responsibility of the State in providing educational facilities to all. However, the legal duties on the part of the State are not clearly stated in the Constitution for the domestic status on education. The remedies in case of violation of the right are also not clearly stated in the present legal frame works other than the remedies available under writ jurisdiction of the Supreme Court and the High Court. The present understanding of compulsory education is limited to right to schooling although the term education means much more than just what is offered in the present school system.

Universalisation of elementary education basically evolves three important things:

- Universalisation of provision,
- Universalisation of enrolment and
- Universalisation of retention.

Universalisation of Provision means that school facilities should be provided to all the children between the age of 6 to 14. Universalisation of Enrolment means that all the children between the age of 6 to 14 must be enrolled. Universalisation of Retention reveals a child who joins primary school; he or she should remain there till he or she completes all their primary education. After the 86th Amendment, Act 2002 inserted Article 21-A in the Constitution of India to provide free and compulsory education of all children in the age group of six to fourteen as a Fundamental Right. The Right of free and compulsory education (RTE) Act, 2009 which represents the legislation under Article 21-A, means that every child has a right to full time elementary education of satisfactory and equitable quality in a formal school which satisfied certain essential norms. Thus education had become a birth right for each and every person of the country. In our country the Right to Education Act came into the effect from 1st April 2010. Now every citizen has an equal opportunity to get education.

At the time of Independence, India inherited a system of education which was not only quantitatively small but also characterised by structural imbalances. Only fourteen per cent of the population was literate and only one child out of three had been enrolled in primary school. The low levels of participation and literacy were aggravated by acute regional and gender disparities. As education is vitally linked with the totality of the development process - education being "the basic tool for the development of consciousness and reconstitution of society," in the words of Mahatma Gandhi - the reform and restructuring of the educational system was recognised as an important area of state intervention.

The need for a literate population and universal education for all children in the age group of 6-14 was recognised as a crucial input for nation building and was given due consideration in the Constitution as well as in successive Five Year Plans. This has resulted in a manifold increase of spatial spread, infrastructural facilities, increased coverage of various social groups; but the goal of providing basic education to all could not be achieved.

Universalisation of Elementary Education (UEE) has been accepted as a national goal in India. Central and State governments are making strenuous efforts to achieve this goal. As a result of these efforts, 94 per cent of the country's rural population has primary schools (grade I-V) within one km and 85 per cent of rural population has upper primary schools (grade VI-VIII) within a distance of 3 km.

The number of primary schools has gone up by three times, from 2.1 lakh to 6.42 lakh and of upper primary schools by about 15 times from 13,596 to 1.98 lakh during 1950-51 and 1999-2000, respectively. Number of teachers in these schools has also increased from 6.24 lakh m 1950-51 to 32.17 lakh in 1999-2000. Expenditure on education as a whole as percentage of GDP also rose from 0.7 per cent in 1951-52 to 3.74 per cent in 2003-04.

The number of primary schools decreased from 6.64 lakh in 2001-02 to 6.51 lakh in 2002-03, whereas that of upper primary schools increased from 2.20 lakh to 2.45 lakh over the period, indicating up-gradation of a large number of primary schools to upper Primary Schools.

The total enrolment at the primary and upper primary levels has witnessed a steady increase. During 2001-02 and 2002-03, the growth rate of enrolment for girls at elementary level was higher than that of boys, Participation of girls at all levels of school education has improved appreciably over the years, but vast disparities amongst the States in gross enrolment ratio (GER) at primary/ upper primary levels still persist.

Of the estimated population of 205 million in the age group of 6-14 years on March 1, 2002, nearly 82.5 per cent was enrolled in schools, compared to 82.4 per cent in 2001-02. The retention rate of students at the primary school stage was about 59 per cent (1992-97).

At the primary level, the drop-out rate decreased from 39.0 per cent in 2001-02 to 34.9 per cent in 2002-03, while at the upper primary level, the drop-out rate decreased from 54.6 per cent to 52.8 per cent over the same period.

In spite of the decline over the years, dropout rate still remains very high, especially in the case of girl students, for whom the rates in 2002-03 were 33.7 per cent and 53.5 per cent, at the primary and upper primary levels, respectively.

The number of teachers at the elementary level rose from 3.4 million in 2001-02 to 3.5 million in 2002-03, while the share of female teachers increased from 37.2 per cent to 40 per cent over the same period. Despite the increase in the number of teachers over the decades, the Pupil Teacher Ratio (PTR) at the primary and upper primary levels has remained more or less constant around 40:1.

Access : Growth of Facilities

There has been a spectacular increase in elementary education during the post-Independence period. The elementary education system of India has expanded into one of the largest in the world. The number of primary schools increased from 209,671 in 1950-51 to 572,541 in 1992-93; the corresponding increase in upper primary schools was from 13,596 to 153,921. These 726,462 schools together with 2.7 lakhs non-formal education centres enrolled 150 million children as compared to 22.3 million in 1951. Universal provision of education has been substantially achieved at the primary stage. According to the Fifth All India Education Survey (1986), 94.5 per cent of the rural population had schools within a walking distance of 1 km and 83.98% of the rural population have an upper primary school within a walking distance of 3 km. The survey estimated that there were 31,815 habitations in the country which had a population of 300 or more but did not have a primary school within the walking distance of one kilometre. Most of these habitations are situated in educationally backward states such as Uttar Pradesh, Rajasthan, Madhya Pradesh, Bihar, Jammu and Kashmir, Assam and Arunachal Pradesh.

Enrolment

Since Independence, there has been a substantial increase in enrolment at all levels of education. Enrolment at the primary stage increased about five fold from 19.2 million to 105.37 million in 1992- 93; the increase in the upper primary stage is far higher from 3.1 million to 38.7 million.

The gross enrolment ratios of children in the age group 6-11 increased from 42.6 per cent in 1950-51 to 105.7 per cent in 1992-93. Likewise, the gross enrolment of 11-14 age group increased from 12.7 per cent in 1950-51 to 67.5 per cent in 1992-93. An analysis of the enrolment data reveals that the population of children moving up from the primary to upper primary stage has been increasing steadily, from 16.3 per cent in 1950-51 to 36.72 per cent in 1992-93.

While the gross enrolment ratios (GER) at the primary stage in the country as a whole and in most of its states exceed 100 per cent there are quite a few states where the ratio is considerably lower. These include Uttar Pradesh, Bihar, Rajasthan, Haryana, Jammu and Kashmir, and Meghalaya. At the upper primary stage these states and in addition, Andhra Pradesh, Orissa and Sikkim have

GERs lower than the national average. Most of these states have literacy rates lower than the national average. There is thus a strong regional dimension of UEE.

The problem. gets more complicated as the drop-out rates, though declining, continue to be high. Nearly half the children who entered Class I drop out before reaching Class V, and two-thirds of the children dropout before reaching Class VIII. Regional disparities also abound in rates of the dropouts.

Gender Disparities

As with any educational indicator, gender disparities are conspicuous in regard to enrolment and retention. Girls' enrolment has grown at the primary stage from 5.4 million in 1950-51 to 42.4 million in 1991-92 and at the upper primary stage from 0.5 million to 13 million. The rate of growth of enrolment of girls has been higher than that of boys but disparities still persist - girls still account for only 45.7 per cent of the enrolment at the primary stage.

Reasons For Children Dropping Out of School

The 42nd round of the National Sample Survey (July 1986 - June 1987) provides valuable information on the reasons for non-enrolment and dropout. Non-availability of schooling facilities seems to account for only about 10 percent of the "never enrolled" in rural India and about 8 percent in urban India; the difference between the sexes is very small in rural areas but somewhat larger in the urban sector.

However, nearly 30 percent of the persons surveyed, both in rural and urban India, gave the reason for "never enrolled" as being "not interested". The difference between the sexes here is large: a larger proportion of "never enrolled" females gave this reason in comparison with the males. The reason for being "not interested" could be considered as a demand side constraint to access: some authorities however, consider it as a supply side constraint rooted in poor facilities and quality of education.

Domestic Restraints

About 52 percent of urban males and 29 percent of urban females could not avail of the educational services because of participation in household economic activity and other economic reasons. Attending to domestic chores restrained around one percent of the males, both in rural as well as urban India, from ever enrolling as students. Nevertheless, this reason was one of the major demand side constraints on access to education for the females: for 9.9 percent of them in the rural and 10.7 percent of them in the urban sector. Most of the young females are denied access to education because they look after their siblings besides performing a variety of domestic, housekeeping chores. Significantly, the proportion of currently "not enrolled" decreases with the increase in per capita household income.

A little over one-fourth of all "drop-outs " in rural as well as urban India gave "not interested in education/further study" as the reason for discontinuance of education - with the proportion among females being somewhat higher - 33.3 percent as against 26.5 percent for males in areas and 28.5 percent as against 23.6 percent for males in urban areas. Another 16.3 percent of rural and 20.3 percent of urban "dropouts" cited 'failure' to pass examinations as the reason for discontinuance. Again, it is a Moot point whether this is a supply side constraint due to the poor quality of education services or a demand constraint, or a combination of both.

The drop-out rates of girls at the primary as well as the upper primary stage are higher than those of boys.

Regional disparities are also conspicuous. High female literacy states (above 50 per cent) have by and large universalised primary enrolments among girls. Even in regard to upper primary enrolments Kerala, Goa, Pondicherry and Lakshadweep fare very well. In states with medium female literacy status (40-50 per cent) enrolment of girls appears to be satisfactory at the primary level. The situation in low female literacy states (20-40 per cent) causes concern. These states have more than half of the country's population, with just four of them (Uttar Pradesh, Bihar, Madhya Pradesh and Rajasthan) accounting for 40 per cent of the country's population.

Scheduled Castes and Scheduled Tribes

According to the 1991 census, the population of Scheduled Castes (SCs) was 138.2 million (16.33 per cent) and that of Scheduled Tribes (STs) 67.8 million (8.01 per cent) of the country's population.

Both SC and ST populations are not homogeneous target groups in all respects. There are wide variations between different SC and ST groups regionally. Thus SC girls in Kerala are likely to be better placed than non-SC boys in some of the more backward states and districts.

Because of the affirmative policies of the government, the enrolment of SCs and STs has increased considerably at the primary stage. The participation of SCs and STs is now more or less in proportion to their share in population at the primary level. Drop-outs, though declining over the years, are significantly large. Gender disparities are very conspicuous among SCs and STs also.

Handicapped Children

Handicapped children are a distinct target group where basic learning needs have to be catered to by special programmes. Handicapped children would include those who are orthopedically handicapped, those with hearing impairments, visual impairments, the mentally handicapped and others.

The POA, 1992 estimates that about10.39 million children with disabilities are to be provided education in the school system. Out of these, about half a million require vocational training.

The statistics on participation of these children are not firm. At the end of 1991-92 about 30,000 disabled children were availing of special benefits under the scheme of Integrated Education for Disabled Children (IEDC). In addition, about 60,000 children with mild disabilities received resource support without special benefits. A large number of children with disability are also receiving education in 1,035 special schools.

Learning Achievement

If the fact that half the children dropout before reaching Class V is shocking, far more shocking is the level of learning achievement of those remaining in school. A sample study of learning achievements of students was conducted in 48 districts as part of the DPEP. In the final year of primary schooling, in none of these districts the maximum average score for reading skills was higher than fifty two per cent; the achievements in arithmetic were worse.

Measures Adopted by the Government of India to Ensure/Achieve UEE

The Right of Children to Free and Compulsory Education Act, 2009, in short RTE Act, is the most important development in the Universalisation of Elementary Education in India. It guarantees universalisation of quality education at elementary level in the country.

Other than RTE Act, the important measures adopted by the Government of India to achieve UEE include the following:

- Disaggregated target setting and decentralised micro-planning, which will provide the framework of universal access and community participation.
- Strengthening alternative channels of schooling such as the non-formal education system for those who cannot avail of conventional full-time schooling.
- Improvement of school facilities by revamping the scheme of Operation Blackboard. The purpose of this scheme was to provide minimum essential facilities to all primary schools in the country. It is aimed at bringing substantial improvement in the facilities of primary schools run by Government, Local bodies and Panchayati Raj and recognized aided institutions.

- Establishing linkages between programmes of early childhood care and education, primary education, literacy and UEE.
- Addressing the more difficult aspects of access, particularly to girls, disadvantaged groups and out-of-school children.
- Restructuring of teacher training in view of the changed strategies and programmes.
- Availing of external financial support for basic education.
- Launching the National Elementary Education Mission (NEEM).
- The Scheme of District Primary Education Programme (DPEP) was launched in 1994 as a major opening to regenerate the Primary Education system and to achieve the objective of Universalisation of Primary Education.
- The Education Commission (1964-66) had recommended a common School system of Public Education (CSS) as the basis of building up the national System of Education with a view to bring the different social classes and groups together. The National Policy of Education 1968 marked a significant step in the history of education in post-independence India. NPE (1968) was introduced with positive attitude but many of its recommendation could not be implemented due to lack of fund and adequate manpower. Therefore the goal of universalisation of elementary education could not be achieved. The New Education Policy 1986 was formulated with a view to preparing students for the 21st century to face the challenges related with global developments, rising technologies and cross-cultural complexities. The NPE (1986) repeated the issues of equality of educational opportunity and free and compulsory education for all children up to 14 years. The Policy of 1986 was modified in 1992 and was tabled in the parliament on 7th May 1992.
- Introduction of Minimum Levels of Learning (MLL) at primary and upper primary stages to improve learner's achievement.
- The National Literacy Mission (NLM) launched on May 5, 1988 as Technology Mission to impart functional literacy to non-literates and modified from time to time aims at attaining a literacy rate of 75 per cent by 2007. The Total Literacy Rate Campaign (TLC) has been the principal strategy of NLM for eradicating illiteracy. However, India continues to lag behind several other developing countries in terms of adult literacy and youth literacy rates.
- Mid-Day Meal Scheme was launched as a Centrally Sponsored Scheme on 15 August 1995. The purpose of this scheme was to be served a prepared Mid-Day Meal with a minimum content of 300 calories of energy and 8-12 gram protein per day for a minimum of 200 days. It also aimed to provide improve the health of the children.

- Non- formal Education has become an effective source of education for those who cannot attend full time schools due to socio-economic reasons. To accomplish the aim of universalisation of elementary education India has been running a programme of NFE for children in the age group of 6-14, since 1979-80. This programme is beneficial for working children who have been drop out from formal schools, children who have to remain at home to do domestic task, and girls who are unable to attend formal schools for a variety of reasons. Today the programme is being implemented in 20 states and union territories through the state governments and voluntary agencies.
- Sarva Shiksha Abhiyan is an effort to universalize elementary education by community ownership of the school system. It is also a great demand for quality education all over the country. This programme is also an effective step to improve human capabilities and provide an equal opportunity of education to all. This programme is included in 86th Amendment to the Constitution of India to provide free and compulsory education to children of ages 6 to 14..
- "The Right of Children to Free and Compulsory Education Act 2009" (popularly called Right to Education Act or RTE Act) was legislated in August 2009, which obtains into effect on April 1, 2010. This act is a detailed and comprehensive piece of legislation which includes provision related to school teachers and specific divisions of duties and responsibilities of different stakeholders.

It is clear that education is a fundamental right of every person and is a basic need of our life. Without education no progress is possible. To universalize elementary education the government of India took significant steps in this field. Time to time different education commission and committees gave their recommendations to realize the goal of universalizing the education. But despite all these policy initiatives and government efforts the goal of universalisation of basic education remained unidentifiable. Universalisation of Elementary Education (UEE) is the provision of education to make education for all children to complete elementary education. So, there is need to draw serious attention and action to achieve the goal of universal elementary education (UEE) in the state within short period.

SKILL DEVELOPMENT PROGRAMMES IN USA

"The land of opportunity" - that is the promise of the United States. And one of the reasons the country has been able to deliver on that promise is that it has been able to develop the talent it needs to create wealth and to adapt to ever-changing economic realities. But there are concerns that the USA can and should be doing better. This will require policies and actions on many fronts, for example on trade, taxation, regulation, education, and fiscal and monetary policy. Preparing people without college degrees for jobs with promising career paths is the need for both business and society.

On the one hand, almost 40 percent of American employers say they cannot find people with the skills they need, even for entry-level jobs. Almost 60 percent complain of lack of preparation, even for entry-level jobs. On the other hand, this "skills gap" represents a massive pool of untapped talent, and it has dire consequences, including economic underperformance, social unrest, and individual despair.

The skills gap takes different forms. In some cases, it is a matter of youth struggling to enter the workforce; in others, it is midcareer learners who have lost their jobs because of factory closings or layoffs, and who now must adapt. Whatever the circumstance, when people are disconnected from the workplace, they often disconnect from other social institutions as well. This is not healthy—neither for those left out nor for the societies in which they live.

Recognizing the importance of this subject, McKinsey has done extensive research on global workforce-development programs and economic strategies. Based on research and experience, it is identified five principles that should be the foundation of workforce-development programs - for funders, participants, and employers.

1. Define geographic assets and identify target professions. To get where they want to go, state and local agencies need to know where they are starting. Even at the local level, economies are complicated. The most promising approach, then, is to identify sectors with high growth potential where there are shortages or a high turnover of workers. Governments should conduct job-market analyses to identify each area's distinctive attributes and supply-and-demand dynamics, as well as the current state of the workforce. This means looking at posted job vacancies, public infrastructure investment, demographics, local university-research commercialization, venture-capital spending, and regulation. The analysis should be done at the city and regional levels, and then buttressed by interviews with major companies in the area.

The best workforce-development solutions happen when leading employers come together to address the talent problem for an entire sector. Assuming there are no antitrust issues, such collaborations can be attractive to industry competitors because the training costs are shared and the risk of poaching is limited. Such efforts typically take three forms: down a supply chain, with an anchor company taking the lead in encouraging its suppliers to participate; by a functional profession (for example, mechatronics) that is in demand by employers in different industries in the same location; and by sector, with competitors collaborating because they all face the same talent problem. One example of the latter is the Automotive Manufacturing Technical Education Collaborative, which includes 19 automotive companies and 26 community colleges in 13 states.

In addition, Government must ask itself whether it has the capabilities to meet the needs of businesses. This can be done simply - ask. Then, based on the responses, work with industry leaders, education providers, government agencies, and trade associations to identify the highest priorities on which to focus.

Successful economic-development efforts develop long-term strategies and make investment decisions based on hard data. A clear-eyed view allows decisions to be made based on a region's actual strengths, and avoids chasing economic-development fads where there is no basis for competitive advantage. The advice is ancient, but pertinent: know thyself.

2. Deliver Return On Investment (ROI) to employers and workers. Hard evidence of *Return On Investment (ROI)* for workforce-development programmes is scarce, for both employers and workers. That lack of proof is why many employers are reluctant to participate in workforce programs, much less to pay for them. Therefore, metrics that link such programs to business performance should be tracked, including the cost of program recruitment and training, employer productivity and quality outcomes, retention, and speed to promotion.

Recent federal legislation, known as the Workforce Innovation and Opportunity Act (WIOA), aims to make the workforce-development system more outcome driven and to emphasize training that leads to jobs. Gathering employer ROI data is not only important for employers but can also help local agencies meet WIOA requirements.

If the ROI case can be proved, the research and experience shows that employers are willing to pay for training programs - up to 15 percent (or roughly two months) of the employee's annual salary, on average. In areas of extreme scarcity, they will do much more. Apprenticeship 2000, a consortium based in Charlotte, North Carolina, comprises eight manufacturers that collaborate with the local community college on a mechatronics apprenticeship. It costs members $175,000 per candidate over four years.

With respect to participants, few employment programs gather evidence of effectiveness. Some track job placement at completion, or retention after one to three months. Few programs, however, follow a range of metrics to show potential participants that their investment in time and effort will pay off with personal and financial well-being. No wonder many job-training candidates are wary. Successful programs, in contrast, can show candidates evidence that the program will place them in jobs with a future after finishing the course.

Once on the job, metrics to track include the income of program graduates before and after completion, continued employment, job promotion, and reliance on public support. These findings can help reveal what works what does not. Programs that fall short can then be cut in favour of those that succeed.

3. Support comprehensive, demand-driven training methods. Local, state, and federal agencies have made numerous efforts to work with businesses, regional groups, education providers, and other stakeholders to deliver effective job training. Some training programs are excellent. Evidence does exist, however, of models that work in a variety of industry and regional contexts.

In successful programs, employers are involved from the start and guarantee interviews for graduates. Once providers decide which sectors and which high-scarcity or high-turnover professions to pursue, the next step is to shadow employees on the job in those professions. The goal is to identify which activities most differentiate high from low performers and to translate this insight into training for the right technical, behavioural, and mind-set skills which include attributes such as punctuality, diligence, and follow-through). Such observation is important, because our experience is that many employers are unable to accurately describe which skills matter most, leading to errors in program design.

In delivering training, one proven approach is to provide two- to three-month "boot camps." During the boot camp, competency is assessed regularly, based on actual demonstrations. Employers collaborate with the training providers and can offer their staff as trainers. The boot camp must be practical, including in-person simulations, on-site apprenticeships, and "serious games" customized to the workplace, where learners can play virtually and repeatedly. Programs need to have a strong in-person component to deliver the necessary dosage of intensive practice and to build the trust that allows providers to support learners—many of whom face multiple life challenges. At the same time, technology-based solutions, such as online applications, mobile apps that track learner performance, and digital workplace simulations can significantly increase the efficiency and effectiveness of these in-person programs.

To reach the people who need these programs most—meaning those at risk of being disconnected from the workforce because of background or education—accessibility is critical. Meeting their needs for transportation or child care during the boot camp, for example, helps make it possible for them to succeed. Programs that respond to these needs see higher completion rates. Some go even further, providing postgraduate mentorship for the first few months on the job, which is the period of greatest vulnerability. If individuals can make it through the first three months on the job, the odds of them continuing to thrive professionally and personally rise significantly.

4. Assess and prepare learners before they start training. Programs need to start by ensuring that learners are ready to train for the professions to which they apply. For example, they must be able to meet job-licensing requirements, such as having a high-school diploma, or pass a background check or a drug test; they also need to show job-appropriate literacy and numeracy levels.

Once this basic screening is done, there are ways to improve retention in the program and in the job. One is simple: make sure that people know what the job is before they start the training. This explanation must cover both positive and negative aspects, and might include things such as showing videos, hosting discussions of a "day in the life" with workers, and spending time at the job site. Someone training to be a certified nursing assistant, for example, needs to know that the position can be physically demanding and requires shift work.

When people understand what it takes to succeed at a given job, they are more likely to choose one that is right for them. That, in turn, improves program completion, job placement, and retention. It also ensures that program resources are spent on those who are most likely to benefit.

5. Coordinate the workforce-development process centrally. Estimated spending on US workforce-development programs for those not going to four-year colleges—everything from federal and state jobs programs, workforce training and certifications, community college, and employer training—is at least $300 billion a year. Most programs, however, are deployed in isolation and are not integrated with other services deployed by other entities. For example, a common scenario is that responsibility lies in different places: job training lies with the state's workforce department, child care and food assistance lies with the social services, and mentorship support lies with a local philanthropy or not for profit. All these components are essential to the learner's success in completing the training, finding a job, and then succeeding at it. Such tight complementarity of service delivery to learners, however, rarely occurs.

State governments can deploy three strategies to ensure effective use of resources. First, have a clear view of all funding and efforts available for target learner segments and professions in a given location, and coordinate these to deliver holistic services to learners. Second, establish a set of outcomes and performance-management processes in which learner employment within 30 days of program completion, retention on the job, and income increases lie at the heart. Finally, ensure the provision of human, technology, and data-analytics capacity for program delivery that supports learners.

Skill Development Courses

Clackamas Community College - DeJardin Hall conducts Skill Development courses on **Conflict Management**. This course is for those interested in managing interpersonal conflict in the workplace or at home. This 2-day course will provide conflict resolution models and interactive exercises to help you manage conflict constructively.

The Mediation course helps to learn the process and skills of mediation through role play exercises with professional coaches. This 5-day, 40-hour training includes and builds off the Conflict Management course. These courses teach the skills and techniques of interest-based mediation. Learn a practical and structured process for helping people in conflict find agreeable solutions. The methods are useful with all kinds of conflicts, including interpersonal, workplace, family, neighbourhood, business, and intercultural.

Enterprise Talent Development programmes of Minnesota State

- **Advanced Project Management:** Participants will learn to take their project management skills beyond the fundamental level and develop an understanding on how to apply advanced project management tools and techniques required for PMP certification. Project managers cannot rely solely on basic skills and must lead teams to a successful project completion as projects become more complex and teams become more distributed and diverse. Various management skills, such as, leadership, team building, procurement, stakeholder relationship, quality and risk will all be discussed. Over this three day course participants will actually plan and manage a complex simulated project that will prepare them to utilize these skills in the workplace or help them pass the PMP exam.
- **Better Communication, Better Teams**: In today's workplace, participating in small group interactions are critical to both individual and organizational outcomes. In order to achieve the best possible outcomes within a team or small group project, it is essential everyone's voice is heard. This course will help you develop skills in leading and participating in small group interaction so that the best outcomes are achieved. A special emphasis will be placed on small group decision making, managing the conversation, and participation from all members.
- **Building a High Performance Team**: Whether you are managing a team to tackle a special project or want your staff to act more collaboratively as they go about their work, there are specific team success factors that should be in place. High performance teams have a shared purpose, clear roles and responsibilities, and a set of team norms. In this course, you will look into what each of these success factors are and more importantly, learn a process for establishing them with your work group.
- **Business Writing Fundamentals:** Effective communication has always played a significant role in career and business success. Today's business professionals engage in written communication more than spoken interactions throughout the work day (i.e., letters, reports, memos, e-mail, text messaging, web pages, etc). Given the strong association between writing skills and professionalism, individuals who are able to write clear, concise and effective

business messages tend to be viewed more favourably in the workplace than those less skilled in this area. In this course learner will explore how to improve their written communication skills to ensure clear and professional correspondence.

- **Citizen Service: Customer Service Skills for Government**: Serving citizens is no different than serving customers at a retail store. One big distinction is that customers of a state agency think they have already paid the bill.
- **Creative Thinking**: How to Think Differently to Get Better Results: When times are challenging, it's often said that everyone needs to start thinking more creatively and come up with more innovative solutions. But how do you actually start doing that in your day-to-day work? This session will provide an overview of what it takes to be innovative, what limits creativity and how to start building a culture that is more open to innovation. It will also provide some practical tools and tips to help you start thinking differently so you can achieve different results.
- **Cultivating Workplace Relationships - In Style**: This session provides leaders and teams with a unique professional development experience focused on individual and team contributions toward goals. Learn and practice interpersonal skills to improve effectiveness with each other for personal satisfaction and professional success using the DiSC assessment.
- **Dealing with Difficult People:** Chances are you have worked with at least one difficult person in your organization. Every organization has them. The problem with being on the opposite end of the continuum is that you give up the power to influence the situation you are in. The painful truth however is you are not going to change them. The only person you have the possibility of changing is 'yourself'. Learning the skills of how to deal with difficult people at work will allow you to approach your work with more enjoyment and satisfaction and your co-workers with greater confidence. This workshop will provide you with assessment tools, methodology, and ways to address your difficult co-workers with proven strategies.
- **Delegation Mastery: Leverage the Power of Your Team:** Often employees are judged by what they personally work on, how fast it's done, and how well the outcome truly is. As a supervisor, it's all about the work your staff completes. Many managers struggle with delegation, but it doesn't have to be so difficult.
- **Diversity and Inclusion: Seeing the Difference:** Only 2.5% of us have the competence to see the full complexity of cultural differences and adapt to them to be our most effective. How effective are you in

your interactions across difference? Learn to unpack your own cultural preferences to identify assumptions generated by cultural unawareness and the impact of such assumptions. Practice using new competence tools and identify specific strategies to continue your development in diversity and inclusion.

- **Effective Performance Reviews and Conversations:** There are both productive and unproductive ways to talk with employees about their performance. Holding performance conversations cannot only strengthen the manager-staff relationship but can also result in improved employee performance, communication, engagement, and teamwork. In this course, you will learn how to reduce anxiety and improve effectiveness of these discussions with employees.
- **Effective Presentations for Subject Matter Experts**: As a subject matter expert, at some point you will likely be called upon to deliver a presentation for others who need to learn from you. Regardless of whether you look forward to speaking in public or if speaking causes you anxiety, this course will provide you the tools for a successful presentation. Learn tips and strategies to translate your knowledge and expertise into a presentation that is effective, dynamic and engaging. The course is delivered in two parts, one day-long session and one half-day session, approximately one week apart, which will enable you to apply the new skills you've learn in a practice presentation on the second day.
- **Exploring Unconscious Bias:** According to research, everyone is subject to their own unconscious bias. Unconscious bias is the result of messages we begin receiving (at an unconscious level) from an early age. These attitudes, which are deeply held, can influence our behaviour towards others and can negatively impact the organization. Because these biases are held at a subconscious level, the first step in addressing them is acknowledging that they exist. In this session participants will learn about unconscious bias and how it shows up in the workplace.
- **Holding Difficult Conversations:** The inability or reluctance to deal with conflict and disagreement can significantly undermine one's effectiveness. In this course, a model is presented and applied that will enable participants to become more comfortable and effective in working through difficult conversations.
- **Holding Meetings in Virtual Environments:** Recent research shows the average American worker spends more than 30% of their work week in meetings, and increasingly those meetings are virtual. This workshop teaches specific skills that assist in effectively accomplishing fundamental communication practices in virtual

environments that come naturally in face to face meetings (think turn taking, participation, engagement). The session addresses the challenges of meeting virtually and provides specific, tactical skills that increase engagement, improve virtual meeting facilitation and improve performance when working and managing from a distance.

- **How to Create and Facilitate a Webinar:** Description: Webinars, virtual classes, webcasts. Whatever you call them, they present new challenges to how we bring people together to meet and learn, especially when attention spans are getting shorter and shorter. The good news? Improving your virtual facilitation and presentation skills is not hard; it's just different.
- **How to Write a Good Email @ Work:** Whether you work in an office or out in the field, one of the biggest components of a 21st century work place is Email. Today, Email is the best way to communicate within your department and across agencies, but often important information can be lost or misconstrued if not written properly. The ability to compose efficient and effective emails is super useful – both in terms of productivity and responsiveness. How can one compose emails that will be read and responded to? How do we effectively email someone who gets a lot of email? This course aims to provide you with tips, tools, and practice in writing effective business emails. This is an online webinar course.
- **Human-Centred Design:** Are you looking for tools to create new and innovative solutions for your customers? Do you want to be able to translate your customer needs into experiences that fulfil them? Human-centred Design (HCD) is about creating new solutions that address the root cause of problems by understanding the people who are experiencing them.
- **Introduction to Agile and Scrum:** This course is a 2 day Simulation Powered Learning class on Agile and Scrum. Participants are introduced via short lectures to Agile tools, techniques and concepts, including: the Agile/Scrum cadence, releases, sprints, user stories, backlogs, daily stand-ups, demos, retrospectives, roles, responsibilities and more.
- **Knowledge Transfer for Individuals:** What would your agency do if you didn't show up for work tomorrow? If you had one day to share all that you do with an incoming person which information would you share?
- **Leading Change:** As the pace of change shows no signs of letting up, many supervisors and managers seek to build and strengthen their own change leadership skills. When leading others through a transition period it is important to identify your own personal

response to change. This session not only addresses the development of personal coping skills, but also discusses specific strategies for leading your staff through organizational changes.

- **Leading Workplace Change:** Guiding employees through workplace transitions is never easy. Even for what you believe to be positive changes, the challenges associated with communicating the change and dealing with people's reactions can be overwhelming.
- **Leading and Managing Project Teams:** Projects and organizations demand more and more from team members and project managers today. Quite often as the project manager your team members are not even direct reports, so how do you lead? The simple answer is you have to be an even better leader to be successful when your team members don't report to you. Project managers who have good leadership and team building skills are more successful in developing high performance teams and meeting demanding project objectives regardless of who their team members report to.
- **Leading and Supervising Virtual Teams:** Today's work environment demands leaders and individual contributors be more adept at communicating at a distance than ever before. The challenges of working in a 24/7, global environment are significant. This workshop teaches specific skills that assist in effectively leading and supervising in virtual environments that may come naturally in face to face situations. The session addresses the challenges of working in a virtual environment and provides specific, tactical skills that increase engagement, improve meeting facilitation and improve performance when working and managing from a distance.
- **Leveraging Your Communication Style:** Communication is an essential skill set for any employee. This course is intended to provide participants with an opportunity to broaden their awareness of their preferred styles of communicating with others. During the session, each participant will complete the DISC instrument. They will also practice the use of proven communication tools and techniques, including a model for giving and receiving effective feedback.
- **Managing Former Peers:** Becoming a supervisor or manager means adjusting your self-image and the relationships you have with your former peers, who now call you "Boss." These shifts do not happen instantaneously when you accept the management role, they happen over time. This transition phase can be a very positive and constructive one, which can establish effective individual and group dynamics to build on over time. This phase can also be mishandled or ignored, usually backfiring at some point, creating conflict and misunderstanding.

- **Managing Priorities and Setting Work Goals:** What is the value of managing priorities? Why set goals? Setting work goals can be intimidating and cumbersome for everyone involved, but it does not have to be that way if the process is done correctly. In this interactive workshop, you will be given the resources to help set SMART goals and performance measurements. You will receive the tools to determine how to respond to the tyranny of the urgent and the value of managing priorities. Participants learn a practical process to effectively consider, plan, document, and manage work priorities. You will refine and master the planning process that helps you create employee work plans with provided advice and guidance from our expert instructor. Learn the importance of preparing work goals and how it allows you succeed from start to finish.
- **Maximizing Meeting Productivity:** You have probably heard or delivered this phrase countless times, "Let's have a meeting and discuss it." Does that statement generate more excitement or dread within your workgroup? With more and more demands on staff members' time, every meeting needs to be purposeful, organized, interactive, and directed at obtaining specific results. Yet most surveys show that attending meetings is considered one of the top five time wasters.
- **Myers-Briggs: Deciphering Your Work Style:** Are you looking for a way to understand why your teammates see different perspectives and utilize different approaches than you do? This course will allow you to gain understanding and clarity about your own type and how you can utilize your strengths.
- **Onboarding: More than a 3 Hour Tour:** Employee engagement, performance, and retention can be greatly influenced by how new staff are brought into an agency. Onboarding is often seen as a burden, but if done correctly it can set your department on the right path. Learn how essential the onboarding process is to helping your new employee succeed in the transition to becoming a part of your team. As the workforce changes, supervisors and managers have the opportunity to design programs which welcome new staff into the organization, offer resources to get them up to speed quickly, and engage them in meaningful work to fulfil their passion. Participants will learn how to design an onboarding program that benefits the employee and the organization.
- **Pass It On: Preserving Knowledge in a Changing Workforce:** One of the biggest threats that agencies will face in the next few years is the loss of expert staff and critical knowledge. In this half day session designed for Supervisors and Managers, participants will learn how to determine knowledge loss risk within their teams,

and identify strategic methods for capturing and transferring it to others. By the end of the session, participants will have a start to a knowledge transfer plan.

- **Power and Influence**: Whether you are leading as an individual contributor or have a team reporting to you, power and influence are critical in getting the work of your organization done. In taking this course, you will better understand how your personal power and influence can impact both work and goal achievement. You will learn the appropriate types of power to use in various contexts, how to influence with and without authority, and how to use power and influence effectively in achieving your career goals.
- **PowerPoint Presentations with Impact:** Avoid falling into that same trap when you create PowerPoint presentations yourself and learn how to make them more impactful for participants. A well-designed presentation will enhance your ability to communicate and help you feel confident about the final product. This course will explain the process of how to create cleaner slides that are both easier for the participant to understand and for you as the speaker to present.
- **Principles of Project Management:** To guide a project to successful completion, there must be a hand on the wheel managing all aspects. Project managers demonstrate a number of critical skills such as, writing a clear vision statement, creating a comprehensive scope definition, organizing resources, working within tight timelines, controlling project costs and generating optimal team performance. This workshop uses a project case study to teach proven project management skills. Participants will learn how to successfully plan, manage, deliver and evaluate excellent results. Additionally, learners walk away from the session with enhanced team building and facilitation skills. This course is intended for employees looking to develop basic project management skills or employees just starting their project management careers.
- **Project Management Fundamentals:** In this course, you will receive hands-on experience in learning, applying, practicing and developing fundamental project management skills. You will have the chance to practice and develop your skills by planning and managing a realistic business project through a computer simulation. After completing this two (2) day course, participants will earn 14 Professional Development Units (PDU's) to accredit towards continuing certification requirements to maintain PMI certifications.
- **Put Your Strengths to Work:** Employees that have the opportunity to do what they do best every day are six (6) times more likely to be engaged in their jobs and three (3) times more likely to report having

an excellent quality of life in general. This course will utilize the Clifton *StrengthsFinder* along with other tools to help you identify what you do best. Learn how to increase productivity and effectiveness for your organization and your own personal job satisfaction as well.

- **Strategic Effectiveness for Aspiring Leaders (SEAL):** Strategic Effectiveness for Aspiring Leaders (SEAL) is ideal for state employees in non-management roles that aspire to become leaders in state government and wish to build skills that will move them towards this goal. Through defining the characteristics of a leader, participants will learn how they can lead more effectively, regardless of title. Topics include strategic problem solving, presenting to senior-level staff, effective communication and integration of your personal strengths into a leadership development plan.
- **Strengths-Based Management:** Levels of employee engagement are seven times greater when leaders focus on the strengths of their employees. Employees experience greater confidence and increased productivity when they are able to utilize their strengths on a daily basis. This session will focus on the value of utilizing the *Clifton Strengths Finder* as a tool to identify and leverage not only individual strengths, but how to utilize other employees' strengths, as well.
- **Team Building for Virtual Teams:** How do you create a sense of "teamwork" when remote employees are typically focused on their own deliverables and rarely interact with their colleagues and manager like they would in a traditional office setting? Discover how to create a sense of team, whether all members work virtually or if you have a hybrid arrangement where some members are collocated and others are working remotely.
- **Technology for Remote Teams:** With so many kinds of technology available, how do you choose the correct ones? Which tools will support the activities your remote team members need to perform in their day to day work? In this course, you will learn about the technology tools, apps and other helpful devices that are available and which kinds of tasks they are best used for. You'll learn how to increase productivity, reduce redundant communication and create norms for your team members.
- **Time Management** - Doing More With Less: Ever wonder where your time goes? Most of us begin our workdays with the veiled hope that we can accomplish most of the tasks on our plate. By the middle of the day, however, we have dealt with everything but what we set out to do. You've handled every question, problem, and interpersonal issue. What about your time? Can you get a handle on what is important and what isn't? In this interactive workshop, you'll learn

some very practical ideas for staying in control of how you use time. You'll also take a time management inventory and review some time wasters to determine how you are spending your workdays.

Federal Mediation and Conciliation Service (FMCS), USA

FMCS mediators are available to provide training in the public, private, and federal sectors on conflict resolution and labour-management relations topics. Customized training programs can be delivered in person or remotely based on the needs of participants. Training modules are tailored to group requirements based on a needs assessment. Core training topics include:

- Communication
- Interest-Based Problem Solving
- Steward/Supervisor Skills
- Conflict Resolution
- Contract Administration
- Facilitation Skills
- Labour Management Committees
- Mediation Skills
- Relationships By Objectives
- Traditional Contract Negotiation
- Collaborative Contract Negotiation
- The Neuroscience of Conflict Resolution
- Maximizing Mediation
- Art of Inquiry
- Mindfulness in Mediation: A Conflict Resolution Tool
- The Art and Science of Dealing with Difficult People
- The 6 Competencies of Outcome-Based Communication for Neutrals

Non-Degree Options

Do you want something a little different from the standard degree program? Maybe you need practical skills or professional contacts more than an educational credential. Perhaps you would prefer a "real world" experience that allows you to travel or work outside of a university environment. Or maybe you are interested in academic study but are unsure about your English fluency, or about the time and financial commitment that a degree program requires. If any of these circumstances describes your situation, you might want to consider a non-degree option. The United States offers many choices. viz;

- Programs Without a Credential
- Summer Coursework

- A Certificate Program
- Training to Build Professional Skills
- Real-Work Opportunities
- Organizations That Can Help

USA offers Skill Development Courses on:

- Home Renovation
- Electrical
- Industrial Millwright Mechanic / Machinist
- Industrial Millwright Mechanic & Electrical Pre-Apprenticeship Program
- Enhanced General Carpentry for Women – Sponsored

Programs Without a Credential

Most universities allow students to take classes on campus without enrolling in a degree program. You may not wish for a credential at the end of the program and simply want the learning experience of studying in the U.S. Many universities offer the opportunity for you to pursue your own interests and choices of courses for a semester or a year without formal matriculation. If you have completed graduate study, you can inquire into postdoctoral research or other opportunities with university departments or particular faculty members who have interests that match your own.

Summer Coursework

During the summer, many U.S. universities offer courses that are open to both non-students and those already enrolled. While there are likely to be some requirements (such as English language proficiency), participants in summer programs generally do not have to go through as complicated and rigorous an admissions process as they would to gain admission to a degree program. Summer classes are often more fast-paced than those offered during the regular academic year, covering material in five to eight weeks that is usually covered in a thirteen- or sixteen-week semester. Classes may be smaller than usual, offering extra contact with professors and fellow students. In some cases, tuition is lower in the summer. However, schools may not offer all of the services (such as student advising, tutoring or even housing) that are available during the regular academic year.

A Certificate Program

If you want a credential at the end of the program but do not have the time for a full degree, consider a certificate program. The term "certificate" does not have a precise meaning in terms of U.S. education, so there are many options available to you. A certificate program may award undergraduate credit, graduate credit, or no academic credit at all. The certificate may simply indicate that particular vocational or professional skills have been mastered. At some schools, certificate programs may be more common at the graduate level. They often take one academic year, or one summer of more intensive study, to complete. Graduate certificate programs are likely to provide credit toward a degree (should you wish to complete one later), and may even provide enough education to allow you to enter your chosen profession. **Department of Health and Human Services (HHS), USA conducts** Cancer Research Education Grants Program. It is a Course for Skills Development.

Training to Build Professional Skills

Many short-term educational programs are offered all across the U.S. that are not intended to result in a degree. Rather, they are designed to build and update practical, professional skills. Courses to meet a variety of career needs are offered by various schools, university departments, businesses, government agencies, associations, and private organizations specializing in providing short-term training.

English language training is the most widely offered type of internationally focused training. English-for-Specific-Purposes (ESP) programs can be particularly valuable to the international professionals who have an intermediate to high level of English proficiency. These programs provide instruction in the terminology of a specific field, such as law or engineering. Many ESP programs combine English instruction with opportunities to take courses in a particular subject, make visits to U.S. organizations, and perhaps even complete a brief internship working in the field. English language programs also offer a range of other options, from test preparation to holiday vacations.

Training suitable for international participants can also be found in hundreds of professional fields, from export management to epidemiology to graphic design. Program length may vary from a day to a year, with most training lasting between one and six weeks. To find programs, check with your local advising centre, U.S. associations in your professional field, and universities that have research facilities or degree programs in the area.

Real-Work Opportunities

Many short-term training programs include brief work experiences in the form of professional internships. Internships are a great way for you to earn hands-on experience in an area of interest without a commitment to a job or career. You may also make contacts with people who may be of help in the future when you are ready to begin your career. Some internships are available to people who are not officially enrolled in a school's academic program, and it may be possible for trainers to arrange an internship on request and/or for an additional fee.

Work as the primary experience of a visit to the U.S. is also possible, with proper preparation. Start early—begin researching internship possibilities at least six to nine months in advance. An added challenge for you will be dealing with the legal regulations designed to protect the jobs of U.S. workers. Non-U.S. citizens who wish to work in the United States must abide by U.S. immigration regulations. Potential employers may not be familiar with these regulations on employing foreign nationals; they may be reluctant to deal with the paperwork involved.

Others can help with visas for all types of professionals internship experiences lasting less than eighteen months, or (in a few cases) with "summer travel/work programs" that allow any type of U.S. employment for a more limited period in the summer (or the winter, for students in the Southern Hemisphere). For a fee, sponsoring organizations may be able to help you locate an internship in your field.

Organizations that Can Help

Peterson's Internships, U.S. consular officials and overseas educational advisers can provide a full list of the organizations authorized to sponsor interns and summer workers for J-1 visas, most of which limit their services to particular work regions and types of work experiences. A few of the larger organizations are:

- AIESEC (American Internationale des Estudiants en Sciences Economiques et Commercials)
- Council on International Educational Exchanges (CIEE)
- AIPT (Association for International Practical Training)

Skills Development is Texas, USA

Skills Development is Texas' premier job-training program. Skills Development provides grants to community and technical colleges to provide customized job training programs for businesses who want to train new workers or upgrade the skills of their existing workforce. Skills Development helps:

- Businesses and employers create new jobs and improve the skills of their current workforce
- Job seekers and employees acquire new skills or upgrade existing skills to advance their careers

A business, consortium of businesses, or trade union identifies a training need, and then partners with a public community or technical college to fill its specific needs. Businesses work with college partners to submit proposals, develop curricula and conduct training. The Skills Development Fund pays for the training, and the college administers the grant. Skills Development is administered by the Texas Workforce Commission, and success is achieved through collaboration with businesses, public community and technical colleges, Workforce Development Boards and economic development partners. The program is funded by appropriations from the Texas Legislature.

Skills for Small Business finances the design and implementation of customized job training programs for newly hired employees of small businesses, successfully merging small business needs and local customized training opportunities into a winning formula for putting people to work in Texas.

The Texas Workforce Commission's (TWC) Skills for Small Business program supports businesses with fewer than 100 employees, emphasizes training for new workers, and helps upgrade the skills of incumbent workers. Through this program, up to $2 million from the Skills Development Fund is dedicated to the backbone of Texas' business community—our more than 433,000 small employers.

Small businesses can apply to TWC for training offered by their local community or technical college or the Texas Engineering Extension Service (TEEX). TWC processes the applications and works with the college to fund the specific courses selected by businesses for their employees. The features of the Program is enlisted below:

- The program emphasizes training newly hired employees—those who have been hired by the company up to 12 months prior to the date that TWC receives an application.
- It funds tuition and fees up to $1,800 per newly hired employee and up to $900 per incumbent employee. An individual employee can participate once per 12-month period.
- Funding for training is for full-time employees.
- All training must be provided by a public community or technical college, or TEEX. No third-party vendor training is allowed.
- Training must be selected from active course catalogues/schedules—credit, continuing education, online or other available unpublished courses.
- Training may focus on occupations within the Governor's six targeted industry clusters: Aerospace and Defence; Advanced Technologies and Manufacturing; Biotechnology and Life Science; Energy; Petroleum Refining and Chemical Products; and Information and Computer Technology.
- Training may also be emphasized for occupations targeted by Workforce Development Boards.
- Employers must pay the prevailing wages in the local labour market for the trainees funded under the grant.

Training and Skills Development at City of El Paso, Texas, USA

City of El Paso's Training & Skills Development Program provides job-specific, evaluation, and professional development services to ESD staff, so they can maintain a competent, professional, and well-trained workforce. viz.

- Division Specific Training Sessions
- Skills Development Training Sessions
- Supervisory and Leadership Training Sessions
- Training Assessments
- Defensive Driving Courses
- HAZWOPER 8 hour refresher courses
- Continuing Education Units (CEUs)

US Department of Education: Skills for Success Programme

The Skills for Success Program supports Local Educational Agencies (LEAs) and their partners in implementing, evaluating, and refining tools and approaches for developing the non-cognitive skills of middle-grades students in order to increase student success. Grants provide funding for the implementation, evaluation, and refinement of existing tools and approaches (e.g., digital games, growth mindset classroom activities, experiential learning opportunities) that integrate the development of students' non-cognitive skills into classroom-level activities and existing strategies designed to improve schools.

Workforce Challenges in America

The High Growth Job Training Initiative is designed to provide national leadership for a demand-driven workforce system that ensures no worker is left behind. It is a strategic effort to prepare workers for new and increasing job opportunities in high-growth/high demand and economically vital industries and sectors of the American economy. Through the initiative the Employment and Training Administration (ETA) identifies high-growth/high demand industries such as energy, works with industry leaders to determine their key workforce challenges, and invests in demonstration projects that ensure individuals gain the skills that they need to get good jobs with good wages in rapidly expanding or transforming industries. The foundation of this initiative is partnerships between the publicly funded workforce investment system, business and industry representatives, and education and training providers, such as community colleges. The purpose of these partnerships is to develop innovative solutions or replicate models that address a targeted industry's workforce issues.

The energy industry was selected as one of 14 targeted industries in the High Growth Job Training Initiative. Industries were selected according to one or more of the following characteristics:

- A substantial number of new jobs will be added in the industry.
- The industry has a significant impact on the overall economy.
- The industry has an impact on the growth of other industries.
- Evolving technology used in the targeted industry requires workers to have new skill sets.
- The industry includes emerging businesses that are projected to grow.

Employment and Training Administration (ETA) included the energy industry in the High Growth Job Training Initiative because of the vital role it plays in the U.S. economy, and due to rapidly evolving technology that requires workers to gain an increasingly technical skill set.

SKILL DEVELOPMENT PROGRAMMES IN INDIA

India is one of the youngest nations in the world with more than 62% of its population in the working age group (15-59 years), and more than 54% of its total population below 25 years of age. Its population pyramid is expected to bulge across the 1559 age group over the next decade. It is further estimated that the average age of the population in India by 2020 will be 29 years as against 40 years in USA, 46 years in Europe and 47 years in Japan. In fact, during the next 20 years the labour force in the industrialized world is expected to decline by 4%, while in India it will increase by 32%. This poses a formidable challenge and a huge opportunity. To reap this demographic dividend which is expected to last for next 25 years, India needs to equip its workforce with employable skills and knowledge so that they can contribute substantively to the economic growth of the country. Our country presently faces a dual challenge of paucity of highly trained workforce, as well as non-employability of large sections of the conventionally educated youth, who possess little or no job skills. Ministry for Skill Development and Entrepreneurship has been set up in November 2014 to give fresh impetus to the *Skill India* agenda and help create an appropriate ecosystem that facilitates imparting employable skills to its growing workforce over the next few decades. Apart from meeting its own demand, India has the potential to provide skilled workforce to fill the expected shortfall in the ageing developed world. As India moves progressively towards becoming a global knowledge economy, it must meet the rising aspirations of its youth. This can be partially achieved through focus on advancement of skills that are relevant to the emerging economic environment. The challenge pertains not only to a huge quantitative expansion of the facilities for skill training, but also to the equally important task of raising their quality.

Skill development, however, cannot be viewed in isolation. Skills are germane to, but not always sufficient for securing adequate economic dividends. Skills need to be an integral part of employment and economic growth strategies to spur employability and productivity. Coordination with other national macroeconomic paradigms and growth strategies is therefore critical.

It is estimated that during the five year period from 2004-05 to 2009-10, only 2.7 million net additional jobs were created in the country. For a skills strategy to be successful it should be complemented by commensurate creation of jobs in the primary, secondary and tertiary sectors which will be a key outcome of overall economic growth including entrepreneurship cutting across all sectors. The Indian capacity for harnessing entrepreneurship has not been fully realized the MSME (Micro, Small and Medium Enterprises) sector contributes to only 17% of GDP as 3 compared to 85% in Taiwan, 60% in China and 50% in Singapore. Given the realities of rapidly changing economic landscape in the country, entrepreneurship opportunities have emerged as an important source of meeting the aspirations of the youth. An all inclusive approach to strengthen the entrepreneurship development scenario in the country which is competent, quality conscious, market savvy, innovative and has globally competitive entrepreneurs, needs to be carefully mentored and encouraged.

Recognizing the imperative need for skill development, National Skill Development Policy was formulated in 2009. Given the vast paradigm shift in the skilling and entrepreneurship ecosystem in the country and the experience gained through implementation of various skill development programmes, there is an imminent need to revisit the existing policy. Moreover, the 2009 Policy itself provides for review every five years to align the policy framework with the emerging trends in the national and international milieu.

National Policy for Skill Development and Entrepreneurship 2015 supersedes the *National Skill Development Policy of 2009*. The primary objective of this policy is to meet the challenge of skilling at scale with speed, standard (quality) and sustainability. It aims to provide an umbrella framework to all skilling activities being carried out within the country, to align them to common standards and link skilling with demand centres. In addition to laying down the objectives and expected outcomes, the policy also identifies the overall institutional framework which will act as a vehicle to reach the expected outcomes. Skills development is the shared responsibility of the key stakeholders viz. Government, the entire spectrum of corporate sector, community based organizations, those outstanding, highly qualified and dedicated individuals who have been working in the skilling and entrepreneurship space for many years, industry and trade organisations and other stakeholders. The policy links skills development to improved employability and productivity in paving the way forward for inclusive growth in the country. The skill strategy is complemented by specific efforts to promote entrepreneurship in order to create ample opportunities for the skilled workforce.

Organisations on Skill Development Programmes in India

Directorate General of Training (DGT)

The Directorate General of Training consists of the Directorate of Training and Directorate of Apprentice Training. This includes a network of Industrial Training Institutes (ITIs) in States; Advanced Training institutes (ATIs), Regional Vocational Training Institutes (RVTIs) and other central institutes. A number of training programmes catering to students, trainers and industry requirements are being run through this network. The building blocks for vocational training in the country - Industrial Training Institutes - play a vital role in the economy by providing skilled manpower in different sectors with varying levels of expertise. ITIs are affiliated by National Council for Vocational Training (NCVT). DGT also operationalises the amended Apprentices Act, 1961.

National Skill Development Agency (NSDA)

The National Skill Development Agency (NSDA), an autonomous body, (registered as a Society under the Society's Registration Act 1860) was created with the mandate to co-ordinate and harmonise the skill development activities in the country, is part of the Ministry of Skill Development & Entrepreneurship (MSDE).

Functions of NSDA

- Take all possible steps to meet skilling targets as envisaged in the 12th Five Year Plan and beyond.
- Coordinate and harmonize the approach to skill development among various Central Ministries/Department. State Governments, the NSDC and the Private sector.
- Anchor and operationalize the NSQF to ensure that quality and standards meet sector specific requirements.
- Be the nodal agency for State Skill Development Missions.
- Raise extra-budgetary resources for skill development from various sources such as international agencies, including multi-lateral agencies, and the private sector.
- Evaluate existing skill development schemes with a view to assessing their efficacy and suggest corrective action to make them more effective.

- Create and maintain a national data base related to skill development including development of a dynamic Labour Market Information System (LMIS).
- Take affirmative action for advocacy.
- Ensure that the skilling needs of the disadvantaged and the marginalized groups like SCs, STs, OBCs, minorities, women and differently-abled persons are taken care of and.
- Discharge any other function as may be assigned to it by the Government of India.

Activities undertaken by the NSDA

Besides anchoring and implementation, the National Skills Qualifications Framework (NSQF), some of the other actions taken by the NSDA are as under:

- **Rationalization of the Skill Development Schemes of the Government of India:** NSDA has worked with the concerned ministries and stakeholders to achieve convergence of norms across the various central schemes for skill development, while at the same time recognizing the special needs of the North Eastern States, the hill States, and other geographies that pose challenging situations for skill development.
- **Creation of an integrated Labour Market Information System:** A national database on all major aspects of skill development is being created in partnership with all other Ministries of the Government of India and the State Governments. This would be a one-shop stop where all the relevant information is freely available to citizens. The government has created a National Steering Committee for setting up the Labour Market Information System (LMIS). The LMIS would bring in operational efficiencies, would be transparent and available to all, and would help reduce considerably the situation of one individual being benefitted under different schemes.
- **Engagement with States:** The NSDA is now actively engaged with the various State governments to plan out their skill development action plan, help them develop their skill development policies, and set up suitable administrative mechanisms. Through Technical Assistance programmes with the Asian Development bank (ADB), European Union (EU) and DFID (Department for International Development of the Government of UK), NSDA is helping the State Skill Development Missions of eleven states build their respective capacities.

- **Skills Innovation Initiative:** A committee has been set up under the Skills Innovation Initiative housed under the NSDA. The NSDA invites innovative ideas, concepts and practices on skill development. The Committee reviews all the proposals of innovations to facilitate their application on a wider scale. Selected innovative practices will be facilitated and propagated for wider application. Five innovative approaches and solutions have already been identified for wider propagation.

National Skill Development Corporation

The National Skill Development Corporation India (NSDC) was setup as a one of its kind, Public Private Partnership Company with the primary mandate of catalysing the skills landscape in India. NSDC is a unique model created with a well thought through underlying philosophy based on the following pillars:

- **Create:** Proactively catalyse creation of large, quality vocational training institutions.
- **Fund:** Reduce risk by providing patient capital. Including grants and equity.
- **Enable:** the creation and sustainability of support systems required for skill development. This includes the Industry led Sector Skill Councils.

The main objectives of the NSDC are to:

- Upgrade skills to international standards through significant industry involvement and develop necessary frameworks for standards, curriculum and quality assurance
- Enhance, support and coordinate private sector initiatives for skill development through appropriate Public-Private Partnership (PPP) models; strive for significant operational and financial involvement from the private sector
- Play the role of a "market-maker" by bringing financing, particularly in sectors where market mechanisms are ineffective or missing
- Prioritize initiatives that can have a multiplier or catalytic effect as opposed to one-off impact.

Partnerships

NSDC operates through partnerships with multiple stakeholders in catalysing and evolving the skilling ecosystem.

- **Private Sector** – Areas of partnerships include awareness building, capacity creation, loan financing, creation and operations of Sector

Skill Councils, assessment leading to certification, employment generation, Corporate Social Responsibility, World Skills competitions and participation in Special Initiatives like *Udaan* focused on Jammu & Kashmir (J&K).

- **International Engagement** – Investments, technical assistance, transnational standards, overseas jobs and other areas.
- **Central Ministries** – Participation in flagship programmes like *Make in India*, *Swachh Bharat*, *Pradhan Mantri Jan Dhan Yojana*, *Smart City*, *Digital India* and *Namami Ganga*, among many others.
- **State Governments** – Development of programs and schemes, alignment to NSQF and capacity building, operationalization of program, capacity building efforts among others.
- **University/School systems** – Vocationalisation of education through specific training programs, evolution of credit framework, entrepreneur development, etc.
- **Non-profit organizations** – Capacity building of marginalized and special groups, development of livelihood, self-employment and entrepreneurship programs.
- **Innovation** – Support to early-stage social entrepreneurs working on innovative business models to address gaps in the skilling ecosystem, including programs for persons with disability.

Achievements

- Over 5.2 million students trained
- 235 private sector partnerships for training and capacity building, each to train at least 50,000 persons over a 10-year period.
- 38 Sector Skill Councils (SSC) approved in services, manufacturing, agriculture & allied services, and informal sectors. Sectors include 19 of 20 high priority sectors identified by the Government and 25 of the sectors under Make in India initiative.
- 1386 Qualification Packs with 6,744 unique National Occupational Standards (NOS). These have been validated by over 1000 companies.
- Vocational training introduced in 10 States, covering 2400+ schools, 2 Boards, benefitting over 2.5 lakh students. Curriculum based on National Occupational Standards (NOS) and SSC certification. NSDC is working with 21 universities, Community Colleges under UGC/AICTE for alignment of education and training to NSQF.
- Designated implementation agency for the largest voucher-based skill development program, *Pradhan Mantri Kaushal Vikas Yojana*.
- Skill Development Management System (SDMS) with 1400 training partners, 28179 training centres, 16479 trainers, 20 Job portals,

77 assessment agencies and 4983 empanelled assessors. Hosting infrastructure certified by ISO 20000/27000 supported by dedicated personnel.

National Skill Development Fund

The National Skill Development Fund was set up in 2009 by the Government of India for raising funds both from Government and Non Government sectors for skill development in the country. The Fund is contributed by various Government sources, and other donors/ contributors to enhance, stimulate and develop the skills of Indian youth by various sector specific programs. A public Trust set up by the Government of India is the custodian of the Fund. The Trust accepts donation, contribution in cash or kind from the Contributors for furtherance of objectives of the Fund. The Fund is operated and managed by the Board of Trustees. The Chief Executive Officer of the Trust is responsible for day-to-day administration and management of the Trust.

The Fund meets its objectives through National Skill Development Corporation (NSDC) which is an industry led 'Not For Profit Company' set up for building skill development capacity and forging strong linkages with the market. NSDC acts as a catalyst in skill development by providing funding to enterprises, companies and organizations that provide skill training. It also develops appropriate models to enhance, support and coordinate private sector initiatives. Till 31st March 2015, NSDF has released ₹ 2333 crore to NSDC towards skill development programmes including National Skill Certification and Monetary Reward Scheme (STAR) and UDAAN Scheme (J&K oriented). NSDC with 160 training partners and 1722 training centres has so far trained around 35 lakh persons across India. Accounts of the Trust are subject to CAG Audit and are also audited by a Chartered Accountant for every financial year and in such manner as may be directed by GOI. The Trust has engaged IL&FS Trust Company Ltd (ITCL), one of the largest Corporate Trustees in India, for providing micro prudential oversight on the implementing partner and monitoring the interests of Trust.

Indian Institute of Entrepreneurship (IIE)

The Indian Institute of Entrepreneurship (IIE) was established in the year 1993 in Guwahati by the erstwhile Ministry of Industry (now the Ministry of Micro, Small and Medium Enterprises), Government of India as an autonomous national institute with an aim to undertake training, research and consultancy activities in small and micro enterprises focusing on entrepreneurship development.

The institute began operating from April 1994 with the North East Council (NEC), Governments of Assam, Arunachal Pradesh and Nagaland

and SIDBI as its other stakeholders. It is also An ISO 9001:2008 Certified Organisation.

Objectives

- To promote and develop entrepreneurship.
- To conduct research and provide consultancy for entrepreneurship development.
- To coordinate and collaborate with other organizations in undertaking training, research and other activities to increase outreach of the institute.
- To provide consultancy and monitoring service to MSMEs/ potential entrepreneurs and enhancing employability of participants.
- To promote greater use of information technology in the activities/ functions of the IIE.
- To comply with statutory responsibility.

Functions

- Designing and organising training activities for different target group and undertaking research in the relevant to entrepreneurship.
- Improving the efficiency, effectiveness and delivery of the change agents and development practitioners i.e. trainers, support organizations engaged in enterprise building. etc.
- Provide consultancy service to the prospective and existing entrepreneurs.
- Increasing the outreach of activities of the institute through collaborative activities and increasing their effectiveness through use of different tools of information technology.

Infrastructure

- The Institute is located at Lalmati, Basistha Chariali, 37 National Highway Bypass, Guwahati.
- The institute has a one Library and Documentation Centre; one seminar hall; a guest house at IIE Residential flat located at RG Boruah Road Ganeshguri chariali, Guwahati; a hostel with 42 fully furnished single rooms with attached bath, 1 auditorium with the seating capacity of 200.
- The institute also has state offices in seven states - Nagaland, Sikkim, Arunachal Pradesh, Mizoram, Manipur, Tripura, and Meghalaya.

Major Activities

- **Trainings**: Are primarily divided into two categories: (i) (Assistance to Training Institutions) ATI Trainings: The institute conducts three ATI Programmes, namely, Announces a Programme on Training of Trainers (ToT); Entrepreneurship and Skill Development Programme (ESDP); and Entrepreneurship and Skill Development Programme (ESDP). (ii) Non-ATI Trainings: The institute conducts 36 trainings related to entrepreneurship ranging from 600 hrs to 15 days. These trainings are conducted free of cost or at nominal charges.
- **Research**: The Institute undertakes research and studies either on its own or on sponsored basis and provides consultancy in the field of growth and development of MSME across North East India and beyond. The Institute also acts as a catalyst and a resource centre for providing various inputs on policy formulation for promoting entrepreneurship and development of MSME to Central and State governments. Another major focus area is evaluation of various Central and State government organisations and schemes. Action Research is also undertaken on development of MSMEs.
- **Consultancy**: It offers advice and consultancy in the various areas of entrepreneurship, including, Enterprise planning; Enterprise Management; Enterprise Expansion, Diversification & Growth; Management Consultancy; Marketing consultancy with specialization on export and border trade; Technology sourcing; Technology propagation; Project and Reports.
- **Seminars and Workshops: The Institute organizes Seminars and Workshops** to share experiences on implementation of programmes of self-employment and entrepreneurship, on current topics and awareness generation. Besides, the institute organizes **Entrepreneurs Meet** to understand and appreciate their problems in launching projects and managing them successfully.
- **Projects:** The institute has also undertaken various projects such as, Centre for Sustainable Livelihood promotion (CSPL); Regional Resource Centre (RRC) for Cluster Development; Science and Technology Entrepreneurship Development (STED) Project; and Rural Industries Programme (RIP)
- **Publications:** The institute publishes Newsletters, Books, Annual Reports, and Results Framework Document.

Collaborations

Indian Institute of Entrepreneurship (IIE) signed a Memorandum of Understanding, signed initially for three years, with Arunachal University of Studies, Namsai, Arunachal Pradesh on 5th March, 2014 at IIE campus,

Guwahati, Assam to promote and develop entrepreneurial environment. The Arunachal University of Studies is authorised to establish and approve new Skill Knowledge Providers (SKP) for facilitating joint certification with IIE.

National Institute of Entrepreneurship and Small Business Development (NIESBUD)

The National Institute for Entrepreneurship and Small Business Development is a society under the Ministry of Micro, Small and Medium Enterprises engaged in Training, Consultancy, Research and Publication, in order to promote entrepreneurship. The institute has been financially self sufficient since 2007-08. The Institute is operating from an integrated Campus in A-23, Sector-62, Noida, Uttar Pradesh. It is established in an area of 10,000 sq. meters with about 40,000 sq. feet of built up area. The infrastructure comprises of 8 class rooms, one auditorium, and one conference hall, besides library. There is also a hostel consisting of 32 rooms, and other facilities.

Major Activities

The major activities of the Institute inter alia include:

- **Training:** The different kind of training programmes being organized by the Institute inter-alia include Trainers' Training Programmes (TTPs); Management Development Programmes (MDPs); Orientation Programmes for Head of Departments (HoDs) and Senior Executives; Entrepreneurship Development Programmes (EDPs); Entrepreneurship-cum-Skill Development Programmes (ESDPs) and specially designed sponsored activities for different target groups.
- **Research/Evaluation Studies:** Besides the primary/basic research, the Institute has been undertaking review/evaluation of different government schemes/programmes, training need assessment- Skill Gap studies, industrial potential survey etc. The broad objective of these activities is the promotion of the MSME Sector.
- **Development of Course Curriculum/Syllabi:** The Institute has developed Model Syllabi for organizing Entrepreneurship Development Programmes. It also assists in Standardization of Common Training programmes.
- **Publications and Training Aids:** The Institute has been bringing out different *Publications* on entrepreneurship and allied subjects. The Institute has also assembled an Entrepreneurship Motivation Training brings out a quarterly *Newsletter*.
- **Cluster Interventions:** The Institute has been actively involved in undertaking developmental programmes (Soft and Hard Interventions) in Clusters in different capacities. The Institute has so far handled a total of 24 Industrial Clusters.

- **Incubation Centres:** The Incubator sponsored by the Ministry of MSME and functioning at the Campus of the Institute, has been instrumental in providing hands-on training and familiarizing the beneficiaries with the real factory/market conditions/ situations in the area of stitching, Mobile Repairing, Home Decor products, Beautician and Art Incubation. Following activities are organized for the same: (a) Self Employment Fair (b) Functioned as Udyami Mitra under Rajiv Gandhi Udyami Mitra Yojana (c) Business plan preparation (d) Institutional arrangements with Financial Institutes/ support organization/s (e) Linkage with Prime Minister's Employment Generation Programme (PMEGP) (f) Post training follow up with the participants.
- **Intellectual Property Facilitation Centre:** The Intellectual Property Facilitation Centre provides facilitation/assistance under one roof to the units located in its vicinity for identification, registration, protection and management of Intellectual Property Rights, as a business tool.
- **The E-Module EDP:** The Institute has developed an E-learning Module *(Hindi and English)* for Entrepreneurship Development Programmes. The course material of the Module has been incorporated in a C.D. which is moderately priced. The Module has been launched in different States.
- **E-learning Modules on Different Subjects:** Eight e-learning Modules have been created on Cyber Security, Communication Skills, Java Personality Development, Mathematical Modelling, Web Designing & Cloud Computing.
- **The Regional Centre, Dehradun:** Undertakes Research and provides Training & Consultancy Services to the beneficiaries specially those belonging to the states of Uttarakhand and Uttar Pradesh.
- **Hand-holding for Enterprise Creation and Employment Assistance to the Trainees:** The Institute provides hand-holding services to candidates interested in self-employment and assists to find suitable wage employment if they do not opt for self-employment. For the same, an interaction platform called *Rojgar Mela(s)* is organized for prospective employees and trained persons.
- **Collaborative Activities:** With different domestic and overseas/ multi-lateral institutions including Government of West Bengal, International Finance Corporation (IFC), a member of the World Bank Group, *Snapdeal* etc. to promote entrepreneurial culture/ provision of support services for different target groups.
- **International Activities:** The Institute conducts 8-weeks' training programmes under the Fellowships of the Ministry of External

Affairs: ITEC/SCAAP/COLOMBO Plan for the participants from different countries. Besides, the Institute also designs and conducts special /request training programmes for overseas agencies and has also been assisting other countries through consultancy assignments primarily in assessing the industrial potential of different Regions.

- **Consultancy Services (National and International):** Offering consultancy services in the area of entrepreneurship especially for MSMEs. It Offers advice and consultancy to other Institutions engaged in entrepreneurial training either in the Government or in the Private Sector. Advising Governments (both Central & State) and foreign Governments as well in the area of entrepreneurship and MSMEs.

Recent Achievements

- The Institute has been certified as compliant to the requirements of Management System ISO 9001: 2008 by TUV NORD CERT GmbH.
- It has been accorded in-principle approval by the All India Council for Technical Education (AICTE) for starting a long term (two years) **Post Graduate Diploma** in Entrepreneurship Management (60 seats).
- **MSME Naukri Portal** *(www.msmenaukri.com)* has been established to bridge the gap between job seekers and job providers. So far, 189 job providers and 10,969 job seekers have been registered on the web portal.
- The **Virtual Cluster** concept consists of a dedicated Web Portal hosted by the MSME Ministry i.e. *www.msmevirtualclusters.in*. It provides an opportunity for the stakeholders in the field of entrepreneurship to register and join. So far, 25,019 industries, 198 Institutions and 120 Experts have registered on the portal.
- The Institute has trained more than 2.60 lakh trainees including 2,600 persons from more than 125 countries till date. Also, in the year 2014-15, the institute assisted 2.40 lakh participants to set up their unit and 22.74 lakh to get wage employment.

Partner Institutions

The Institute, at present, has 58 Partner Institutions spread over 12 States/ U.T engaged in educational activities including those pertaining to entrepreneurial education/development.

Sector Skill Councils (SSC)

Sector Skill Councils are set up as autonomous industry-led bodies by NSDC. They create Occupational Standards and Qualification bodies, develop competency framework, conduct Train the Trainer Programs, conduct skill gap studies and Assess and Certify trainees on the curriculum aligned to National Occupational Standards developed by them. Till date, the NSDC Board has approved proposals for 38 Sector Skill Councils. There are approximately 450 Corporate Representatives in the Governing Councils of these SSCs. The Ministry of Skill Development & Entrepreneurship has been actively engaging with these SSCs.

- Ministry of Skill Development & Entrepreneurship under the Chairmanship of the Hon'ble MoS (I/C) held meetings with all the Sector Skill Council (SSC) in the months of December, 2014 and January, 2015 to integrate them into the National Agenda on Skilling.
- The Hon'ble MoS was also part of the Governing Councils meeting of 6 Sector Skill Councils viz. Beauty & Wellness, IT & ITeS, Telecom, Aviation & Aerospace, Rubber and Hospitality & Tourism Sector Skill Councils which were held over the last 3 months.
- The Ministry also organized meetings at the Joint Secretary level with the line Ministries of Sector Skill Councils like Capital Goods, Telecom, Mining, Shipping to align the activities of the SSC completely with these Ministries.
- The Ministry, along with NSDC and Sector Skill Councils, organized sectoral workshops on National Occupational Standards in February 2015.
- The Ministry has issued a notification that enables SSCs to join the list of non-statutory bodies which issue nationally recognised skills certificates

Various Schemes for Skill Development in India

Pradhan Mantri Kaushal Vikas Yojana (PMKVY)

Pradhan Mantri Kaushal Vikas Yojana (PMKVY) is the flagship scheme of the Ministry of Skill Development & Entrepreneurship (MSDE). The objective of this Skill Certification Scheme is to enable a large number of Indian youth to take up industry-relevant skill training that will help them in securing a better livelihood. Individuals with prior learning experience or skills will also be assessed and certified under Recognition of Prior Learning (RPL). Under this Scheme, Training and Assessment fees are completely paid by the Government. The scheme will be implemented through the National Skill Development Corporation (NSDC).

Key Components of the Scheme

- **Short Term Training:** The Short Term Training imparted at PMKVY Training Centres (TCs) is expected to benefit candidates of Indian nationality who are either school/college dropouts or unemployed. Apart from providing training according to the National Skills Qualification Framework (NSQF), TCs shall also impart training in Soft Skills, Entrepreneurship, Financial and Digital Literacy. Duration of the training varies per job role, ranging between 150 and 300 hours. Upon successful completion of their assessment, candidates shall be provided placement assistance by Training Partners (TPs). Under PMKVY, the entire training and assessment fees are paid by the Government. Payouts shall be provided to the TPs in alignment with the Common Norms. Trainings imparted under the Short Term Training component of the Scheme shall be NSQF Level 5 and below.

- **Recognition of Prior Learning:** Individuals with prior learning experience or skills shall be assessed and certified under the Recognition of Prior Learning (RPL) component of the Scheme. RPL aims to align the competencies of the unregulated workforce of the country to the NSQF. Project Implementing Agencies (PIAs), such as Sector Skill Councils (SSCs) or any other agencies designated by MSDE/NSDC, shall be incentivized to implement RPL projects in any of the three Project Types (RPL Camps, RPL at Employers Premises and RPL centres). To address knowledge gaps, PIAs may offer Bridge Courses to RPL candidates.
- **Special Projects:** The Special Projects component of PMKVY envisages the creation of a platform that will facilitate trainings in special areas and/or premises of Government bodies, Corporates or Industry bodies, and trainings in special job roles not defined under the available Qualification Packs (QPs)/National Occupational Standards (NOSs). Special Projects are projects that require some deviation from the terms and conditions of Short Term Training under PMKVY for any stakeholder. A proposing stakeholder can be either Government Institutions of Central and State Government(s)/ Autonomous Body/Statutory Body or any other equivalent body or corporates who desire to provide training to candidates.
- **Kaushal and Rozgar Mela:** Social and community mobilisation is extremely critical for the success of PMKVY. Active participation of the community ensures transparency and accountability, and helps in leveraging the cumulative knowledge of the community for better functioning. In line with this, PMKVY assigns special importance to the involvement of the target beneficiaries through a defined mobilisation process. TPs shall conduct Kaushal and Rozgar Melas every six months with press/media coverage; they are also required to participate actively in National Career Service Melas and on-ground activities.

- **Placement Guidelines:** PMKVY envisages to link the aptitude, aspiration, and knowledge of the skilled workforce it creates with employment opportunities and demands in the market. Every effort thereby needs to be made by the PMKVY TCs to provide placement opportunities to candidates, trained and certified under the Scheme. TPs shall also provide support to entrepreneurship development.
- **Monitoring Guidelines:** To ensure that high standards of quality are maintained by PMKVY TCs, NSDC and empanelled Inspection Agencies shall use various methodologies, such as self-audit reporting, call validations, surprise visits, and monitoring through the Skills Development Management System (SDMS). These methodologies shall be enhanced with the engagement of latest technologies.

Skills Acquisition and Knowledge Awareness for Livelihood Promotion (SANKALP)

Skills Acquisition and Knowledge Awareness for Livelihood Promotion (SANKALP) project aims to implement the mandate of the National Skill Development Mission (NSDM), which was launched on 15th July by Ministry of Skill Development & Entrepreneurship, through its core sub-missions. The project will be implemented in mission mode through World Bank support and is aligned with the overall objectives of the NSDM. The main objectives of the project include strengthening institutional mechanisms at both national and state levels, building a pool of quality trainers and assessors, creating convergence among all skill training activities at the state level, establishing robust monitoring and evaluation system for skill training programs, providing access to skill training opportunities to the disadvantaged sections and most importantly supplement the Make in India initiative by catering to the skill requirements in relevant manufacturing sectors. SANKALP is an outcome oriented project supported by World Bank. The project will focus on the overall skilling ecosystem covering both Central (MSDE, NSDA and NSDC) and State agencies, and outcomes will be measured through Disbursement Linked Indicators (DLIs) agreed between MSDE and the Bank. A DLI verification protocol has also been established to measure DLIs on a periodic basis.

UDAAN

Udaan is a Special Industry Initiative for Jammu & Kashmir in the nature of partnership between the corporate of India and Ministry of Home Affairs and implemented by National Skill Development Corporation. The programme aims to provide skills training and enhance the employability of unemployed youth of J&K. The Scheme covers graduates, post graduates and three year engineering diploma holders. It has two objectives: (i) To provide an exposure to the unemployed graduates to the best of Corporate India; (ii) To provide Corporate India, an exposure to the rich talent pool available in the State.

The key stakeholders are:

- Ministry of Home Affairs (MHA) - Chief Benefactors
- State Government (Jammu & Kashmir)
- Corporate Training Partners
- Implementation Agency (IA) - NSDC

The Scheme aims to cover 40,000 youth of J&K over a period of five years and ₹ 750 crore has been earmarked for implementation of the scheme over a period of five years to cover other incidental expenses such as travel cost, boarding and lodging, stipend and travel and medical insurance cost for the trainees and administration cost. Further corporates are eligible for partial reimbursement of training expense incurred for the candidates who have been offered jobs.

Standard Training Assessment and Reward (STAR) Scheme

The National Skill Certification and Monetary Reward Scheme, known as STAR (Standard Training Assessment and Reward), was operational between August 2013 and September 2014. NSDC is the designated implementing agency of the scheme and is working through various Sector Skill Councils (SSCs), Training Providers (TPs) and independent Assessment Agencies (AAs).

Polytechnic Education

Polytechnic education in our country constitutes an important segment of Technical Education and contributes significantly to the economic development. Aimed at creating a vast amount of technical manpower, the polytechnics have played a pivotal role in providing skilled manpower at various levels for organized, unorganized and Service Sectors. Generally, the polytechnics in the country have been offering three year diploma courses in conventional disciplines such as Civil, Electrical and Mechanical Engineering. However, during the last two decades many polytechnics have started offering courses in emerging disciplines such as Electronics, Computer Science, Medical Lab technology, Hospital Engineering, Architectural Assistantship etc. In addition, many institutions are also offering specialized diploma programmes in areas such as Leather Technology, Sugar Technology, and Printing Technology etc. Many diploma programmes are also being offered suited to women such as in Garment Technology, Beauty Culture and Textile Design etc. Polytechnics are meant to provide skills after class X and the duration of diploma programmes is 3 years. Polytechnics are also offering post diploma and advanced diploma programmes of 1-2 year's duration in different specializations.

Centrally Sponsored Scheme of Vocationalisation of Secondary Education

The Centrally Sponsored Scheme of Vocationalisation of Secondary Education of Ministry of HRD, Government of India lists out a crucial role for NSDC and its Sector Skill Councils (SSCs) in implementation of NSQF. The trainings conducted in the scheme are based on the National Occupational Standards set by NSDC through its Sector Skill Councils. The scheme also mandates the SSCs to conduct assessments and certification jointly with the State Board.

NSDC is currently working with the State Governments of Haryana, Himachal Pradesh, Karnataka, Punjab, Uttarakhand, Madhya Pradesh, Nagaland, Maharashatra, Chhattisgarh and Rajasthan for implementation of the scheme in their states through its approved and funded Sector Skill Councils. Sector Skill Councils support the States in Identification of Trades/ Occupations, Accrediting curriculum with PSSCIVE, Recommendation for Appointment of Vocational (Industry) Coordinator, Quality Control of Training, Training of Trainers, Student Assessment and Certification and Industry Interface. NSDC funded Training Partners take the responsibility of entire Training Delivery including deploying and managing faculty, setting up of labs, organising Guest Lectures/Industry Visits.

Role and Responsibilities of the Stakeholders

- **State Government:** Policy, Providing infrastructure, Mobilisation of Students through Principals, Monitoring, Regulatory, Aligning vocational to mainstream scheme of studies of the State Board, Extensive advocacy and marketing of the project.
- **NSDC:** Conceptualize and operationalize the project, Selection of NSDC partners in various trades to implement the project across schools, Setting Standards & Quality Processes, MIS and Monitoring, Management Review.
- **Sector Skill Council:** Identification of Trades, Accrediting curriculum, Recommendation for Appointment of Vocational (Industry) Coordinator, Quality Control of Training, Student Assessment and Certification and Facilitating Industry Interface.
- **NSDC Training Partner:** Curriculum development aligned to National Occupational Standards, Development and Printing of Courseware, Providing Vocational trainers, Industry Participation through OJTs and Internships, MIS & reporting, Interfacing with all Stakeholders.

Skill Based Trainings in Higher Education

In order to bridge the industry academia gap – NSDC has developed a unique model to integrate skill based trainings into the academic cycle of the Universities. These are based on National Occupational Standards set by industry through sector skill councils. The job roles offered are designed to be progressive in nature – from Level 5 – level 7 on National Skills Qualification framework. The key highlight of the model are as given below:

- Based on state skill gap report – identification of Sectors and job roles
- Development of implementation model and Integration into time table as per university norms
- Training of Trainers by Sector Skill Council
- Curriculum Alignment and Capacity Building workshops
- Student orientation sessions to take an informed choice of sector/job role based on career aspiration
- Standardised Training Delivery by NSDC Training Partners
- Internships and On- the-job Training
- Assessment and certification by Sector Skill Council
- Last Mile Employability and Entrepreneurship Opportunities for the students

NSDC is working with 21 Universities, UGC and AICTE catering to more than 1200 colleges and 400 community colleges across the country. Some of the organization include:

- Savitribai Phule University of Pune : 663 colleges and 57 autonomous institutions
- University of Delhi: 67 colleges
- University Grants Commission: 150 community colleges and 127 colleges for B.Voc. and Degree programmes
- Tamil Nadu Open University (TNOU): 155 learning resource centres and 204 community colleges
- Centurion University: 4 colleges
- Haryana and Punjab Universities
- AICTE : 100 Community Colleges

NSDC funded training partners affiliated to respective SSCs are involved in imparting trainings to the students under these partnerships. The infrastructure is allocated by the respective colleges of the University. A project management team ensures monitoring and evaluation of ongoing trainings. Academia recognise the benefits of this model for integration of industry recognized skills with regular studies and post assessment the students receive industry endorsed and recognized certificate.

Skill India

Skill India is an initiative of the Government of India which has been launched to empower the youth of the country with skill sets which make them more employable and more productive in their work environment. National Skill Mission is chaired by the Hon'ble Prime Minister himself.

India is a country today with 65% of its youth in the working age group. If ever there is a way to reap this demographic advantage, it has to be through skill development of the youth so that they add not only to their personal growth, but to the country's economic growth as well.

Skill India offers courses across 40 sectors in the country which are aligned to the standards recognised by both, the industry and the government under the National Skill Qualification Framework. The courses help a person focus on practical delivery of work and help him enhance his technical expertise so that he is ready for day one of his job and companies don't have to invest into training him for his job profile.

The Skill Mission launched by the Prime Minister on 15 July 2015, has gathered tremendous steam under the guidance of Union Minister of State for Skill Development and Entrepreneurship. The target to train more than a crore fresh entrants into the Indian workforce has been substantially achieved for the first time. 1.04 Crore Indians were trained through Central Government Programs and NSDC associated training partners in the private sector.

For the first time in 68 years of India's independence, a Ministry for Skill Development & Entrepreneurship (MSDE) has been formed to focus on enhancing employability of the youth through skill development. The skill ecosystem in India, is seeing some great reforms and policy interventions which is reinvigorating and re-energising the country's workforce today; and is preparing the youth for job and growth opportunities in the international market. The Hon'ble Prime Minister's flagship scheme, Pradhan Mantri Kaushal Vikas Yojana (PMKVY) alone, has till date seen close to 20 lakh people get skilled and prepared for a new successful India.

Skill India harbours responsibility for ensuring implementation of Common norms across all skill development programs in the country so that they are all standardized and aligned to one object. The ITI ecosystem has also been brought under Skill India for garnering better results in vocational education and training.

The success of a nation always depends on the success of its youth and *Skill India* is certain to bring a lot of advantage and opportunities for these young Indians. The time is not far when India will evolve into a skilled society where there is prosperity and dignity for all.

EDUCATIONAL ADMINISTRATION IN USA

Department of Education

Twenty years before the Hatch Act of 1887, the United States established an agency for keeping track of statistics, administration, and educational concerns to the nation at large. Originally known as the Department of Education, it was abolished in 1868, and its successor became part of the Department of the Interior under the name of the Office of Education, from 1868 to 1869. In 1869, its name changed to the Bureau of Education, remaining under the Department of the Interior. After restructuring again in 1939, education fell under the Federal Security Agency, moving again in 1953 following the establishment of the Department of Health, Education, and Welfare (HEW). HEW was reorganized in 1972 under the Education Division. In 1980 a new Department of Education was created.

One of the characteristics of American education is that all levels of government actively participate in decision making, budgetary concerns, and research funding. Education is thus highly accountable to taxpayers, but the many layers of federal Department of Education bureaucracy make reform slow and costly to implement. Essentially, the mandate of the Department of Education is to supplement the educational functions headed by the individual states. The department tracks educational statistics and trends, plus takes responsibility for overseeing research and the delivery of some non-state educational services, such as school lunch programs.

Primary responsibility for education is that of states and some localities. Exceptions include the District of Columbia, Pacific islands, and Indian reservations in the United States, where the U.S. Department of the Interior or Department of Education oversees operations. For example, in Guam the Department of Education oversees K-12, vocational, and community college schooling for civilian and military dependents. In 2001, an estimated 32,000 students were enrolled in Guam's K-12 single school district system.

Funding & Expenditures

Early funding of public education was uneven from state to state and even from school district to school district, particularly during the late nineteenth century. Perhaps the most important test case benefiting school funding was the 1874 Michigan Supreme Court decision on behalf of a Kalamazoo high school board, affirming its right to assess taxes as a basis of support. Subsequently, other schools in many states that had been operating under precarious circumstances seized the opportunity to gain financial backing.

While federal contributions are considerable, the primary responsibility for funding public schools rests with states, districts, and public and private organizations. According to federal figures in 2001, only about 9 percent of the $600 billion spent annually for education is supplied by the U.S. government. About three percent of all federal money goes to various school and Head Start lunch programs.

Moneys have been earmarked since 1981 to aid financially disadvantaged elementary and secondary school youth through Chapter I of the Education Consolidation and Improvement Act. Title I, as it most commonly is called, has since appropriated billions of dollars to thousands of school districts whose populations contained a significant number of persons falling below the poverty line. Figures from the most recent census are used to apportion future federal aid to states and school districts to provide additional learning resources for poverty-level students. Essentially, the higher a district's number of persons living in poverty, the higher that district's federal aid.

Each State in America has the power to establish its own system of education. The local districts under the States also have the power to establish schools boards and to found schools as well. The power of the States to set up schools does not in any way prevent the church from establishing schools in any of the states. The Education Levels in America include:

- Nursery Education
- Elementary or Primary Education
- Secondary Education
- Teacher Education and
- University and Adult Education.

Nursery Education

At the beginning, nursery education was part of primary school between 1868 and 1873. By 1888, nursery education had spread to many places in America. The Lanham education Act of 1940 also enhanced the development of nursery education in America by giving subventions from the federal government to nursery education. Later, individuals who had interest in the education of children started to part-take in the running of nursery schools. Also, the churches were participating in the running of nursery school.

The Primary Education

Primary Education in America is the education given to the children which has the duration of six years. The purpose of American primary education includes:

- Turning out well-adjusted citizens
- Helping the children to be active participants in the building of their own lives and also to assist them in understanding the roles expected of them in establishing a better American society.

- The primary school subjects include: Mathematics, Science, Geography, History, Social Studies, English language, English literature, French, German and Spanish. However, religious subjects are not included in the school curriculum as Americans have freedom of worship.
- In the primary schools, the promotion of the pupils is always based on continuous assessment and not on any promotion examination. It is the duty of the Local Schools Board to provide some of the school materials.

A public primary school is headed by the principal who is the administrative head of the school. While the primary school teachers are expected to have a university degree, the principals are in addition expected to have master's degree of educational administration and supervision. The failure of the Federal Government to include Religious Instructions in the school curriculum was one of the reasons that forced the Catholic to establish their own schools where religious instruction was included in the school curriculum. By implication, there are both private and public primary schools in America.

Secondary Schools in America

Secondary education in America is the type of education given to the adolescents on the basis of three years in the Junior Secondary School and three years in the Senior Secondary School. This can be referred to as 3 - 3 secondary education system.

The aims and objectives of American Secondary Education include:

- Creating a strong egalitarian society where everybody will have Equal opportunity.
- Preparing students for survival in the future
- Preparing the students for their colleges and universities. Some States in America provide free secondary education and free textbooks for their citizens particularly up to the age of sixteen years. The products of primary schools are always admitted into the secondary schools.

There are both public as well as private secondary schools in America. The Ordinance Act 1785 which made it mandatory for each township to set its sixteenth section for the use of education as well as the North West Ordinance of 1887 greatly enhanced the development of education in America. However, the problem of sub-standardized secondary schools and willingness to provide secondary education for many American children led to the introduction of Junior High School. In the Junior High School, the students are expected to spend three years after their primary education that is between the age of 12-15 years. After successfully completing the Junior Secondary Education, the students will start their Senior High School Education which is meant for the students, who are academically inclined. The public senior high schools are tuition free. Provision of learning materials for schools and the general financing of schools are responsibilities of the local schools district. In America, private high schools or secondary schools are also allowed by the constitution. However, unlike the public high schools, tuition is not free and the teaching of religious education is allowed. It is on record that America has started operating 6-3-3-4 education system, yet, the old system of 8-4 years is still in operation.

Teacher Education in the United States of America

Teacher education in USA like in other places refers to the professional training being given to the would-be teachers. The aims and objectives of American Teacher Education include;

- Preparing teachers for the needs and aspirations of American as a democratic nation.
- Preparing teachers who will later assist in the training of American children for the purpose of promoting their culture. The establishment of Jefferson College in Washington among others in the 1800s marks the beginning of teacher education in America.

The preparation of primary school teachers is always done by the normal schools. These normal schools are recognized by the State Boards of Education for the training of primary school teachers. The subjects being offered in the training institutions include: Administration, Psychology, Philosophy, History of Education. On the other hand, the secondary school teachers are expected to be university degree holders after a period of four years either in a college or in the university. In most cases, teachers' appointment is always on contract basis and it is renewable yearly, provided the concerned teacher is still interested in working in his school. At the same time, the school district board of education has the constitutional power to terminate the contract appointment of any of its teachers.

The American University Education

In America, higher education is provided in the colleges of education, higher technical institutes and universities. In 1862, the American Government passed the Morrill Act which made it compulsory for the Americans to make land available to the American Federal Government for the development of Universities and higher institutions of learning. There are two major categories of higher education in America, they are:

- The state universities and colleges which are maintained by the state and
- Independent universities and colleges which are run by various churches and private individuals. In these private colleges and

universities, high school fees are changed. A degree programme lasts for four years.

Adult Education in America

The beginning of Adult education can be traced to the establishment of Lyceum in Massachusetts in 1826. Also, the Smith Lever Act of 1914 as well as the Adult education Association of the United States in 1951 greatly contributed to the development of Adult Education in America. Adult education in American is run by private individuals such as lawyers, physicians, architects, teachers and musicians for the purpose of self culture, community instruction as well as the mutual discussion of common public interest. In 1906, the university extension was started and this has been extended to most of the universities in America.

Technical Education

There have been some technical institutions as early as the middle of 19th century. But there was no serious attempt to promote technical education until when the Mosco technical school was able to perform creditably well at the international exhibitions in the 1970s. Thereafter, more technical institutions began to spring up in America. Also, the Morill Act of 1862 assisted in the development of technical education, private individuals started founding both commercial as well as business colleges. The Smith-Hughes Act among other things recommended that a Federal Board of vocational education should be set up. It was on the basis of this that the Federal Board of vocational education was established in which a substantial amount of money was set aside by the federal government for the general promotion of vocational and technical education throughout America.

Administration of Education in America

Education in America is decentralized. Therefore, it is the responsibility of each State as well as the private individuals to take care of their schools. In 1867, the National Officer of Education was set up and it is being headed by the Education Commissioner who is an appointee of the president of America. The federal government always assists the state governments in the funding of technical and vocational education. The state universities are financially aided by the Federal Government. At the State level, there is a state department of education under the headship of Education Director who is elected by the people within the state for a period of two to four years. Locally, each local government has a local board of education, usually headed by a Superintendent of schools in the district. His duties include: appointing teachers and other personnel who will be working with him. He also works on the finance of schools founded by the local government.

Finance of Education in America

In the whole of America, less than 60 per cent of the total cost of both public primary and secondary schools comes from the taxes levied by the local schools boards. Also, the state government always sets aside about 40 per cent of its annual budget for the running of the public schools. The bulk of this money is generated from the state taxes as well as the taxes paid by the state workers. In the private schools, starting from the primary school up to the university, the students pay school fees in addition to the taxes being paid by the parents. Also, some well to-do individuals in America always assist the private schools financially.

EDUCATIONAL ADMINISTRATION IN UK

The administration of education policy in the United Kingdom began in the 19th century. Official mandate of education began with the Elementary Education Act 1870 for England and Wales, and the Education (Scotland) Act 1872 for Scotland. Education policy has always been run separately for the component nations of the United Kingdom, and is now a devolved matter (by the Northern Ireland Constitution Act 1973, the Scotland Act 1998, and the Government of Wales Act 1998 - each as amended).

As there is no devolved government for England, the administration of education policy for the nation has been carried out by a number of different British central government departments since the 19th century. Key events in Education in England have been the Elementary Education Act 1870, the Education Act 1902, the Education Act 1944, and the Education Reform Act 1988.

19th Century

Before the latter-part of the 19th century education was a private matter, and there was no governmental policy lead. Some education services were provided by the Church (dating back to a Papal proclamation in the 11th century).

A Committee of the Privy Council was appointed in 1839 to supervise the distribution of certain Government grants in the education field. The members of the Committee were the Lord President of the Council, the Secretaries of State, the First Lord of the Treasury, and the Chancellor of the Exchequer. From 1857 a Vice President was appointed who took responsibility for policy, leading to the creation of the Education Office.

With the 1870 Act the Education Office was given the task to manage the national process and commission local school boards in boroughs and parishes where they were requested.

The Board of Education Act 1899 took effect in 1900, renaming the Education Office to the Board of Education was created which managed the national process and commissioned local school boards in boroughs and parishes where they were found to be needed.

20th Century

The 1902 Act formalised the relationship between central government and education delivery by abolishing the 2568 school boards set up by the 1870 Act, and transferring their duties (and schools) to local government (borough and county councils) in a new guise as local education authorities.

The 1944 Act changed the system of education in England by forming the Tripartite System wherein secondary schools were mandated in one of four forms (Grammar, Comprehensive, Secondary Modern, and Secondary Technical schools), and renamed the Board of Education to the Ministry of Education.

The Department of Education and Science (DES) was created in 1964 as the merger of the Ministry of Education with that of the Ministry of Science following the Prime Minister Harold Wilson's focus on the "white heat of technology".

The 1988 Act brought in the concept of external validation of teacher performance and a support framework for teachers to use as the core of their syllabus, in the form of the National Curriculum.

In 1995 the DES was merged with the Benefits Agency and split off the Office of Science and Technology to become the Department for Education and Employment (DfEE).

21st Century

After the 2001 General Election, the DfEE and the Department for Social Security were combined and re-split into the Department for Education and Skills (DfES) and the Department for Work and Pensions.

In 2007, when Gordon Brown became Prime Minister, he split the education ministerial portfolio into two. The Department for Children, Schools and Families (DCSF) was formed with board responsibilities for children up to the age of 14, and for some aspects up to 19, taking on some social care responsibilities from the Department for Health. The Department for Innovation, Universities and Skills (DIUS) took over responsibility for all higher and further education and science policy, taking on the Government Office for Science, which by then included the Office of Science and Technology that had split off from DES in 1994.

In 2009, DIUS was merged with parts of the Department of Trade and Industry to form the Department for Business, Innovation and Skills (BIS), but with no change in the scope of its education policy remit.

Evaluations & Inspections

In 1993, a decision was reached by the government to engage outside agencies to rate the quality of courses in higher education institutions. Schools are held accountable for the aims and objectives they have stated in a self-assessment and goals statement. After 1997, institutions in England, Wales, and Northern Ireland are assessed by representatives engaged by the Quality Assurance Agency for Higher Education (QAA). The results are published for the public record.

Funding & Resources

The Higher Education Funding Council For England, a council that promotes and funds teaching and research in universities and colleges, reports that funding in excess of 11 billion pounds was distributed during the 1996-1997 academic year. Moneys came from four UK funding bodies—the Higher Education Funding Council for England; the National Council for Education and Training in Wales; the Department of Education, Northern Ireland; and the Scottish Higher Education Funding Council provide the lion's share of funding in a formula based upon faculty research and teaching. These four funding organizations receive their funding from Parliament but look only for standards and guidance to Parliament, being fully self-determining with funding priorities reflecting their respective educational needs and missions. In addition to providing funds for teaching and research, these bodies advise Parliament on status of education and changing needs such as technology. The remaining funding obtained by universities and colleges for operation come from private sources, including tuitions, conferences, gifts, and other services. Income from non-UK students for tuition amounted to approximately 563 million pounds in 1996-1997, according to the Higher Education Funding Council for England. As of 1996-1997, some 200,000 overseas students reside in the United Kingdom, hailing from more than 180 countries. European Union countries made up 44 percent of overseas representation.

Appropriations

Northern Ireland: Moneys appropriated in the education budget for Northern Ireland in 1993-1994 came to approximately 1.23 billion pounds (US$1.8 billion), according to the DENI Compendium of Northern Ireland Statistics. The moneys are for preschool, primary, secondary, and university schools.

School finances are overseen by the Education and Library Boards. Additional financial responsibility for budgetary matters goes to the Boards of Governors of individual schools through a Local Management of Schools (LMS) orderly plan.

Pre-primary, primary, and secondary schools receive moneys based on a formula that primarily is figured through enrolment numbers and the cost of infrastructure and other operational considerations. As in the Republic of Ireland, spending per pupil is most deficient at the primary level and is highest at the university level.

Education in England

Education in English at the initial stage was provided by voluntary agencies including the churches. However, such schools founded by the voluntary agencies were financially aided by the government. With the rapid growth in population as well as the expansion in the Industrial Sector and the enactment of education Act of 1870, schools' boards were established to assist the Voluntary Schools, later, the parliamentary Acts Elementary Education made elementary education compulsory and free. The beginning of a national education system in Britain can be traced to the *Hadow Report of 1926*. It was this report that brought about the reorganization of the elementary education. In the same vein, the SPENS report of 1938 also assisted the reorganization of the elementary education and the recommendation of technical secondary education. In the development of education in Great Britain, the Catholic played significant roles as quite a number of the Voluntary Schools were founded by them. However, the education Act of 1902 gave the following three levels of education.

The Elementary School

This school is designed for the children aged 5-14 years, in order to ensure that majority of the children attend elementary school, elementary education in England was not only tuition free but it is also compulsory for all the children who are within the age of 5 and 14 years.

Secondary School

This school was designed for children who have already completed the elementary education. It is designed for children whose parents are rich enough to pay the school fees. Unlike elementary education, it is not compulsory at all. Secondary education after graduation offers the products clerical jobs among others.

Preparatory and Public Schools

These schools were very expensive and were meant for children of the upper class (the Aristocrats). These preparatory and public schools gave birth to the establishment of both the University of Oxford and the Cambridge University.

Types of Schools in England

The following types of schools are in existence in England.

Nursery Education: A nursery school is school designed for children aged 3-5 years. Nursery school also serves as a temporary home for the children whose parents are working. Nursery education can be dated back to 1850, through the efforts of Friedrich Frobel as well as Maria Montessori.

It should be noted that day-nurseries where the children of working parents are kept are not the same thing as nursery school. The reason is that, real nursery education is for the children aged 3-5 years and it is also part of the school system. It is tuition free. The Hadow Report of 1933 and Plowden report of 1967 greatly enhanced the development and improvement of nursery education in England.

Primary Education: The Balfour-Morant Act of 1904 gave the following as the objectives of primary education in England.

(a) Recognising the child from 7-11 is a total being whose character, intelligence as well as physical abilities are moulded and trained.

(b) Arousing in the pupils a lively interest in man's ideals, achievements, literature, history as well as language.

(c) Developing an awareness in the pupils limitation; and

(d) Demonstrating to the pupils how to acquire knowledge as well as learning for themselves. Primary school in England could be divided into:

- Elementary and
- Higher elementary schools.
- According to statistics, about 93 percent of the children within the age of twelve years were in the elementary school.

The Fisher education, Act of 1918 made primary education compulsory for children up to the age of fourteen years and it also recommended the re-organization of primary education. Simply, primary education in England can be described as the education of young children below the age of eleven years. For the purpose of administration, all the public primary schools were being administered by the local education Authorities. It was also the responsibility of the Local Education Authorities to control all forms of secular education in the privately owned (Voluntary) primary schools. Also in England, there are some primary schools called Direct Grant School. Parents pay school fees in these schools. Primary school head is always given contract appointment. Inspectors only visit schools on request. Primary school subjects include:

History, Geography, Nature study, Crafts, Arts and Physical Education, French, Religious Education. Also, the extra school activities include: Gymnastic, Swimming, music among others. The 1944 Act increased the compulsory education in England to 15 years. It also recommended that the number of pupils in each class should be reduced to make it more manageable. The plowing report of 1967 had recommended a change in the age at which school pupils may transfer from eleven to twelve's years. It was also recommended that the junior schools were recommended for pupils aged 8-12 years or 9-13 years to enable the Local Authorities have a better reorganization of the secondary schools.

Secondary Education

Secondary school in England may be day or boarding school which offers to each of its scholars, up to and beyond the age of 16, a general, education, physical, mental and moral, given through a complete graded course of instruction of wider scope and more advanced degree than that in elementary schools. About four types of secondary education can be identified in England. They are:

- Secondary Modern Schools
- Secondary Grammar Schools
- Technical High School and
- Comprehensive School

Secondary Modern Schools are designed for students who are not academically inclined after their Primary Education. Secondary Modern Schools cater for secondary education for academically weak students up to the age of fifteen (15) years.

Secondary Grammar Schools are designed for the students who are academically inclined after their primary education. These schools in addition to giving sound formal education to the students also serve as the Custodian of English Tradition.

Technical High Schools are provided for students who have an intension of working in the industry later in life. In other words, these schools are established to cater for the needs of commerce and industry. The products of this school are admitted into the faculties of engineering for engineering courses in the British Universities.

Comprehensive Schools: These schools are established to caterfor children aged 11-18 years. The students in these schools offer the same subjects up to their second year. At the end of their third year, the students will be expected to choose three subjects apart from English language and Mathematics which they will like to study in their last two years. In the school, the students will have opportunity of learning one vocation or the other. As from the third year, the students will be exposed to one vocation or the other which he may want to do later in life. To assist the students, career officers are always provided by the school for the purpose of counselling the students on their future vocation.

Technical or Further Education in England

These are the institutions provided for young person's for the purpose of assisting them to develop their various aptitudes and also to train them to become responsible adults in life. Such schools among others include physical, practical as well as vocational training. An increased interest in the development of British Industry after the World War II for the training of skilled manpower in the area of technology greatly contributed to the development of further or technical education in England. At the end of the course, the students could be presented for the examination of the city and guilds of London Institute or any other related professional examinations. For children under the age of sixteen years, tuition is free while those who are above the age of 16 years and are working have to pay fees. Technical colleges or further education are run on both part time and full time basis.

Teacher Education in England

Teacher education is the professional training designed for teachers of all categories starting from the nursery school to the university. Perhaps, the first teachers' College for the training of secondary school teachers was the college of preceptors which was founded in the year 1846. With effect from 1904, the local education authorities were allowed to establish their Teachers Colleges. As from 1921, the British Universities include Teacher education programme in their curricula. For the degree in education, students would spend three years and the fourth year would be for their teaching practice after which a university diploma or certificate in education would be awarded. In 1943, the Board of education recommended that more Teachers' colleges should be founded so as to be able to solve the problem of inadequate qualified teachers. The Me Nair report of 1944 among others, recommended that universities as well as Teacher Training Colleges should work hand in hand for the general improvement of teacher education. However, before the education Act of 1944, the primary school teachers were of four categories:

- Certificated
- Un-certificated
- Supplementary and
- Specialist teachers.

In case of secondary schools, the teachers are expected to specialize in a particular subject. While the teachers for the old elementary schools were trained in the two-year colleges after their secondary education, the secondary school teachers were trained in a one-year teachers' diploma course at the university departments after graduating either from the faculty of Arts or Science. On the other hand, the teachers of independent public schools were degree holders.

Adult Education in England

Adult education in England can be described as education designed for people who have left school, adequate facilities for leisure-time occupation in organized cultural training and recreative activities for persons who are above compulsory school age and can benefit from such educational programmes. The beginning of Adult education in both England and Wales could be traced to the activities of British Philanthropists who initiated the idea by first of all establishing *Sunday Schools* for the Literacy Education of both the children as well as the adults. Many children and adults profited from this kind of education. The success recorded from this kind of education led to the establishment of London Mechanics Institution for the training of Mechanics in 1823. Within a very short time, similar institutions were cited in both England and Wales. The formation of the workers' educational Association which was affiliated to the Oxford University also contributed to the development of Adult Education in England. The association used to organize tutorial classes for its members in England. With effect from 1907, the Board of Education in England started to assist the university tutorial classes for general enhancement of Adult education. Also, for the promotion of Adult education, an Adult education Committee was set up in 1921. Primarily, the committee was to assist in the co-ordination of all the Adult education Voluntary Agencies. To crown it all, an open University was founded between 1960 and 1970 to provide better education for both the Adults as well as the workers. With the Open University education, workers in particular, were able to improve their working condition even though such Open University education was not tuition free.

University Education in England

Higher institutions in both England and Wales include: the Universities, colleges of education as well as the polytechnics. The most popular universities are the Oxford University founded in 1185 and Cambridge University in 1230. The two oldest universities were founded by the Church of England. In order to break the monopoly of both the Oxford University and the University of Cambridge, London University was established in 1828. School fees are being charged by the universities with which the universities are being financed in addition to financial aid from the public. Each university is autonomous in respect of admission, examination and award of degrees among others.

Administration of Education in England

The Education Minister is always appointed by the prime Minister.

The Minister has Permanent Secretaries to help him in carrying out his official duties. The Minister is the controller as well as the Director of Education Board. He has the power to organize the schools at any time. The Local Education Authorities are elected bodies for the purpose of controlling schools under them. They also have voluntary schools under them. They employed teachers and pay their salaries as well. Each school has the power to select the textbooks for the use of its pupils. However, unlike primary and secondary schools, higher institutions are not under control of the Ministry of Education.

Financing of Education

Money is always voted for the Ministry of Education from the national revenue by the parliament. The Minister of Education will also disburse part of the money in the form of grants to local Education Authorities.

EDUCATIONAL ADMINISTRATION IN INDIA

The Indian government is quasi federal in nature. The union government and the state government together are responsible for the development of education in the country. Hence separate ministries are formed for smooth functioning of the departments. On 26th September 1985 the Government of India created a new ministry in the name of **Ministry of Human Resource Development**. This ministry is responsible for educational development of the country. The ministry has two departments viz. Department of School Education and Literacy and Department of Higher Education.

Under the former, there are two sub categories viz.

- Elementary Education
- Secondary Education and Adult Education

Under the later, there are six sub categories viz.

- University and Higher Education
- Technical Education
- Book Promotion and Copy Right
- Scholarships
- Languages
- Minority Education

The ministry is headed by a cabinet minister called HRD minister followed by two state ministers, one for Higher Education and other for School Education and Literacy. Again a number of secretaries are also appointed by the ministry for administrative purpose.

State Ministries

The states of India have their separate ministries for education. The ministry for education of a particular state consists of a cabinet minister followed by a state minister. The state governments also formulate policies for education. There is also provision of acts and bills in the state legislature. These are brought whenever necessary. The minister is responsible to present the bill in the State Legislative Assembly for receiving grants and aids. Over the years, since Independence in 1947, there has been a shift in the process of educational planning from 'centralisation to decentralisation', from macro-planning to micro-planning and the district has been accepted as the most appropriate unit of planning.

Primary Education

At the pre-primary stage (0-6 years) there is the attempt to establish a linkage between ECCE and other development programmes including the Integrated Child Development Scheme (ICDS), for which Balwadis/ Anganwadis or Day-Care Centres and Schemes are run by Government and NGOs and State Governments.

The principle of decentralisation has been extended to the management of primary education and Village Education Committees (VECs) have been set up in many parts of the country. These Committees are responsible for the enrolment and retention of children in schools, supervise the functioning of schools, check teacher absenteeism and mobilise additional resources for the schools. Thus, attempts have been made to elicit community participation not only in the preparation of educational plans but also in the administration of education including mobilisation of additional resources.

District Boards of Education (DBE) plan and administer education at the district level. District-specific plans have been developed to increase infrastructural facilities, develop instructional material, train teachers, etc.

Secondary Education

At the state level, it is usually the Departments of Education that administer secondary education. At the national level, the Kendriya Vidyalaya Sangathan, New Delhi runs the Kendriya Vidyalayas (Central Schools) while the Navodaya Vidyalaya Samiti, New Delhi runs the Navodaya Vidyalayas, i.e., schools for talented rural children.

The Central Board of Secondary Education (CBSE), New Delhi functions under the overall supervision of the Department of Education, Ministry of Human Resource Development, Government of India. It deals with activities related to affiliation, academics and examination, and is known for introducing innovations and reforms at the secondary and senior secondary levels so as to bring education at par with international standards. At present, there are 4,308 schools affiliated to the Board. There are Boards of Secondary Education in each state as well.

Higher Education

In the tertiary sector, the following bodies determine and maintain standards for higher education and funding at the national level:

- University Grants Commission
- All India Council for Technical Education
- Medical Council of India
- Indian Council of Agricultural Research
- Veterinary Council of India
- National Council for Teacher Education.

Some states also have Higher Education Councils as also senior government functionaries (Secretaries) for higher education at the State Government level to effectuate higher education administration in the state.

All India Council for Technical Education (AICTE)

The administration of technical education is done through the AICTE. Set up as an advisory body in 1945, it was given a statutory status through an Act of Parliament in 1987, which came into effect in March 1988. The main functions of the statutory AICTE include proper planning and coordinated development of technical education in the country, qualitative improvement at all levels in relation to planned growth as well as regulation and maintenance of norms and standards. The AICTE performs its statutory functions through seven Regional Committees, All India Boards of Studies and various innovative schemes and programmes.

Adult Education (AE)

The National Literacy Mission (NLM) provides technical support and leadership in targeting the estimated 121 million non-literates in the 15-35 age-group. There is a central scheme of assistance to voluntary agencies in AE in which the agencies are encouraged to take up area specific TLC/PLC projects, establish and run post literacy centres called JSNs.

Vocational education

The CIVE/NCERT was set up in Bhopal, Madhya Pradesh, in 1993 to serve as an apex research and development institute for vocational education in the country. This institute's activities revolve around the review and standardisation of curriculum / textbooks / instructional material, teacher training programmes, and inter-state interaction to facilitate and share information and experiences related to vocational education.

Non Formal Education (NFE)

All the NFE centres are organised on the basis of projects. Mostly, each NFE project comprises of 100 NFE centres. However, in hilly, coastal or tribal areas, the project may have a smaller number of centres. A Project Officer is in charge of the project and looks after both the academic and administrative needs of the project. The monitoring of the programme is done on a continuous basis at the village, district and state through VECs, District Institutes of Education and Training (DIETs), State Councils of Educational Research and Training (SCERTs) and Directorate of Education, respectively.

Apex institutions

The NCERT is the apex resource organisation assisting and advising the central and state governments on academic matters related to school education. The constituents of the NCERT include:

- National Institute of Education, New Delhi.
- Central Institute of Educational Technology, New Delhi.
- Four Regional Institutes of Education, located at Ajmer, Bhopal, Bhubaneswar and Mysore.
- Pandit Sundarlal Sharma Central Institute of Vocational Education, Bhopal.
- Field Offices in major states.

During the year 1995-96, the NCERT has reprioritised some of its programmes to respond to national concerns in school education. At the state level, functions similar to the NCERT are performed by the SCERTs. The apex institution concerned with educational planning and administration is the National Institute of Educational Planning and Administration (NIEPA). This institution conducts research, organises training, provides consultancy services and disseminates important information on innovations, changes and developments in the areas of planning and management. Many states are also in the process of setting up SIEMTs, State Institutes of Educational Management and Training, to assist state level educational planning and training of educational planners and administrators.

Non-Governmental Organisations (NGO)

A large number of NGOs are working in the areas of Adult Education (AE), Non-Formal Education (NFE), Special Education for Children with Disabilities, Early Childhood Care and Education (ECCE) and teacher training. NGOs are also engaged in education and welfare of working children and street children. Some NGOs have been established to undertake innovative programmes in teaching, curriculum development and teacher training. For example, a large number of teachers and teacher educators are involved in the activities of organisations like *Eklavya* in Madhya Pradesh, and *Digantar* and *Sandhan* in Rajasthan, which are engaged in teacher training, curriculum development, educational research and NFE.

Statutory Councils and Apex Bodies

The Statutory Councils and Apex Bodies play important roles in reforming the education system of the country. These councils or apex bodies are either established by the state governments or by the central government. They are responsible for recognition of courses, promotion of professional institutions and providing grants to undergraduate and post graduate programmes and various awards. The Important National councils of the country include:

- All India Council for Technical Education (AICTE)
- Indian Council for Agriculture Research (ICAR)
- National Council for Teacher Education (NCTE)
- Rehabilitation Council of India (RCI)
- Medical Council of India (MCI)
- Indian Nursing Council (INC)
- Dentist Council of India (DCI)
- Central Council of Homeopathy (CCH)
- Central Council of Indian Medicine (CCIM) etc.

DISTANCE EDUCATION AND CONTINUING EDUCATION IN AUSTRALIA

Australia is an advanced industrial nation with a population of sixteen million and in the late 1980s a budget outlay of $41,628 billion (1986/87). Within that budget outlay the amount allocated to education was $2,898 billion. While there has been some small variation since then this percentage (7%) has been reasonably consistent. The Commonwealth of Australia is a federation of States - New South Wales, Victoria, Queensland, South Australia, Western Australia and Tasmania - together with Territories administered by the Commonwealth. The most important of these are the Northern Territory and the Australian Capital Territory where the nation's capital, Canberra, is located. Federation combined the previous colonies of states in 1901. Most of Australia's sixteen million people live in large coastal cities - either the state capitals or major cities on the south and east coast. It is a multicultural nation with over 20% of the population born overseas. Most were born in either the United Kingdom or Ireland, but a significant proportion of those arriving in recent decades have come from southern Europe and the Middle East. Refugees from

Indo-China constituted the greatest proportion of Australia's refugee intake during the 1980s. The indigenous people of Australia - Aborigines and Torres Strait Islanders - make up about 1% of Australia's population. Many of these live in rural and outback areas, especially in Queensland, New South Wales, Western Australia and the Northern Territory, rather than in major cities. Nevertheless there are substantial communities of Aborigines in the cities, particularly Sydney and Brisbane. Some Aboriginal community schools teach traditional languages, as do ethnic community schools, usually outside school hours but it must be considered that the primary language of instruction in Australia is English. Nevertheless there are many opportunities to study in other languages in high schools. Constitutionally education is the responsibility of the States. But the Federal Government has become heavily involved in higher education particularly because of funding arrangements. Within the states, education in government schools (75%) is controlled by State Education Departments usually headed by a Director-General of Education and responsible to a government minister.

Centralization is a feature of the administration of public education in all states of Australia. Staffing, curriculum planning and resources are the responsibility of the department. The goal of public education in Australia is equality of opportunity for all students, urban or rural. This is expressed in a common curriculum within each state. Across Australia, curriculum difference is more a matter of degree or emphasis rather than content. Distance education in Australia fits into the ethos of equality of education and uniformity of practice. The public schools are financed through a redistribution of federal tax. Australia's universities and Colleges of Advanced Education (CAEs) are autonomous institutions established under Acts of State Parliament and are the only institutions with the power to establishment of universities and colleges is a state responsibility and traditionally they were state funded. Tertiary education is now almost completely funded by the Commonwealth. Under a series of trade-off agreements in 1974, the Commonwealth undertook total funding responsibilities for the tertiary sector in order to achieve its policy objective of free tertiary education. Thus since 1975 there have been no tertiary tuition fees. In the 1986/87 budget an administrative charge of $250.00 (Aus) was introduced. In 1988/89, charges were introduced and levied as a tax on future or present income, known as the Higher Education Contribution Scheme (HECS). Technical and Further Education Colleges (TAFE) are essentially vocationally orientated but also provide adult non-vocational education and are funded mainly by the states (75% State and 25% Commonwealth). Federal Education Commissions formulate and administer federal education policy within the government's financial guidelines. Australia is a large continent covering an area of approximately seven million square kilometres. Nevertheless it has a very extensive telephone and telecommunications system. Most Australians, except those in the most remote outback, have telephones and/or radio phones and can receive at least one national carrier both on television and over radio - the Australian Broadcasting Commission (ABC). Australia is known as one of the leaders in digital telecommunications. The postal system is efficient, with mail between capital cities taking between two and three days and mail to the outback, even to some of the smaller rural stations, usually takes no more than two weeks unless there is inclement weather. Newspapers tend to be state based with two major chains. Television ownership and provision is similarly state based. The national carrier, the ABC, provides both national and local state programs. It would be true to say that the communications system in Australia is an efficient one with the variety of modes of distribution becoming a modem industrial nation. Satellite communications to the outback are increasing with the use of satellite dishes.

The Legal Status of Distance Education

The legal status of distance education is difficult to delineate, largely because it has been an integral part of the education system in Australia since its creation in 1901. From the beginning, state school departments were offering educational opportunities to students in remote areas through correspondence and later through the School of the Air. Technical and Further Education colleges from the 19305 onwards also offered in rural and remote areas similar courses to those they were offering on-campus students. At the higher education level, the University of Queensland in 1910 and the University of Western Australia in 1911 in their initial charters had to provide education for those unable to attend on-campus studies. An example of the enabling by-law is the University of New England Bill (Act 34, 1953) which was passed in December 1953 and gave the Council of the new autonomous university power to: establish within the university a Department of External Studies for the purpose of providing appropriate tuition for students who are unable to attend lectures at the university and of enabling degrees to be conferred upon such of them as, by examinations satisfy the requirements of the university.

Aims and Objectives of Distance Education

There are no overall aims and objectives of distance education as they vary from institution to institution. They tend to be concerned with issues of access and equity. The following are examples: The college endeavours to meet the needs of groups which have, for many reasons, been disadvantaged in the education system. It seeks to break down the barriers that have denied access to higher education by Aboriginal people, women and people with disabilities. (External Studies Guide, The South Australian College of Advanced Education, 1991). External Studies has a vital role to play in ensuring access to higher education for people in rural and geographically isolated areas. The university considers it has a valuable role to play in using external studies to provide access to higher education for educationally and socio-economically disadvantaged adults.

Control, Organization and Management Structure of Distance Education

The levels of distance education provision include the schools, TAFE Colleges and the higher education level. Provision of these services is State and Federal Government funded, it is neither private nor jointly established. At the school level the funding comes as part of the normal state education department budget. A proportion of that is given to the state correspondence school, which is part of the management structure of the Department of Education, responsible to the minister. Likewise, the TAFE correspondence schools come within the Technical and Further Education Department, which is responsible through the Director-General to the State Minister.

Funding for the universities and CAEs comes from the Federal Government, but they are autonomous institutions. All of them are dual mode institutions so again distance education is not a separate establishment within the universities. There are Distance Education Centres but they come within the established university structures. The net result is that there is actually no overall governing body for distance education in Australia. In the last three years the National Distance Education Council was established, with sub-committees considering areas such as technology, data base and standards. This is not a governing body; but rather a policy development committee.

The responsibilities of administration, setting academic standards, resource planning, management and dissemination of information are distributed throughout the management structure of the state schools and TAFE departments, and also within the autonomous management structures of the university. Thus the relationship between distance education and other education institutions is difficult to determine because distance education is part of the same structure and is not a separate institution. In many ways this might be seen as the strength of the Australian model.

Financing Distance Education

The source of financial support for Distance Education Centres and programs is largely from State and Federal funding. However, while the Commonwealth is by far the dominant source of financial support (for instance in higher education it provided 84.5% of net income in 1986) other sources have steadily increased in importance over recent years. Total income from non-Commonwealth sources rose to 15.5% in 1986. Growth in the different items of non government revenue has been uneven, reflecting in part the different strengths of the university and advanced education sectors. For instance the universities, particularly the long established ones, appear better able to derive income from endowments, bequests and donations, whereas some of the old CAEs are benefiting from their traditionally close links with industry. In the Commonwealth sector there has been a growth in university funding through sources such as the Australian Research Grants Committee; these sources provide funds earmarked for specific research projects.

Instructional Systems

The primary method of delivery utilized for distance education at all three levels is print despatched by mail. There are some significant exceptions to this, such as the internationally famous School of the Air. Nevertheless even they have very strong print components. The radio component is more for tuition and interaction. The TAFE system is using satellite transmission for one-way video/two-way audio and also for graphic transfers in some states.

The Distance Education Centres at the higher education level also use print as the core medium but include other technologies as part of their teaching materials. Audio has been used since the mid-1960's particularly in the development of language teaching at a distance. Video has been used since the 1980's and some universities, especially the University of New England, have developed a wide range of video material. The University of New England also uses broadcast radio and broadcast television. An interesting development in the provision of the instructional systems of distance education will occur in 1992 when a two-year trial of television based open learning (at tertiary level) will occur. Eight to ten first year accredited university courses will be presented with integral television components. These will be accompanied by print material which will remain the core learning medium.

Enrolment in Distance Education

The most recent figures available for distance education are based on 1990 enrolments. The statistics for higher education (Universities, CAEs, TAFE) are published in the Selected Higher Education Statistics 1990 by the Federal Department of Employment, Education and Training. Due to the nature of higher education funding and administration the data is more readily available for universities. The state based primary and secondary correspondence schools data is not as easy to collect. The type of enrolment is broken down into external and internal full-time and internal part-time; for the purposes of this paper full-time and part-time internal will be grouped together as internal In 1990 there were 52,712 external students and 432,363 internal students enrolled in higher education institutions in Australia. Therefore the ratio of external to internal students is one external student to eight internal students. Of those 52,712 external students, 22,666 were new to their course of study. Data pertaining to higher education graduates is not defined in terms of internal or external study; the combined graduates from all disciplines at higher education institutions in Australia was 90,482 in 1990.

International Affiliation and Co-operation

Many individuals and departments in Distance Education Centres are members of The Australian and South Pacific External Studies Organization (ASPESA) - which covers Australia, New Zealand, The South Pacific and Papua New Guinea. Many of ASPESA's members also hold membership of the International Council for Distance Education (ICDE). Their membership is now in excess of eighty individual members as well as significant institutional participation.

Growth and Expansion

There appears to be no planned expansion to distance education in Australia in the next 5-10 years. Growth may come from the Distance Education Centres at the tertiary level if those centres cannot fill their student quotas by internal on-campus students. It is unlikely that growth will occur in correspondence schools as there is a slow de-population of the rural and remote areas. Whilst the service will continue it is doubtful that the population will increase in those areas. This is probably also the case for TAFE correspondence colleges.

Australian Higher Education: The current situation with regard to distance education

Within Australia, there has been little movement in the provision of distance education with institutions that traditionally cater for external students maintaining their market share of the domestic market.

The 'no or limited growth' scenario for domestic external students has meant that distance education is of little strategic interest to institutions in their quest to gain income through new markets or by gaining a greater share of existing markets. There is, however, strategic interest in maintaining market shares of domestic internal students by ensuring that study arrangements are convenient and enable students to 'earn and learn.' Many institutions have therefore added to their existing 'design configuration' (Gibbons, 2004) to develop more flexible delivery approaches (Nunan, 2000), while at the same time maintaining face-to-face as the predominant mode. This has meant the provision of parts of a program by distance or online education or at the very least the use of distance teaching techniques within courses or programs.

In Australia, the enrolment category of mixed mode records instances where students use a mix of internal and external studies. This provides a measure of flexibility at a macro level as it enables student choice about how frequently they will need to attend at a campus. The use of micro in-course mechanisms of introducing flexibility using distance education or online teaching and learning techniques is much more difficult to measure as three categories have been identified and institutional and national figures are not available.

The provision of mixed mode attendance within a program has seen major changes in demand and provision. In New South Wales, changes between the 2002 and 2003 mode of attendance patterns show that the total of part and full-time external and multi-modal students went from 28,699 to 58,785 – an increase of some 105 percent. Closer inspection of the figures reveals that the changes represent a number of universities providing external mode within multi-modal attendance. Institutions with existing external delivery capacity have used this to provide more flexible arrangements for studying programs at their institutions.

New forms of 'distance education' have become integrated into the delivery processes of universities as 'flexible delivery'. Universities are undergoing a paradigm shift with regard to the provision of teaching and learning – their first decision is more likely to be what type of variant of fifth generation intelligent flexible learning (Taylor, 1999) is needed, rather than whether either traditional internal face-to-face or distance teaching should be used. Indeed, the changes to distance education are such that it is arguable whether it is useful to consider it as a distinctive and organizational entity (King, 2003).

Distance education has but a small and tangential role to play in the main game for Australian higher education, which is generating income from international enrolments. Currently international students make up nearly one in four of all Australian university students and contribute AUS $5 billion to the system. There are predictions for further expansion. Vidovich (2004) comments upon this situation, noting that Australian universities: . . . are heavily into the 'business' of international marketing, and this emphasis is set in a context of reduced Commonwealth Government funding, creating pressures for universities to actively seek private sources of income, especially from overseas (p. 344).

So important has been this source of funds to the economic survival of particular institutions that within them the national and local have become driven by the global.

Conventional distance education has not been part of exporting education. Where students are taught in their home country the model has been largely one of an Australian satellite campus or of 'education centres' through partner institutions. However, the products of distance education in the form of printed course guides and their resources often play a role in defining the syllabus of the area and in assuring the quality of the face-to-face teaching and learning experiences provided by a partner institution. This use of distance teaching materials in conjunction with local tutors enables the capacity to reach wider in-country markets and has assisted in gaining income for some institutions.

DISTANCE EDUCATION AD CONTINUING EDUCATION IN UK

The United Kingdom (UK) comprises four countries: England, Northern Ireland, Scotland and Wales. The four United Kingdom (UK) nations share a common quality assurance (QA) framework for higher education. Nevertheless, due to the three devolved national administrations of Northern Ireland, Scotland and Wales, some aspects of the framework are nation-specific. The UK regulatory framework is 'integrated' (Kirkpatrick, 2012), in that it makes no distinction between modes of higher education. However, there are a range of other agencies which influence the regulatory framework for distance higher education in the UK, including the British Standards Institute, the British Accreditation Council, and the Open and Distance Learning Quality Council. Universities and colleges in the UK are independent of the state and autonomous in their activities. Most receive government funding through national funding councils. A range of requirements is associated with that funding, which differs considerably in each of the four UK nations. The Quality Assurance Agency (QAA) oversees academic standards in institutions. An organization independent of government, it provides guidance on and conducts reviews of HE provision. QAA areas of focus include a regular cycle of audit and review, identifying good practice, making recommendations for improvement and publishing guidelines to help institutions develop effective systems to ensure that students have high quality experiences. The QAA makes no distinction between on-campus and distance provision. The British Accreditation Council is responsible for quality assurance in the independent further and higher education sector. This includes private colleges providing access to higher education courses and validated HE courses in partnership with universities and awarding bodies. The British Accreditation Council works with the British Council which accredits English language centres and the Online and Distance Learning Quality Council (ODLQC), both of which predominantly focus on courses below higher education level.

England

Higher education provision in England is regulated through three main organizations: the Higher Education Funding Council for England (HEFCE), the Office for Fair Access (OFFA) and the Quality Assurance Agency. The Higher Education Funding Council for England (HEFCE) is the funding body for higher education in England and plays a central role in ensuring proper accountability for public funds. The Office for Fair Access (OFFA) promotes and safeguards fair access to higher education for lower income and other under-represented groups. It provides regulatory oversight by approving and monitoring 'access agreements', documents which set out how a higher education institution intends to support access to higher education for underrepresented groups using the additional fee income that they choose to charge. There has been some recent pressure for these three 'regulators', each with very different briefs, to be merged into a single higher education regulator for England (Future of Higher Education Commission, 2013) which would include within its remit monitoring of the financial health of higher education institutions.

Wales

The Higher Education Funding Council for Wales (HEFCW) currently holds regulatory oversight by applying terms and conditions to the annual round of funding provided to each Welsh Higher Education Institution (HEI) charging annual student fees above £4,000. These terms and conditions relate to the financial stability of the HEI, its efforts to widen access to under-represented groups, and the quality of its provision.

Scotland

In Scotland regulatory oversight is the responsibility of the Scottish Funding Council (SFC) which distributes funding to HEIs and Further Education Colleges (FECs) in Scotland. Responsibilities are delegated from the UK-level QAA Board to QAA Scotland. One distinguishing aspect of the Scottish system is a central focus on the Quality Enhancement Framework (QEF), introduced in 2003, which places the improvement of the student experience at the forefront of quality assurance work. Enhancement-led Institutional Reviews focus on institutional management of the standards of academic awards and the quality of learning opportunities provided to students.

Northern Ireland

In Northern Ireland the Quality Assurance Agency works closely with the Department for Employment and Learning and higher education institutions. Reviews of higher education are conducted by the Quality Assurance Agency, following the Institutional Review process used in England and Wales. Reviews of further education colleges which provide higher education awards are conducted through the Integrated Quality and Enhancement Review (IQER) process.

The Size and Shape of Distance Education in UK

There are no explicit national policies concerning distance education in any of the separate nations of the UK. However, a range of factors and policies have a bearing on distance education. For example, recent tightening of Visa approvals processes and immigration control, which threaten international student fee income, have encouraged universities to sell more distance courses to international students to be completed in their home nation. Some politicians in England, amidst a turbulent few years for higher education policy, have advocated distance education as a way through the difficulties (The Guardian, 2010). Distance education in the UK is included within the provision of a wide range of institutions. A small number of specific institutions cater to a very large proportion of all distance learning students, most notably the Open University UK.

The generally held view is that many institutions pursue distance education for economic reasons, often exploiting the potential of academic globalization to reach international students (Rovai and Downey, 2010). Furthermore, in order to pursue such students in a competitive marketplace, many institutions draw in the services of private organizations to deliver their distance provision.

In the UK, for example, the University of Liverpool works in partnership with Laureate to offer a range of online postgraduate courses in management, IT, health, law and psychology; the University of Essex works in partnership with Kaplan, offering a limited range of online undergraduate and postgraduate degrees. Both target a broad market of working professionals, both UK based and international. The UK higher education sector includes an increasing number of private providers. Many of these make use of online provision, although not exclusively so. One major private provider, BPP University College, which has held degree awarding powers since 2007, describes all its students as online students, although it also offers face-to-face engagement on many of its programmes.

Advances in technology in recent years have meant that for many institutions, and for the UK sector in general, the terms 'distance learning' and 'online learning' are often used interchangeably. This means that it is difficult to find robust data on numbers of distance education and online education programmes separately. The major contribution to the literature is a study conducted by the University of Oxford in 2010 (White et al., 2010). The UK Higher Education Statistics Agency also provides limited statistics on distance higher education provision.

The majority of UK distance learning offered by HEIs is at Level 74 (postgraduate level) and is offered as a form of professional development, often directed at business, law, medicine, science and education. Nevertheless, there is also significant provision at Level 45, also in vocational areas (White et al., 2010)

Although technology has enhanced much of what is possible in distance and online learning, UK institutions have articulated a range of other factors which are critical for its success. These include course and programme design, management, student and tutor support, and marketing (White et al., 2010), all of which must be delivered in a very different manner compared with campus-based higher education (Kirkup, 2014)

Costs of Distance Education in UK

Undergraduate higher education fees are controlled differently in each of the four UK nations. In England, tuition fees are capped at £9,000 per year for a full-time course; there are no fees in Scotland for Scotland-domiciled students; and in Wales, although fees of up to £9,000 per year are chargeable, Welsh students are supported through government grants to reduce the fee cost to the student to £3,685 per year. The vast majority of full-time degree courses in England and Wales charge the maximum fee, but distance learning undergraduate tuition fees vary considerably, from less than £2,500 per year for the equivalent number of credits to a full time course, up to the maximum £9,000. Postgraduate course fees are not regulated, and some more prestigious qualifications, particularly MBAs, attract significantly higher fees.

What is known about Students in Distance Education?

Distance education students in the UK can be separated into those who are UK-based or UK-funded (which includes Crown servants in the Services studying overseas) and wholly overseas students (which includes students registered with or studying for an award at a UK Higher Education Institution). In 2012/13 there were a total of 226,420 UK based/funded and 123,635 wholly overseas students studying by distance education through UK-based Higher Education Institutions (HEI). Students of the Open University UK constitute a large proportion of all undergraduate and postgraduate distance learning students in the UK. Changes to fees and funding for higher education in England which came into effect in 2012/13 saw a dramatic reduction in the numbers of part-time students. This is reflected in the Open University numbers for 2012/13. Wholly overseas provision grew between 2011/12 and 2012/13, with overall growth in undergraduate and postgraduate distance learning students represented by growth in non-EU students (6.1% for undergraduate and 10.1% for postgraduate), cancelling out a contraction in EU students.

Barriers and Enablers

Advances in technology have increased the range of what is possible in distance learning, but some have suggested that this pace of technological change can be out of step with learners' skills (White et al., 2010). However, there are indications that students' familiarity with the main tools most often used by distance and online providers – virtual learning environments, blogs, wikis and forums – is increasing. There appears to be general agreement that distance and online students have different expectations to 'traditional' campus-based students. It has been suggested that this relates to the fact that many distance learning students are working professionals and are as a rule older than campus-based students. White et al. identified that distance learning students 'generally expect to be engaged, challenged, consulted and supported in a professional manner' (2010, p. 43). Some institutions providing distance and online learning offer a range of supporting activities, including open days, online graduation services, and induction programmes. Advances in technology appear to support such developments, which aim to improve the social aspects of learning online.

Number of Adult Learners in UK

The dominant application route into HE in the UK is the Universities Central Admissions System (UCAS). Across the 162 HEIs in the UK, total numbers for full-time undergraduate (UG) degrees showed some decline following the effective tripling of HE tuition fees in England in 2012. However, numbers have remained relatively stable since then (378,000 entrants in England in 2013/14, 27,000 more than in the previous year). Some subjects reflect this recent increase (Sciences, including Engineering and Computing) while others (Languages, Architecture) have continued to decline. On the UCAS website, it is noted that around one third of all undergraduates are mature students (defined as adults aged 21 or over at the commencement of studies). This is broken down into:

- 40% aged 21-24
- 20% aged 25-29
- 40% aged 30+

Two thirds of these entrants have had no prior experience of HE. The proportion of fulltime adult HE students from low participation neighbourhoods is dropping, suggesting that efforts to widen adult participation have stalled. If non-degree qualifications are included (certificates, diplomas, institutional credit), the proportion of adult learner enrolment rises to 52%. Crucially, 92% of part-time HE entrants in the UK in 2012/13 were aged 21 or over. In order to understand the UK's somewhat ambivalent attitude to adult HE students, it is thus vital to take into account that the numbers of part-time UGs almost halved between 2010 and 2014 (48% drop from 320,000 to under 200,000 (HEFCE, 2014), especially on courses that are not first degrees (numbers on foundation degrees, certificates and diplomas (38%) and institutional credit (35%) all dropped significantly). There may be significant social justice issues here, since a greater proportion of females (60%) study part-time.

Success Rate / Drop Out

Across UK Higher Education (HE), adult learners studying full-time tend to drop out in slightly greater proportions than young students (10% vs. 6%), which is attributable to the additional responsibilities (life pressures) that adult learners carry while studying. Of the 2011/12 cohort of mature access students, 10% withdrew from their UG degree programmes – the same proportion as for adult students with traditional entry qualifications. The more significant issue is withdrawal from part-time HE courses. This stands at 35%, a figure aligned with the experience of adults studying courses with the Open University. Supporting persistence for adult learners studying part-time is therefore of crucial importance, given that adult learners who see their degree through to the end perform at least as well as younger students and enjoy a significant 'graduate premium' in terms of subsequent career earnings, according to Open University evidence.

Courses and Programmes of Study

The most popular HE subject choices for adults are:

- Subjects allied to medicine
- Business
- Education

The contrast with young full-time students is striking: 28% of adult UGs study subjects closely linked to public sector employment (subjects allied to medicine and education) compared to only 12% of young students. Higher Apprenticeships have been advocated as a contemporary solution for adult learners. However, for at least fifty years, reports have bemoaned the relative absence of higher level technical/vocational skills provision below degree level in HE in England (Association of Colleges, 2014), blaming the gravitational pull towards the academic in HE, as manifest in a system dominated by three-year residential degrees. This contributes to a decline in the recruitment of part-time adult students and a shortage of advanced technical skills. A key criticism is that HE qualifications are not fit for purpose: they are too generic, with insufficient skills elements and limited employer involvement. If Higher Apprenticeships are a solution, support will be needed in the HE in FE sector, which enrols 130,000 HE students, about 10% of the total, of whom half study part-time and 60,000 study for professional certificates and diplomas.

Although the absence of credit places them outside this report, could free Massive Open Online courses (MOOCs), Badged Open Courses (BOCs) and Open Educational Resources (OERs) address the needs of adults in HE though informal learning? This would potentially bring together modes of learning familiar from distance education and an innovative re-engagement with adults seeking HE learning. The evidence is not yet clear, but poor retention and cohorts consisting of existing graduates suggest that MOOCs may not widen participation, and that OERs in their present forms may not start UK adults on a journey to formal HE learning.

DISTANCE EDUCATION AD CONTINUING EDUCATION IN INDIA

Open and Distance Learning (ODL) system is a system wherein teachers and learners need not necessarily be present either at same place or same time and is flexible in regard to modalities and timing of teaching and learning as also the admission criteria without compromising necessary quality considerations. ODL system of the country consists of Indira Gandhi National Open University (IGNOU), State Open Universities (SOUs), Institutions and Universities offering education and includes Correspondence Course Institutes (CCIs) in conventional dual mode universities. This is becoming more and more significant for continuing education, skill-updation of in service personnel and for quality education of relevance to learners located at educationally disadvantageous locations. With the dissolution of the Distance Education Council of the IGNOU, the regulatory powers on ODL is currently vested with the University Grants Commission (UGC).

Adult Education After Independence

An important responsibility of a democratic government is to educate its citizens for a better living. The education given to them must be related to their daily life. It must be related to the economic development of the people. It should provide the manpower at all levels to increase output, by training people in needed skills. An effective, planned educational programme, in relation to the life of participants, can make desirable changes in them. After independence the national government realized the need to educate the adults so as to enable them to understand their rights and responsibilities and to participate meaningfully in the developmental programmes of the country. The investment in education therefore was given much emphasis and importance. The budget allocation for education during the first five year plan was 153 crores. It steadily increased to ₹ 19600 in eight five year plans. Increased investment in education has brought a remarkable change in literacy percentage of the country. The literacy rate was only 16.65 percentages in 1951. This has risen to 65.36 percent in 2001, four-fold increase over a period 50 years. Female literacy, which was around 8 percent in 1951, has risen to 55 percent - around seven-times increase during the same period. It is not the investment in education alone that is responsible for sharp increase in the literacy level of the country. Special attention attached to adult education also played a key role in improving the literacy level of the population. The Government of India felt that it was not possible to effectively tackle the problems of illiteracy through formal education alone as there was vast chunk of population outside the field of formal education. Further, a vast majority of the illiterate population was from poorer sections of the community, which could be reached only through non-formal adult education. That was why, the Government of India enhanced the budget allocation for adult education in the country. The proportion of budget allocation for adult education to total investment in education has steadily gone up though there were fluctuations in between plan periods. During the 8th plan period the allocation for adult education was around 10 percent of the allocation for education.

Major Adult Education programmes

The Government of India realizing the need to educate the vast number of illiterate adults introduced special programmes in the sphere of adult education. A brief description of each of the programmes is given, as it would provide a backdrop for the study.

Social Education

The main attention of the Government and the leaders after independence was focussed on the problem of rehabilitation of refugees. The idea of developing an appropriate adult education programme for the refugees as well as on- refugees continued to be the concern of officials and non-officials in the early years of freedom. The Indian Adult Education Association (IAEA), a non-governmental organization of professional adult educators took up the task of reviewing the role of adult education and reinterpreting its function in a democratic set up in their annual conference held in Rewa in December 1947. It was observed that 'adult education must aim at enabling the common man to live a richer life in all its aspects- social, economic, cultural and moral' and for the first time, the social aspect of adult education was emphasized by the professional adult educators.

Gram Shikshan Mohim

A Movement "Grama Shiskhan Mohim" was started in 1959 in Satara District of Maharastra and extended to all districts of the state within a period of two years (1961-63). 10 lakhs adults in the age of 14 years and above were made literate. It clearly enhanced the literacy rate in Maharastra. The literacy rate which was 34.2 percent in 1961, increased to 44.9 percent in 1971. But, the survey carried out later by the Planning Commission made it clear that there was a widespread relapse of the adults into illiteracy, which was attributed to the lack of well-organized follow- up services.

Farmer's Education and Functional Literacy

The concept of functional literacy emerged during 1960s. A series of international and national events during 1950s paved the way for its emergence. The World Conference of Education Ministers on 'Eradication of illiteracy', held in Tehran (1965) defined functional literacy with greater precision. It discussed in detail the close link between literacy and social and economic progress.

National Adult Education Programme (NAEP)

An ambitious adult education programme was launched on October 2, 1978 with the objective of providing adult education to ten crore adults in the age group 15-35 within five years. This nation-wide programme sought to enable majority of our active citizens to play a positive role in bringing about social, economic and cultural changes so that social justice and equity could be achieved.

Rural Functional Literacy Programme (RFLP)

Farmer's Functional Literacy Programme (FFLP) was renamed and reshaped as Rural Functional Literacy Programme (RFLP) by the Govt, of India immediately after the launching of NAEP. RFLP mainly aimed at all rural illiterates and it has a wider coverage of the rural population, which included farmers also.

20-point programme of the Govt, of India

This programme as a part of the sixth Five Year Plan, aimed at the socioeconomic development of the people. Item number 16 of the programme lays special attention on the eradication of illiteracy among adults especially in the age group 15-35, with the help of voluntary organizations and university and college students.

Mass Programme for Functional Literacy (MPFL)

Mass Programme for Functional Literacy (MPFL) was introduced on 1st May 1986, to give a boost to adult education work. It aimed at involving two lakhs students to work about 150 hours within 3-4 months on purely voluntary basis. It was really a people's programme ensuring community support and assistance. It also aimed at involvement of teachers for eradication of illiteracy. Mass movement is a unified attempt by a large number of individuals to effect social change by working as a group. Teachers and students of universities, colleges and schools, workers of trade unions, panchayat raj agencies and voluntary agencies were involved in the programme.

Jana Shikshan Nilayams (JSNs)

With a view to preventing the relapse of neo-literates into illiteracy and ensuring that the basic literacy skills acquired by them are reinforced, retained and applied in day to day life situations, National Literacy Mission envisaged institutionalization of post literacy and continuing education arrangements through setting up of Jana Shikshan Nilayams (JSNs) throughout the country.

National Literacy Mission (NLM)

The Govt, of India has identified eradication of illiteracy as one of the national missions with a view to applying technology and scientific research for the benefit of the deprived sections of society. The 'Technology Mission for Eradication of Illiteracy now known as the 'National Literacy Mission' (NLM) was drawn up in 1988 as a comprehensive central programme in the field of adult education. The NLM concentrate on 15-35 age group, which is crucial for country's development.

Total Literacy Campaigns (TLC)

The total literacy campaign model is now accepted as the dominant strategy for eradication of adult illiteracy in India. These campaigns are area-specific, time-bound, volunteer-based, cost-effective and outcome-oriented. The thrust is on attainment of functional literacy through prescribed forms of literacy and numeracy. The learner is the focal point in the entire process and measurement of learning outcome is continuous, informal, participatory and non-threatening. The campaigns are implemented through district level literacy committees in which a number of individuals and organizations work together. It is delivered through volunteers without any expectation of reward or incentive. To enable every learner to achieve measurable levels of literacy, the new pedagogy known as "Improved Pace and Content of Learning (IPCL)", has been translated in the shape of a set of multi-graded and integrated teaching/ learning materials and training.

Post Literacy Campaigns

Post literacy is considered as a 'bridge' between primary schooling and its equivalent and further study. Learning skills acquired by neo-literates during the short span on the literacy campaign are at best fragile. The aim of the National Literacy Mission's Post Literacy Programme is to consolidate the basic literacy skills of speaking, reading, writing, numeracy and problem solving and at the same time, transform these learners into an educated 'whole person' who is a productive socio-economic asset to the community.

Continuing Education Programmes

Continuing education is regarded as any education which adults voluntarily undertake, and it is for literate youth and adults; it responsive to needs and wants; it includes experiences provided by all education sub-sectors; and it can be defined in terms of opportunity to engage in life-long learning. Continuing education, stresses the unity of the concept of education, both child and adult. It continues throughout life though the phrase has come to have at least two other rather narrower meanings: all education for adults returning to the educational system, and professional vocationally oriented training programmes at an advanced level for adults who have already received a good deal of education. Establishment of Continuing Education Centres (CECs) and Nodal Continuing Education Centres (NCECs) are the principal modes of implementing continuing education programmes. The centres follow an area-specific, community-based approach. The scheme envisages one CEC for each village to serve a population of about 1500 to 2000 people. Eight to ten such centres form a cluster in which one of them acts as the nodal CEC.

Indira Gandhi National Open University (IGNOU)

Indira Gandhi National Open University (IGNOU) was established in 1985 by an Act of Parliament with the dual responsibilities of (i) enhancing access and equity to higher education through distance mode and (ii) promoting, coordinating and determining standards in open learning and distance education systems. Since then, the IGNOU has undergone rapid expansion and emerged as an international institution in the field of Open and Distance Learning. As per the provisions of the IGNOU Act, the University is to:

- offer of degree, diploma and certificate programmes related to the needs of employment as necessary for building the economy of the country;
- provide opportunities for higher education to a large cross-section of people, in particular the disadvantaged segments of society;
- promote acquisition and up-gradation of knowledge and offer opportunities for training retraining in the contests of innovation and research;
- encourage an innovative system of university level education, flexible and open with regard to methods and pace of learning, combination of courses, eligibility for enrolment, age of entry, conduct of examination and delivery of the programmes to encourage excellence; and
- coordinate, promote, assess and accredit institutions and programmes offered by open and distance learning system as also to prevent through such measures as are considered appropriate, institutions from offering sub-standard courses and programmes.

IGNOU practices a flexible and open system of education in regard to methods and place of learning, combination of courses and eligibility for enrolment, age for entry and methods of evaluation etc. The University has adopted an integrated strategy for imparting instruction. This consists of providing print materials, audio-video, tapes, broadcast on radio and educational TV Channels, teleconferencing, video conferencing as also the face to face counselling, at its study centres located throughout the country. The University has adopted the method of continuous assessment and term-end examination for evaluation of the performance of its students enrolled in various subjects.

Educational development of North-East Region (NER) is another focus area and 10% of the Annual Plan Budget used to be extensively earmarked to the development of this region. The University has established 8 Regional Centres in the North-East Region. One of the significant focuses of IGNOU is to pay special attention to disadvantaged sections of the society and regions. The university has developed a number of programmes for women and special study centres were established in the backward areas and districts with low female literacy rate.

IGNOU makes use the Information and Communication Technologies (ICTs) extensively for imparting education. In addition to self-instructional printed materials, the university utilizes Audi/Video programme tapes, teleconferencing, Gyan Vani (FM Radio), Gyan Darshan (educational TV Channels), computer networks for imparting instructions. With the launce of "One Stop Education Portal SAKSHAT'; in October 2006 by the then President of India, Dr. A.P.J. Abdul Kalam, IGNOU developed plan to use this platform, extensively to provide knowledge resources and impart education to its students.

IGNOU has a large number of programmes, ranging from purely academic to technical, professional and vocational at various levels leading to award of Competency Certificates, Diplomas, Bachelor's, Master's and Doctor's degree to successful candidates. Many of these programmes are modular in nature.

State Open Universities (SOUs)

There are at present 13 State Open Universities set up by the respective state grants are single mode institutions, which means they provide education only in the distance mode. These universities cater to people who are unable to pursue regular courses due to various reasons. These Universities are also instrumental in shaping the career growth of learner who are already employed.

Commonwealth of Learning (COL)

Commonwealth of Learning (COL) was established through a Memorandum of Understanding between Governments of Commonwealth countries in the year 1988. The Commonwealth of Learning (COL) is an intergovernmental organisation created by Commonwealth Heads of Government to encourage the development and sharing of open learning/ distance education knowledge, resources and technologies. COL is helping developing nations to improve access to quality education and training.

Headquartered in Vancouver, Canada, COL is the world's only intergovernmental organisation dedicated solely to promoting and delivering distance education and open learning, and is the only official Commonwealth agency located outside Britain.

COL is voluntarily funded by the Commonwealth countries and India is third major donor after United Kingdom and Canada. India is represented on the Board of Governors and Executive Committee of COL through Secretary, in-Charge of Higher Education.

COL has focused its attention on activities in the instructional materials, telecommunication technology and training and information service. COL has located its Educational Media Centre for Asia (CEMCA) in India and Joint Secretary in charge of Distance Learning is a member on Advisory Council of CEMCA.

SAKSHAT: A One Stop Education Portal

SAKSHAT - a One Stop Education Portal launched on October 30, 2006 to facilitate lifelong learning for students, teachers and those in employment or in pursuit of knowledge free of cost to them. The content development task for 'SAKSHAT' was looked after by the Content Advisory Committee (CAC) for the respective subject, which consisted of representatives from educational institutions like IGNOU, Delhi University, Kendriya Vidyalaya Sangthan (KVS), Navodyaya Vidyalaya Sangthan (NVS), National Institute of Open Schooling (NIOS) and National Council for Educational Research and Training (NCERT) and prominent academicians in the field. In addition, some NGOs had also provided the contents developed by them free of cost for this portal.

The vision is to scale up this pilot project 'SAKSHAT' to cater to the learning needs of more than 50 crore people through a proposed scheme of 'National Mission in Education through Information and Communication Technology (ICT). The scheme is to provide connectivity to all institutions of higher learning to world of knowledge in the cyber space, to leverage the potential of ICT, in providing high quality knowledge modules with right e-contents, to address to the personalized needs of learners, in order to take care of their aspirations. These modules are to be delivered through 'SAKSHAT'. The scheme may also have a provision of certification of competencies of the human resources acquired through formal or non-formal means as also to develop and maintain the database of profile of human resources.

MODEL QUESTIONS

Very Short Answer type Questions. Each question carries 1 Mark. To be answer in about 20 words each.

1. What is the structure of education in Sri Lanka.

2. Enlist the different skill development programmes/courses in USA.

3. Enlist the Organisations on Skill Development Programmes in India.

4. Write a short note on *Udaan* Scheme for Skill Development in J&K.

Short Answer type Questions. Each question carries 2 Marks. To be answer in about 150 words each.

5. Illustrate Buddhist influence over the education of Sri Lanka.

6. Describe the issues of UEE in Bangladesh.

7. Discuss the reasons for children dropping out of school in India.

8. Compare and Contrast UEE efforts in India and Sri Lanka.

Multiple Choice Questions. Each Question carries 1 Mark.

9. —————, are Buddhist educational institutions in Sri Lanka.

(a) Gramodaya Mandalayas

(b) Pirivenas

(c) Gurukulas

(d) Sarvodaya Vidyalayas

10. In India, RTE Act came into the effect from:

(a) 1st April 2008

(b) 1st August 2009

(c) 1st April 2010

(d) 1st April 2011

11. "The land of opportunity"- This slogan related to:

(a) India

(b) Sri Lanka

(c) Bangladesh

(d) USA.

12. Indian Institute of Entrepreneurship located at:

(a) New Delhi

(b) Mumbai

(c) Guwahati

(d) Kolkata

Answer Key:

9: B 10: C 11: D 12: C

Reference

Indira Gandhi National Open University (IGNOU). retrieved on 28-03-2018 from http://mhrd.gov.in/technology-enabled-learning-3

Chapter 1: Adult and Continuing Education In India: An Overview. retrieved on 28-03-2018 from http://shodhganga.inflibnet.ac.in/bitstream/10603/108536/9/09_chapter%201.pdf

Boampong, A.O. & Holmberg, C. (2015). *Distance Education in Europian Higher Education - The Potential - UK Case Study.* Hamburg: UNESCO. retrieved on 28-03-2018 from http://uil.unesco.org/i/doc/adult-education/ideal/ideal-united-kingdom-case-study.pdf

Nunan, T. Markets, Distance Education, and Australian Higher Education. *International Review of Research in Open and Distance Learning*. Volume 6, Number 1. March – 2005. retrieved on 28-03-2018 from https://files.eric.ed.gov/fulltext/EJ846612.pdf

United Kingdom - Administration, Finance, & Educational Research. retrieved on 28-03-2018 from http://education.stateuniversity.com/pages/1622/United-Kingdom-ADMINISTRATION-FINANCE-EDUCATIONAL-RESEARCH.html

Education administration in the United Kingdom. retrieved on 28-03-2018 from https://en.wikipedia.org/wiki/Education_administration_in_the_United_Kingdom

Arger, G. (1993). *Distance Education in Asia and the Pacific: Australia*. UNESCO. retrieved on 28-03-2018 from http://www.unesco.org/education/pdf/53_23a.pdf

Standard Training Assessment and Reward (STAR) Scheme. retrieved on 28-03-2018 from http://www.skilldevelopment.gov.in/star.html

National Institute of Entrepreneurship and Small Business Development (NIESBUD). retrieved on 28-03-2018 from http://www.skilldevelopment.gov.in/NIESBUD.html

National Policy for Skill Development and Entrepreneurship 2015. retrieved on 28-03-2018 from http://www.skilldevelopment.gov.in/assets/images/Skill%20India/National%20Policy%20on%20Skill%20Development%20and%20Entreprenurship%20Final.pdf

The U.S. Department of Labor; Employment and Training Administration (2007). *Identifying and Addressing Workforce Challenges in America's Energy Industry*. retrieved on 28-03-2018 from https://www.doleta.gov/BRG/pdf/Energy%20Report_final.pdf

Envisage International Corporation (2018). *Non-Degree Options*. retrieved on 28-03-2018 from https://www.internationalstudent.com/study_usa/choosing-the-usa/usa-education-system/non-degree/

Cancer Research Education Grants Program - Courses for Skills Development. retrieved on 28-03-2018 from https://grants.nih.gov/grants/guide/pa-files/PAR-18-477.html

OECD (2014), *Employment and Skills Strategies in the United States*, OECD Publishing, Paris. retrieved on 28-03-2018 from http://dx.doi.org/10.1787/9789264209398-en

Developments in Sri Lankan Education in the Nineties. retrieved on 28-03-2018 from http://edu.cmb.ac.lk/nerec/wp-content/uploads/2014/11/Chapter-01-Introduction.pdf

UNESCO (1984). *Towards Universalization of Primary Education in Asia and the Pacific: Country Studies-Sri Lanka*. retrieved on 28-03-2018 from https://files.eric.ed.gov/fulltext/ED274457.pdf

Aturupane, Harsha et.al. (2013). *Transforming Primary Education in Sri Lanka : From a 'Subject' of Education to a 'Stage' of Education*. retrieved on 28-03 2018 from https://openknowledge.worldbank.org/handle/10986/16287?show= full

Gnanawasa, R.M. *A study of a few recognized Educational Issues faced by Sri Lanka at present*. Fourth Asia Pacific Conference on Advanced Research (APCAR, Melbourne, March, 2017). Asia Pacific Institute of Advanced Research (APIAR). Page 35. retrieved on 28-03-2018 from https://apiar.org.au/wp-content/uploads/2017/04/6_APCAR_MAR_2017_BRR739_education-35-42.pdf

Universalisation of primary education in Bangladesh: formal approaches. retrieved on 28-03-2018 from http://shodhganga.inflibnet.ac.in/bitstream/10603/14240/11/11_chapter%204.pdf

World Bank; Human Development Sector South Asia Region (September 28, 2013) *Bangladesh Education Sector Review.* retrieved on 28-03-2018 from https://openknowledge.worldbank.org/bitstream/handle/10986/16768/806130ESW0BD0E00Box379859B00PUBLIC0.pdf

Rabbi, F. *Primary Education in Bangladesh: Viability of Achieving Millennium Development Goals.* retrieved on 28-03-2018 from http://bigd.bracu.ac.bd/jdownloads/WORKING%20PAPERS/32.Primary%20Education%20in%20Bangladesh.pdf

UNICEF Bangladesh: *Quality Primary Education in Bangladesh.* retrieved on 28-03-2018 from https://www.unicef.org/bangladesh/Quality_Primary_Education (1).pdf

Mondal, P. *Universalisation of Elementary Education in India.* retrieved on 28-03-2018 from http://www.yourarticlelibrary.com/education/universalisation-of-elementary-education-in-india/20899

Importance of Universalisation of Elementary Education (UEE) in India. (November 9, 2016) retrieved on 28-03-2018 from https://heignotes.com/2016/11/09/importance-of-universalisation-of-elementary-education-uee-in-india/

Bala, I. Universalization of elementary education under different schemes. *International Journal of Advanced Research and Development.* Volume 2; Issue 1; January 2017; Page No. 13-15. retrieved on 28-03-2018 from www.advancedjournal.com

Universalisation of Elementary Education (UEE). retrieved on 28-03-2018 from http://www.teindia.nic.in/mhrd/50yrsedu/r/2R/7Q/2R7Q0101.htm

Pradhan Mantri Kaushal Vikas Yojana (PMKVY). retrieved on 28-03-2018 from http://www.skilldevelopment.gov.in/pmkvy.html

Pradhan Mantri Kaushal Vikas Yojana (PMKVY). retrieved on 28-03-2018 from http://www.skilldevelopment.gov.in/pmkvy.html

Laboissiere, M. & Mourshed, M. (Feb 2017). *Closing the skills gap: Creating workforce-development programs that work for everyone.* retrieved on 28-03-2018 from https://www.mckinsey.com/industries/social-sector/our-insights/closing-the-skills-gap-creating-workforce-development-programs-that-work-for-everyone

Distance Learning. retrieved on 28-03-2018 from http://mhrd.gov.in/distance-learning

Commonwealth of Learning (COL). retrieved on 28-03-2018 from http://mhrd.gov.in/technology-enabled-learning-2

SAKSHAT: A One Stop Education Portal. retrieved on 28-03-2018 from http://mhrd.gov.in/technology-enabled-learning-1

Administration of the Education System. retrieved on 28-03-2018 from http://www.teindia.nic.in/mhrd/50yrsedu/r/2Q/A2/2QA20501.htm

Educational Administration. retrieved on 28-03-2018 from http://www.indiaeducation.net/indiaedudestination/structure/

United States - Administration & Finance. retrieved on 28-03-2018 from http://education.stateuniversity.com/pages/1633/United-States-ADMINISTRATION-FINANCE.html

Skill India. retrieved on 28-03-2018 from http://www.skilldevelopment.gov.in/background.html

Note on SANKALP. retrieved on 28-03-2018 from http://www.skilldevelopment.gov.in/assets/images/sankalp/note.pdf

UDAAN. retrieved on 28-03-2018 from http://www.skilldevelopment.gov.in/udaan.html

Polytechnic Education – An Overview. retrieved on 28-03-2018 from http://mhrd.gov.in/sites/upload_files/mhrd/files/upload_document/Revpolytech.pdf

Vocationalisation of Secondary Education. retrieved on 28-03-2018 from http://www.skilldevelopment.gov.in/school-education.html

Higher Education. retrieved on 28-03-2018 from http://www.skilldevelopment.gov.in/higher-education.html

Directorate General of Training (DGT). retrieved on 28-03-2018 from http://www.skilldevelopment.gov.in/DGT.html

National Skill Development Agency (NSDA). retrieved on 28-03-2018 from http://www.skilldevelopment.gov.in/nationalskilldevelopmentagency.html

National Skill Development Corporation. retrieved on 28-03-2018 from http://www.skilldevelopment.gov.in/nationalskilldevelopmentcorporation.html

National Skill Development Fund. retrieved on 28-03-2018 from http://www.skilldevelopment.gov.in/nationalskilldevelopmentfund.html

Sector Skill Councils (SSC). retrieved on 28-03-2018 from http://www.skilldevelopment.gov.in/ssc.html

Skills for Success. retrieved on 28-03-2018 from https://www2.ed.gov/programs/skillssuccess/index.html

Training and skills development. retrieved on 28-03-2018 from https://www.elpasotexas.gov/environmental-services/training-and-public-programs/training-and-skills-development

Skills for Small Business - Program Overview. retrieved on 28-03-2018 from http://www.twc.state.tx.us/programs/skills-small-business-program-overview

Skills Development - Program Overview. retrieved on 28-03-2018 from http://www.twc.state.tx.us/programs/skills-development-program-overview

Skills Development Training. retrieved on 28-03-2018 fromhttps://www.fmcs.gov/services/education-and-outreach/skills-development-training/

Enterprise Talent Development. retrieved on 28-03-2018 from https://mn.gov/mmb/etd/skills-development-courses/open-enrollment-courses/

Skill Development courses. retrieved on 28-03-2018 from http://www.clackamas.us/ccrs/upcomingtrainings.html

Chapter 1: Introduction. retrieved on 28-03-2018 from http://shodhganga.inflibnet.ac.in/bitstream/10603/39731/7/07_chapter%201.pdf

Unviersalisation of elementary education. retrieved on 28-03-2018 from http://wikieducator.org/UEE_and_ELL

Indian Institute of Entrepreneurship (IIE). retrieved on 28-03-2018 from http://www.skilldevelopment.gov.in/IIE.html

Index

B

C

T